D0848820

THE ANGLICAN EPISCOPATE

AND

THE AMERICAN COLONIES

BY

ARTHUR LYON CROSS

ARCHON BOOKS

HAMDEN, CONNECTICUT

1964

Originally Published 1902
HARVARD HISTORICAL STUDIES IX

Reprinted 1964 in an
unabridged and unaltered edition

LIBRARY OF CONGRESS CATALOG CARD NUMBER: 64-7768
PRINTED IN THE UNITED STATES OF AMERICA

PREFACE.

This monograph, in its original form, was accepted as a dissertation for the degree of Doctor of Philosophy at Harvard University; it also was awarded the Toppan Prize in 1899. Since that time the work has been, to a considerable extent, recast, revised, and enlarged.

The author feels greatly indebted to the help of many friends for whatever merit his book may possess. Among his former teachers at Harvard his chief acknowledgments are due to Professor Edward Channing, under whose guidance the work was prepared, and who has liberally contributed advice and assistance at every stage of its progress; to Professor Albert Bushnell Hart for many valuable suggestions; and to Professor Charles Gross, who kindly consented to read the proof. Miss Addie F. Rowe, of Cambridge, rendered efficient service in getting the manuscript ready for the press. The extensive privileges and courteous assistance received from authorities and officials at the Harvard University Library, the Library of the Massachusetts Historical Society, and John Carter Brown Library, in this country, and at the British Museum, the Public Record

Office, and Lambeth Palace, in England, are gratefully acknowledged. Especially the author wishes to express his deep obligations to Mandell Creighton, late Bishop of London, for generously placing at his disposal the rich collections at Fulham Palace relating to his subject.

ARTHUR LYON CROSS.

University of Michigan,
April, 1902.

CONTENTS.

CHAPTER X.

CHAPTER XI.

CHAPTER XII.

APPENDICES.

THE ANGLICAN EPISCOPATE AND THE AMERICAN COLONIES.

CHAPTER I.

THE BEGINNINGS OF EPISCOPAL CONTROL OVER THE COLONIES.

THE history of the relations between the Anglican episcopate and the English plantations in North America may be studied under two aspects. One aspect has to do with the jurisdiction which the Bishop of London exercised over the colonial Church of England; the other is concerned with the attempts which were made from time to time to introduce resident bishops into the colonies, and to transfer his powers into their hands.

In the study of this subject, the origin, nature, and actual workings of the Bishop of London's authority as colonial diocesan will be considered first. After that, the earlier attempts to establish bishops resident in the colonies will be examined, and an effort will be made to explain the motives actuating the authors of this movement. The next step will be to describe the opposition which gradually manifested itself against the project. This will bring us to the outbreak of the controversies between those who sought to secure, and those who strove to prevent, the settlement of resident bishops. After tracing at some length the details of this struggle, and endeavoring to estimate its significance, a short account will be given of the steps which finally, after the United States became an independent nation, led to the establishment of a native American episcopate. The work will close with a general survey and summing up of the conclusions to be drawn from the whole discussion.

The subject thus sketched in bare outline would seem at first glance to be one of purely ecclesiastical concern; but, while this feature is largely predominant, there is also a political aspect, claiming the attention of any one who aims at an understanding of our pre-Revolutionary history. At the very outset we find secular considerations playing an important part in the Laudian project to establish episcopal control over the colonies, as a preliminary step toward the founding of a state church. After the failure of this plan, religious and political questions cease for more than a century to have any perceptible connection. With the approach of the War for Independence, however, ecclesiastical issues become involved with those of practical politics, and exhibit a phase, not altogether uninteresting or unimportant, in the final struggle leading up to the separation from Great Britain. But, waiving for the present any further considerations on this point, let us see what kind of authority the bishops of London exercised over the colonies, and how they came to be vested with it.

Among the functions which, according to English ecclesiastical law, appertained to a bishop of the Church of England, those which concern us in this survey may be grouped under two heads.[1] The first, or more purely ecclesiastical, function had to do mainly with administering the government and discipline of the church, — with consecrating sacred edifices, for example, and with confirming, ordaining, suspending, and degrading ministers. The second function, which was rather civil, or ecclesiastico-civil, in its character, comprised a certain jurisdiction over the probate of wills, the issue of marriage licenses, and the presentation to benefices.

Although these functions, and many others, were constantly and successfully exercised by every bishop in the mother country, it is easy to see how difficult, nay, how impossible, it was for a bishop resident in England to perform them for the distant colonies with any satisfaction to himself or to those committed to his charge. Hence, many devices were employed,

---

[1] Nothing need be said here of the bishop's legislative functions, or of his competence in causes not purely ecclesiastical, for these were never extended to the colonies.

with more or less success, to avoid the difficulties necessarily attendant upon this unfortunate condition of things. Some of the offices, such as ordination, required the personal participation of a bishop; accordingly, since the bishop could not or would not come to America, candidates for orders were obliged to go to England. The hardships and expense which these journeys involved were one of the most frequent complaints of those who argued for the necessity of an American episcopate.[1]

Other episcopal functions related chiefly to the oversight and discipline of the church and clergy. These duties were, by the end of the seventeenth century, delegated to commissaries,[2] officers whom bishops of the Church of England are accustomed to appoint to exercise ecclesiastical jurisdiction in particular parts of their dioceses, where, owing to distance or to other causes, they cannot attend in person. A commissary may be empowered to hold visitations, to call conventions, to superintend the conduct of the clergy, and, in general, to exercise the authority of officer-principal or vicar-general. Appeals, however, lay not to his bishop, but to the archbishop, or to some great officer of state.[3] The workings of the commissarial sys-

[1] See, for example, Abbey, *English Church and Bishops in the Eighteenth Century*, i. 362–363.

[2] There is possibly a solitary earlier instance. The Reverend William Morell, who came to New England in 1623, is said to have exercised some sort of commissarial jurisdiction. He returned to England in 1624, and we hear of no other commissary in the colonies until the appointment of the Reverend James Blair in 1689 (cf. Simeon E. Baldwin, in American Antiquarian Society, *Proceedings*, New Series, xiii. 192: citing Charles Francis Adams, *Three Episodes of Massachusetts History*, i. 142, 154–155, 229; Massachusetts Historical Society, *Collections*, 4th Series, iii. 154; Perry, *American Episcopal Church*, i. 81, 395, ii. 600). The statement of the Reverend Richard Peters, in a letter to Bishop Terrick, November 6, 1766, that there had been commissaries since 1620, seems to be almost entirely without foundation. The letter is printed in Perry, *Historical Collections relating to the American Colonial Church*, ii. (Pennsylvania) 409–410.

[3] See Dalcho, *Protestant Episcopal Church in South-Carolina*, 78–79, citing *Constitutions and Canons Ecclesiastical*, Article 127, where the qualifications for a commissary are enumerated. Cf. also Burn, *Ecclesiastical Law*, i. 290, ii. 8. The commission printed below in Appendix A, No. ii., will serve to show what was expected from a colonial commissary.

tem will be examined when we come to consider historically the relations between the Bishop of London and the several colonies.[1]

The more properly civil part of the bishop's jurisdiction — such as had to do with probate of wills, marriage licenses, and collations to benefices — was vested, not in these episcopal representatives, but in the colonial governors as ordinaries or lay bishops. These powers were expressly excepted out of the Bishop of London's commission (when he came to have one) as diocesan of the plantations.[2] The reason for this limitation seems to have been that in the early days of the colonies, long before the bishop's authority had come to be permanently recognized, the governors had been accustomed to perform these functions,[3] and that, by the time a commission was issued to the

---

[1] Much light on this subject is to be obtained from the letters of the various commissaries to the bishops of London: *e.g.*, James Blair, November 18, 1714, and February 10, 1723–24, in Perry, *Historical Collections*, i. (Virginia) 130–131, 250–251; Alexander Garden, February 1, 1751, *Fulham MSS.*; Roger Price, April 19, 1751, *ibid.*; Robert Jenny, May 23, 1751, *ibid.*; William Dawson, July 15, 1751, in Perry, *Historical Collections*, i. (Virginia) 377–379. Some of the letters which have not hitherto been printed may be found below in Appendix A, No. x.

[2] See the commissions and instructions to various governors after 1685; *e.g.*, to Governor Fletcher of New York, *New York Documents*, iii. 821.

[3] See, for example, an act of the Virginia legislature of 1662: " That for the preservation of purity and unity of doctrine and discipline in the church, and the right administration of the sacraments, no minister shall be admitted to officiate in this country, but such as shall produce to the governor a testimonial that he hath received his ordination from some bishop in England, and shall then subscribe, to be conformable to the orders and constitutions of the Church of England, and the laws there established: *upon which the Governor is hereby requested to induct the said minister into any parish that shall make presentation of him:* and if another person pretending himself a minister, shall, contrary to this act, presume to teach or preach, publicly or privately, the governor and council are hereby desired and empowered to silence the person so offending, and upon his obstinate persistence to compel him to depart the country with the first convenience." (Trott, *Laws*, No. VI., p. 116; Hening, *Statutes*, ii. 46; Hawks, *Ecclesiastical Contributions*, i. (Virginia) 53). Cf. also the following statement: " The judicial office of Commissary had at first been vested in Governors of Colonies; but, in 1695, the Governor and Assembly of Maryland agreed in a petition to William and Mary, to transfer it, as a purely ecclesiastical office, to the Bishop of London, and wrote to the

Bishop of London defining his jurisdiction, the practice had become so firmly fixed by custom and legal enactment that the English authorities feared to excite the jealousy of the various colonial governments by removing from the secular arm duties involving such dignity and profit. Or it may have been that the government felt the need of having a stronger coercive force behind these important functions than could have been guaranteed either by a non-resident bishop or by his commissarial representative. The governor's power of ordinary did not include that of patronage, or of presentation in any way except by lapse; nor did it carry with it the right to prefer any minister to an ecclesiastical benefice without a certificate from the Bishop of London vouching for the soundness of his orthodoxy and his morals.[1]

In the royal colonies,[2] the candidates for clerical appointments were presented by the vestries, and were inducted into their cures by the governors. In case of a vacancy or a lapse, the governor or the commissary recommended a successor, who, after the vestry had received him, officiated as rector. If he happened to be inducted by the governor, he enjoyed full legal possession. But commonly the vestries, either from arbitrariness or from a desire to guard themselves from unworthy pastors, failed to present their ministers for induction, and consequently could and did remove them at will. This power of

Bishop, requesting him to send over a Clergyman to discharge its duties" (Anderson, *Colonial Church*, ii. 383).

[1] For a full discussion of the relative powers of bishop and governor by a contemporary authority, see Commissary Blair's "Remarks" in the Virginia convention of 1719, in Perry, *Historical Collections*, i. (Virginia) 218–245, from the original manuscripts of the convention.

[2] What is here said applies particularly to Virginia, where the establishment was more of a reality than in any of the other colonies. The royal provinces were Virginia, the Carolinas, New York, New Jersey, New Hampshire, and Georgia; the proprietary, Maryland, Pennsylvania, and Delaware; the charter, Massachusetts, Rhode Island, and Connecticut. The Carolinas, New Jersey, and Georgia, were, however, originally granted to proprietaries. New Hampshire for a time formed a part of Massachusetts. The Church of England was established in Virginia, Maryland, South Carolina, and in three counties of New York. At a later period a partial establishment existed in North Carolina also.

removal was their only safeguard ; for an appeal to a non-resident diocesan, possessed of inadequate powers of coercion, was,
to say the least, uncertain.[1]

In the proprietary colony of Maryland the case was somewhat
unique. Practically the whole control over the appointment of
ministers was here vested in the hands of the proprietary, by virtue
of the right of presentation which he enjoyed, and owing to the
fact that the governor, in whom the right of induction lay, was
subject to appointment and removal by him alone. Obviously,
then, it depended solely upon his personal will to say what
powers the bishop or his commissary might exercise in the
colony. To be sure, the bishop enjoyed a certain negative control, in that he issued the license to the clerical candidate ; but
this done, his power really ceased, for, when the minister was
once inducted into office, neither the bishop, his commissary,
nor the vestry had any authority to deprive him of the tempo-
ralities of his living.[2] Accordingly, whatever jurisdiction the
bishop or those who represented him might seek to exercise,
although it might have moral weight, could have no legal or
coercive force.

To sum up : so far as one can safely generalize, one may say
that in both royal and proprietary colonies the governor possessed the power of induction, while the Bishop of London
issued the certificate empowering the candidate to perform the

---

[1] See, for example, Governor Culpeper's "Report to the Lords of Trade
and Plantations, on the Present State of Virginia," December 12, 1681, in
Sainsbury, *Calendar of State Papers, Colonial Series, America and West
Indies,* 1681–1685, p. 155. There were innumerable disputes over this matter
of presentations, particularly in Virginia (cf. Perry, *Historical Collections,* i.
(Virginia), *passim*).

[2] One writer has put the case thus : " Lord Baltimore selected a clergyman
in England, and appointed him to a living ; the Bishop of London gave him a
license ; the Governor of the province inducted him ; if he did wrong the
commissary tried him, if there chanced to be a commissary ; and, when
convicted, no power *punished him ;* for after induction, even his lordship the
proprietor could not remove him ; and the Bishop of London, nominally his
diocesan, could neither give nor take away the meanest living in the province "
(Hawks, *Ecclesiastical Contributions,* ii. (Maryland) 190). Cf. also Tiffany,
Protestant Episcopal Church, 75–76 ; McConnell, *American Episcopal Church,*
107–108.

clerical functions ; that in the royal colonies the power of the diocesan was restricted enough, in the proprietary it was practically subject to the arbitrary will of the proprietor.

In the Northern and Middle colonies, where, with the exception of three counties of New York, the Church of England had no legal footing, the governors had little or nothing to do with clerical appointments. In those churches which were assisted by the Society for Propagating the Gospel, the ministers were appointed by that body; in the other churches nominally by the Bishop of London, but in many cases — particularly in the later years — practically by the congregations themselves.[1] In all these colonies, commissaries were the exception rather than the rule;[2] but, as will be seen later, where they did exist — in Pennsylvania and New York, for example — they exercised a more or less active supervision.

This brief preliminary survey is intended to show in outline the nature of the authority of the Bishop of London over his charges beyond the seas, and of his relations to the other colonial officials in fields where their jurisdictions came in contact. It has been made evident that the exercise of such authority as his Lordship legally possessed was hampered by many adverse circumstances, particularly by the confusion of

---

[1] Since there seems to have been no fixed rule, it is hard to generalize on this matter. Later on in the course of this discussion a few particular cases will be examined. This much one may say : that the larger churches in the more important towns, — for example, Christ Church, Philadelphia, and King's Chapel, Boston, — which kept up an intimate and regular intercourse with their diocesan, allowed themselves in the main to be ruled by his judgment (cf. Baldwin, in American Antiquarian Society, *Proceedings*, New Series, xiii. 197). After the resignation of Roger Price in 1746, however, the congregation of King's Chapel began to choose its rectors without reference to the Bishop of London (cf. Baldwin, *ibid.*, 199–200, citing Greenwood, *History of King's Chapel*, 105, 179). For fuller references, see Perry, *Historical Collections*, ii.–iii. (Massachusetts and Pennsylvania), and Foote, *Annals of King's Chapel, passim.*

[2] During the entire colonial period (leaving out of account the brief term of the Reverend William Morell, noticed above, p. 3, note 2) there was only one commissary for all New England, and one for New York. Pennsylvania, whose commissarial district included Delaware, was a little better off in this respect.

functions between the ecclesiastical and the secular powers in the various colonies, and by the fact that the bishop enjoyed so small a share in the appointment of the clergy committed to his care. Furthermore, since he could only confirm and ordain such candidates from across the water as chose to come to him, thereby being deprived of all initiative in propagating his faith through American agencies, his activity, not only in governing, but also in fostering and strengthening the growth of the colonial branch of the Anglican church was checked on almost every side. Nevertheless, by virtue of long-established custom, which linked his name with the control of the colonial churches, his authority and influence were exerted and felt in many ways: through the powers conferred on him, at one period by a clause inserted in the commissions of the various colonial governors, at another by a patent from the crown; through the visitations and exhortations of his commissaries, when there happened to be any commissaries; and, finally, through his connection, as an officer of state, with that part of the English government which was vested with the oversight of the ecclesiastico-political affairs of the colonies. Let us now pass on to a brief consideration of the origin of such ecclesiastical jurisdiction as the Bishop of London, in his capacity as colonial diocesan, came to possess.

At the time of the Restoration, a tradition prevailed to the effect that the Bishop of London's colonial authority rested on an order in council issued in the Laudian period. When, however, a careful search, made about 1675, failed to reveal the existence of any such document, it became necessary to account for the origin of the jurisdiction in some other way. The explanation which was finally adopted, and which has since been generally accepted, was as follows: As soon as the territories of the Virginia Company had come to be reasonably well populated, a bishop was necessary to ordain ministers and to exercise a general supervision over the church and clergy in those parts; since the Bishop of London for the time being happened to be a member of the company, and had manifested some interest in the church beyond the seas, the charge was intrusted to him, and from the precedent thus established may be traced the beginnings of the diocesan control of the bishops of London over the English plantations.[1]

The facts on which this view is based were first presented at length by Bishop Sherlock, in a " Report on the State of the Church of England in the Colonies," laid before the king in council in 1759. Sherlock begins his narrative with the issue of the first Virginia charter, April 10, 1606, by which each of the companies thereby created was to have a council for governing "according to such Laws Ordinances and Instructions *as sho^d in that behalf be given and signed by His Majesty's hand or sign manual & pass under the Privy Seal of England.*" "On the 20th Nov^r, 1606," he continues, "the King in pursuance of the right reserved to himself, gave divers orders under his Sign manuall and the Privy Seal, one of which

---

[1] A work published in 1706, entitled *An Account of the Society for Propagating the Gospel in Foreign Parts,* remarks (p. 11) with regard to the early tradition : " An Order of King and Council is said to have been made to commit unto the Bishop of London, for the time being, the Care and Pastoral charge of sending over Ministers into our Foreign Plantations, and having the Jurisdiction of them. But when the present Lord Bishop of London was advanced to that See in 1675, his Lordship found this Title so defective that little or no Good had come of it." For the facts that apparently form the basis of the view which afterward came to be held, see Bishop Sherlock's " Report on the State of the Church of England in the Colonies," *New York Documents,* vii. 360–369. References in later works are : Hawks and Perry, *Connecticut Church Documents,* i. 31–32 ; Hawks, *Ecclesiastical Contributions,* i. (Virginia) 36–38 ; Evans, *Theophilus Americanus,* 310–312 ; Anderson, *Colonial Church,* i. 261–262 ; Wilberforce, *Protestant Episcopal Church,* 36– 37 ; Tiffany, *Protestant Episcopal Church,* 23 ; Brodhead, *New York,* ii. 456–457 ; Perry, *American Episcopal Church,* i. 154–155 ; Foote, *Annals of King's Chapel,* i. 171–172. Whitney, in his *History of South Carolina* (a doctoral dissertation in the Harvard College Library), ii. 410, thinks that the jurisdiction was a usurpation in the first instance, and cites as authority for his opinion the following works : Rivers, *South Carolina,* supplementary chapter, 87 ; Dalcho, *Protestant Episcopal Church in South-Carolina,* 100 ; South Carolina Historical Society, *Collections,* ii. 178 ; Chalmers, *Opinions,* 18–23. Anderson (*Colonial Church,* i. 410–412) and Makower (*Constitutional History and Constitution of the Church of England,* 141–142) have something to say on the beginnings of the Bishop of London's jurisdiction abroad, particularly about an order in council which was actually issued in 1633, and which will be considered below.

was as follows: 'That the President Council and Ministers should provide that the true word and service of God should be preached planted and used, *according to the Rites and Doctrine of the Church of England.*' "[1]   Sherlock says that when the second charter was issued, May 23, 1609, George Abbot, then Bishop of London, was made one of the grantees.[2]

But during the early years there was little need of any episcopal supervision; for as late as 1620 there appear to have been only five clergymen in the colony of Virginia. As time went on, however, and as the colony began to grow, the necessity for more ministers became apparent, and the council for Virginia applied to John King, at that time Bishop of London and a member of its body, for his aid in furnishing them with "pious, learned, and painful ministers." The Bishop, who had, as early as 1619, shown his zeal for the welfare of the colonies by raising £1000 toward a fund for educating the Indians, quickly responded.[3]   In this way, according to the authorities cited above, grew up the Bishop of London's colonial jurisdiction; but neither now or later was any attempt made by him to incorporate Virginia or any other American colony into the diocese of London.[4]

---

[1] This " Report " is printed in full in *New York Documents*, vii. 360 ff. There is a complete text of the charters and of the supplementary royal ordinance in Hening, *Statutes*, i. 57 ff.   The citations above are in the words of Sherlock, which differ in some respects verbally, though not substantially, from Hening's text.

[2] This is evidently an error.   Abbot did not join the Company until after the charter was issued, though his name was inserted in later copies intended for American use.   Cf. Baldwin, in American Antiquarian Society, *Proceedings*, New Series, xiii. 180, note 2.

[3] Hawks, *Ecclesiastical Contributions*, i. (Virginia) 36–38 ; Abbey, *English Church and Bishops*, i. 75.

[4] See, particularly, Tiffany, *Protestant Episcopal Church*, 23.   Baldwin (American Antiquarian Society, *Proceedings*, New Series, xiii. 179–181) discusses the subject of the early connection between the bishops of London and the colony of Virginia.   He points out that it had begun before the time of King, with his predecessors Ravis and Abbot, and that though he " increased, . . . he did not originate, the supervision of the Bishop of London over the

From several indications it is evident that Bishop King's connection with the colonial churches was only a passing one. He himself died in the year following the application just alluded to; and his successor either made no effort to supply the colony with ministers, even if he went so far as to make the attempt, and secured no recognition of his power over the churches there. As a proof of the first assertion, we have a statement in a report of the Virginia assembly in 1624, that there were many officiating clergymen who had no orders.[1] In support of the second assertion, is the fact that among the thirty-five "articles" passed by this assembly, the first seven of which concern the church and the clergy, there is not one that intimates in the slightest degree that the Bishop of London had any authority or jurisdiction in the province at that time;[2] and also the fact that, in an enumeration of the appurtenances of the diocese of London, made by a contemporary biographer of Laud at the time of his accession to that see, in July, 1628, the colonies are not mentioned.[3] In one respect, however, the connection of Bishop King (and possibly that of his predecessors, Ravis and Abbot) with Virginia may have had some significance: it may have established a precedent in favor of the Bishop of London when the need of a colonial

Virginia settlements, until it gradually came to be recognized as authoritative on both sides of the Atlantic."

[1] Sherlock's "Report," *New York Documents*, vii. 361.

[2] *Ibid.* Among other things it was enacted "that there be an uniformity in our Church, as near as may be to the Canons in England, both in substance and circumstance; and that all persons yield obedience to them under pain of censure" (Hening, *Statutes*, i. 122–124). See also Cornelison, *The Relation of Religion to Civil Government in the United States*, 7; Tiffany, *Protestant Episcopal Church*, 11–12, 20–21, where, however, the acts of 1623–24 are assigned to the year 1619. Note also that, neither in the new constitution which Sir Francis Wyatt brought over for the colony in 1621 nor in his commission and instructions, is there among the provisions with regard to religion, any mention of the Bishop of London. For the texts of these documents, see Hening, *Statutes*, i. 110–118.

[3] "As for the Diocess of London, it contains in it the whole counties of Middlesex and Essex, so much of Hertfordshire as was anciently possessed by the East Saxons, together with the peculiar Jurisdiction of the Church of St. Albans" (Heylyn, *Cyprianus Anglicus*, 175).

diocesan came to be felt.   This is all that can reasonably be made of the incident.[1]

In seeking for a more satisfactory answer to the obscure question of the origin of the Bishop of London's colonial authority, we are not much helped by those who have written on this point.   Bishop Wilberforce, for example, says that it is uncertain whence the jurisdiction sprang, if not from John King's exercise of episcopal functions as a representative of the Virginia Company.   Indeed, he regards this precedent as the sole basis of the Bishop of London's authority till 1727, when a royal commission under the broad seal was issued to Bishop Gibson.[2]   Many writers follow Wilberforce in this view.   Others, without making any positive assertion, have hinted at the possibility of the existence of some sort of royal grant originally vesting the Bishop of London with the powers which he came to exercise.[3]   Only two or three modern writers have even touched what appears to be the clue to the best solution of the problem.[4]

The proper place to look for the origin of the precedent — for it had a basis no more definite or authoritative — on which the Bishop of London's colonial jurisdiction rested, is in the Stuart policy, instigated by Laud, of seeking to extend the Church of England establishment to every part of the known

---

[1] The continuity of this connection has undoubtedly been overestimated. See, for example, Anderson (*Colonial Church*, i. 261), who says: " So far, one channel of direct and authoritative communication was established between himself [the Bishop of London] and the Clergymen whom he nominated, and over whom he was to exercise, as far as it was practicable, Episcopal controul."

[2] *Protestant Episcopal Church*, 37.

[3] For example, Evans (*Theophilus Americanus*, 313) says: " The authority of the Bishop of London has been believed to have rested on some grant from Great Britain; but it is by no means certain that such a document existed although some of the bishops of London had something of the sort which was in force for their lives."   The last clause is, of course, a vague reference to the royal commission issued to Bishop Gibson.   For other references, see above, p. 9, note 1.

[4] Anderson and Makower (see above, note 3), following Laud's contemporary biographer, Peter Heylyn, who was court chaplain to both Charles I. and Charles II., and Judge Baldwin (American Antiquarian Society, *Proceedings*, New Series, xiii. 181–182), who cites Anderson.

world where the English government had a foothold.[1] It will
be necessary to consider somewhat in detail the steps taken to
carry this policy into effect.

In the month of July, 1628, William Laud was translated to
the see of London.[2] For the three or four years next ensuing
he devoted himself to the work of reducing the people of
England and Scotland to conformity to the established church.
When at length he found time to look abroad, he discovered
a state of affairs well calculated to make him apprehensive:
the infection of Calvinism was spreading among the English
trading stations and regiments in the Low Countries. Laud
seems to have cared nothing for what the Protestants of other
countries might do, — they might accept whatever form of
doctrine and discipline they liked, so far as he was concerned,
— but when it came to Englishmen living abroad the case was
different. He shuddered to think of members of the Anglican
communion becoming tainted with foreign heresies, and, what
was infinitely worse, coming back and spreading the contagion
at home. Yet this was precisely what was likely to happen:
the congregations of the commercial settlements at Delft and
Hamburg, for example, had gone so far as to reject the Church
of England form of worship and to seek the ministration of
Presbyterian divines.[3]

Having once realized the danger, Laud was not slow to act.
Early in the year 1632 he sent suggestions to the Privy Council
for the purpose of extending conformity to the national church
to the English subjects beyond the seas.[4] The story of this

---

[1] See Gardiner, *History of England,* vii. 314–316. The most complete
account of the whole question of Laud's procedure is in Heylyn, *Cyprianus
Anglicus,* 218 ff., 259 ff. Other references are: Collier, *Ecclesiastical History
of Great Britain,* ii. 752–753; Anderson, *Colonial Church,* i. 411; Makower,
Constitutional History and Constitution of the Church of England, 141.

[2] Heylyn, *Cyprianus Anglicus,* 175; Le Neve, *Fasti Ecclesiæ Anglicanæ,*
ii. 304.

[3] Gardiner, *History of England,* vii. 314–316.

[4] " Our Bishop," says Heylyn, " offereth some considerations to the Lords
of the Council, concerning the Dishonour done to the Church of *England* by
the wilful negligence of some Chaplains and other Ministers, both in our Factories and Regiments beyond the Seas; together with the Inconveniences

action and of his subsequent procedure is quaintly told by Heylyn: Laud, he says, "not thinking he had done enough in order to the peace and uniformity of the Church of *England*, by taking care for it here at home, his thoughts transported him with the like affection to preserve it from neglect abroad. To which end he had offered some considerations to the Lords of the Council, as before was said, *Anno* 1622,[1] relating to the regulation of Gods publick Worship amongst the *English Factories*, and Regiments beyond the Seas, and the reducing of the *French* and *Dutch* Churches, settled in divers parts of this Realm, unto some conformity. In reference to the first he had not sate long in the Chaire of *Canterbury* when he procured an Order from the Lords of the Council, bearing date *Octob*. I, 1633. By which their *English* Churches and Regiments in *Holland* (and afterwards by degrees in all other Foreign parts and plantations) were required strictly to observe the *English* Liturgie with all the Rites and Ceremonies prescribed in it. Which Order contained the sum and substance of those considerations which he offered to the Board touching that particular." [2]

which redounded to it from the *French* and *Dutch* Congregations, settled in many places amongst our selves. He had long *teemed* with this Design, but was not willing to be his own *Midwife* when it came to *Birth*; and therefore it was so contrived, that *Windebank* should make the Proposition at the Council Table, and put the Business on so far, that the Bishop might be moved by the whole Board to consider of the Several Points in that weighty Business: who being thus warranted to the execution of his own desires, presented two *Memorials* at the end of the year, *March* 22. The one relating to the Factories and Regiments beyond the Seas; the other to the *French* and *Dutch* Plantations in *London, Kent, Norfolk, Yorkshire, Hampshire*, and the *Isle of Axholme* . . . But it will not be long," continues Heylyn, "before we shall behold him sitting in the Chair of *Canterbury* [August 6, 1633], acting his own Counsels, bringing these *Conceptions* to the *birth*, and putting the design into execution" (*Cyprianus Anglicus*, 218, 222). Cf. also Collier, *Ecclesiastical History of Great Britain*, ii. 752–753. Anderson (*Colonial Church*, i. 410) cites both these authorities, and Makower (*Constitutional History and Constitution of the Church of England*, 141) cites Anderson.

[1] This should be 1632.

[2] *Cyprianus Anglicus*, 259. Heylyn puts a rather optimistic construction on the motives that actuated Laud. For a less favorable view, compare the following: "The length of this great Prelate's Arm would have reached not only to the Puritans in England, but the Factories beyond Sea, if it had been in

This order in council of October 1, 1633, provided, among other things, " That the Company of Merchant Adventurers should not hereafter receive any minister into their Churches in foreign parts without his Majesty's approbation of the person, and that ye Liturgy and Discipline now used in ye Church of England should be received and established there, and that in all things concerning their Church Government they should be under ye Jurisdiction of ye Lord Bpp. of London as their Diocesan." [1] Here the Bishop of London's jurisdiction abroad began; and here it stopped, at least so far as the American colonies were concerned,[2] until after the Restoration. But a precedent had been established, and, although incomplete, it was probably the basis of the tradition which came to connect the name of the Bishop of London with the diocesan control of the English colonies in all parts of the world, in America as well as elsewhere.[3]

his Power. The English Church at Hamburgh managed their Affairs according to the Geneva Discipline, by Elders and Deacons. In Holland they conformed to the Discipline of the States, and met them in their Synods and Assemblies, with consent of King James and of his present Majesty, till Secretary Windebank, at the Instance of this Prelate, offered some Proposals to the Privy Council for their better Regulation " (see Neal, *Puritans*, ii. 237–238, based on Prynne, *Canterbury's Doom*, 389). Laud's plan of seeking to enforce conformity to the doctrine and discipline of the Church of England in Holland was never carried out; for the churches there were supported by the States, and, as the English ministers represented in a letter to the king, would be in danger of losing their maintenance if they submitted to any innovations.

[1] *State Papers, Domestic Series*, Charles I., No. 247, October 1–15, 1633.

[2] This remark does not, of course, apply to his activity in connection with the churches at Delft and Hamburg. A careful search through the English *State Papers*, under the guidance of the *Calendars*, has failed to reveal a single instance of the Bishop of London's diocesan control over the churches in America during the Laudian period.

[3] The persistence of this tradition is attested by the following incident: In 1675 Henry Compton desired to ascertain the basis of the colonial authority which was usually regarded as belonging to his see. To that end he applied to the Lords of Trade and Plantations. At a meeting of a committee of that body held January 21, 1675, this entry was made: " Their Lordships desire that enquiry be made touching the Jurisdiction which the *Bps. of London* hath over the Foreign Plantations; in order to wch see the Charter of Virginia and New England, or by any other order since, *but most probably about the year* 1629, *when Bp. Laud was in Chief Authority*." [The last italics are

To one who reads the whole document,[1] it will be at once apparent that the authority which it conferred upon the Bishop of London did not extend to the colonies in general, but was limited to the churches of the Merchant Adventurers Company at Delft and Hamburg.   Heylyn seems to imply that its provisions were afterward extended to all other English plantations abroad, including those in America; for, in concluding his account of the events just narrated, he says : " And now at last we have the face of an English Church in Holland, responsal to the Bishops of London for the time being, as a part of their Diocess, directly and immediately subject to their Jurisdiction.   The like course was also prescribed for our Factories in Hamborough, and those farther off, that is to say, in Turkey, in the Moguls Dominions, the Indian Islands, the Plantations in Virginia, the Barbadoes, and all other places where the English had any standing Residence in the way of Trade." [2]   In spite of Heylyn's statement, there are good reasons for concluding that, whatever may have been the original intention, no authoritative action based on this order was taken, in the Laudian period, to extend the Bishop of London's jurisdiction to the American plantations, or to incorporate the churches there into his diocese.   In the first place, there is no record of anything of the sort among the *State Papers*, where one would naturally expect to find it;[3] in

the present author's.]   Sherlock's " Report," *New York Documents*, vii. 362 ; cf. also Sainsbury, *Calendar of State Papers, Colonial Series, America and West Indies*, 1675–1676, pp. 337–338.   This is, of course, a question of origins. The Bishop of London received no legal authority to act as diocesan of the colonies until after the Restoration.

[1] Those parts of the order in council which relate to the subject in hand are printed below in Appendix A, No. i., from the original manuscript in the British Public Records Office.

[2] " It was now hoped," he adds fervently, " that there would be a Church of *England* in all Courts of *Christendom*, in the Chief Cities of the *Turk*, and other great Mahometan Princes, in all our Factories and Plantations in every known Part of the world, by which it might be rendered as diffused and *Catholick* as the Church of *Rome*" (*Cyprianus Anglicus*, 260).   Compare also what he says above, p. 14.

[3] Note also that, although the successive governors of Virginia (the only colony where as yet the Church of England had anything like a legal status) were encouraged to support and foster the Church of England, they were not

the second place, Laud, as will subsequently be shown, employed other methods for administering the affairs of the Church of England in this country.

The question naturally arises why the Bishop of London, rather than any other, was chosen to act as diocesan of the foreign churches which Laud was seeking to reduce to conformity. It is hardly probable that the previous relations of Bishops Ravis, Abbot, and King with the colony of Virginia had any weight in determining the choice: the independent character of the Laudian procedure detracts from the likelihood of this hypothesis. Moreover, there are other reasons to account for the selection, if it needs to be accounted for at all. Laud, it should be remembered, held the see of London when he began negotiations for the control of the churches abroad, though he was translated to Canterbury before he completed them. As primate, he had enough to do at home without undertaking the administration of church affairs abroad; and in selecting another to perform these functions it was natural for several reasons that he should choose the Bishop of London. In the first place, London was the see which he himself had occupied during the transactions leading up to the issue of the order.[1] In the second place, William Juxon, his successor, was a man thoroughly in sympathy with his policy, he was, in fact, the primate's own nominee. Finally, London, as the great centre of trade with the continent, was more closely associated than any other city of the kingdom with foreign trading settlements; indeed, evidence is not lacking to indicate that since the

instructed, as they came to be after 1685, to sustain the jurisdiction of the Bishop of London. In one case, at least, the encouragement to support the established church was couched in very specific terms. For example, Article 1 of the instructions issued to Sir William Berkeley in 1650, provided "that in the first place you be careful, Almighty God may be duly and daily served, according to the form of Religion established in the Church of England, both by yourself and all the people under your charge, which may draw down a Blessing upon all your Endeavors. . . . Suffer no Innovation in matters of Religion, and be careful to appoint sufficient and conformable ministers to each Congregation, that they may Catechise and Instruct them in the Ground and Principle of Religion" (Perry, *Historical Collections*, i. (Virginia) 1-2).

[1] Laud became Archbishop of Canterbury in August; but since William Juxon was not consecrated till October 3, 1633, the see was probably not altogether out of Laud's hands at the time of the issue of the order in council.

2

previous century its bishops had had more or less connection with foreign affairs and foreign churches.[1]

Having considered the attempts to work out the Laudian policy in the Low Countries, so far as they affected the origin of the American jurisdiction of the Bishop of London, it should be beyond our province to follow the subject farther. It may be well to note, however, that the order in council was at once put into practical operation, as is shown by a letter of July 17, 1634, from Archbishop Laud to the merchants at Delft, commending to them Mr. Beaumont, who had been chosen preacher by the consent of their Company.[2] Beaumont's commission, issued July 17, 1634, instructed him "That he should punctually keep and observe all the Orders of the Church of England, as they are prescribed in the Canons and Rubricks of the Liturgy ; and that if any person shall shew himself refractory to that Ordinance of his majesty, he shall certifie the name of any such offender, and his offense to the Lord Bishop of London for the time being, who was to take order and give remedy accordingly." [3]

Leaving at this point the history of the jurisdiction of the Bishop of London in the Netherlands, let us turn our attention to the English colonies in America. Although there is no evidence, before the Restoration, of any act performed by the Bishop of London which would lead one to suspect that he had any diocesan authority in the colonies, and not the faintest trace of any theoretical recognition of his title there, there are, on the other hand, several instances of attempts by Laud to control the American branch of the Church of England in other ways.

His first step in this direction was to secure the issue, by writ of privy seal, of a commission " erecting and establishing a board

[1] For example, Vaughan, who succeeded Bancroft as Bishop of London in 1604, received from the French and Dutch ministers in his diocese a petition for protection and favor. In his reply he speaks of Edmund Grindal, Bishop of London from 1559 to 1570, as one of the "superintendents of your Churches" (Neal, *Puritans*, ii. 40, from Strype's *Annals*, iv. 390).

[2] Anderson, *Colonial Church*, i. 411.

[3] Heylyn, *Cyprianus Anglicus*, 260. Anderson, Makower, and Collier also quote something of the correspondence relating to this subject.

for the purpose of governing the colonies." [1] This board was to consist of William Laud, Archbishop of Canterbury, the lord keeper of the great seal, the Archbishop of York, the high treasurer, the lord keeper of the privy seal, and seven other members of the privy council. These, or any five of them, were given "power for the rule and protection of the colonies" in both political and civil affairs and (in consultation with two or three suffragan bishops, who were to be called in for the purpose) in ecclesiastical affairs also. To insure the enforcement of the laws and ordinances made in pursuance of their authority, the commissioners might inflict fitting punishments. They might also require from every colonial governor, and magistrate, ecclesiastical or civil, an account of his office, and might, with the royal assent, remove or otherwise punish him for causes which should seem to them just and reasonable. Furthermore, they were authorized, in consultation with the Archbishop of Canterbury and some of his suffragans, to establish courts and tribunals as well ecclesiastical as civil, forms of judicature, and modes of proceeding, and to decide what offences should appertain to the ecclesiastical and what to the civil administrations, and to act as a court of appeal for settling any disputes which might arise in the colonies. They had also the right to provide for the endowment of churches by means of tithes and other sources of revenue, and to revoke such

[1] For the complete text of this commission in Latin, and for a draft in English, see Baldwin (American Antiquarian Society, *Proceedings*, New Series, xiii. 213 ff.). In the body of his article (pp. 182–187) Judge Baldwin discusses this and the second commission, of April 10, 1636. A rather curious English translation of the Latin original may be found in an appendix to Bradford's *Plymouth Plantation* (Massachusetts Historical Society, *Collections*, 4th Series, iii. 456). For references to other translations, see Baldwin as above, 182, note 2, and an editorial note in Bradford, Appendix, 456. The Latin edition of the second commission is in Pownall, *Administration of the British Colonies*, ii. 155 ff., from whom it is copied by Hazard, *State Papers*, 344 ff., with the date erroneously given as 1634. The supposition of the editor of Bradford that the Latin version in Pownall is the original, from which Bradford's is a translation, is incorrect. Pownall's version is dated April 10, and names Juxon as high treasurer, an office which he did not begin to hold till 1635. In the Bradford edition the Earl of Portland, who died in 1635, is mentioned as high treasurer.

charters as seemed to infringe upon the royal prerogative.
In short, they had supreme control over every branch of colonial
affairs, ecclesiastical and civil.

Two years later, April 10, 1636, a second commission was
issued to Archbishop Laud and others for the government of
all persons within the colonies and plantations beyond the seas,
according to the constitutions there, with power to constitute
courts as well ecclesiastical as civil, for determining causes.[1]

During these years the strenuous attempts of the English
government to execute the new Stuart-Laudian policy of enforcing unity and conformity caused an access of emigration,
particularly to New England.   Notwithstanding the measures
which Laud had undertaken for the supervision and regulation
of the ecclesiastical affairs in the new world, he thought that
he could maintain a firmer check on the spread of dangerous
opinions by keeping their suspected adherents at home.   Proceeding on this assumption, he induced Charles I. to issue,
April 30, 1637, the following proclamation: "The King, being
informed that great numbers of his subjects are yearly transported into New England, with their families and whole estates,
that they might be out of reach of ecclesiastical authority, his
Majesty, therefore, commands that his officers of the several
ports should suffer none to pass without license from the commissioners of the several ports, and a testimonial from their
ministers, of their conformity to the order and discipline of
their church." [2]

On the first of May the king issued a second proclamation,
extending the restriction to the clergy and vesting the right to
issue testimonials in the Archbishop of Canterbury and the
Bishop of London.   "Whereas it is observed," reads this
proclamation, "that such as are not conformable to the dis-

[1] The Latin form of this commission may be found in Pownall, from whom
it was copied by Hazard (see above, p. 19, note 1).   The first and second
commissions seem to be substantially the same, except that in the second the
name of Juxon, the new high treasurer, is substituted for that of the Earl of
Portland, deceased. Cf. Sainsbury, *Calendar of State Papers, Colonial Series,*
1574–1660, p. 232.

[2] Rushworth, *Historical Collections,* ii. 409–410, quoted by Vaughan, *Stuart
Memorials,* i. 487–488.

cipline and ceremonies of the Church, do frequently transport themselves to the plantations, where they take liberty to nourish their factions and schismatical humours, to the hindrance of the good conformity and unity of the Church, we, therefore, do expressly command you, in his Majesty's name, to suffer no clergyman to transport himself without a testimonial from the Archbishop of Canterbury and the Bishop of London." [1]

Trusting to this means to stop the growth of the dissenting element from without, Laud's next step was to devise a way to gain a hold on those who had already got beyond his reach. To this end he made arrangements, in 1638, to send a bishop to New England; but, owing to the sudden outbreak of troubles in Scotland, he was forced to abandon the design.[2]

[1] Rushworth, *Historical Collections,* as above. The appearance of the Bishop of London's name in this connection is interesting, but it furnishes no proof that he was regarded as diocesan of the colonies at this time.

[2] Heylyn's account of the affair gives us a most striking picture of the way in which the New Englanders were regarded by a contemporary royalist and high-churchman : " Not much took notice of at the first," he says, " when they were few in Numbers, and inconsiderable for their Power : but growing up so fast both in Strength and multitude, they began to carry a face of danger. For how unsafe must it be thought both to Church and State, to suffer such a Constant Receptacle of discontented, dangerous, and schismatical Persons, to grow up so fast ; from whence, as from the Bowels of the *Trojan* Horse, so many Incendiaries might break out to inflame the Nation ? *New England,* like the Spleen in the Natural Body, by drawing to it so many sullen, sad, and offensive Humours, was not unuseful and unserviceable to the General Health : But when the Spleen is grown once too full, and emptieth itself into the Stomach, it both corrupts the Blood, and disturbs the Head, and leaves the whole man wearisome to himself and others. And therefore to prevent such mischiefs as might thence ensue, it was under the Consultation of the chief Physicians, who take especial care of the Churches Health, to send a Bishop over to them, for their better Government, and back him with some Forces to compel, if he were not otherwise able to persuade Obedience. But this Design was strangled in the first Conception, by the violent breakings out of the Troubles in *Scotland*" (*Cyprianus Anglicus,* 347). Compare with this an account from the opposite standpoint : " In the reign of Charles I. . . . Laud attempted to subjugate the Colonies, then in their infancy ; he was not content with striving to cramp their trade by foolish proclamations [see Rushworth, *Historical Collections,* i. 718] : but to complete their ruin, was upon the point of sending them a bishop [see Heylyn, as quoted above], with a military force to back his authority . . ." (*Pennsylvania Chronicle,* 7 July, 1768). This quotation, taken from a contro-

The few instances given in this chapter will suffice, it is hoped, to convey some idea of the plan, pursued during the decade 1630–1640, when Charles I. and Laud guided the policy of the English church and state, of extending the Anglican ecclesiastical system in the English colonies throughout the world, as well as some idea of the methods employed for the control of the colonies. Naturally, the Archbishop of Canterbury, by virtue of his office as primate and metropolitan, was the nominal head of the whole English ecclesiastical system both at home and abroad; but, for purposes of more immediate supervision, he made various arrangements for the control of the colonial churches. Thus, he granted to the Bishop of London jurisdiction over the churches of the Merchant Adventurers Company at Delft and Hamburg; he set up a commission for regulating the ecclesiastical affairs of the American colonies; and he made an attempt to establish a bishop in New England to take charge of the churches there.

But a crisis in the course of English history brought the work thus begun to a standstill. Following the rising of the Scots, came the meetings of the Short and the Long Parliament in quick succession, and in the rush of events which ensued the king and his archbishop were allowed no time for the consideration of colonial church affairs. The execution of Laud took place in 1645, and that of Charles followed in 1649. Then came the Commonwealth and the Protectorate, a government hostile, not only to the extension, but even to the existence, of the episcopal establishment. These facts will serve to explain why there are no records of any official connection between the Anglican episcopate and the colonies during the period 1638–1663. With Laud's death his vast plan passed out of consideration, leaving no trace behind save a shadowy tradition, which came to serve as a precedent to the succeeding bishops of London for the exercise of their colonial authority.

Soon after the Restoration the episcopal hand begins to

versial article, written at the time when the agitation against the establishment of American bishops was at its height, will serve to show that the attempts of Laud were regarded with no small anxiety by our colonial forefathers.

appear again in the management of colonial concerns, and one of the names most frequently noticed in connection with the movement is that of the Bishop of London. For example, when an order was passed June 24, 1663, to enforce the British Navigation laws in the plantations, his Lordship was one of the privy counsellors assembled at Whitehall for the consideration of colonial affairs.[1] This is only one of six cases occurring at this time in which his name is mentioned in the list of those members of the Privy Council who served on committees on colonial questions. To cite one more specific instance: the first connection of the Bishop of London with the Carolinas is his presence, November 25, 1664, with that of the Archbishop of Canterbury, at a meeting of this committee, on business relating to the administration of colonial detail.[2]

As time went on, indications began to appear that the Bishop of London was regarded as having the peculiar charge of the concerns of the Church of England in the American colonies. Perhaps the best illustration which can be given is an extract from a letter, dated July 18, 1666, from Thomas Ludwell, secretary of Virginia, to Secretary Lord Arlington, enclosing a description of the province. In that part of his letter which is devoted to ecclesiastical affairs, he says that the clergy "are subject to the See of London and have no superior clergyman among them . . ."; he "wishes my Lord of London and other great clergymen would take them a little more into their care for the better supply of ministers."[3] Another example of a

---

[1] *New York Documents,* iii. 44.

[2] *North Carolina Records,* i. 73–74. The following example, also, may not be without significance. In 1661, an anonymous writer, who signed himself "R. G.," sent to Gilbert Sheldon, Bishop of London, an account of the Church of England in Virginia, in which he lamented the low state into which it had fallen, and suggested measures of reform. The full title of the work is *Virginia's Cure, or an Advisive Narrative concerning Virginia, discovering the True Ground of the Churches Unhappiness, and the only True Remedy. As it was presented to the Right Reverend Father in God, Guilbert Lord Bishop of London, by R. G. September 2, 1661.* This pamphlet will be considered somewhat more in detail in a following chapter.

[3] Sainsbury, *Calendar of State Papers, Colonial Series, America and West Indies,* 1661–1668, p. 400.

recognition of the Bishop of London's special interest in the plantations occurred a few years later. On August 2, 1676, the Archbishop of Canterbury enclosed in a letter to Bishop Compton a complaint addressed to him by one John Yeo, setting forth the " Deplorable Condition of Maryland for want of an Established Ministry." The archbishop makes the following comment: "Received the enclosed from a person altogether unknown. The design of the writer seems very honest and so laudable that I conceive it concerns us by all means to promote it. If his Lordship will remember it when Lord Baltimore's affair is considered at the Council Table, [his grace] makes no question but there may be a convenient opportunity to obtain some settled revenue for the ministry of that place as well as the other plantations. When that is once done it will be no difficult matter for us to supply them with those of competent abilities both regular and conformable." [1] Whether his Lordship ever brought the matter before the Council does not appear.

Certainly at the time of the Restoration the opinion was more or less prevalent that the charge of colonial ecclesiastical affairs belonged to the Bishop of London; and, according to the scattered instances related above, he seems even thus early to have taken some share in the administration of such matters. There was, however, apparently no effort to place the jurisdiction on a legal footing, or to exercise it in anything like a systematic and efficacious manner, until the accession of Bishop Compton, whose activity in this direction will be considered in the next chapter.

The only permanent results, then, of the period to which this chapter has been mainly devoted were the establishment of the Church of England in Virginia,[2] and the fixing of the precedent that the diocesan control of the English plantations in North America should be vested in the Bishop of London.

---

[1] Sainsbury, *Calendar of State Papers, Colonial Series, America and West Indies,* 1675–1676, p. 435.

[2] This was brought about by royal ordinance in 1606, confirmed by enactment of the Virginia assembly, and reaffirmed — in one case, at least, specifically — in the instructions to the early governors. See above, pp. 9, 11, 16, note 3.

CHAPTER II.

THE POLICY AND WORK OF BISHOP COMPTON, 1675-1714.

No sooner was Henry Compton translated to the see of London, in December, 1675,[1] than he interested himself in the affairs of the colonies. In a letter dated March, 1676, he writes : "As the care of your churches, with the rest of the plantations, lies upon me as your diocesan, so to discharge that trust, I shall omit no occasions of promoting their good and interest."[2] Reports from several quarters indicate that in some of the colonies the need of such episcopal guidance and assistance was felt. For example, Sir Thomas Lynch, in his account of the state of the church in Jamaica, written in May, 1675, had suggested that "if the king would affix to that island two considerable prebendaries as of Eton, Westminster, Lincoln, etc., such person, by the Bishop of London's direction, might have a superintendence of Church affairs, keep people in their duty, convert sectaries, and suppress atheism and irreligion, which the people there much incline to."[3] Evidently, something would now be done, if the united efforts of the new bishop and divers earnest men abroad could bring it to pass.

Compton's first important step was to find out what legal basis he possessed for the authority over the colonies which tradition attributed to his see. To that end, he instituted the inquiry which has already been noticed in another connection.[4] Finding nothing to warrant the exercise of any formal jurisdic-

[1] Le Neve, *Fasti Ecclesiæ Anglicanæ*, ii. 304; *New York Documents*, vii. 373, editor's note.

[2] Wilberforce, *Protestant Episcopal Church*, 107, citing *Fulham MSS*. The name of his correspondent is not given.

[3] Endorsed, "Sir Thos. Lynch, his acct. about the Church in Jamaica, May, 1675" (*Colonial Papers*, Vol. 34, No. 83). See also Sainsbury, *Calendar of State Papers, Colonial Series, America and West Indies*, 1675–1676, pp. 237–238. For an earlier instance, see above, p. 22.

[4] See above, p. 15, note 3.

tion on his part, and at the same time realizing the necessity of some sort of episcopal supervision over the ministers and churches beyond the seas, he induced the government to insert the following provisions in the instructions issued to colonial governors after this time : " That God be duly served, *The Book of Common Prayer as is now established, read each Sunday and Holy Day, and the Blessed Sacrament administered according to the rules of the Church of England.* . . . And our will and pleasure is that no Minister be preferr'd by you, to any Ecclesiastical Benefice in that Our Colony *without a Certificate from the Lord Bp. of London, of his being conformable to the Doctrine of the Church of England.*" [1] It will be noticed that the powers thus conferred upon the Bishop of London were of a purely ministerial nature.

The practical condition of things was this : first, the status of the Church of England in the colonies was upon an extremely insecure footing ; and, secondly, the Bishop of London and a few ardent churchmen resident beyond the seas desired to remedy the matter. The truth of these statements is evident both from the complaints made by some of the colonists to him whom they regarded as their diocesan, and from the latter's attempts to bring these complaints before the council. The following incident will serve as an illustrative example. At a meeting of a committee of the Lords of Trade and Plantations at Whitehall, July 17, 1677, Bishop Compton presented a memorial enumerating nine abuses which had crept into the government of the church in the plantations,[2] — including offences against ecclesiastical law, lax morality, and the like. Of these nine enumerated abuses, it will be necessary to repeat at length only the first and the seventh. The former asserts, " That the Kings Right of Patronage & presenting to all benefices and Cures of Souls which happen to be void in any of the Plantations

---

[1] These clauses first appear in the instructions to Governor Culpeper of Virginia, Articles 15 and 16, *New York Documents,* viii. 362.

[2] " A Memorial of what abuses are crept into the Churches of the Plantations : " *New York Documents,* iii. 253 ; *North Carolina Records,* i. 233–234 ; Sainsbury, *Calendar of State Papers, Colonial Series, America and West Indies,* 1677–1680, pp. 117–118.

is not duely asserted & practised by the several Governors in so much as some parishes are kept vacant where a lawfull minister may be had, and some persons are commissionated to exercise the ministerial function without Orders both in Virginia, Barbados, & other places." The latter declares " That the vestries there [in Virginia] pretend an Authority to be intrusted with the sole management of Church Affaires, & to exercise an arbitrary power over the Ministers themselves." The other subjects of complaint were as follows: the fact that the people converted the profits of the vacant parishes to their own uses; the precarious tenure and small compensation of the ministers; the want of a settled maintenance for ministers in Maryland; the fact that in Virginia no places were allotted for the burial of the dead; the power of the vestries over their ministers; the failure to enforce the marriage laws in Virginia; the law requiring all Church of England ministers to have their orders from some bishop in England; and the fact that no care was taken for the passage and accommodation of such ministers as were sent over, except in the case of those sent to Virginia.

The Bishop's memorial seems to have had some weight with their lordships; for, after considering the enumerated grievances in order, they recommended that the governors be directed to see that each was remedied. Moreover, it was noted in the Council's journal of November 10, that, in relation to the law for the maintenance of the ministry, their lordships thought all the particulars in the memorial very necessary to be observed, and were of opinion that they ought to make part of the governor's instructions.[1] Again, January 14, 1680, on a motion of Compton concerning the " state of the Church in His Majesty's Plantations," the king issued an order in council directing " that the Lords of Trade and Plantations signify His Majesty's pleasure unto His respective Governors in America, that every Minister within their government be one of the Vestry in his respective parish, and that no vestry be held without him except in case of sickness, or that after notice of a vestry summoned he absent himself." [2]

[1] Sainsbury, *Calendar of State Papers, Colonial Series, America and West Indies*, 1677–1680, p. 176.　　　　　　　　　　[2] *Ibid.* 469.

It must be always kept in mind that at this time Virginia was the only American colony where the Church of England had anything like a firm foothold.   From New England, for example, comes the following testimony in the words of Governor Andros: "I have not heard of any Church or Assembly according to ye Church of England in any [of] the Collonyes; their Ecclesiasticall government is as in their law bookes and practice most or wholly independant."[1]   This statement is hardly surprising in view of the fact that in 1680 there was only one Episcopal clergyman in New England, Father Jordan of Portsmouth.[2] Indeed, in 1679, when several of the inhabitants of the town of Boston petitioned Compton for a minister, there appear to have been only four Church of England clergymen in North America outside of Virginia and Maryland.[3]   In the former colony there were forty parishes and something like twenty clergymen, and in the latter twenty-six parishes, about one-half of which were supplied with ministers.[4]

This paucity of means for supplying the spiritual needs of Episcopalians dwelling outside of Maryland and Virginia opened Compton's eyes, and caused him to set about remedying the defect.   To this end he induced King Charles to allow the New England church a building; whereupon, in 1689, the society formed in accordance with the royal sanction built King's Chapel, and King William began the practice, which was continued till the Revolution, of sending an annual bounty of £100 for the support of assistant ministers.[5]

The energetic Compton also obtained from Charles II. a bounty of £20 for each minister and schoolmaster taking passage to the West Indies, and caused instructions to be given to the respective governors, to permit no man to serve in the cure of souls, or to teach school, unless licensed by the Bishop of

[1] Report, dated April 9, 1678, in answer to inquiries of the Council of Trade concerning the plantations of New England, *New York Documents*, iii. 264.

[2] McConnell, *American Episcopal Church*, 41.

[3] *Account of the Society for Propagating the Gospel in Foreign Parts* (1706), 12 ; David Humphreys, *Historical Account of the Society*, etc., 8.

[4] Humphreys, *Historical Account*, 41–42.

[5] *Account of the Society*, etc., 11 ; Humphreys, *Historical Account*, 7.

London. This provision for sending out regular clergymen and schoolmasters under the certificate of the Bishop of London did much for the Church of England in America, both in the West Indies and in the colonies on the mainland where it came to be applied.[1] Apparently Sir Thomas Lynch of Jamaica was the first among the West Indian governors to have a clause inserted in his instructions, relating to the ministerial supervision of the Bishop of London. It is worded precisely the same as that issued to Culpeper two years before,[2] with the following additional direction : " And you are to enquire whether any Minister preaches or administers the Sacrament without being in *due Orders;* whereof you are to give notice to the Bp. of London." In regard to this clause, a later bishop, Thomas Sherlock, who seemed always to be on the lookout for a chance to find a limitation in the scope of any grant of power to the Bishop of London, remarks : " What the Bp. of London could do upon such notice, does not appear. The Plantations being no part of his Diocese, nor had he any authority to act there." [3]

Compton's next step was to obtain a more effective control over the clergy and the laity.[4] In view of the extremely insecure position of the Church of England in the colonies, he particularly needed more power to secure himself against unworthy ministers. Consequently, soon after the accession of James II. he sent a letter April 15, 1685, to Blathwaite, secretary to the Lords of Trade and Plantations, embodying the following propositions : " That he [the Bishop of London] may have all *Ecclesiastical Jurisdiction* in the West Indies, excepting the disposal of parishes, licences for Marriage, &ᶜ, Probate of Wills," and " That no Schoolmaster coming from England,

---

[1] *Account of the Society,* etc., 12 ; Humphreys, *Historical Account,* 8–9.

[2] See above, p. 26. Lynch's instructions are dated 1681 (*New York Documents,* vii. 362).

[3] Sherlock's " Report," *New York Documents,* vii. 362).

[4] Compare a contemporary writer : " And for the better ordering of them, his Lordship prevailed with the King, to devolve all Ecclesiastical Jurisdiction in those Parts upon him and his Successors, except what concern'd Inductions, Marriages, Probate of Wills and Administrations, which was continued by the Governors as profitable Branches of their Revenue " (*Account of the Society,* etc., 12–13).

be received without Licence from His Lordship, or from other His Majesty's Plantations without they take the Governor's licence." [1]

The lords, having heard the letter, agreed to consider its proposals further when the bishop should be present. Accordingly, on April 27, when Compton happened to be in attendance, the letter was again read, and the lords agreed to move the king to insert the articles in the governors' instructions. As a result of this resolution, the following clauses were added to the instructions of Sir Philip Howard, governor of Jamaica, in a commission of the same year : [2]

"*And to the end the ecclesiastical Jurisdiction of the s^d Bp. of London may take place in that our Island, as far as conveniently may be, we do think it fit that you give all countenance and encouragm^t in the exercise of the same excepting only* the Collating Benefices, granting licences for marriages, and probate of wills, which we have reserved to you our Governor, and the Commander in chief for the time being.

" And we do further direct that no schoolmaster be henceforward permitted *to come from England* and to keep school within that our Island *without the licence of the said Bishop.*" [3]

Like instructions were afterward given to the governors of nearly all the royal provinces. Under the authority thus conferred, Bishops Compton, Robinson (and Gibson also for the first two or three years following his promotion to the see of London),[4] exercised ecclesiastical supervision over the colonies, except in matters relating to collations to benefices, licenses for marriages, and probate of wills, which, as we have seen, were reserved to the governors in their respective provinces.[5] An assertion made by some writers, that the authority granted to Compton and his successors was afterward confirmed by an

[1] *New York Documents*, vii. 362.

[2] The clause already inserted in the instructions to Culpeper and Lynch (see above, p. 29, and note 2, *ibid.*) was naturally incorporated in these and subsequent instructions.

[3] *New York Documents*, vii. 363.

[4] Perceval, *Apostolical Succession*, Appendix, 109–121.

[5] For a full account, see *New York Documents*, vii. 363 ; Perry, *American Episcopal Church*, i. 154–155 ; Brodhead, *New York*, ii. 456–457.

order in council,[1] while not capable of direct proof, has evidence to support it. Though the original order is not to be found in the council books, yet, at about the time when it is said to have been issued, there is a blank left on the books for the insertion of something which was never inserted. The missing document, whatever it may be, is very likely among the papers of Mr. Blathwaite, who was then acting chief clerk of the council; but where those papers are, or whether they are still extant, the present writer has not as yet been able to discover. In the opinion of Commissary Gordon of Barbadoes, it is very probable that such an order was issued. His reasons are as follows: in the first place, because at about that time an order in council was issued adding the Bishop of London to the body of Lords Commissioners for Trade and Plantations, all of whom were then members of the Privy Council; secondly, because the clauses quoted above were inserted in governors' commissions and instructions;[2] in the third place, because in a copy of a letter, dated September, 1685, from Bishop Compton to Lord Howard, governor of Virginia, the order is expressly mentioned, with the reasons for vesting the power in the bishop;[3] and, finally, because there is the indirect evidence of two orders in council, dated October, 1686, one suspending the Bishop of London from his diocese and vesting the exercise of his authority in a

---

[1] Abbey, *English Church and Bishops*, i. 82; cited by McConnell, *American Episcopal Church*, 97.

[2] The commentator adds that the words "which we have reserved," etc., seem "to refer to something done before; for every Reservation necessarily implies some previous Grant out of which the Reservation is made." It is more likely, however, that the reservation is from the ordinary jurisdiction which the bishops of London exercised in England.

[3] ". . . I do most humbly thank your Lordship for the great care you have taken in setting the Church under your Government. There is a constant Order of Council remaining with Mr. Blaithwaite that no man shall continue in any Parish without Orders; nor any to be received without a License under the hand of the Bishop of London for the time being, and that the Minister shall always be one of the vestry. This order was made four or five years since, and I can make no doubt, among others you have it in your instructions. This King has likewise made one lately that Except Licenses for marriages, Probat of Wills, and disposing of the Parishes, all other Ecclesiastical Jurisdiction shall be in the Bishop of London" (*Fulham MSS.*).

board of commissioners, the other,[1] issued a week later, suspending him, with the same formality, from his authority in the plantations and conferring it on the same commission.[2] Though these reasons do not conclusively prove that there was a standing order in council, issued about 1685, vesting the ecclesiastical jurisdiction of the colonies in the Bishop of London, they at least make it appear highly probable that there was such an order, even though no entry appears in the council books.

Of course the temporary orders in council embodied in every governor's instructions had, while they continued, the force of standing orders; but they lacked the advantage of stability. For instance, take the case just alluded to: Bishop Compton fell out with King James because of his opposition to the Test Act; whereupon, on his refusal to suspend Dr. Sharpe for a sermon against popery, he was removed from the Privy Council, his see was put into commission, and his colonial authority was delegated to the Archbishop of Canterbury.[3] It was not long, however, before Archbishop Sancroft himself incurred the king's displeasure on account of his ecclesiastical opinions. For this reason the jurisdiction over the colonies was taken from his hands and transferred to the bishops of Durham, Rochester, and Peter-

---

[1] October 27, 1686: "Whereas His Majesty has thought fitt to appoint Commissioners for exercising the Episcopal Jurisdiction within the City and Diocese of London, His Majesty in Council does this Day Declare his pleasure that the Ecclesiastical Jurisdiction in the Plantations shall be exercised by the said Commissioners; and did order & it is hereby ordered that the R^t Honble the Lords of the Commñ for Trade & Plantations do prepare instructions for the several governors in the Plantations accordingly" (*Fulham MSS.*).

[2] For a discussion of the whole subject see a letter of November 3, 1725, from Commissary Gordon of Barbadoes to Bishop Gibson, in regard to his jurisdiction (*Ibid.* The letter is printed in Appendix A, No. iv.).

[3] See instructions to Governor Dongan of New York, issued May 29, 1686, in which, in the articles relating to religion (Articles 31–38), the words "Archbishop of Canterbury" are substituted for "Bishop of London" (*New York Documents*, iii. 369–375). For details, see *An Account of the whole Proceedings against Henry, Lord Bishop of London, before the Lord Chancellor and the other Ecclesiastical Commissioners* (pamphlet, London, 1688); *Life of Henry Compton* (anonymous), 16–42; Foote, *Annals of King's Chapel*, i. 166–167. See also Brodhead, *New York*, ii. 455–456, who cites various other references.

borough, who administered the see of London in commission during the suspension of Compton. With the change of dynasty which soon followed, Compton was restored to royal favor.[1] He must at once have resumed his interest in colonial concerns; for, in an ordinance of February 16, 1689, by which King William nominated twelve great officers of state, or any three of them, to constitute a "Committee of the Privy Council for Trade and Foreign Plantations," the Bishop of London is the only ecclesiastic on the list.[2] In the instructions to Henry Sloughter, January 31, 1689, Compton's name again appears as diocesan.[3]

Being here concerned only with the basis and scope of the Bishop of London's jurisdiction after the Restoration, we must reserve for another place a consideration of the relations between Compton and the particular colonies. However, some of the more general evidences of his activity may be noted here. In 1671 there were hardly more than thirty Church of England clergymen in Virginia and Maryland, and less than forty in the whole country. By the year 1700 the number had increased to nearly sixty, of whom twenty exercised their functions outside the two great Episcopal centres.[4] And this was in the days before the foundation of the Society for Propagating the Gospel, by whose efforts so many clergymen were sent to America.[5]

Compton also instituted the practice of appointing commissaries, who from this time until the middle of the eighteenth century continued to exercise delegated authority in the colo-

[1] Brodhead, *New York*, ii. 456; Perry, *American Episcopal Church*, i. 154–155.

[2] *New York Documents*, iii., Introduction, xiv.; *Life of Henry Compton* (anonymous), 43.

[3] *New York Documents*, iii. 685–691.

[4] McConnell, *American Episcopal Church*, 87. Tiffany, however, says that at the beginning of the eighteenth century there were six outside Virginia and Maryland, and about fifty including the clergymen of these two colonies.

[5] In 1725 this Society had thirty-six missionaries in America, in 1743 sixty-seven, in 1750 seventy, and at the beginning of the Revolution over one hundred. See Abbey, *English Church and Bishops*, i. 348; Caswall, *American Church*, 68.

nies.[1]   The first commissary to receive an appointment was the
Reverend James Blair, who was sent to Virginia in 1689;[2] the
second was the Reverend Thomas Bray, sent in 1695 to inquire
into the state of the colonial church as a whole.   It was due to
the influence of Dr. Bray's pamphlet, *A Memorial, representing
the State of Religion in the Continent of North America,* that the
Society for Propagating the Gospel was founded.   Since this
society contributed more than any other single organization
toward fostering the growth of the Church of England in
America, perhaps a few words concerning its origin and aims
will not be out of place.

Not only did the enthusiasm of Compton rouse the English
government to the need of doing something to strengthen the
Episcopal church abroad, but various indications show that his
efforts among private individuals were equally successful.   For
example, Sir Leoline Jenkyns, in his will (proved November 9,
1685), provided for the establishment of two fellowships at Jesus
College, Oxford, on condition that the holders take holy orders
and go to sea when summoned by the Lord High Admiral,
"and in case there be no Use of their Service at Sea, to be
called by the Lord Bishop of London, to go out into any of His
Majesty's Foreign Plantations, there to take upon them the Cure
of Souls, and exercise their Ministerial Function."[3]   This meant
a great deal at a time when there were, with one or two exceptions, no Church of England ministers in Pennsylvania, the
Jerseys, New York, or New England;[4] for the earliest Episcopal churches in Massachusetts and Rhode Island had not yet
been built, and seven years were to elapse before the church
secured its partial establishment in New York.[5]

---

[1] In one colony, at least, there were commissaries up to the Revolution.
In the others, however, few if any appointments were made after the time of
Gibson.

[2] See above, p. 3, note 2.

[3] *Account of the Society for Propagating the Gospel in Foreign Parts* (1706).

[4] There was a Church of England chaplain in the fort at New York, and, as
we have seen, one clergyman at Portsmouth, New Hampshire (above, p. 28).

[5] In 1693, owing to the efforts of Governor Fletcher, clergymen were settled
in three or four New York counties, each supported by a grant of from £40 to
£60 a year.

While isolated efforts such as this were an encouraging sign of a laudable missionary zeal, it was evident, nevertheless, that, if effective results were to be secured, they would have to be supplemented by an organized movement. Realizing this fact, Archbishop Tennison and Bishop Compton applied to the king to charter a missionary society; and as a result of their efforts the "Society for Propagating the Gospel in Foreign Parts" was incorporated by royal charter under the great seal on June 16, 1701.[1] All the bishops of the realm were to canvass for such clergymen as were willing to go out as missionaries; those secured for the purpose were to report their names to the secretary of the Society, who, after consultation with the Bishop of London, was to decide to what places they should be sent.[2] Among other things it was provided "that before their departure, they should wait upon his Grace the Archbishop of Canterbury, their Metropolitan, and the Lord Bishop of London, their Diocesan, to receive their Paternal Benediction and Instructions."[3] They were further required to keep up a constant and regular correspondence with the secretary; to send, every six months, a statement of the condition of their respective parishes; and to communicate what was done at the meetings of the clergy, and "whatsoever else may concern the Society."[4]

From this time the Society continued, on the whole, to be a refining and elevating force, striving to devote itself wholly to spiritual concerns, rarely meddling with politics as such, and apparently not desiring to meddle with them. Thus, when the "Church Act" of South Carolina arrived in England for confirmation, November 4, 1704, the Society, at a meeting held in St. Paul's, declared that by the act in question "the ministers of South Carolina will be subjected too much to the pleasure of the people, and therefore they agree to recommend this matter to the Wisdom of the Lord Archbishop of Canterbury and the Lord Bishop of London to take such care herein as they shall

---

[1] *Account of the Society*, etc., 14 ff. For the text of the Society's charter, see its *Collection of Papers* (1715), 1–13.

[2] *Account of the Society*, etc., 14.

[3] *Ibid.* 19.

[4] *Ibid.* 26.

think proper." [1] In the interim, until a decision should be
reached, it declined to send any more ministers to the Carolinas. As it did not wish to rule the people, so it did not wish
the people to rule the Society or its ministers; it sought only
sufficient independence for the free scope of its missionary activity, and wished to leave all other matters to its civil and ecclesiastical superiors — the king, the Archbishop of Canterbury, and
the Bishop of London. This was its policy, or rather its ideal.

Unfortunately this ideal was not always fully realized; for
no sooner was the Society established on a firm foundation
than it began to direct its efforts toward substituting a control
by bishops resident in the colonies for the jurisdiction of the
Bishop of London. However innocent this intention may have
been, the Anglican Episcopal organization was too closely interwoven with the English governmental system to make it possible to keep the matter within the spiritual field. Moreover,
the Independent congregations in America knew the Church of
England bishop only as an oppressive tyrant, backed by the
strong arm of the civil power. For these reasons, the attempt
of the Society to secure an American episcopate involved not
only itself but the whole colonial church in a series of political
contests, the outcome of which marked the first great crisis in
American history. Just how this crisis came about will be shown
in a later chapter.

At this point it may be of interest to consider a few typical
cases of the activity of Compton and of his successor, Robinson.
A striking instance of Compton's watchful care over the church
beyond the seas may be found in a clause in the Pennsylvania charter, which makes an extremely liberal provision for
such Episcopalians as may wish to found a church or churches
in the colony. [2] The insertion of this provision was due to the

---

[1] *Account of the Society*, etc., 75–79.

[2] Extract from the grant of Pennsylvania, March 4, 1680–1681 : " And Our
further pleasure is, and wee doe hereby, for us, our heirs and Successors,
charge and require, that if any of the inhabitants of the said Province, to the
number of Twenty, shall at any time hereafter be desirous, and shall by any
writeing, or by any person deputed for them, signify such their desire to the
Bishop of *London* that any preacher or preachers, to be approved of by the
said Bishops, may be sent unto them for their instruction, that then such

bishop's efforts. At a meeting of the Lords of the Committee of the Privy Council for the affairs of Trade and Plantations, held at Whitehall January 22, 1680, to consider the draft of the patent constituting William Penn absolute proprietary of the tract of land later known as Pennsylvania, he presented a paper desiring "that Mr. Penn be obliged, by his patent, to admit a chaplain, of his Lordship's appointment, upon the request of any number of planters." As a result of this application, the Lords, in a meeting held on the 24th of February, passed the following resolution : "The Lord Bishop of *London* is desired to prepare a draught of a law to be passed in this country, for the settling of the Protestant religion."[1] Thus, in consequence of Compton's efforts, the Church of England was at least insured of a definite recognition in the colony of Pennsylvania.[2] Penn seems to have been on a friendly footing with him, and on one occasion at least thankfully accepted and followed one of his suggestions.[3]

Occasionally during this period the Bishop of London was called upon to exercise his authority in a case of discipline. Perhaps the best example is that of the Reverend Francis Philips, curate of the Reverend Robert Jenney, rector of Christ Church,

preacher or preachers shall and may be and reside within the said province, without any denial or molestation whatsoever " (Poore, *Charters and Constitutions*, ii. 1515). See also Perry, *Historical Collections*, ii. (Pennsylvania) 5 ; Perry, *American Episcopal Church*, i. 224 ; Proud, *Pennsylvania*, i. 186.

[1] Perry, *American Episcopal Church*, i. 224, note 1 ; Perry, *Historical Collections*, ii. (Pennsylvania) 497–498 ; Hazard, *Register of Pennsylvania*, i. 269–270.

[2] Stillé, in his *Address delivered on the two hundredth anniversary of Christ Church, Philadelphia*, November 19, 1895, says (p. 8) that even the missionaries in Pennsylvania had the privileges of membership in the " Established Church of America," accountable only to the Bishop of London and his "Church Courts." One wonders what the "Established Church of America" was. "Church courts " is a rather formal name for the small powers of jurisdiction which the commissaries generally exercised ; moreover, the Society certainly claimed some accountability for its missionaries.

[3] In a letter dated Philadelphia, August 14, 1683, Penn says : " I have followed the Bishop of *London's* counsel, by buying and not taking away the natives' land ; with whom I have settled a very kind correspondence " (Proud, *Pennsylvania*, i. 274). See also Perry, *American Episcopal Church*, i. 224, note 1.

Philadelphia. Early in the year 1715, Philips, being accused of misdemeanors, was put into prison. On promising to behave himself he was released; but no sooner did he regain his liberty than he raised a mob of his supporters and resumed his place, announcing that he would stay in it in spite of any orders of the Bishop of London to the contrary. On March 17 the clergy of Pennsylvania took occasion, in their congratulatory message to Robinson on his accession to the see of London, to review the case of Philips up to the point where he had defied the authority of his diocesan, and to pray for his removal. Philips's friends were equally active; several of them, headed by Lieutenant Governor Gookin and including many prominent members of the vestry, drew up and signed a memorial to the Bishop of London in which they exonerated Philips from all blame and prayed for his continuance among them. Philips himself wrote to the secretary of the Society, beseeching him to interest the new bishop in his behalf. In this letter he denies all the charges against himself, as mere fabrications of his enemies. Of one of his chief accusers, he says, and appeals to Reverend Evan Evans, a prominent Pennsylvania clergyman, to support his statements: "It was his daily practice in the last reign in all companies to rail at the church and state; and as to the canons — he has more than once in my hearing at a public meeting of the Vestry declared that they were of no force here, so that I take it for granted that though he is no member of the Vestry now, his next assertion will be that we are not under the cognizance of the Bishop of London [1] and consequently that the people may call or displace a minister after the independent mode when they please but this I believe he will scarcely be able to accomplish during my abode here." The next step in the controversy was an appeal from the wardens and vestry of the church in Philadelphia in behalf of Philips, who evidently had a large party behind him. Their argument for restoring the offending clergyman to his curacy is certainly a curious one. After assuring their Bishop of their recognition of his jurisdiction over the behavior of the

[1] The allusion to the Bishop of London has the appearance of being lugged in for the sake of currying favor, particularly in the face of the alleged defiant attitude which Philips had shown a short time before.

clergy in all except criminal cases, they beg his Lordship to reinstate Philips because they do not want the decision of a Quaker court of judicature upon the conduct of a Church of England clergyman to prevail, for the reason that it may give justification for attempts upon his Lordship's prerogative in the future. But all these attempts of Lieutenant Governor Gookin, and of the wardens, vestry, and members of the Philadelphia church, proved unavailing. When Bishop Robinson finally decided against them, they submitted and gave up possession of the church. Although Philips went home to plead his cause in person, it does not appear that he was ever reinstated.[1]

In the proprietary colony of Maryland, although the Church of England was established there, the Bishop of London exercised very little authority except during the administration of a governor who happened to be friendly to his interests. This fact is well illustrated in the struggle over the appointment of a successor to Thomas Bray, the first commissary.[2] Soon after Bray's return from Maryland, finding that in all likelihood he would never be able to go there again, he resigned his office, and in August, 1700, reminded his diocesan of the urgent necessity of sending over a successor. At once the question arose as to how means might be obtained for his support. In 1694–1695 the governor and assembly had passed an act vesting the office of judge in testamentary causes in such ecclesiastical person as the Bishop of London for the time being should commissionate under him; the income attached to the office was to be £300. Although Bray had obtained the position, he had been deprived of the stipend by an intrigue. His constant aim was to strengthen the authority of the Church of England in the colony. Having failed in an effort to secure the appointment of a suffragan bishop,

[1] For the documentary evidence on the case, see Perry, *Historical Collections,* ii. (Pennsylvania) 81, 87–89, 90–93, 97–98.

[2] See an account of the whole matter by Bray himself, in "a Memorial giving a true and Just account of the affair of the Commissary of Maryland, with respect to which the New Governor, Col! Seymour, has made so great Complaints of his ill usage by me," etc., 1705 (Perry, *Historical Collections,* iv. (Maryland) 57–63).

he now returned to the plan of governing by a commissary, who was, however, to be invested with the power of induction hitherto exercised by the governor.[1] He recommended as his successor in the commissarial office the Reverend Michael Huetson, Archdeacon of Armagh, a candidate who proved acceptable to the Bishop of London. To provide for his support, Bray proposed that the judgeship of testamentary causes be given to him. This proposal he justified on the following grounds: "since the office of Judge in Testamentary Causes is an office of an Ecclesiastical nature; an office that the Country have desired might be vested in an Ecclesiastical person, and more particularly in the Bishop of London's Commissary for his support; and since it is an office that He, the Governor, could not execute himself, being that appeals lie from that court to himself, as Chancellor, or at leastwise to himself in Council; an office, too, that must be bestowed on some one." The Bishop felt the force of Bray's reasoning, and, during a dinner held at Fulham, at which Bray, Huetson, and Colonel Seymour, the governor-elect, were all present, made the proposal to the new governor. Seymour not only refused to grant the request, but violently denounced the negotiations of Bray as underhanded, and slandered him, in this and many other particulars, not only to Bishop Compton but to the Archbishop of Canterbury as well. In a word, he betrayed so curious a behavior that Bray hazarded the suspicion in his memorial that there must have been some fundamental ground for his opposition to a commissary.[2] However that may have been, Seymour gained his point, Huetson did not go to Maryland, and for many years the Bishop of London remained without an official representative in the colony.

In the absence of a commissary, a plan was evolved by the assembly to establish a spiritual court made up of the governor

---

[1] Hawks, *Ecclesiastical Contributions*, ii. (Maryland) 121 ff. Hawks regards this as a very effective scheme for giving to the commissary control over the admission of clergy for whose conduct he was responsible. But the fact that presentation remained with the governor was somewhat of a handicap.

[2] Possibly the fact that the new commissary was to have the power of induction may account for Seymour's attitude.

and three laymen.   This court was "to superintend the conduct
of the clergy" and to take "cognizance of all cases of immorality on the part of a clergyman, and of non-residence in his
parish for thirty days at one time"; its power was also to
extend to the deprivation of livings and to suspension from the
ministry.   The bill passed both houses, but was not signed by
the governor for want of instructions.   Naturally, the scheme
was opposed by the clergy, who wrote to their diocesan that
"it would be establishing presbyterianism in the colony, upon
the neck of the Church, and raise an effectual bar to the introduction of Episcopacy, which is generally wished for by the
clergy of this province." [1]

Commissarial authority was resumed in Maryland soon after
the accession of Governor Hart, a man most friendly to the
interests of the Church of England in the province.   In a
letter written to the Bishop of London, September 6, 1715, he
recommended the appointment of two commissaries, if a suffragan could not be secured.[2]   The nominees suggested by him
were Christopher Wilkinson for the Eastern, and Jacob Henderson for the Western Shore.   The nominations were confirmed
in the following year by the bishop, and the commissaries at
once entered office.[3]   In spite of the friendliness of the governor, however, they had a difficult time in the exercise of their
functions; for the assembly and the people of the higher
classes were extremely hostile to the established clergy and to
the attempts to extend the jurisdiction of the ·Bishop of London.[4]   "It is a sad truth," write the commissaries, "that we
must declare that we have not one friend in the province,
except our governor to make our application to; nor any
access to, nor place, nor employ in the government, nor friend
in the world that we know of, but your lordship to stand by us." [5]

---

[1] Hawks, *Ecclesiastical Contributions*, ii. (Maryland) 129–131.

[2] Perry, *Historical Collections*, iv. (Maryland) 80–82.

[3] Hawks, *Ecclesiastical Contributions*, ii. (Maryland) 150.

[4] See the correspondence between Bishop Robinson and his commissaries
in Perry, *Historical Collections*, iv. (Maryland), and in *Fulham MSS., passim.*

[5] Hawks, *Ecclesiastical Contributions*, ii. (Maryland) 154.   For the whole
letter, see Perry, *Historical Collections*, iv. (Maryland) 89–91.

The Bishop seems to have exercised his good offices with Lord Baltimore, who wrote to the commissaries, March 23, 1718, that he acknowledged the establishment and the authority of the Bishop of London, and would do all in his power to further the interests of the Church of England in Maryland.[1]

Failing in an attempt to get a bill through the assembly acknowledging the authority of the Bishop of London in the province,[2] Wilkinson sought from that body an authorization of his right to punish two clergymen accused of immorality, one of drinking and swearing, the other of an incestuous marriage. Owing to the political influence of the accused, and to the fear of setting a precedent, which prevailed among the independent elements in the colony, the proposal was defeated.[3] These two failures were a sore blow to the development of any ecclesiastical authority in Maryland; and henceforth the commissaries found it harder than ever to exercise ecclesiastical discipline. An indication of their discouragement is seen in the fact that they found it no longer worth while to require church wardens to present offenders.[4] Even the indomitable Henderson, who was far more aggressive than his colleague Wilkinson, at length recognized the futility of attempting to exercise anything save an advisory and exhortatory control over the clergy under his charge.[5]

---

[1] Perry, *Historical Collections*, iv. (Maryland) 99.

[2] The bill passed the council and was supported by the governor.

[3] For an account of this affair, see Hawks, *Ecclesiastical Contributions*, ii. (Maryland) 162; also two letters from Wilkinson to Bishop Robinson, dated respectively April 25 and May 26, 1718, in Perry, *Historical Collections*, iv. (Maryland) 106–109. There seems to have been considerable discussion as to the relative limits of civil and ecclesiastical power. In the letter of April 25, for example, Wilkinson reports that it has been decided that, when the ecclesiastical punishment is not corporeal or pecuniary, temporal punishment may follow. He thus shows that the status of ecclesiastical punishment was at least recognized.

[4] Hawks, *Ecclesiastical Contributions*, ii. (Maryland) 170.

[5] Henderson to Bishop Robinson, June 17, 1718: "As there is no hopes of an Act of Assembly to support it [the jurisdiction of the Bishop of London], and your Lordship has been pleased to order me not to set up a Court in form, I have faithfully obeyed ever since the receipt of your Lordship's Letter, and my only endeavours for the future shall be to keep a decorum amongst the Clergy" (Perry, *Historical Collections*, iv. (Maryland) 109–112).

Although in Maryland it was possible for a hostile governor to prevent the commissarial representative of the Bishop of London from taking up the duties of his office, in Virginia precisely the reverse was true. Commissary Blair became involved in quarrels with two successive governors, Edmund Andros and Francis Nicholson,[1] concerning the extent of the ecclesiastical functions intrusted to them as ordinaries and their methods of administering those functions; and he was able eventually to procure the dismissal of Andros, and probably to contribute an important influence toward the recall of Nicholson.[2]

The departure of his enemies was not so clear a victory for Blair as he might have had reason to hope. The struggle had stirred up much feeling among the clergy, who were particularly annoyed by what they regarded as the commissary's excessive and uncalled-for meddling in their affairs; nor were their diocesan's efforts to smooth matters over of much avail.[3] Eventually quiet was restored, but only at the cost of great concessions on Blair's part. He was forced to resign himself to comparative inactivity, contenting himself, for the most part, with the exercise of the bare routine duties of his office.

The extent of these duties can be best understood from a letter which he wrote, November 18, 1714, to Robinson, the new Bishop of London. Having acknowledged the receipt of his commission and thanked his Lordship for it, he expresses a hope that he may fulfil his duties in a manner satisfactory to his new diocesan. "But," he adds, "it is necessary that I acquaint your Lordship that this Country having a great aversion to spiritual courts, the late Lord Bishop of London directed

---

[1] Andros was governor from 1692 to 1698, Nicholson from 1698 to 1705.

[2] The history of the quarrels, particularly of that with Nicholson, is very complicated, and is much obscured by the violent recriminations of the respective parties. The documents printed in Perry, *Historical Collections*, i. (Virginia) offer an opportunity to one who cares to trace the contentions through their various ramifications. For a recent account, see Daniel Esten Motley, *Life of Commissary James Blair*, 43 ff., a work which only came to the author's hands after the present chapter was in type.

[3] The whole story of the relations between the Bishop of London, his commissary, and the clergy of Virginia may be found in Perry, *Historical Collections*, i. (Virginia) 144 ff.

me, to make use of the power granted me, in a like commission by him, chiefly to restrain the irregularities of the Clergy without meddling with the Laity, except our Virginia Laws & Govt should give countenance to a further exercise of the ecclesiastical discipline, so that the Chief of my business has been, where I have heard of any complaints of the Clergy, first to try to reclaim them by monitory letters; & when that would not do, I have had a publick visitation of their Church, and upon an open trial of the facts, have either acquitted or suspended the Minister as the case required. I have made in all my time but few examples of this Kind, but I find it necessary not to be too slack as on the other hand I am not suspected of too great severity, the great Scarcity of clergymen among us, obliges me of the two to incline rather to the methods of gentleness. My Lord, I inform your Lordship, truly of these things, that if you Judge it necessary to give any further directions, you may take measures accordingly."[1] From this account it is evident that the Virginia commissary, like his Maryland colleagues, at this time pretended to no coercive jurisdiction, but confined himself to mere supervision and admonition, with an occasional attempt at discipline. Indeed, the commissary often found it difficult to exercise even this small amount of oversight; for it appears from an address of the clergy to Bishop Robinson, dated April, 1719, that, although visitations were attempted by the commissary, he met with so many difficulties, from the refusal of the church wardens to take their oaths or to make presentments, as well as from the general aversion to anything like a spiritual court, that little could be done in that direction.[2]

In the opinion of a careful contemporaneous observer, the commissarial office was not, on the whole, a success.[3] The commentator suggests, as a remedy for the evils of his time,

[1] Perry, *Historical Collections*, i. (Virginia) 130–131.

[2] See "Journal of the Proceedings of the Convention held at the College of William and Mary in the City of Williamsburgh, in April, 1719," *Ibid.* 199–217.

[3] "Which Office and Name has not appeared well-pleasing to the People and Clergy, for Reasons I can't account for; neither has it obtained the Power and Good Effect as might have been expected" (Jones, *Present State of Virginia*, 99).

the appointment of "a Person whose Office upon this Occasion should be somewhat uncommon, till a Bishop be established in those Parts;[1] who might pave out a Way for the Introduction of Mitres into the *English America,* so greatly wanting there. This Person," he continues, "should have Instructions and Powers for discharging such Parts of the Office, of a Bishop, of a Dean, and of an Arch-Deacon, as Necessity requires, and the Nature of those sacred Functions will permit;" he should reside in some parish in Virginia, and be obliged to make a "Progress (for the People will not approve of a Visitation)" every spring and autumn in Virginia and North Carolina, "as his Discretion shall best direct him." He suggests a salary of £100 a year for travelling expenses, which might be secured from the government out of the quitrents, as the commissary's salary was obtained. "As for the Establishment of Episcopacy in *Virginia,* it would be of excellent Service, if Caution was taken not to transplant with it the corrupt Abuses of spiritual Courts, which the People dread almost as much as an Inquisition; but these their Fears would soon be dissipated, when by blessed Experience they might feel the happy Influence of that holy Order among them, free from the terrible Notions that Misrepresentations of regular Church Government have made them conceive." He conceives the salary to be one of the chief drawbacks to the establishment of an episcopacy, but thinks that a contribution toward it might be taken from the superior clergy and collegians of the universities, until the usefulness of a bishop had been proved by trial; afterward some other means might be employed, as, for example, the appropriation of a tract of land.[2] Jones's scheme was never even considered by those in power; but his observations are of

---

[1] This suggestion of a bishop for Virginia is the third I have met. The other is in a merely casual letter from "Mr. Nicholas Moreau to the Right Honorable the Lord Bishop of Lichfield and Coventry, his Majesty's High Almoner," April 12, 1697. After a panegyric of Nicholson, the writer says: "An eminent bishop of the same character being sent over with him will make Hell tremble and settle the Church of England in those parts forever" (Perry, *Historical Collections,* i. (Virginia) 29–32).

[2] Jones, *Present State of Virginia,* Appendix, Scheme ii., *passim,* particularly pp. 98–99, 110.

interest as an instance of contemporary opinion on the existing ecclesiastical situation in Virginia.

The attempts which culminated in the establishment of the Church of England in the Carolinas afford an interesting instance of the Bishop of London's influence with the English government. From both charters, as well as from the Fundamental Constitutions, although these instruments specifically provided that toleration should be granted to all Christians, it is evident that the establishment was contemplated in the minds of the founders. The first step in the direction of an exclusive establishment was taken on May 6, 1704, when Governor Nathaniel Johnson procured the passage of a bill to exclude dissenters from the House of Representatives. Henceforth every man who hoped to become a member of the assembly would be obliged to take the oaths and subscribe to the declarations appointed by that body, to conform to the religion and worship of the Church of England, and to receive the sacrament according to the usages of that church.[1] This proceeding at once raised a protest in the colony, particularly from the members of Colleton County, who sent an agent, one John Ash, to England by way of Virginia. He had an interview with the Palatine, from whom, however, he obtained no satisfaction. He died in England soon after.[2]

Not content with the passage of the act mentioned above, Governor Johnson took the further step of instituting a high commission court, composed of twenty laymen, who should form a corporation for the exercise of ecclesiastical jurisdiction, with full power to remove ministers not only for immorality but also for imprudence, that is to say, for any prejudice which

---

[1] Alexander Hewit, *South Carolina* (Carroll, *Historical Collections*, i.), 147; Grimké, *Laws of South Carolina*, No. 224 (May 6, 1704). This act, which was on its face contrary to the charters and the Fundamental Constitutions, was carried in the South Carolina assembly by the close vote of 12 to 11 (Dalcho, *Protestant Episcopal Church in South-Carolina*, 53). Its purpose, according to a good authority, was not "religion's sake," but the sudden exclusion of the dissenters, most of whom were on the side of those who were seeking to make an inquiry into the illegal practices of the ruling party (Rivers, *South Carolina*, 222; cf. Oldmixon, in Carroll, *Historical Collections*, ii. 431).

[2] Hewit, *South Carolina* (Carroll, *Historical Collections*, i.), 148–149.

might be taken against them.[1] Here, of course, was a direct
encroachment on the jurisdiction of the Bishop of London, an
argument of which the greatest possible use was made in the
later complaints against the measure. In England the two
acts, though opposed by John Archdale, were ratified by the
requisite four proprietors, who further manifested their approval
of the proceedings by sending Johnson a letter lauding him for
his zeal in the service of the church. After the death of Ash,
his papers came into the hands of the governor and council,
who suppressed them.[2]

But the dissenters were still far from discouraged, so long as
the acts remained unratified by the crown. To prevent this
final step they sent Joseph Boone to England to argue their
cause. He presented a memorial to the House of Lords in the
name of his constituents, and the lords addressed the queen,
who in turn referred the matter to the Commissioners of Trade
and Plantations. Soon afterward the commissioners returned
a report declaring that the assembly of Carolina had abused its
powers, and recommending the queen to revoke the charter by
a writ of *scire facias*. In pursuance of this advice, her Majesty
declared the acts null and void, without issuing the *scire facias*,
however.

Boone's memorial, in which he was joined by some influential
London merchants, is chiefly interesting to us from its discussion
of the effect of the second of these acts on the jurisdiction of the
Bishop of London. Its last, and evidently its weightiest, argument is as follows: "That the ecclesiastical government of the
colony is under the Bishop of London; but the governor and
his adherents have at last done what the latter often threatened
to do, totally abolished it; for the same assembly have passed
an act, whereby twenty lay-persons, therein named, are made a
corporation for the exercise of several exorbitant powers, to
the great injury and oppression of the people in general, and
for the exercise of all ecclesiastical jurisdiction, with absolute

[1] Hewit, *South Carolina* (Carroll, *Historical Collections*, i.). For a
complete description of the two acts, see *North Carolina Records*, i. 635–
637.

[2] Hawks and Perry, *South Carolina Church Documents*, 32, note.

power to deprive any minister of the Church of England of his benefice, not only for immorality but even for imprudence, or incurable prejudices between such minister and his parish, . . . which the inhabitants of the province take to be an high ecclesiastical commission-court, destructive to the very being and essence of the Church of England, and to be held in the utmost detestation and abhorrence by every man that is not an enemy to our constitution in church and state." [1] Considering the interest of Bishop Compton in the colonies, and the fact that he was one of the commissioners to whom the act was referred, we may assume with reasonable safety that it was largely due to him that the acts were nullified. On November 30, 1706, the very day on which the governor and deputies repealed the measures which the English government had declared void, the assembly passed a new act, which, being ratified in England as lacking in objectionable features, continued to be the basis of the established Church of England in South Carolina up to the Revolution. [2]

The first commissary of the Carolinas was the Reverend Gideon Johnson, who was appointed to that office and also to the rectorship of St. Philip's, Charleston, in 1707. He continued to officiate in both positions until he met his death by drowning, May 23, 1716. [3] Apparently he performed his duties to the satisfaction of both people and diocesan, but he exercised very little jurisdiction. It is even uncertain whether he held visitations; if he did, the records have been lost. [4]

Johnson was succeeded in 1717 by the Reverend William Treadwell Bull, who served till 1723. Bull, who was the incumbent of St. Paul's, Colleton, seems to have held annual visita-

---

[1] Hewit, *South Carolina* (Carroll, *Historical Collections*, i.), 151–154; *North Carolina Records*, i. 639.

[2] For the act of March 30, 1706, see Dalcho, *Protestant Episcopal Church in South-Carolina*, 75; Rivers, *South Carolina*, 230; Trott, *Laws*, No. 2, pp. 5–22; Grimké, *Laws of South Carolina*, No. 258. For additional acts supplementing that of November 30, 1706, see Grimké, i. *Laws*, No. 284 (April 24, 1708); No. 293 (April 8, 1710); No. 313 (January 7, 1712); No. 475 (January 23, 1722).

[3] Letter to Bishop Robinson, May 31, 1716, *Fulham MSS.*

[4] Dalcho, *Protestant Episcopal Church in South-Carolina*, 116.

tions and to have maintained some sort of discipline ;[1] but the first man to exercise anything like real commissarial functions was the Reverend Alexander Garden, who arrived at Charleston in 1719, and was soon afterward made rector of St. Philip's. Appointed commissary for North and South Carolina and the Bahama Islands in 1726, he held his first visitation in 1731, and from this time was very active in the performance of his duties.[2]

Although the commissary's authority apparently amounted to very little in practice till the advent of Garden, his relations to the clergy under his supervision had been well defined some time before. This fact is shown by the following set of instructions issued by Bishop Robinson, presumably upon the appointment of Johnson's successor : —

1. "That they [the clergy of the Carolinas] do in all things Conform themselves to the Canons and Rubrickes, and in Case of any Difficulty apply themselves to the Commissary for his Advise.

2. "That no Clergyman, the Commissary excepted, presume to officiate, or by any means concern himself in the affairs of another Parish, unless the Minister be sick, and that his consent be thereunto first had, or except he be absent, and at so great a distance from his Parish that his leave cannot be timely obtained ; In which Case any perquisit receiv'd by the Ministers officiating shall be by him without the least deduction given to the Incumbent unless he refuse to receive the same.

3. "That no Minister for the time to come shall take upon him to supply any vacant Parish without a License from the Bishop to officiate in the Province of N. or S. Carolina, and the Commissary's appointment for the particular Parish ; and that as to the Care of such Parishes, the Clergy shall govern themselves by such Directions as the Commissary shall give them, till such time as the Bishop's pleasure can be known.

4. "That when the Banns are superseded by a Grant of a License, the Minister shall not join together any Persons in the holy estate of Matrimony, but such as his own Parishioners,

[1] Tiffany, *Protestant Episcopal Church*, 230.
[2] Dalcho, *Protestant Episcopal Church in South-Carolina*, 98, 103, 116.

E

or at least that the Woman be so. And that when the Minister shall have married such couple, He shall notify the same within a Month after to the Commissary.

5. "That the Commissary shall strictly and punctually hold a general Visitation of the Clergy each Year, and that he shall visit them parochially and call them together at other times, as often as the good of the Church and the Necessity of affairs shall require it. And that at such Visitations, He shall earnestly recommend them so to frame their own Lives as may adorn the doctrine of Christ our Lord; and so to discharge all the parts of their Ministerial Office as may best lead to the Edification of those intrusted to their care." [1]

Even during this period, when the Bishop of London had as yet no commission, one comes across frequent instances not only of the actual exercise, but of the formal recognition, of his general powers as diocesan. For example, at a meeting of January 20, 1711, convened and presided over by Dr. Sharpe, Archbishop of York, and attended by Dr. Robinson, Bishop of Bristol, Dr. Bisse, Bishop of St. Davids, Atterbury, prolocutor of the lower house of convocation, and Drs. Smallridge and Stanhope, the archbishop made a proposition concerning the providing of bishops for the plantations; but "as the Bishop of London, who from his recognized relation to the colonial churches had a right to be first consulted on such a project, was not present, the matter was dropped." [2] Again, Nicholas Trott, who published his *Laws* in 1721, dedicated them to "William . . . Archbishop of Canterbury, Primate of all England and Metropolitan . . . and to the . . . Reverend and Honourable the Members of the Society for the Propagation of the Gospel in Foreign Parts; and particularly to . . . John . . . Lord Bishop of London, to whose Jurisdiction in Matters Ecclesiastical the British Plantations in America do belong." [3] Moreover, not only was the Bishop of London's position as colonial diocesan well recog-

---

[1] *Fulham MSS.*, April 22, 1717, "Somerset House J. L." [John, London].

[2] Thomas Newcome, *Life of Archbishop Sharpe*, i. 532, cited by Perry, *American Episcopal Church*, i. 399.

[3] *The Laws of the British Plantations in America relating to the Church and Clergy, Religion and Learning* (London, 1721).

nized, but also — on the part of the mother country, at least — great care was taken not to encroach on his province.[1]

So far we have followed the results of the work of Compton and his successor Robinson, a work in which the former had taken the distinctively leading part. He had reëstablished the authority of the Bishop of London in the colonies; he had stimulated individual enterprise toward the extension of the Church of England in those territories; he had instituted the custom of sending commissaries to exercise delegated authority; and most particularly, he had been one of the chief moving causes in the formation of that society which did more than any other organization toward the foundation of the present Protestant Episcopal church in the United States.

[1] Compare a commission issued by the Society for Propagating the Gospel to Francis Nicholson, October 17, 1712: "Now know all men by these Presents that the Said Society Have and by these presents Do (as much as in them is and ought to be in most humble Submission to his Majesty's Royal Prerogative and Power and the Jurisdiction of the R^t Rev^d the Lord Bishop of London) Request and Desire the said Francis Nicholson to make Enquiry in the best manner and by such Ways and Means as to him shall be thought fitt and requisite, of the Society's Missionaries, Schoolmasters, and Catechists, with respect to the good Purposes and Designs of the Society relating to them, And of the present State of the Churches, Glebes, Parsonage-Houses, and Libraries (Sent by the Society) within all and every Such Parts of Her Majesty's Dominions and Countries as are comprised in the Commission now granted to the said Francis Nicholson from his Majesty for the purposes therein mentioned," etc. (Foote, *Annals of King's Chapel,* i. 216–217, where the whole instrument is cited.)

CHAPTER III.

EDMUND GIBSON took control of the see of London in 1723,[1] and with his accession a conscientious and enthusiastic prelate was again at the head of the Anglican church in the colonies. In his first address, delivered November 2, he said: " Being called by the providence of God to the government and administration of the diocese of London, by which the care of the churches in the foreign plantations is also devolved upon me, I think it my duty to use all proper means of attaining a competent knowledge of the places, persons, and matters entrusted to my care. And as the plantations, and the constitutions of the churches there are at a far greater distance, and much less known to me, than the affairs of my diocese here at home, so it is the more necessary for me to have recourse to the best and most effectual methods of coming to a right knowledge of the state and condition of them, which knowledge I shall not fail, by the grace of God, faithfully to employ to the service of piety and religion, and to the maintenance of order and regularity in the church." [2] What a similarity in spirit to Compton's first letter! Moreover, emulating the example of his zealous predecessor, Gibson did not long delay the execution of his purpose to find out all that it was possible to know concerning the religious condition of the colonies under his charge; for in the ensuing year he sent out sets of questions to be answered by every Episcopal commissary and clergyman in America. Since the form of these queries is in all cases practically the same, those addressed to Commissary Blair of Virginia may be taken as a sample: —

" Queries to be answered by Persons who were Commissaries to my Predecessor.

[1] Le Neve, *Fasti Ecclesiæ Anglicanæ*, ii. 305.
[2] Wilberforce, *Protestant Episcopal Church*, 107-108.

" [1.] What public acts of assembly have been made & confirmed, relating to the Chh or clergy within that Gov^t ? . . .

" [2.] How oft hath it been usual to hold a visitation of the Clergy ? how oft have you Called a convention of them ? & what has been the business ordinarily done, & the method of Proceeding in such meetings ? . . .

" [3.] Does any Clergyman officiate who has not the Bp'8 licence for that Gov^t ? . . .

" [4.] What Parishes are there which have yet no Churches nor Ministers ? . . .

" [5.] How is the revenue of the Churches applied which arises during the vacancies ? . . .

" [6.] What are the ordinary prices of the necessaries of life there ? . . .

" [7.] Can you suggest anything that may be serviceable to religion & conduce to the ease of the Clergy & their more comfortable subsistence, which you believe to be fairly practicable & which will in no way interfere with the Authority of the Governor nor be judged an infringment of the rights of the People ? " [1]

This list was replied to, query for query, by Commissary Blair, July 17, 1724.[2] The other commissaries and clergymen answered with more or less regularity. At this point, however, attention will be given solely to the reply of the Reverend William Gordon, commissary of the Barbadoes ; for in his answer general rather than particular interests dominate.

On the receipt of Gibson's letter, Gordon applied for advice to Worsley, governor of the island ; for he was unwilling to do anything without the approbation of his excellency.[3] To this application the governor made the following reply : " From the perusal of the Rt. Rev. Lord Bishop of London's Letter to you, I find his Lordship is of opinion that there is a great uncertainty in the ground and extent of his Jurisdiction in the Plantations, and as I can't authorize any Jurisdiction the Bishop of London may

---

[1] Perry, *Historical Collections*, i. (Virginia) 257–260.

[2] *Ibid.*

[3] See Gordon to Worsley, Barbadoes, February 10, 1723–1724, *Fulham MSS.*

have till I know what it is, I must consider his Lordship's Letters and Queries to you and the rest of the Clergy of this Island, as private Letters and Queries to you and them, to which I think you ought all to pay the honour and respect, that is due to so learned, so good, so wise, and so great a Prelate. Your prudent Conduct in this affair is very comendable and praiseworthy." Authorized by this letter, Commissary Gordon — unofficially, as it would seem — answered the queries, and wrote to his diocesan a long letter concerning the basis and the scope of the Bishop of London's colonial jurisdiction, as he understood it.

He begins by expressing the current view that the Bishop of London enjoys his authority by prescription or ancient right. In regard to the rumor that it rests on an order in council granted to Laud, he says that he has searched the Council books from Queen Elizabeth to King Charles without finding any trace of such a document. He then goes on to give his reasons for believing that the colonies were put under the care of the Bishop of London either at the end of the reign of King Charles or in the beginning of that of James II. Having completed his survey of the origin and basis of the jurisdiction, Gordon proceeds to a theoretical discussion of its scope. In his opinion, even if no order in council had ever been issued, the temporary orders in every governor's instructions answer the same purpose, " as being themselves not only Solemn Orders of Council pass'd and establish'd but also referr'd to and expressly enforc'd by Letters Patent under the Broad Seal." Hence, since the king orders the various governors "to give all countenance and encouragement to the exercise of the Ecclesiastical Jurisdiction of the Bishop of London excepting as before excepted[2] . . . the exercise thereof is well warranted by . . . Instructions and Authorities and by the Commission under the Great Seal by which these are especially enforced." It may very well be objected, he argues, that the words, " so far as conveniently may be," leave it to the dis-

---

[1] Worsley to Gordon, February 15, 1723–1724, *Fulham MSS.*
[2] The exceptions related to powers especially reserved to the governors.

cretion of the particular governors as to whether they will allow the commissaries to exercise authority in their respective provinces. He thinks that this is a serious limitation, but that when the commissary proceeds with the governor's consent, the instructions are a sufficient warrant for every legal act of his. Of course the Bishop of London's powers are of uncertain tenure, resting, like the commissions and instructions, on the king's pleasure; but, concludes Gordon, "until the king actually Determines, Alters, or Revokes his Commissions & Instructions they are (with all Deference to Superior Judgments) in my humble Opinion, very Sufficient to warrant the appointment of a Commissary to proceed in a *Judicial* manner, with the Leave & Countenance of a Governor." [1] From this, the most careful and thorough of the answers returned to the queries, it would seem that the Bishop of London would be seriously hampered in any authority that he might choose to exercise over ecclesiastical concerns in the colonies.

After weighing the opinions which he received, Gibson came to the conclusion that the powers embodied in the instructions to the royal governors, under which Compton, Robinson, and he himself had hitherto exercised their authority, were insufficient. [2] He accordingly appealed to the crown to establish his jurisdiction on a more definite basis, and even refused to send out any more commissaries until an understanding should be reached. The reason which he assigned for his doubts and for his subsequent action was the fact that the colonies lay beyond the proper limits of his diocese, and that the only basis of his jurisdiction there was the rather transitory authorization from the crown embodied in the commissions to various governors. He said that he had made a vain search for the order supposed to have been issued to Compton, but had failed to find it either in the

---

[1] Gordon to Gibson, November 3, 1725, *Fulham MSS*.

[2] For further comments on the order in council supposed to have been issued in Compton's time, see Wilberforce, *Protestant Episcopal Church*, 107; Abbey, *English Church and Bishops*, i. 82; McConnell, *American Episcopal Church*, 175, who erroneously cites Abbey, to the effect that the ecclesiastical jurisdiction of the Bishop of London over the colonies was confirmed by an order in council in 1703.

Council books or in the Council Office; that, moreover, able lawyers whom he had consulted had informed him that, even if such an order existed, " it would not warrant the Bishop to grant Commissions to others, unless he himself should be first Empowered so to do by a Commission from the king under the great seal; the Plantations being not a part of any Diocese but remaining under the sole and immediate Jurisdiction of the King; and that Jurisdiction not to be legally delegated but under the Great Seal." [1]

In a " Humble Representation " to the king in council, Gibson indicated a further reason which influenced him to the step he then took. It was, in effect, that, under existing conditions, the commissaries appointed by his predecessors were in a very anomalous position. Although in general strictly refraining from any interference with collations, wills, or benefices,[2] they had been absolutely prevented from holding any courts at all, or indeed from proceeding in any judicial manner whatever. As an instance of the extent to which the matter had been carried, he cited the case of Governor Lowther, late of the Barbadoes, who procured an " Act of Assembly and Council," prohibiting the issuance of any kind of ecclesiastical citation or process, under penalty of a fine of £500. Owing to this and other restraints, he argued, the jurisdiction of the Bishop of London had become merely nominal, and his commissaries were unable to proceed judicially against any sort of immoralities or irregularities. In addition to this, a clause inserted in many of the governor's instructions providing that " if any person already preferr'd to a Benefice shall appear to you to give scandal, either by his Doctrine or Manners you are to use the best means for the Removal of him," seemed to give to the governor what little power the bishop possessed even over the clergy. In view of all these circumstances, Gibson deemed it advisable to secure a more sufficient basis for his power, and, as has been said, declined to exercise any further jurisdiction or to appoint

[1] *London Weekly Miscellany* (edited by Richard Hooker, London, 1736–1738), i. 81.

[2] There had been one or two instances of such interference by Blair in Virginia and by Bray in Maryland (see above, pp. 40, 43).

any more commissaries until an understanding as to the precise limits of his authority could be reached.[1]

"Convinced that any attempt to exercise jurisdiction over the whole body of the laity would be resisted, or would at least occasion great dissatisfaction, he suggested to the king and council, that in case they saw fit to grant him a commision under the great seal, they should make it extend only to the Clergy, and to such other Persons and Matters as concern'd the Repair of Churches, and the decent Performance of Divine Service therein."[2] His petition was referred to the attorney and solicitor generals, who reported "that the authority by which the Bishops of London had acted in the Plantations was insufficient," and that ecclesiastical jurisdiction in America "did belong neither to the Bishop of London, nor to any Bishop in England ; but was solely in the Crown by virtue of the Supremacy, and that the most proper way of granting to any person the exercise of such jurisdiction, was by Patent under the Broad Seal." In pursuance of this advice, such a patent was granted to Gibson, but, according to Sherlock[3] and other contemporaries, only to Gibson personally and not to his successors ; hence the grant expired with his death, and the jurisdiction reverted to the crown.[4]

The instrument, in its final form, was dated April 29, 1728.[5]

---

[1] "The Humble Representation of Edmund, Bishop of London, to the King's most Excellent Majesty in Council " (*Fulham MSS.*).

[2] *London Weekly Miscellany*, i. 83–86.

[3] See his Report, 1759, *New York Documents*, vii. 363.

[4] Brodhead, *New York*, ii. 456–457, note 3. Other references are : Wilberforce, *Protestant Episcopal Church*, 108 ; Whitney, *South Carolina*, ii. 413 ; Protestant Episcopal Historical Society, *Collections*, i. 137, 159 ; Forsyth, *Cases and Opinions*, 45 ; *New York Documents*, vii. 363 ff. ; Perry, *American Episcopal Church*, i. 154–155.

[5] South Carolina Historical Society, *Collections*, i. 225 ; *New Jersey Archives*, v. 126–128. **The text of this commission may be found in *New York Documents*, v. 849–854** (reprinted below, Appendix A, No. v.). There were two patents. The first, issued by George I., was superseded by that of his successor, George II. The former seems (although the writer has been unable to find a copy of it) to have been more full than the one under which Gibson and his commissaries exercised their powers. Cf. *London Weekly Miscellany*, i. 86 : "The Commission above mentioned expired upon the Death of his late

Its full title is, " A Royal Commission for exercising Spiritual and Ecclesiastical Jurisdiction in the American Plantations." In the preamble the King, George II., grants to the Bishop of London "full power and authority," by himself or by his "sufficient commissary or commissaries," to be by him "substituted and named to exercise Spiritual and Ecclesiastical Jurisdiction in the special causes and matters hereinafter expressed and specified, within our several Colonies, Plantations, and other dominions in America, according to the laws and canons of the Church of England, in England lawfully received and sanctioned." Four causes are then specified in which the Bishop is to have jurisdiction: (1) the visitation of all the churches in which the rites and liturgy of the Church of England are used ; (2) the citation of all rectors, curates, and incumbents, as well as of all priests and deacons in Church of England orders, and the right to inquire, by witnesses duly sworn, into their morals and conduct, with power to administer oaths in the ecclesiastical courts, and to correct and punish any of these clergy by suspension, excommunication, or like measure ; (3) the appointment of commissaries, removable at pleasure, for the exercise of this jurisdiction ; (4) the right of appeal, before certain of the Privy Council enumerated in the commission, for all those who should feel themselves wronged by any decision of the local ecclesiastical courts of the commissaries.

Bishop Sherlock, in his report on the church in the colonies presented to the king in council, February 19, 1759,[1] discusses this part of his predecessor's commission in some detail. He is inclined to regard the powers conferred by it as very vague and,

Majesty ; and before a new one could pass the Great Seal, it was represented to the Bishop, That insomuch as the Laws of the Several Governments have already provided for the Repair of Churches, and the furnishing of such things as are necessary for the decent Performance of Divine Service ; the taking that care out of the Hands of the Vestries, who are chiefly interested with it, would probably give Uneasiness, and be the Occasion of leaving the Fabricks and Furniture of Churches not so well taken Care of as they are at present : Whereupon the Bishop, desiring as much as possible to avoid the giving Offense, and the raising any uneasiness, was Content that the New Commission should be confined to a Jurisdiction of the Clergy alone : and so it stands."

[1] *New York Documents*, vii. 363-364.

in many respects, inadequate. Let us follow him as he takes
up the four points one by one. He shows (1) that, although
the bishop, or his representative, has authority to visit all the
churches, he has no power whatever over church wardens or
vestries; (2) that, although he has the right to summon and discipline all regularly-ordained clergymen of the Church of England, he has not the least control over those making false
pretences to such profession; (3) that although he is empowered
to examine the conduct of the clergy under oath, he has no
authority to summon lay witnesses, however necessary such a
step may be to the purposes of the trial; (4) that, although he
may appoint commissaries, he has no control over their judgments, since an appeal lies, not to him, but to the Privy Council.
His conclusion is that the bishop's only resource was a power
of absolute removal. After pointing out how defective the
Bishop of London's jurisdiction was under this grant, and how
futile it must ever be to invest a bishop with a charge beyond the
seas which could not be duly executed except in person, Dr. Sherlock goes on to discuss his favorite remedy — an American
bishop. The reasons which he adduces in favor of his plan,
and the difficulties he urges against it, will be considered
later; for they are brought forward by him and by others again
and again during the century.

The limitations in the grant of ecclesiastical jurisdiction
may have been as formidable as Sherlock maintains; but it
must be remembered that this commentator was hardly an un-
biassed critic, and also that, like most written instruments, the
commission was susceptible, under a liberal interpretation, of
far-reaching implied powers. As a matter of fact, however,
owing to the position in which the commissaries found themselves in the colonies, they usually confined their activities to
visitation, exhortation, supervision, and administration, making
very few attempts to exercise a punitive jurisdiction, or to set
up courts. Indeed, outside of Virginia, the only instance known
in which a commissary subjected a priest to formal trial and
sentence is the case of Commissary Garden of South Carolina
against Reverend George Whitefield.[1]

[1] See below, p. 80 ff.

Whatever flaws Sherlock may have picked in the royal grant of 1728, and however eloquently he may have argued in favor of an American episcopate as the only possible system by which the Church of England in America could be ruled, Gibson found his commission, for the time being at least, a basis quite adequate for his purposes ; and that the English government so regarded the patent is evident from the fact that it at once took steps to enforce its provisions.   To this end, Newcastle ordered the following clause to be inserted in each succeeding governor's instructions : [1] —

" Having been graciously pleased to grant unto the Right Reverend Father in God Edmund Lord Bishop of London a Commission under our Great Seal of Great Britain whereby he is empowered to exercise Ecclesiastical Jurisdiction by himself or by such Commissaries as he shall appoint in our several Plantations in America.   It is Our Will and Pleasure that you give all countenance and due encouragement to the said Bishop of London or his Commissaries in the legal exercise of such Ecclesiastical jurisdiction according to the laws of the Province under your government and to the tenor of the said Commission a Copy whereof is hereunto annexed and that you do cause the said Commission to be forthwith registered in the public records of that our Province." [2]

Moreover, in another article of all subsequent instructions was inserted a provision from a draft prepared by an order in council of May 3, 1727, in accordance with a petition from Bishop Gibson 'that all laws against blasphemy, adultery, drunkenness, swearing, etc., be vigorously put in

[1] See Newcastle's communication to the Board of Trade, January 21, 1729–1730, and the Board's reputed draft of instructions, April 20, 1730, in South Carolina Historical Society, *Collections*, i. 227.   See also an address to the king on this subject from the Board of Trade, March 17, 1729–1730, *New Jersey Archives*, v. 264–265.

[2] The first instructions in which the clause seems to have been embodied were those to Governor George Burrington of North Carolina, issued December 14, 1730.   The other clauses on which the authority of Compton and his successors rested (quoted above, pp. 26, 29, 30) were also inserted in these instructions, and continued to be reinserted in all the later commissions.   See *North Carolina Records*, iii. 90–118 ; *New Jersey Archives*, v. 264–265.

force."[1] This is only one of many instances which prove, not only that the bishop manifested a warm paternal interest in the colonies, but also that his right to such an interest was well recognized by the authorities of the English government.

Having set his colonial jurisdiction upon a secure legal basis, Gibson next formulated a plan for regulating the legal procedure of his commissaries in any trials of immoral or irregular clergymen which they might be called upon to undertake. The rules which he drew up are embodied in a pamphlet which he sent to each of his commissaries.[2] He begins by notifying the commissary in question of his appointment, and then enumerates a list of directions which are to guide him in the performance of his functions. These duties are distinctly grouped under several heads. In the first place, he is to proceed by private admonition against clergymen guilty of irregularity or negligence in the performance of their duties, and, in the case of graver crimes, by public or even judicial measures; in the latter event, he is to use a short and summary process according to the directions laid down in the *Methodus Procedendi*, and is always to act with the assistance of at least two clergymen chosen by himself; except in case of very serious crimes he is to confer the sentence of suspension *ab officio et beneficio* rather than of deprivation, in order to give the guilty person time to repent. Secondly, he is to hold a visitation every year, and is to send an account of it to the Bishop of London; he is to inquire into the state of parsonages and glebes, and to find out if there be any clergymen officiating without a testimonial from the bishop. In the third place, he is to inform the bishop what steps have been or are to be taken to obtain an act of assembly for presentment of crimes and vices to be made to the temporal courts twice every year. Next, he is to give notice to his diocesan of any hardships or

---

[1] *North Carolina Records*, iii. 111–112; South Carolina Historical Society, *Collections*, i. 225; *London Weekly Miscellany*, i. 83–86 (an account of the clause, with text).

[2] There is a copy in the Fulham library. It is a quarto of sixteen pages, entitled *Methodus Procedendi contra Clericos Irregulares in Plantationibus Americanis*. It has no date or place of publication, but it was issued by Gibson, September 28, 1728. It is reprinted below, Appendix A, No. vi.

oppressions to which he finds the clergy exposed in relation to the rights to which they are entitled by the laws and constitutions of the government. Finally, he is directed "to take all proper opportunities to recommend to the clergy a loyal and dutiful Behaviour towards the present Government, as vested in his Majesty King George, and established in the Illustrious House of Hanover, and that they pay all due Submission and Respect to the Governor sent, as well in regard to his Commission and Character, as to engage his Favour and Protection to the Church and Clergy." It was left to the judgment and prudence of the commissary to apply these rules in particular cases.

So much for the duties of the commissary in general. A consideration of the particular method to be employed in proceeding against irregular clergymen will now be taken up.

The special irregularities for which a clergyman might be brought to account were as follows: officiating without a license; marrying without banns or license; neglect in catechising, or the omission of any other church duty; a refusal to baptize or to bury; and immoralities of various kinds, such as incontinence, profanity, intemperance, and the like. In each case the trial was to be held in a church, either that of the commissary or that of the person accused. The prosecution was to be conducted either by a promoter appointed by the commissary or by a voluntary accuser. In the latter case the accuser was to deposit a sum of twenty pounds, by way of security for the costs of the trial should he fail to prove his accusation. The process was to be summary, beginning with a citation under the seal of the commissary, and this citation was to be served on the party personally if possible, if not by a process *viis et modis*, to be hung on the door of his church or of his dwelling-house. If he did not appear, he should be called contumacious, and the proceedings should go on without him; that is, the witnesses should be admitted, sworn, and examined, their depositions published, and a day assigned for the sentence. If the defendant appeared and confessed, he should be sentenced according to the character of the offence, either by admonition, suspension, or deprivation, and should also pay the costs. If he denied the charge, witnesses should be produced, who, after being duly sworn, should be examined before a notary public, or other person skilful in taking depositions. Witnesses properly summoned and refusing to appear, or appearing and refusing to undergo examination, might be compelled by ecclesiastical censure. The depositions were to be taken in the presence of the commissary (who acted as judge) and his assessors. Forty-eight hours were then granted the defendant to inquire into the character of the witnesses and to arrange whatever questions he might see fit to ask them. Beyond that, the defendant, by his proctor or advocate, might put in a defensive plea. If the proof advanced by the prosecution were legally insufficient to convict, the defendant was to be dismissed with his costs. He was allowed to appeal, any time within fifteen days, to the judges appointed by the king's commission. The record of the trial was to be preserved in a book kept by the registrar.[1]

It will be noticed that this process was strictly ecclesiastical in almost every respect. The only secular element was the question of the costs, to recover which a civil suit might be required. Whether such a suit could ever have been successful it would be hard to say. All the penalties in the hands of the commissary, even those for forcing the attendance of witnesses, were strictly ecclesiastical. Processes according to the procedure laid down in the *Methodus* were tried to some extent in South Carolina and Virginia. Whether or not they were used elsewhere is extremely uncertain; probably they were not.

During Gibson's occupancy of the see of London, he seems to have become aware of the evil of licensing promiscuous applicants for churches in the American plantations. In order to avert the danger, he issued the following proclamation, July 13, 1743: —

"There having been of late, a greater number of Persons than usual who have come from the Plantations for Holy

---

[1] The various forms of citations, articles, sentences, appeals, etc., in both Latin and English, may be found below in Appendix A, No. vi., where the whole pamphlet is given.

Orders; I find it convenient to have it understood, that no
Person may come over for that Purpose with any Hope of
Success, unless he bring with him,

" 1° A Testimony and Recommendation from the Commissary
for that Government, in which his usual residence has been.

" 2° An Account, from the Same Hand, of the Truth of his
Title, and if it be for an Assistant, what Occasion the Incumbent has to desire one, and whether the Salary which he proposes to allow be sufficient with regard to the value of the
Living, and the Duty to be performed.

"The several Commissaries are hereby requested, to take the
proper Methods of making these Things known, in the respective Governments to which they belong.

" EDM' LONDON." [1]

Having made such earnest efforts to establish his colonial
jurisdiction on a definite legal basis, and to provide for the due
exercise of his authority, personally and through his commissarial representatives, Bishop Gibson naturally identified himself
closely with the concerns of the Church of England in the
various colonies.

In Massachusetts he met with considerable opposition, — in
one case, at least, from his own people. The congregation of
King's Chapel, composed chiefly of Tories, had but a cold
welcome for a diocesan who was a Hanoverian Whig; they
sent him no letter of congratulation, and sought to oppose the
exercise of powers which they had accepted from previous
bishops.[2]   Governor Dummer, on the contrary, although an
Independent, seems to have been more favorably disposed
toward the new bishop.   He wrote, April 29, 1724: "I have
the honour of Y^r Lordship's Letter of the 29th Novemb^r, which
I received not till the Middle of April.   I heartily Congratulate
Your Lordship upon y^r Promotion to the See of London, — To
which your eminent piety and Learning, Moderation and firm
Attachment to his Majesty's Interest and Government and the

---

[1] A printed circular apparently distributed among the colonies (original in
Fulham MSS.).

[2] Foote, *Annals of King's Chapel*, i. 321.

protestant Succession do So Justly Entitle You; and I do Assure Your Lordship that this Government have a Good part of the Gen[ll] Satisfaction in Your Lords[ps] Translation to a place of that Important Trust in the Church of England. I shall always Use my best endeavours to answer Your Lordships Desire and Expectation by Countenancing and Encouraging the Church and the Ministers thereof in their endeavours to promote Piety, Loyalty, and good manners, So long as I have the Hon[r]. to Serve his Majesty in the Chief Command over this province." [1]

Soon after his accession, Bishop Gibson, following his customary procedure with regard to the several colonies, sent a set a queries concerning ecclesiastical conditions to all the Church of England clergymen in Massachusetts.[2] From their answers it appears that there were no parishes in the province, that the governor had no power of induction, that clergymen took possession of their livings and held them solely by virtue of the license of the Bishop of London, and that ministers were supported partly by voluntary contributions from the congregations and partly by stipends from the Society for Propagating the Gospel.[3] Since there was as yet no commissary in New England, the Reverend Samuel Myles, rector of King's Chapel, replied for the district. He reported that there had never been any visitation or convention there. In answer to the query, "What public Acts of Assembly have been made & confirmed, relating to the Church or Clergy within that Gov[t]?" he said: "There are Several laws for the Establishing of Independants, & Settling Orthodox Ministers chosen by the people. The Church of England only indulged, as the Anabaptists & Quakers for never in any of the Laws is the case supposed that the clergy of the Chh of Engl[d], should be here Supported." "It would tend very much to the advantage of the Church & comfort of the Clergy," he suggests in answer to another query,

---

[1] *Ibid.* 292–293, from *Massachusetts Archives*, li. 403. Probably the bishop's letter, to which this is a reply, was destroyed in the fire which burned the Court House, December 9, 1747 (cf. Foote, as above).

[2] See above, pp. 52–53.

[3] Perry, *Historical Collections*, iii. (Massachusetts) 149–150.

"if the members of the Chh were freed from any compulsion to pay to the independant ministers, as they are forced to do in many places Particularly in Bristol where the Church people have been imprisoned for not paying their rates towards the maintenance of M^r. Cotton a Dissenting Minister of that Town."[1] Such was the condition of the church and the church people whose interests Gibson was to protect and further in New England.

The first case in which his hand is distinctly seen is the celebrated Checkley controversy.[2] This trouble was due to the fact that John Checkley was a violent and unreasoning partisan of the Church of England among people who were bitterly hostile to the claims he advanced in her behalf. The conflict began in 1723, when he published in London a reprint of Leslie's *Short and Easy Method with Deists*, to which he added a "Discourse concerning Episcopacy in Defense of Christianity and the Church of England." In this work, passing beyond the proper limits of his argument, he rudely attacked the clergy and people of New England. For this he was tried at Boston in 1724, and was fined. Frequent appeals were made to Gibson for advice and support; but the bishop showed his tact and moderation by standing aloof as far as possible from the actual controversy, intervening only to exhort both parties to peace and unity. Nevertheless, his utterances show that, in quarters to which his authority extended, he would see to it that no essential principle of the Church of England was infringed upon.[3] His efforts toward conciliation seem to have been

---

[1] Myles to Gibson, June 1, 1724, Perry, *ibid.* 153–154.

[2] For good accounts of this controversy based on the sources, with liberal excerpts from them, see Foote, *Annals of King's Chapel,* i. ch. viii., Slafter's *Checkley* in "Prince Society Publications," and Perry, *American Episcopal Church,* i. ch. xv. Some of the documents are printed in Perry, *Historical Collections,* iii. (Massachusetts), *passim.*

[3] See Gibson to Myles, September 3, 1724, in Perry, *Historical Collections,* iii. (Massachusetts) 166–167; Foote, *Annals of King's Chapel,* i. 331–332; Douglass, *Summary,* i. 228–229. The copy in Massachusetts Historical Society, *Proceedings,* 1865, p. 226, is there stated to have been written to the Honorable Thomas Graves of Charlestown; but a more authentic copy of it, addressed " To ye Revd Mr Miles, at Boston, New England," may be found in

appreciated. For example, December 17, 1724, the Reverend David Mossom, the clergyman at Marblehead, wrote to thank him for his "pathetick exhortations and authoritative injunctions to Peace and amity." Yet Mossom continues in a tone of sadness: " Such is the flaming zeal of this Mr Checkley and the party which abets him, that, be your Lorship's decisions what they will, except they agree with their ways of thinking, they put 'em behind 'em and take no notice of them; and . . . we . . . the poor inferior Clergy . . . are the Butts of their vehement and ungoverned heat."[1] Checkley went to England in 1727, intending to take orders and settle in Marblehead; but Gibson was wise and politic enough to refuse to ordain a man who, whatever the merits of the question he defended, had rendered himself so obnoxious to the people of Massachusetts. Subsequently he secured ordination from the Bishop of Exeter and went to Rhode Island, where he passed the rest of his life.

The Checkley controversy was still in progress when a new question arose in which Gibson was called upon to play a leading part. On May 27, 1725, a convention of New England ministers petitioned the governor, council, and House of Representatives of Massachusetts for permission to hold a synod for the purpose of correcting certain abuses which had crept into the church. On June 3, the council voted to grant this request; but on the eleventh the House of Representatives voted to hold the matter over until the next session for further consideration. In this decision of the lower house, the governor and council finally concurred.[2] On June 19, the very day on which the authorities voted to postpone the matter, Samuel Myles and Timothy Cutler, two Church of England clergymen of Boston,[3] presented a counter petition to the assembly, in which they protested against the synod for reasons which they enumerated as fol-

the *Proceedings* of the same society for 1866–1867, p. 342 (see Foote, *Annals of King's Chapel*, i. 331, note 2).

[1] Foote, *Annals of King's Chapel*, i. 333; Perry, *Historical Collections*, iii. (Massachusetts) 169.

[2] Chalmers, *Opinions*, i. 4–14.

[3] Rectors of King's Chapel and Christ Church respectively.

lows : first, because it purposed to concern itself with all churches, among them the Church of England, with which it had no right to meddle; secondly, because various utterances in the petition — as, for example, one referring the council to a time when there was no Church of England in the province — indicated that the synod would probably be prejudiced against that church; thirdly, because the prime movers in the affair had not consulted the Episcopal ministers, who were, equally with all other denominations, concerned in the moral and religious life of the colony; in the fourth place, because the ministers of this body felt that they should be represented in the synod, and yet thought it improper, "it being without the knowledge of their R^t Revd Diocesan the Lord Bishop of London." Their final reason was stated as follows : "Whereas by Royal Authority the Colonies in America are annex'd to the Diocese of London, & inasmuch as nothing can be transacted in ecclesiastical matters without the cognizance of the Bishop, We are humbly of opinion that it will neither be dutiful to his most sacred Majesty King George nor consistent with the rights of our R^t Revd Diocesan to encourage or call the said Synod until the pleasure of His Majesty shall be known therein." This last proposition hinted at possibilities in the way of an extension of the control of the crown and the Bishop of London over the ecclesiastical affairs of New England which must have been most startling to the authorities in that province. This consideration very likely impressed the council; for it voted, June 22, that the petition be dismissed as containing an "indecent reflection" on the proceedings of that board, and "groundless Insinuations." The next day the lower house concurred in this vote.[1]

As soon as the matter of the synod came to the ears of the Bishop of London, he despatched a letter (August 17) to the Duke of Newcastle discountenancing the project. In his letter he indicates two points that should be kept in mind in considering the advisability of allowing such an assembly : first, what the ministry purpose to do; secondly, whether, if the right to

---

[1] Perry, *Historical Collections*, iii. (Massachusetts) 170–171 ; see also an extract from the *New England Courant*, July 10, 1725, *Ibid.* 173.

hold synods be granted, it may not furnish a new handle of complaint to the English dissenters in England, who are already
clamoring for a sitting convention.[1] In a second letter, written
four days later, he takes a firmer stand. He doubts whether, in
view of the Act of Union between England and Scotland, the
Independents of New England "are any more than a Federal
Ministry and People." He admits that the Act of Uniformity[2]
"extends no further than the Realm of England, the Dominion
of Wales, and town of Berwick on Tweed, and therefore left the
Crown at liberty to make such Worship and Discipline as the
King and Queen for the time being think proper, the Established
worship and discipline of the territories;" but he adds that "by
the act of union,[3] every King and Queen at their Coronation
shall take and subscribe an oath to maintain and preserve inviolably the settlement of the Church of England, and the Doctrine,
Discipline, Worship, and Government thereof as by Law established within the Kingdoms of England and Ireland, the dominions of Wales, and town of Berwick upon Tweed, *and the
territories thereto belonging.*" By this clause, he affirms, the
establishment of the Church of England extends to the American plantations, and in view of this fact, the Independent clergy
are simply a tolerated body as in England. Such being the
case, the Bishop maintains that to grant them permission to
hold a synod would be to do an injustice to both the established
and the dissenting clergy at home, neither of whom were permitted by law to hold synods.[4]

Gibson's letters appear to have roused the English authorities
to action; for on September 24, 1725, the lords justices wrote to
him informing him that his communications to the Duke of
Newcastle concerning the proposed New England synod had
been laid before them, and that they had sent them to the
attorney and solicitor generals for an opinion. Having received

---

[1] Perry, *Historical Collections*, iii. (Massachusetts) 179.

[2] 13 & 14 Charles II., c. 4.

[3] 6 Anne, c. 5.

[4] Chalmers, *Opinions*, i. 4–6; Perry, *Historical Collections*, iii. (Massachusetts) 180–181. During most of the eighteenth and part of the nineteenth
centuries, convocations were not allowed to be held.

no official account of the matter, they desire his Lordship to aid them with all the information in his power.[1]

On September 29 the attorney and solicitor generals rendered an opinion, to the effect that there was no such regular establishment of a national or provincial church in New England as to warrant the holding of a synod or convention ;[2] that, should the clergy presume to hold such an assembly without the royal license, the king's prerogative would be sufficient to declare the meeting illegal, even though it had been sanctioned by the council and the House of Representatives.[3] Yet, in the opinion of the crown lawyers, such an assembly, being only a voluntary society, could not be illegal if it did not seek to pass any authoritative acts.[4]

After receiving and considering these decisions, the lords justices sent a communication, through the hands of Secretary Charles de la Faye, to the governor of Massachusetts, in which they expressed surprise that he, contrary to his instructions, had neglected to inform the government of the proposed synod. Their letter reported the opinion of the attorney and solicitor generals that such an assemblage could not be legally held without the king's consent, and directed that, if it were already in session, it should be dissolved, but not by any formal act, lest by that step the authorities might seem to imply that such a body had some shadow of right to assemble. This ended the matter : the synod never met.[5]

In the long struggle which New England Episcopalians carried on during the greater part of the first half of the eighteenth century, in their efforts to secure exemption from taxation

---

[1] Perry, *Historical Collections*, iii. (Massachusetts) 186–187.

[2] Based on the Massachusetts Provincial charter of October 7, 1691 : see statute 3 William & Mary, and *Acts of the Massachusetts Assembly to* 1722.

[3] Chalmers, *Opinions*, i. 12.

[4] *Ibid*. 14.

[5] December 17, 1725, the Reverend Benjamin Colman, a prominent Boston clergyman, wrote to Bishop Kennett giving an account of the discussion relating to the calling of the synod, with his own opinions on the subject. His personal allusions to the Bishop of London are interesting, coming as they do from a liberal Congregationalist. Any one interested in his presentation of the case may find it completely stated in Turell, *Life of Colman*, 136–141.

for the support of Congregational ministers and churches, they frequently called upon their diocesan for aid; but although he labored earnestly in their behalf, they were unable to obtain such a settlement as they desired until the advent of Shirley to the governorship of Massachusetts.[1] Shirley proved a powerful ally. He had not been long in the province when he secured the passage of a perpetual act, providing that the taxes levied on Episcopalians should be applied to the support and maintenance of their own religious institutions, and not to those of the Congregationalists.[2]

In 1730 Bishop Gibson appointed Roger Price, rector of King's Chapel, to be his commissary for New England. Indeed, it seems to have been his custom, after he received his commission, to place a commissarial representative in every important colony which had hitherto been without one.

Passing southward through the various colonies, we find little to interest us until we come to Maryland. The situation of the Church of England here was much confused, and in spite of the fact that, relatively speaking, its membership was larger in Maryland than in any other province, its condition was very discouraging to those who had its best interests at heart. This unsatisfactory state of affairs was due partly to the fact that the respective rights of the Bishop of London and the lord proprietary had never been definitely marked off from each other, a circumstance which gave rise to frequent misunderstandings and conflicts. In theory the chief control of the ecclesiastical affairs of the colony was in the hands of the Bishop of London and his

---

[1] Shirley was ordered by his instructions to " give all Countenance and due Encouragement to the . . . Bishop of London or his Commissaries in the legal exercise of . . . [their] Ecclesiastical Jurisdiction, according to the Laws of the Province under . . . [his] Government." For the whole extract relating to ecclesiastical matters, see American Antiquarian Society, *Proceedings*, New Series, xiii. 221, from *Massachusetts Archives*, xlix.

[2] For a detailed account of the struggle of the Episcopalians to secure exemption from religious taxation for the support of the Congregational church, see Foote, *Annals of King's Chapel*, i. *passim*, and Perry, *Historical Collections*, iii. (Massachusetts) *passim*. There had been acts previous to that of 1743 granting exemption to Episcopalians ; but they had been only temporary in scope.

representatives; but practically the proprietary and his agent, the governor, had a not inconsiderable share in the management of these affairs. The situation was all the more complicated by the variable attitude of the latter two toward the establishment. At one moment they were most friendly, at another they seemed to wish to do everything in their power not only to check its progress but even to imperil its very existence. This circumstance, together with the fact that most of the Maryland clergy refused either from principle or from self-interest to acknowledge the delegated jurisdiction of the commissary, combined to render the authority of the Bishop of London extremely uncertain. His power was still further hampered by the independent position of the fully-installed parish priest. Selected by the proprietary, licensed by the Bishop of London, and inducted by the governor, he was secure from removal. He might be tried by the commissary, if there happened to be one; but it was more than uncertain that whatever sentence the latter pronounced against him could be enforced; in theory, to be sure, the commissary was, by the *Methodus Procedendi*, issued by Gibson, empowered to punish convicted clergymen by suspension or by deprivation of orders.[1]

An instance of the limitations under which the commissarial authority suffered at this time is seen in an extract of a letter from one Giles Rainsford to a friend, April 10, 1724. Rainsford writes that he had expressed a desire to the commissary of the Western Shore that he would convene the clergy for the purpose of addressing the present bishop on his promotion to the see of London, and that the commissary had expressed his willingness to do so, but had said that he had not the requisite power. Whereupon Rainsford adds that the clergy know who their bishop is, and if they forget their oath of canonical obedience it is no fault of his.[2] Soon after this, at the governor's suggestion, the clergy of the Western Shore convened and drew up a

[1] Hawks, whom I have followed closely on this point, is particularly strong in his emphasis on the unassailability of the inducted clergyman. For his opinion, see above, p. 6. It should be noted, however, that he is not sufficiently careful to distinguish between theory and practice.

[2] Perry, *Historical Collections*, iv. (Maryland) 233–234.

message of congratulation to their new diocesan. Their attitude toward him seems to have been particularly encouraging; for, after assuring him that he had gone to work more resolutely than any of his predecessors, they agree to answer all his queries, and promise him their obedience and aid in sustaining his jurisdiction.[1] In a few weeks the clergy of the Eastern Shore, evidently convoked by their commissary, sent a letter of congratulation to their new bishop. In it they spoke in high terms of the friendly attitude of Lord Baltimore, deplored the want of a regular spiritual jurisdiction, and for more specific information referred to their answers to his Lordship's queries.[2]

These answers, which are given in full in Perry's documents, shed considerable light on the existing ecclesiastical situation. They show, for example, what laws have been made in the province in relation to the church, the clergy, and the schools. On the Western Shore it seems to have been the custom for the commissary to hold a visitation of all the churches, schools, and glebes once in three years. A meeting of the clergy and church wardens was usually held once a year. At this time clergymen who were accused of any faults were presented, and six months afterward the commissary visited the several parishes of such parsons as had been accused.[3]

A letter written in the autumn of this year (1724) by Wilkinson, of the Eastern Shore, gives an interesting account of his methods of procedure as commissary under Gibson's predecessor. Foreseeing that the exercise of ecclesiastical jurisdiction which had been committed to him was "of no great moment and new" in that province, and that the management of it would be attended with difficulties, and realizing particularly that a false step at first would be fatal to its future success, he convoked the clergy at once for consultation. In convention they agreed upon certain articles, which Wilkinson laid before the government and also sent to Bishop Robinson, in both cases securing approval of them. He then delivered these articles to his clergy, and, among other things, ordered them to present for

---

[1] May 29, 1724, Perry, *Historical Collections*, iv. (Maryland) 234–235.
[2] July 16, 1724, *Ibid.* 239–241.
[3] *Ibid.* 131 ff.

punishment none but such as were "notoriously guilty"; others they should privately admonish in the presence of the church wardens and vestry of the parish. The commissary next proceeded to make personal visitations of the parish churches, glebes, and houses, to examine their condition, and to advise necessary repairs. During these visitations he licensed such schoolmasters as he found qualified to teach, and issued citations to the church wardens to appear at the general conventions. They came at the time appointed, bringing their presentments with them; whereupon Wilkinson proceeded, "after the same manner used in the spiritual courts in England, as near as the circumstances of the country would permit." He did everything gratis himself, without proctor or registrar.

In the opinion of Wilkinson, the plan of ecclesiastical censures seems to have worked well. He says that it caused a "visible reformation" in that part of the province, and that "the sight of one person performing penance struck a greater terror upon all offenders than all the pecuniary and corporal punishments which the secular courts inflict, as some of 'em have publickly acknowledged." [1] Wilkinson was undoubtedly optimistic as to the success of his plan; but he certainly was a popular commissary, at least so far as such an officer could be popular among the conflicting elements of colonial opposition to the institution; and there can be little doubt that, among those willing to recognize his authority, his punitary measure had some efficacy.

The class of well-disposed individuals was all too small, however; and it was evident that among the churchmen at large in Maryland this form of exercising ecclesiastical discipline was far from satisfactory. In view of this fact, a motion was made in the lower house of the Maryland assembly to erect "a Jurisdiction for the better Government of the Church and Clergy." This immediately called forth a "Humble Representation" from the clergy to the governor and upper and lower houses. Their chief complaint against the proposition lay in the fact that it

[1] Wilkinson to Gibson, September 9, 1724, in Perry, *Historical Collections*, iv. (Maryland) 244–246.

purposed to place the jurisdiction in the hands of laymen, a proceeding which the petitioners pronounced "inconsistent with the Lord Proprietary's Charter and with the rules of good reason, repugnant to the laws of the realm of Great Britain, destructive to the constitution of the Church of England, & w^t they can't in conscience submit to as being altogether opposite to the ordination vow." They admitted, however, that there was need of a law for the enforcement of ecclesiastical jurisdiction in the province, and expressed their willingness to confer with the legislature upon the proper heads of a bill for that purpose.[1]

The reply of the lower house to this petition was extremely favorable. It believed that the scandals which at that time were manifest in the lives of the clergy were due to the want of some jurisdiction to correct offenders; for since the Bishop of London's commissaries were not strong enough to correct clerical offenders, and since the clergy claimed exemption from lay jurisdiction, there was practically no power over them. But while insisting that something be done, the assembly expressed a readiness to accept the clergy's offer of assistance in drafting a bill to stop these infringements against law and morality.[2] Ultimately, however, the assembly decided to adhere to the original purpose of establishing a jurisdiction of lay persons over the clergy; and, in the words of Wilkinson, nothing could prevent the execution of the measure unless the governor, the only friend in the province upon whom the clergy could rely, refused to give his consent.[3] At this juncture Governor Calvert intervened, in the interest of the Bishop of London. He gave two reasons for refusing to sanction the proceedings of the assembly: first, because the clergy were under the bishop's inspection, and it was for him to see to it that they were properly disciplined; secondly, because in his opinion there was no ground for the

---

[1] Petition enclosed in a letter to Gibson, November 20, 1724, in Perry, *Historical Collections*, iv. (Maryland) 247–248.

[2] Reply enclosed in the same letter, *Ibid.* 248–249.

[3] Wilkinson to Gibson, June 15, 1726, *Ibid.* 254–255. It appears from a letter of Governor Calvert to Gibson that this step was due to the machinations of one Thomas Bardley, a lawyer, who was an enemy of the governor.

extravagant charge against their conduct.[1]   However cogent his reasons may have seemed, the interference of Calvert was all that was necessary to block the measure.[2]

In 1730 Gibson made the energetic Henderson commissary of the Eastern as well as of the Western Shore.[3]   At his first visitation, held in the former district June 24, 1730, he stated that the objects of his coming were to examine credentials, to bespeak the assistance and concurrence of the clergy for a strict and orderly administration of the divine offices, and to exhort them to a suitable and exemplary life and conversation ;[4] and at a meeting held on the other Shore he repeated the speech.[5]   At both convocations his acts and recommendations were necessarily of a purely spiritual nature ; for Henderson, much as he might perhaps have wished, was in no position to go further.   In the first place, he was unpopular with the governor, against whom he had appealed to Lord Baltimore through his diocesan, and also with a great majority of the people ; in the second place, he dared not set up any jurisdiction until he had received an exemplification of the royal commission ; for, had he attempted to act without the authority of this instrument, undoubtedly the provincial court would have stayed him.[6]   A copy of the commission from the late king was in his possession, but that was of course superseded.   Probably one of the new copies had been sent to him, but had either been lost on the way, or, as he suspected, had been suppressed by his enemy the governor.[7]   In spite of his zeal, therefore, Henderson continued impotent.

[1] Calvert to Gibson, June 22, 1725, Perry, *Historical Collections*, iv. (Maryland) 249–250.

[2] There is considerable evidence even from their own midst that the moral condition of the clergy was bad : see, for example, the admission of the petitioners themselves (above, p. 75), and compare also Wilkinson to Gibson, December 4, 1727 (Perry, *Ibid.* 259–260).

[3] Hawks, *Ecclesiastical Contributions*, ii. (Maryland) 204.

[4] For Henderson's address to the clergy, with all the proceedings of this visitation, see Perry, *Historical Collections*, iv. (Maryland) 288–296.

[5] For the second visitation, see *Ibid.* 297–299.

[6] See Henderson to Gibson, August 12, 1730, *Ibid.* 300–301.

[7] Henderson to Gibson, March 13, 1731–1732, *Ibid.* 302–303. Notwithstanding these handicaps, Henderson continued for a time as an active worker in the

In 1733 the proprietary visited the colony. Although he took pains to prevent any further encroachments upon the clergy, and did all he could to reconcile clergy and laity; and though he placed no hindrance in Henderson's way in the exercise of the powers conferred by his commission, he stood, nevertheless, upon the provisions of his charter as he understood them, and strictly maintained his rights in the ordering of the affairs of church discipline within the boundaries of the province.[1] Owing to the difficulty, or rather the impossibility, of obtaining the enforcement of the powers entrusted to him, Commissary Henderson resigned in 1734, and from this time the Bishop of London ceased to be officially represented in the province of Maryland.[2]

After Henderson's resignation the situation grew rapidly worse. Owing to a quarrel with the proprietary, Bishop Gibson took little interest in the Maryland church during the last years of his life.[3] The clergy, left to themselves, fell into greater disorders than ever. "Enthusiasm, deism, and libertism (with all which we abound) make no small advantage," writes the Reverend Hugh Jones to Gibson, October 19, 1741, "especially seeing these sons of Eli are permitted to persevere with impunity, and without censure or admonition, since the offation of the exercise of M^r. Henderson's commissarial power." Having sketched the situation, he suggests a remedy: "The vast importance . . . [of] the affair obliges me in conscience to inform your Lordship of the great necessity there is for a strict spiritual discipline over the Clergy here, either by an effectual restitution of your Lordship's delegated Jurisdiction, or by the Proprietor's exertion of his power (according to the Ecclesiastical jurisdiction of England, to which his Charter refers)

interests of the clergy; he made visitations regularly, and resisted laws made to curtail the clerical stipends. August 7, 1731, he again urged his diocesan to send him an attest of the royal commission, in order that he might proceed against one Mr. Urmston, who had been complained of by his parishioners for leading a scandalous life.

[1] Henderson to Gibson, June 5, 1733, *Ibid.* 311–313.

[2] Perry, *American Episcopal Church*, i. 309–310; Hawks, *Ecclesiastical Contributions*, ii. (Maryland) 222.

[3] Hawks, *Ecclesiastical Contributions*, ii. (Maryland) 230.

if the right be really invested in him; or else by a conjunction of your Lordship's authority & his; or finally by an Act of Parliament or Assembly obtained for the purpose or by what other method your Lordship's prudence and Interest can accomplish so great & necessary a work." But no heed was paid either to Jones's representation or to his suggestions, and at the time of Gibson's death the theoretical jurisdiction of the Bishop of London had no basis in fact.[1]

The Nestor among American commissaries, Blair, of Virginia, lived nearly through the Gibson period. In a letter to his diocesan of February 10, 1723–24, he gives some account of his work. Bishop Compton had directed him, many years before, to make no further use of his commission than was necessary to keep the clergy in order. In consequence of this advice and of the conditions that he had to face, Blair had never attempted to exercise coercive jurisdiction by setting up a spiritual court. Indeed, unless an accused clergyman were notoriously delinquent, he had been accustomed to proceed no farther than to admonition; for, owing to the dearth of clergymen,[2] it was difficult to fill the place of one suspended.[3] During the interval between Gibson's accession and the issue of the royal commission of 1727, some of the clergy, "looking upon it as a time of misrule . . . became exceeding scandalous," apparently worse than usual.[4] Blair chafed under the temporary restraint which deprived him of his accustomed authority, though even when he was vested with full commissarial powers he seems never to have been a very keen disciplinarian.[5]

---

[1] Perry, *Historical Collections*, iv. (Maryland) 323–324.

[2] Blair states that at the time of writing there were at least two vacancies with no clergymen to supply them.

[3] May 13, 1724, Blair writes that he has made only two suspensions in the thirty-four years that he has been commissary. He wants his commission in order to suspend two more clergymen accused of drunkenness. It was evidently the custom for each successive Bishop to renew the commissarial commissions. For Blair's letter, see Perry, *Historical Collections*, i. (Virginia) 252–253, and *Fulham MSS.*

[4] Blair to Gibson, June 21, 1725, *Fulham MSS.*

[5] Blair rarely prosecuted except when public opinion required him to do so, and even then he never resorted to coercion. A letter which he wrote to

Throughout the Gibson period the precariousness of the clerical tenure in Virginia was a matter of much concern to the parish priests and the ecclesiastical authorities. From an examination of the answers which the Virginia pastors returned to his queries, Gibson first learned how dependent many of them were on the arbitrary will of their flocks. A large number of them he found to be without institution or induction, the parishes having disregarded the law directing them to make presentations to the governors, and the governors having neglected to make use of their powers as ordinaries to induct without presentation when such lapses occurred. In order to remedy this state of affairs, Gibson petitioned the king to instruct the governors, in case of neglect of presentation by parishes, *jure devoluto*, to collate and induct suitable clerks. The bishop thought, however, that six months, the term allowed to patrons by English ecclesiastical law, was too short a time for the colonies, particularly when the clergyman came from England, as was most often the case. In view of these facts, he recommended that in the colonies the term be lengthened to eighteen months.[1] Later, William Gooch, who came over as governor in 1727, undertook to adjust the matter in the interest of the establishment;[2] but he was evidently unable to effect a settlement.

As years went by, the establishment steadily lost ground in Virginia, and cognizance of spiritual affairs came more and more into the hands of the governor and council. Much blame

Bishop Gibson, March 24, 1734, concerning accusations of drunkenness among the clergy, is characteristic. While admitting that the charges are in a measure true, he adds: " It is neither so general, nor to such a degree as he [an anonymous accuser] represents it. Some of the persons he names I have admonished both in discourse and writing, and have found some good effects of these admonitions. But it is a mighty hard matter to prove any of these things upon them; it is an office which everybody declines; except when the scandal is very great; and then when they fear a public prosecution, they contrive to leave the country. I shall take occasion to renew my admonition to some persons on this subject; but I may safely tell your L^{dp} it is not near so bad as that anonymous person represents " (*Fulham MSS.*).

[1] The petition, dated 1724, is printed in Perry, *Historical Collections*, i. (Virginia) 345–346.

[2] See Blair to Gibson, October 28, 1728, *Ibid.* 352–353.

was laid on Blair. It was admitted that he was a good man; but he was advancing in years, and it was generally felt that he was not equal to the requirements of the office. Accordingly a wish was expressed for a deputy commissary, "a clergyman of known zeal, courage, & resolution & such as could redress some great neglects of duty," among the clergy, "and bring Episcopacy to be better regarded."[1] But Blair's life was drawing to a close. He died in 1743, and was succeeded by William Dawson, who had been recommended by Governor Gooch.[2] Dawson received his commission July 18, 1743, having been previously elected president of William and Mary College by the unanimous choice of the visitors.[3]

By far the most energetic of Gibson's commissaries was Alexander Garden of Carolina. He made visitations almost every year, examined letters of orders and licenses, heard complaints, regulated disorders, enforced the instructions of the bishop, and transmitted accounts of his proceedings, both to his ecclesiastical superior and to the Society for Propagating the Gospel. He was very active as a disciplinarian, and was somewhat of a stickler for formality, seeking to conduct his trials more in accordance with canonical form than any other commissary in the colonies.

From the many prosecutions which Garden undertook, that against the celebrated preacher George Whitefield, may, although it came to nothing, be selected for consideration, as perhaps the most interesting.[4] On his first visit to Charleston, in September, 1738, Whitefield was well received by the com-

---

[1] Reverend Anthony Gavin to Gibson, October 5, 1738, *Fulham MSS.*; partly printed in Perry, *Historical Collections*, i. (Virginia) 360–361.

[2] Gooch to Gibson, May 10, 1743, in Perry, *Ibid.* 367.

[3] Dawson's commission may be found in the *Fulham MSS.* As commissary, Blair had no salary or perquisites, though the governor allowed him £100 a year out of the quitrents. Probably Dawson received the same. See Hartwell, Blair, and Chilton, *Present State of Virginia.*

[4] These letters are in the *Fulham MSS.* The most complete account of the affair yet written may be found in Tyerman, *Life of Whitefield*, i. *passim.* (See index, under "Garden.") Tyerman, however, had not examined the letters at Fulham. He errs in saying (i. 399–400) that it was "the first Episcopal Court in the British Colonies."

missary.[1] This was before he began to exhibit to such a marked
degree those qualities of enthusiasm and radicalism which afterward caused the orthodox among his clerical brethren to regard
him with suspicion. By the time of his second visit to South
Carolina, he had come to be distrusted by Garden; hence,
when he called at the latter's house in Charleston, March 14,
1740, he was very coolly received. In the course of the interview which followed, the commissary charged him with
breaking the canons of the church as well as his ordination
vows, and warned him that, if he preached in any public church
in the province, he would suspend him. Whitefield replied, " I
shall regard that as much as I would a Pope's Bull." After
some further discussion, which became more and more heated,
Garden ordered him to leave the house.[2] Disregarding the
commissary's warning, Whitefield continued to preach, and was
in consequence brought to trial.[3]

The citation was issued on the eleventh of July, and on the
fifteenth the trial was opened.[4] Whitefield refused to answer

[1] " I was received in a most Christian manner by the Bishop of London's
commissary, the Rev. Mr. Garden, a good soldier of Jesus Christ " (Tyerman,
Life of Whitefield, i. 143).

[2] *Continuation of Whitefield's Journal, after his arrival at Georgia,* March
14, 1740.

[3] During the interval between the interview of March 14 and the opening
of the trial, Garden took occasion more than once to denounce Whitefield
from his pulpit, and wrote several letters, later published in pamphlet form, in
answer to some printed utterances of Whitefield upon various subjects, including an attack on Archbishop Tillotson and strictures on Southern slave-
holders. See Tyerman, *Life of Whitefield,* i. 359–364.

[4] The most detailed description of the trial is in Tyerman, *Life of Whitefield,* i. 396–401. A full account which Garden sent to his diocesan is unfortunately missing, as appears from a remark in a letter of July 8, 1743, from
Garden to Gibson, to the effect that the account which he sent with his letter
of January 28, 1741, had probably miscarried, since he had heard nothing of
it. It is certainly not among the manuscripts at Fulham. For Garden's side
of the story we have to depend on a rather meagre report of the case embodied
in his answer to Bishop Sherlock's " circular letter." This may be found
among the Carolina manuscripts at Fulham, under date February 1, 1750.
Tyerman apparently never saw this letter. The form of citation was that
provided by Gibson's *Methodus Procedendi* (see below, Appendix A, No. vi.,
where the complete text is given).

the articles of accusation presented against him until he was satisfied that the court had the requisite authority to examine him. After the commissary's commission had been produced, Whitefield proceded to question the jurisdictional authority of the Bishop of London over his case. He argued, first, that neither the bishop nor his agent had power to exercise legal jurisdiction in special cases in South Carolina unless supported by acts of the colonial assembly ; and secondly, that in any case he was, as a resident of Georgia, beyond the scope of Garden's commissarial court. He said, moreover, that "though he had preached in the fields near London, the bishop had never attempted to exercise such authority over him; and that the Trustees of Georgia, to his knowledge, doubted whether the Bishop of London had *any* jurisdiction in the transatlantic colonies." [1]

At Whitefield's request a day was given him in which to secure information as to the extent of the commissary's jurisdiction. When the court opened on the next day he presented a *recusatio judicis*, that is, a refusal to accept Garden as his judge. This *recusatio* was based on the ground that the commissary had no power to proceed against him, since, as a clergyman of Georgia, he was out of the limits of Garden's jurisdiction.[2] Moreover, he alleged that Garden was his enemy and had written and preached very bitterly against him.[3] Then a dispute arose as to who should pass upon the *recusatio*. The commissary's attorney wanted it to be tried in court, but Whitefield wished it to be referred to six arbitrators, three to be chosen by each party. Thereupon Whitefield named as the three who were to act on his part two Independents and one French Calvinist, all of whom, according to Garden, were "zealous admirers" of the accused.

[1] Garden to Sherlock, February 1, 1750, *Fulham MSS.*

[2] Whitefield to Gibson, September 8, 1740, *Fulham MSS.*

[3] Garden, in his letter of February 1, 1750, mentions only the latter reason, and Tyerman (*Life of Whitefield*, i. 399) makes the same statement. Possibly this was the real reason ; for Whitefield would hardly have wished to be tried by a prejudiced judge. Nevertheless, an exception based on want of jurisdiction would have been more easy to sustain than one founded on merely personal grounds ; and this cause was probably the one insisted on then and in the subsequent appeal.

Garden saw many obstacles in the way of submitting the exception to the ruling of the arbitrators. In the first place, there was the difficulty of securing a non-partisan judgment from such a board; in the second place, if the members failed to agree, the case would probably have to be dropped, as the law made no provision for such an exigency; and, finally, if they decided against the commissary, the laws were equally silent as to who should be appointed as judge in his place. In view of these difficulties, the commissary refused to allow the *recusatio* to be arbitrated, whereupon Whitefield appealed to the English authorities.[1] In compliance with the legal formalities in such a case, he was conducted before the commissary by the latter's apparitor, and took an oath to lodge his appeal within twelve months, depositing ten pounds as a guarantee that his oath would be observed.

Garden kept the court in regular adjournment for five months after the expiration of the judicatory term allowed for such appeals, that is, twelve months, waiting for an official notification of the result of the appeal.[2] This did not come to hand; but, inferring from a letter which he received that "Whitefield had deserted his Appeal, notwithstanding his solemn oath, in open court, *bona fide* to prosecute it," the commissary decided to carry on the case. Accordingly, he again summoned Whitefield to appear before the court; and as the latter neither came nor answered his summons, he proceeded to examine witnesses, and on their evidence found him guilty of preaching in dissenting

[1] Whitefield, according to his own words, "appealed, according to law, to four of His Majesty's commissioners for reviewing appeals, to know whether the commissary ought not to have accepted a *recusatio judicis*, which I lodged in the court" (Whitefield to Gibson, September 8, 1740, *Fulham MSS.*, and Tyerman, *Life of Whitefield*, i. 405). Although it is uncertain whom his appeal ultimately reached, it is certain that it was not, as Tyerman asserts (*Ibid.* 400), directed to the High Court of Chancery.

[2] See Garden to Gibson, January 28, 1741: "I could have wished that the council your Lordship employed had, on the expiration of the Juratory Term, transmitted a proper Certificate from the Office, that Whitefield has deserted his Appeal w^ch (if I am rightly informed) is the Method in Cases of Appeals in Civil Matters from America, and would not have been denied them" (*Fulham MSS.*). But the evidence is not altogether clear that Whitefield actually deserted his appeal.

meeting-houses and conducting service without the forms prescribed in the Book of Common Prayer.   At the conclusion of
the trial he pronounced upon him the sentence of suspension
from the exercise of his functions as a minister of the Church
of England.[1]   In a subsequent letter to his bishop, Commissary
Garden informed him that, if the lords appellees did not approve
of his sentence, they might annul it.   In any case he regarded
the matter as ended so far as he was concerned, having done all
he could with the means at his disposal.[2]

The evidence concerning the history of Whitefield's appeal
to the authorities in England is very obscure and conflicting.
Unfortunately, as he ceased to keep up his Journal after his
arrival in England in the spring of 1741, his side of the story
can be gathered only from occasional allusions in his letters.
On the whole, however, one is inclined to doubt Garden's assertion that Whitefield deliberately deserted his appeal.   Certainly
there is good evidence to show that he intended at the start
to prosecute it in all earnestness.   In the first place, he took
an oath and deposited a money pledge in the commissary's court
to lodge his appeal within a year before the proper authorities.[3]
Secondly, on September 8, 1740, he wrote to Bishop Gibson
informing him of his action, and seeking his Lordship's
opinion as to the extent of the jurisdiction of the court of the
commissary of the Carolinas.[4]   Again, and this is a far more
certain proof of the honesty of his intention at this time, he
wrote to a friend in London : " The bearer brings the authentic
copy of my appeal.   I sent you another copy from Carolina.
Be pleased to keep this I have now sent, till you hear of my
coming to England.   If I come in the spring, I will lodge it
myself ; if not, be pleased to lodge it for me, and I will pay all

---

[1] Garden to Sherlock, February 1, 1750, *Fulham MSS.*   The sentence was
apparently in the form prescribed by Gibson in the *Methodus Procedendi* (see
below, Appendix A, No. vi.).   An English form of the sentence is given in
Tyerman, *Life of Whitefield*, i. 400.

[2] Garden to Gibson, January 28, 1741, *Fulham MSS.*

[3] Tyerman, *Life of Whitefield*, i. 399.

[4] There is a copy of this letter in the *Fulham MSS.*   It is printed in Tyerman, *Life of Whitefield*, i. 405–406.

expenses." [1] Finally, there are two bits of evidence showing that, although he may have been glad to get rid of the matter, it was not through any neglect on his part that the case was dropped. The first piece of evidence is in a letter to a friend, dated April 10, 1741, a month after his arrival in England, in which he says, "My 'Appeal' will come to nothing, I believe." [2] The second is at the end of a letter to James Habersham, December 7, 1741, where he writes triumphantly: "The Lords see through Mr. Garden's enmity, and will have nothing to do with my Appeal; so that a hook is put into the leviathan's jaws." [3]

All this goes to show that, although Whitefield would have been glad to see the matter at an end, he was zealous enough to push it until he saw that nothing was going to be accomplished. The delay which prolonged the proceedings beyond the regular judicial term was evidently due to a misunderstanding as to where the appeal should go, but it is difficult to know just where to place the blame. Whitefield himself expressly says, in his letter to Bishop Gibson, that he had appealed "according to law, to four of His Majesty's commissioners for reviewing appeals." On the other hand, an account in a communication from the Council Office seems to indicate that he had not appealed to the proper persons. Early in May, 1742, he called at the Office to obtain some information about his appeal, not being able to understand from his solicitor exactly what had been done about it. William Sharpe, who received him, informed him that it had been returned to his solicitor "as improper to be laid before his Majesty in Council, his Majesty having Appointed Commissioners for hearing and Determining Appeals of that Nature." Whereupon, Whitefield said that he would forthwith appeal to the Archbishop of Canterbury, the first named in the commission, to obtain a hearing. [4] Bishop Gibson, to whom Sharpe had written for advice, evidently applied in his turn to Commissary Garden, who sent a reply

---

[1] Tyerman, *Life of Whitefield*, i. 406.

[2] *Ibid.* 477.

[3] *Ibid.* 539.

[4] Letter from the Council Office to Gibson, May 15, 1742, *Fulham MSS.*

which serves only to confuse the case still more. "Mr. White-field's pretence of Mistake in lodging his Appeal," he says, "is manifestly idle & groundless. Your Lordship knows that his Appeal was directed not only in general To the most rev^d and most noble & right hon^ble the Lords Commiss^nrs &c. but to them, by each of the Names and Titles at length set down as specified; so that any such mistake was impossible."[1] And again in a later letter he says decidedly: "He interposed an Appeal to the Lords named in the Royal Patent; but . . . either wilfully or ignorantly neglected to prosecute [it] until the Juratory Term . . . was expired."[2]

There was evidently a mistake somewhere; but it seems almost certain that the blame lay rather with the ecclesiastical and civil authorities in England than with Whitefield. All the evidence available, especially the letter from the council, indicates that Whitefield certainly meant to apply to the proper persons and to get a hearing. But the upshot of the matter was that his appeal was never granted, the suspension pronounced upon him *in absentia* was never removed, and, when he continued to disregard it, Garden was only by lack of authority restrained from excommunicating him.[3]

This is the last important case which occurred during the term of the Reverend Alexander Garden. In the beginning of 1749 he resigned his office as commissary. With his resignation the visitations, which had been held since 1731, ceased, and were replaced by annual meetings of the clergy, the first of which was held April 5, 1749.[4] Garden resigned the rectorship of St. Philip's October 29, 1753. Not long after his return

---

[1] Garden to Gibson, July 8, 1743, *Fulham MSS.*

[2] Garden to Sherlock, February 1, 1750, *Ibid.*

[3] "Sentence of Suspension from his Office . . . still stands against him, — But this Sentence having had no effect upon him for his Reformation and Submission, I should have long since have proceeded, pursuant to the Canon, to that of Excommunication, but for a Defect in the Law, which would have rendered it as ineffectual as the other, vizt, that the Writ *de excommunicato capiendo*, could not be issued against him here, because the Statutes of Queen Eliza^bth on which that Writ is grounded, do not extend to America " (Garden to Sherlock, February 1, 1750, *Ibid.*).

[4] Dalcho, *Protestant Episcopal Church in South-Carolina*, 162.

from a visit to England he died in Charleston, September 27, 1756, at the age of seventy-one years.[1] He was the last commissary who ever held office in the Carolinas.

Such is the history of Gibson's connection with the colonies. Beginning with a consciousness that he had a binding duty to perform toward his charges beyond the sea, he took pains to find out all that was possible concerning their condition; endeavored to have his authority set upon a secure footing; and then, having formulated rules for the action of his representatives, he faithfully did his duty in each particular case as it arose. His ideal was to carry on the organization of the colonial churches under his charge, to check disorder and strife, and to supply the people with earnest and worthy ministers. In the midst of all his activity, he seems to have been guided by purely spiritual considerations. While he doubtless recognized the limitations of his power, he saw that the time was not yet ripe for the introduction of any other system, and so held his peace.

With his successor, however, came a change of policy. For reasons to be explained later, Sherlock, refusing to carry on the jurisdiction in the manner of his predecessors, sought to secure the appointment of bishops resident in the colonies who should exercise the powers hitherto in the hands of the Bishop of London. But, before considering Sherlock's work and its consequences, it will be necessary to trace the history of the efforts to establish an American episcopacy which were made previous to his accession.

[1] Dalcho, *Protestant Episcopal Church in South-Carolina*, 176.

CHAPTER IV.

ATTEMPTS TO OBTAIN AN AMERICAN EPISCOPATE, 1638–1748.

THE scheme of entrusting the government of the Church of England in America to resident bishops is almost as old as the jurisdiction of the Bishop of London. The early attempts to secure such an establishment came from the side of the English government and the Anglican hierarchy. No sooner was the Society for Propagating the Gospel founded, however, than the initiative began to be taken by the missionaries of that body who were resident in America. From that time on, the matter passed out of the hands of the English government, and, so far as it was considered at all in England, into those of the Society and of such bishops as were connected with that body either as officers or as members. After many discouragements and delays the hopes of those interested in the project seemed about to be fulfilled, when they were suddenly shattered by the death of Queen Anne. The new king and his advisers had so many other affairs claiming attention that they could not give any consideration to a matter of so little importance in their eyes; and the agitation, which almost ceased after this set-back, was not revived again till the conversion of Timothy Cutler and the other Connecticut ministers, in 1722. Thenceforth, from time to time, the Episcopal clergymen of the northern and middle colonies,[1] both individually and collectively, appealed for what they characterized as an indispensable limb of their church system; but their petitions received little attention. Whether this inattention was due to indifference, or to a feeling that the Bishop of London under his new commission possessed powers sufficiently adequate to render the erection of an episcopal hierarchy unnecessary, it would be hard to say. Certainly the English government was not held back then, as it was later, by any fear of opposition from the colonial Independents. At any rate, from

[1] Particularly in New England in this period.

whatever cause, the subject was rarely discussed in public from the end of the reign of George I. to about 1740, when Thomas Secker, then Bishop of Oxford, again opened the question in a sermon before the Society for Propagating the Gospel. During the next few years the movement was much strengthened by the aid which Bishop Sherlock lent it, particularly after his elevation to the see of London in 1748, when the question began to assume a public, political importance. Sherlock's accession, therefore, marks a new epoch in the episcopal question; for, from the time of the failure of the Laudian projects until Sherlock began his activity, the attempts to settle bishops in America concerned only the church as such.[1] The truth of this statement will at once be evident from a short historical examination of the character of these early attempts.

They may be classed under a few main heads, namely, the efforts made by the English government, those made by the missionaries resident in the middle colonies, those of the Society and of the higher clergy in answer to the Society's appeals, and finally those of the Episcopal clergy of New England from 1722 onward. It is worthy of remark that the centre of agitation lay chiefly in the middle and northern provinces, where the missionaries felt the need of a strong organization. Few of the petitions emanated from the southern colonies; for, since those provinces in which the Church of England was established by law felt no need of a stronger system, the clergy were not willing to curtail their accustomed liberty by submitting to the rigid supervision and authority of a superior, and the laity were not inclined to drain their purses to supply revenue for what they regarded as an unnecessary appendage. Let us now consider the history of this subject somewhat more in detail.

As early as 1638, Laud seems to have had in mind a plan to send a bishop to New England, but to have been prevented by the disorders in Scotland from carrying out his purpose.[2] The next attempt to establish a colonial bishop occurred shortly after

---

[1] With the possible exception of the efforts of the Society in the time of Anne; and even these were apparently actuated by purely missionary motives.

[2] Heylyn, *Cyprianus Anglicus* (see above, p. 21); Hawkins, *Missions of the Church of England*, 376.

the Restoration, when Lord Chancellor Clarendon made preparations to send Dr. Alexander Murray to Virginia.[1] The plan got so far as to receive the approval of the king in council, with letters patent for the execution of it;[2] but from some cause or other it came to nothing. Some writers attribute the failure to the sudden accession to power of the Cabal ministry, and the consequent dismissal of Sir Orlando Bridgman, to whose care the matter had been intrusted;[3] other writers ascribe it to the opposition excited because the "endowment was payable out of the customs."[4]

[1] The draft of a patent for the creation of a bishopric in Virginia was found in a manuscript of All Souls' College, Oxford, and a copy was brought to the United States by the Bishop of Virginia in 1867. It was among the papers of Sir Leoline Jenkins, whom we have already met as an earnest friend of the plan of extending the Church of England in America (above p. 34), and was probably drafted by his hand. Very likely this was the patent under which Sir Alexander Murray was to exercise his functions. This instrument (printed in Perry, *Historical Collections*, i. (Virginia) 538 ff., and in Foote, *Annals of King's Chapel*, ii. 229–230) provides that all the provinces — with the exception of New England, which was to be free from episcopal control — should be annexed to the diocese of Virginia. The aim, as the patent states, was " to establish and confirm under one and the same order and rule, and under one doctrine, discipline, authority, and jurisdiction all our remaining regions and plantations in America."

[2] Archbishop Secker (*Letter to Walpole*, 17) informs us that he first heard of the design from his examination of the papers of the late Bishop Gibson; and that the " Letters Patent for that Purpose are still extant." Cf. Chandler, *Appeal Farther Defended*, 148, note.

[3] Hawkins, *Missions of the Church of England*, 376 (from Gadsden, *Life of Bishop Dehon*, 5). Murray says that Sir Orlando Bridgman, to whom, together with the new Bishop of London, the case was referred, was put out of office by the incoming Cabal ministry (see Protestant Episcopal Historical Society, *Collections*, i. 139). According to Chandler (*Appeal Farther Defended*, 148), a writer who furnished an extract from Cranmer's *Catechism* in a letter of February 28, 1770, said that he had seen an original letter — which fell into his hands by executorship — from Dr. Alexander Murray giving an account of the proposed establishment and dated, so far as he could recollect, October 16, 1673; he supposed that the " matter died, by the Cabal's throwing out Sir Orlando in the November following, before the bishop and he had made their report." The same view is expressed by Chandler (*Free Examination*, 1), who cites as reference " Some papers in the late Duke of Bedford's Office."

[4] Hawkins, *Missions of the Church of England*, 376. Secker promulgated their view, which was based on an opinion of Gibson (Secker, *Letter to Wal-*

The next attempt seems to have been in 1664. It was rumored that the "Commissioners for New England" sent out in that year were to establish bishops there;[1] but even if the English authorities had any such original intention, they soon changed their minds, for, in the set of private instructions issued to the commissioners, they ordered them to take no steps in the direction of substituting episcopacy for the existing form of religion.[2]

The next instance of an attempted establishment was that associated with the name of Chaplain Miller of New York, who made a vain effort to have the Bishop of London consecrate a suffragan who should also be charged with the secular government of the province.[3]

Perhaps the most interesting of these abortive plans which took rise in England was the attempt to make Dean Swift Bishop of Virginia. Our knowledge of this affair is based on the correspondence between Swift and Colonel Hunter, who, designated as lieutenant governor of Virginia, but failing to get the position, went out in 1713 as governor to New York.[4] From this correspondence it appears that Swift did not take the prospective appointment very seriously, but re-

pole, 17). What Gibson has to say on the matter may be found in his "Letter and Memorial on sending Bishops to the American Plantations Abroad," in the manuscripts of the General Convention of the Protestant Episcopal Church (Protestant Episcopal Historical Society, *Collections*, i. 139).

[1] The "Chamber at Amsterdam" wrote to the governor and council of New Netherlands, April 21, 1664, that it had received news from England "according to which his Royal Majesty of Great Britain, being inclined to reduce all his kingdoms under one form of government in Church and State, hath taken care that Commissioners are ready in England to repair to New England to install Bishops there the same as in Old England" (*New York Documents*, ii. 235).

[2] *Ibid.* iii. 59; cf. American Antiquarian Society *Proceedings*, New Series, xiii. 202.

[3] Perry, *American Episcopal Church*, i. 160–161 ; McConnell, *American Episcopal Church*, 65–67.

[4] Extracts from this correspondence are cited in Hawkins, *Missions of the Church of England*, 378 ; Perry, *American Episcopal Church*, 398–399, citing Swift, *Works* (edited by Walter Scott), xv. 295, 308, xvi. 48. See also the life of Swift, in his *Works*, i. 98.

garded it as a sinecure and a last resource in case he could get nothing better. On January 12, 1708–9, Swift wrote to Colonel Hunter : " *Vous savez que — Monsieur Addison notre bon ami est fait secrétaire d'état d'Irlande ;* and unless you make haste over and get my Virginia bishoprick, he will persuade me to go with him, for the Vienna project is off ; which is a great disappointment to the design I had of displaying my politics at the Emperor's Court." [1] On March 22 of the same year he wrote : " Being not able to make my friends in the ministry consider my merits or their promises enough to keep me here, . . . all my hopes now terminate in my bishoprick of Virginia." [2] After Hunter became governor of New York, he wrote to his friend intimating that he should like to have him occupy the bishopric for which he had purchased a seat by order of the Society.[3] But the plan dropped here. And so too did the project of Archbishop Sharpe, which miscarried because the Bishop of London was not present at the meeting.[4]

The attempts made by clergymen resident in the colonies to obtain one or more bishops to take charge of their church affairs will now be considered. With one exception I know of no plea from this source before the foundation of the Society for Propagating the Gospel, in 1701. This exception is to be found in the work called *Virginia's Cure*, written in 1662. The author attributes the low state of religion in Virginia, not to the absence of a bishop, but to the scattered condition of the population, and beseeches the Bishop of London's aid in securing a closer population and more city life.

[1] Swift, *Works*, xv. 295–296.

[2] *Ibid.* 308. In a note on the same page we find the following statement : " There was a scheme on foot at this time to make Dr. Swift Bishop of Virginia with power to ordain priests and deacons for all our colonies in America, and to parcel out that country into deaneries, parishes, chapels, &c., and to recommend and present thereto ; which would have been of the greatest use to the protestant religion in that country had it taken effect."

[3] Hunter to Swift, March 1, 1712–1713 : " I have purchased a seat for a bishop, and by orders from the Society have given directions to prepare it for his reception. You once upon a day gave me hopes of seeing you there. It would be to me no small relief to have so good a friend to complain to (*Ibid.* xvi. 48).

[4] See above, p. 50.

He suggests, however, as the fifth of seven means by which the condition of the Virginia church might be improved, "that there being divers persons already in the Colony fit to serve the Church in the office of deacon, a Bishop be sent over, so soon as there should be a City for his See, as for the other needs of that Church, so also, that after due Probation and Examination, such persons may be ordained Deacons and their Duty and Service be appointed by the Bishop."[1] Yet this is a bare suggestion and is not insisted on. Not only is it the sole request for a bishop coming from the colonies in the seventeenth century, but it is one of the very few that came from the southern colonies during the whole colonial period.

It may safely be said that it is with the foundation of the Society for Propagating the Gospel that earnest efforts began to be made for the establishment of bishops in North America. The first proposal seems to have come from Dr. Thomas Bray,[2] who even received some contributions in answer to his appeal; but the matter resulted in nothing. Next to Dr. Bray, the most energetic and zealous among the early missionaries was the Reverend John Talbot, who, with his fellow-worker George Keith, may be regarded as the pioneer of the Society in the middle colonies. Beginning in 1702,[3] Talbot continued to agitate the question upon every possible occasion. Out of his many appeals the following may be selected as one of the most characteristic: "The poor Church," he writes in a letter to the Society, dated September 1, 1703, "has nobody upon the spot to comfort or confirm her children; nobody to ordain several that are willing to serve, were they authorized, for the work of the Ministry. Therefore they fall back again into the herd of the Dissenters, rather than they will be at the Hazard and Charge to goe as far as England for orders: so that we

---

[1] *Virginia's Cure, an Advisive Narrative*, 21.

[2] Perry, *American Episcopal Church*, i. 396. Bray's *Memorial, representing the Present State of Religion, on the Continent of North America*, in which he agitated the subject of an American episcopate, appeared in 1700–1701. Although the Society was not definitely established till June, 1701, Bray had some time earlier begun his efforts toward organizing it.

[3] Talbot's first appeal was sent from New York in 1702. See Hawkins, *Missions of the Church of England*, 376.

have seen several Counties, Islands, and Provinces, which have hardly an orthodox minister, am'st them, which might have been supply'd, had we been so happy as to see a Bishop or Suffragan Apud Americanos."[1] It will be noticed that Talbot desired a bishop for purely spiritual purposes, such as ordaining, confirming, and the like offices. Though it is not certain just how, in his opinion, a bishop would be supported, it would seem, from a letter written to his colleague Keith, in regard to one John Livingstone's purpose to go to England to seek an episcopal consecration, that he regarded a contribution of tenths from the clergy as ample means for a bishop's maintenance.[2] But it is difficult to see how a handful of ministers, most of them depending upon a stipend from the Society, could furnish for their diocesan "a provision as honorable as some in Europe."

Talbot did not confine his efforts to writing; in 1706 he went to England to press his cause in person.[3] Evidently he received some encouragement there, for on his return to America he selected a house for a bishop's seat.[4] In 1712 the Society closed the bargain, and directed that the residence be prepared for habitation,[5] an action which is explained by the

[1] Society for Propagating the Gospel, *Digest of the Records*, 11. Probably by an "orthodox minister" he means one of the Church of England.

[2] October 20, 1705: "Mr. John Livingston designs, it seems, to go for England next year; he seems to be the fittest person that America affords for the office of a suffragan, and several persons, both of the Laity and Clergy, have wished he were the man; and if my Lord of London thought fit to authorize him, several of the Clergy both of this Province and of Maryland have said they would pay their tenths unto him, as my Lord of London's Vicegerent, whereby the Bishop of America might have as honorable provision as some in Europe." (Protestant Episcopal Historical Society, *Collections*, i. 58.)

[3] *Ibid.* 59.

[4] Letter to the secretary of the Society, June 30, 1709, *Ibid.* 63.

[5] See Evan Evans and Talbot to the Society, December 4, 1712, *Ibid.* 65–66. This was the house to which Hunter alludes in his letter to Swift (above, p. 92, and note 3). An account of the affair may be found in the sermon of William Fleetwood, bishop of St. Asaph's, before the Society, February 16, 1710-11, printed in the Society's *Abstract*, 1709–1710 (London, 1711), pp. 22–28. In the *Abstract* for 1713, p. 44, there is a statement that the Society, through the agency of Governor Robert Hunter, has obtained from John Tathouse the house at Burlington for £600 sterling.

hopes which it then had of obtaining, by the aid of Queen Anne, some sort of episcopal establishment. These hopes were blasted by the queen's death in 1715.

Meantime, Talbot's endeavors were supplemented by those of his brother missionaries, acting both singly and collectively. In 1705, for example, fourteen clergymen assembled at Burlington, New Jersey, and sent to the archbishops and bishops a petition setting forth their needs.[1] Assigning, in addition to the considerations ordinarily urged, such as the need of some one to officiate at confirmations and ordinations, several reasons of a more special nature, they appeared to contemplate an establishment of a kind more likely to arouse opposition among the dissenters than that usually projected by the missionaries in this period.

Two years later, however, in 1707, Evan Evans, in a letter entitled "The State of the Church in Pennsylvania, most humbly offered to the Venerable Society for the Propagation of the Gospel in Foreign Parts," brought out some distinctively new points. His main reason for wanting a bishop was to have an officer capable of deciding in the disputes between clergymen ; since they, standing on a level with regard to authority, could not very well manage such things for themselves. He divides his argument into three main heads. Starting with the general proposition, " I take it for granted, that the ends of a mission can never be rightly answered without establishing the discipline

---

[1] " The presence and assistance of a Suffragan Bishop is most needful to ordain such persons as are fit to be called to serve in the sacred ministry of the Church. We have been deprived of the advantages that might have been received of some Presbyterian and Independent Ministers that formerly were, and of others that are still willing to conform and receive the holy character, for want of a Bishop to give it. The baptized want to be confirmed. The presence is necessary in the councils of these provinces to prevent the inconveniences which the Church labours under by the influences which seditious men's counsels have upon the publick administration and the opposition which they make to the good inclinations of well affected persons ; he is wanted not only to govern and direct us but to cover us from the malignant effects of those misrepresentations that have been made by some persons empowered to admonish and inform against us who indeed want admonition themselves " (Society's *Digest*, 744, citing its *Journals*, Appendix A, 508-513). Cf. Hawkins, *Missions of the Church of England*, 377-378.

as well as the doctrine of the Church of England in those parts,"
he argues as follows : first, that a bishop is needed to supply and
ordain ministers, for only a resident bishop can judge of the
fitness of a candidate to serve in a particular region, he only can
know the "true state of ecclesiastical things or persons," and
can " best see into all the secret causes and springs of things ";
secondly, that "a Bishop is absolutely necessary to preside over
the American clergy, and oblige them to do their duty and to
live in peace and unity with one another. . . . Wheresoever
Presbytery is established," he continues, "there they have the
face and appearance of an Ecclesiastical jurisdiction and authority after their way to resort to upon all occasions. But our
clergy in America are left destitute of any advantage of this
kind, and are exposed to the mercy of their very often unreasonable passions and appetites ; which are by many degrees the
worst masters they can truckle with." Here, and in one place
earlier in the same letter, where he asserts that there is not the
least shadow of authority to keep the clergy within bounds,
Evans plainly disregards the fact that the Bishop of London's
authority had any efficacy in the colonies. His Lordship's
authority certainly was weak ; but Evans may have exaggerated
a bit, using purposely strong expressions to add emphasis to his
argument.

His third point is that the clergy themselves are handicapped
for want of a bishop, since, being dependent upon the laity for
support,[1] they cannot, even in cases of the grossest irregularities
of living, denounce the leaders among their people without the
aid of episcopal sanction. In reference to a possible official
censure of immoral laymen, he says : " But now nothing of this
kind is heard of or attempted there, and men commit adultery,
polygamy, incest, and a thousand other crimes, of which the
minister can hardly admonish them in private, without manifest
hazard and disadvantage to himself, because there is no ecclesiastical jurisdiction established in those parts, and though there
were, there are no laws in being, which make the inhabitants of
those countries liable and obnoxious to it. No statute of the

---

[1] This was, of course, not true in the case of the missionaries of the
Society.

28 H. VIII.; no writ de excommunicato capiendo, to oblige spiritual delinquents to submit to the censures of the Church for the good of their own souls." What Evans here says is perfectly true; but the crimes which he enumerates were under the competence of the secular courts, and could be handled much more safely and surely by those bodies than by any ecclesiastical authorities. Such assertions as these of Evans would, had they been uttered half a century later, have raised a storm of abuse among the laity not only of the Independent, but even the Episcopal churches. This is, as a matter of fact, one of the few instances in which a petitioner for a bishop ventured to advocate strongly the disciplinary side of the office, particularly in its relations to the laity. To be sure, only the laymen of the Church of England were meant; but they were, as a rule, as adverse to ecclesiastical oversight in matters temporal, both public and private, as the members of any other religious body. Finally, at the close of his other arguments, Evans adds that a bishop is needed for the exercise of the office of confirmation.[1]

It is interesting to note that, in the same year in which Evans wrote this letter, — indeed, perhaps because of the letter, — the Bishop of London drew up a series of observations concerning the advisability of providing a suffragan for America. Agreeing with the Society's missionaries, he thinks that a bishop would be a proper remedy for the disordered condition of the Church of England there. But what sort of a bishop? An absolute one? Such a one would, he thinks, be impracticable for several reasons, of which the chief is that the colonists would not suffer such control.[2] The cause of this opposition, however, he ascribes not to the fear of a politico-ecclesiastical tyranny, — the time was hardly ripe for that, — but to the apprehension that a bishop clothed with full powers would exercise too close

---

[1] Hazard, *Pennsylvania Register*, iii. 337–340 (May 30, 1829). This is one of a series of articles on the history of the Episcopal church in Pennsylvania, originally printed in the *Episcopal Magazine.*

[2] He says of the attempt in " K. Charles ye 2^{ds} time," that "there came over Petitions and addresses with all violence imaginably." Presumably he alludes to the attempt made in 1662 (see above, pp. 89, 90); but there seems to be no record of any such resistance as the bishop alludes to. We have seen the probable causes why that attempt failed (above, p. 90, notes).

a supervision over the lives and morals of the clergy and the laity, which were, in many cases, in a very bad condition. For this reason his lordship advocates a suffragan, a functionary who would be too much like a commissary, to whose office they were already accustomed, to excite much aversion. Such a suffragan, having the necessary Episcopal orders, could, he argues, perform all the needed offices, such as confirmation, ordination, and consecration, and would thus have all the necessary requisites without any of the disadvantages. The implication seems to be that a suffragan might be tried as an experiment; if the experiment succeeded, well and good, and perhaps later an absolute bishop might be substituted; if it failed, the suffragan might be quietly withdrawn. It does not appear that this proposition was much considered at the time, although afterward many of the petitioners made their pleas for a suffragan rather than for an absolute bishop.[1]

All the applications which have thus far been considered came from the middle colonies; but later, after the matter had been taken up by the Society for Propagating the Gospel, the efforts of the missionaries of the middle colonies began to be reënforced by those of the New England brethren, particularly those in Boston, the only place in Massachusetts where the Church of England had as yet gained any definite foothold. The first New England petition, dated December 8, 1713,[2] came from the ministers, church wardens, and vestry of King's Chapel. Not only did they make representation to the Society, assuring that body how gladly they welcomed its efforts to secure a bishop for them, but they also sent a "Humble Address to the Queen's Most Excellent Majesty."[3] All evi-

[1] *New York Documents,* v. 29. The whole document is reprinted below, Appendix A, No. iii.

[2] For the text of the representation, see Foote, *Annals of King's Chapel,* i. 224; Massachusetts Historical Society, *Collections,* 1st Series, vii. 215.

[3] Massachusetts Historical Society, *Collections,* 1st Series, vii. 215–216. These petitions were never delivered, having been in some way intercepted. They are said to have been found among Sir Charles Hobby's papers by Mr. Mason, his administrator, and to have been sent by him to Boston. The members of the Episcopal party were endeavoring to obtain the ascendancy in New England, as appears from a letter of the Reverend Samuel Myles, in which

dence goes to show that these representations and addresses owed their origin to Governor Nicholson.[1] The movement for bishops seems to have been fairly general at this time; for there are records of simultaneous petitions from New York, New England, and Rhode Island asking for bishops for the northern colonies as a measure against the "Whigs and fanaticks" who "swarme[d] then in those parts."[2] Prominent members of the episcopin in the mother country were in correspondence with some of the leading Independent ministers in New England, seeking in this way to feel the temper of the clergy and laity of the various sects that would probably be hostile to such an innovation as the introduction of bishops.[3]

he writes, under date February 17, 1713–14: "I am humbly of opinion, the church here, and also in other parts of this province, would increase much more under a Governor that was a constant communicant thereof, from whom we might reasonably expect all requisite protection and encouragement" (*Ibid.* 216–217).

[1] See a letter from Nicholson to the Archbishop of Canterbury, in which he says that "unless a Bishop be sent in a short time, the Church of England will rather diminish than increase in North America" (Hawkins, *Missions of the Church of England*, 379, citing the Society's *MS. Letters*, 94).

[2] J. Redknap to Sir Charles Hobby and Jonathan Jekyll (London, April 27, 1714), in Foote, *Annals of King's Chapel*, i. 226–227.

[3] Bishop Kennett to Dr. Benjamin Colman, September 15, 1713: "It is our being *misinformed* and misguided in Some Ways," he says, "that increases our Desires of having *Bishops* settled in those *foreign Parts* committed to our Care; that *they may judge* better of *Things* and *Persons* within their own view. . . . But alas, there is so much of an *Ecclesiastical* and of a *Civil* Nature in this Affair, and such a *Concurrency required* here at Home and Abroad, that what Issue it may come to we are yet uncertain, — And whether at this *Juncture* we should make a fit Choice of *discreet* Men for this Office; I dare not pretend to *guess*. — I hope *your Churches* would not be *jealous* of it, they being out of our *Line*, and therefore beyond the *Cognizance* of any *Overseers* to be sent from hence. What *Time* may do, with the Spirit of *Knowledge and Charity* to make the English in America all of one Heart, and of Way of *Discipline* and Worship, I recommend to *your Prayers*, and add my own" (Turell, *Life of Colman*, 128). "Which needful Provisions," he says in another letter to the same person, March 13, 1716–17, alluding to the proposed establishment, "will not break in upon your national Rites and Customs, at least no other Way than by laying a Foundation (*we will* hope, and *you will* agree) for the Union of all Protestants in some future Age, when Charity and Peace shall prevail above Interest and Passion" (*Ibid.* 130).

So much for the movement concerning the work of individuals and groups of individuals in the early eighteenth century. It will now be necessary to see what had in the meantime been accomplished by the Society for Propagating the Gospel, to which most of the petitions for a suffragan had been referred. As early as 1703 a committee of the Society formulated a statement entitled " The Case of Suffragan Bishops briefly proposed," which was referred to the attorney general without result.[1] This was the first in a series of steps culminating in a plan which seemed on the verge of success when the death of Queen Anne, who had finally agreed to take the matter in hand, checked its progress. The following memorial will serve as a sample of the Society's addresses to the throne: " We cannot but take this opportunity further to represent to your Majesty, with the greatest humility, the earnest and repeated desires, not only of the Missionaries, but of divers other considerable persons that are in communion with our excellent Church, to have a Bishop settled in your American plantations (which we humbly conceive to be very useful and necessary for establishing the gospel in those parts), that they may be the better united among themselves than at present they are, and more able to withstand the designs of their enemies; that there may be Confirmations, which, in their present state, they cannot have the benefit of, and that an easy and speedy care may be taken of all the other affairs of the Church, which is much increased in those parts, and to which, through your Majesty's gracious protection and encouragement, we trust that yet a greater addition will daily be made."[2] This memorial was

---

[1] This case refers to a revival of suffragans (statute 26 Henry VIII., c. 13), and asks (1) whether the bishops suffragan of Colchester, Dover, Nottingham, and Hull might not be used for foreign parts; (2) whether archbishops and bishops would incur penalties for consecrating bishops with no more than common jurisdiction; (3) whether the queen, by statute Edward VI., c. 2 (for the election of bishops), might not appoint foreign suffragans. See the Society's *Digest*, 743–744, citing its *Journal*, November 17–December 15, 1704, Appendix, 258; Protestant Episcopal Historical Society, *Collections*, i. 139, note 3, citing the *Account* of the Society published in 1706.

[2] Hawkins, *Missions of the Church of England*, 377–378; Protestant Episcopal Historical Society, *Collections*, i. 140.

reënforced by a sermon before the Society in 1712 by Bishop Kennett, who urged the need of "discipline and Episcopal government" to be "there settled to compleat the face of decency and order." Apparently neither of these pleas gained the desired attention; for, March 27, 1713, a petition for bishops, entitled "A Representation to be laid before Her Majesty, for procuring Bishops and Bishopricks in America," was reported from a committee. It was read, amended, and ordered to be delivered to the Archbishop of York, with instructions that it be presented to the queen after the seal of the Society had been affixed.[1] Queen Anne finally decided to grant the request of the Society; and a bill was drafted and about to be introduced into Parliament, when her Majesty's death put a stop to further proceedings.[2]

Not discouraged by this set-back, the Society, on June 12, 1715, sent a petition to the new king. It was never considered, however, perhaps (as Hawkins suggests) because of the advent to power of Sir Robert Walpole and the Whigs, and of the Tory rising in 1715.[3] This was the last attempt made by the Society for Propagating the Gospel, as a body, to induce the crown to establish bishops in America.

After this the missionaries in America seem to have been too much discouraged to send many more petitions for some years to come, although there is record that a few were sent from time to time. Chief among these was an address, dated June 2, 1718, from the clergy and vestries of Christ Church, Philadelphia, and St. Anne's, Burlington, and some others. The petitioners based their plea on the customary grounds, such as the need of some one to consecrate churches and to perform the offices of confirmation and ordination. With regard to the latter function they said: "For the want of that sacred

---

[1] See the Society's *Report*, 1713, in Foote, *Annals of King's Chapel*, i. 222–223; also its *Abstract*, 1713–1714, pp. 27–28, and 1714–1715, pp. 52–54. See also Hawkins, *Missions of the Church of England*, 380; Protestant Episcopal Historical Society, *Collections*, i. 140–141.

[2] Protestant Episcopal Historical Society, *Collections*, i. 141.

[3] Hawkins, *Missions of the Church of England*, 380–383, citing the Society's *MS. Letters*, x. 28.

power which is inherent to your apostolick [office] the vacancies which daily happen in our ministry cannot be supplied for a considerable time from England, whereby many congregations are not only become desolate, and the light of the gospel therein extinguished, but great encouragement is thereby given to sectaries of all sorts which abound and increase amongst us, and, some of them pretending to what they call the power of ordination, the country is filled with fanatic teachers, debauching the good inclinations of many poor souls who are left destitute of any instruction or ministry." [1] This plea, like all those made by the Society for many years to come, obtained no encouragement from the authorities in England.

The majority of the petitions thus far considered came from the missionaries in the middle colonies. Soon, however, a movement was begun in New England, — or one might better say in Connecticut, — which never ceased till the consecration of Samuel Seabury as Bishop of Connecticut in 1784. The first step was taken by the Reverend George Pigot, who had come to Connecticut as a missionary in 1722. According to his representation, "besides the deficiency of a governor in the Church, to inspect the regular lives of the clergy, to ordain, confirm, consecrate churches, and the like . . . there . . . [was], also, a sensible want of this superior order, as a sure bulwark against the many heresies that are already brooding in this part of the world." [2] This step was only a forerunner; the determined effort on the part of the New England episcopacy did not make itself felt until the passing over of Cutler, Johnson, Brown, and Wetmore from the Presbyterian to the Episcopal communion. This event in itself had a great influence in strengthening the already latent apprehension of the New Englanders as to the dangers of episcopacy; and the efforts which the new converts made to secure the settlement of native bishops certainly did nothing to allay the apprehension. In a

[1] Hawkins, *Missions of the Church of England,* 384–385, citing the Society's *MS. Letters,* xiv. 44; Hazard, *Pennsylvania Register,* iii. 382 (June 13, 1892). This was followed, April, 1729, by another petition of the same sort (cf. *Ibid.* 383).

[2] Beardsley, *Episcopal Church in Connecticut,* i. 50–51.

later chapter an attempt will be made to follow the constantly-increasing hostility between the two communions, which finally broke into a controversy that was only ended by the War of Independence, which it helped to promote.

As early as 1723 Johnson realized and commented on the need of bishops resident in the colonies ; and according to his biographer, Chandler,[1] he succeeded in interesting Bishop Gibson in the project, particularly after the rumor that Talbot and Welton had received Episcopal consecration from the non-juring bishops.[2] The evidence, however, is hardly sufficient to prove that Gibson took any decided steps to further the plan, although Johnson in one letter to him suggests that he use his influence with the king for that purpose.[3]

Dr. Johnson was seconded in his efforts by Dr. Cutler and by the other New England clergy both singly and collectively.[4]

[1] Chandler, *Life of Johnson*, 38–39.

[2] The subject of non-juring bishops in America is very fully treated by the Reverend John Fulton, in Perry, *American Episcopal Church*, i. 541 ff. For another account, see Protestant Episcopal Historical Society, *Collections*, i. *passim*.

[3] See a letter from Johnson to Gibson, January 28, 1724, in Hawkins, *Missions of the Church of England*, 386–387. Chandler, in his *Life of Samuel Johnson*, says that Bishop Gibson sought to interest the ministry in the project, but failed. The two following extracts indicate that some such proceeding on the part of the bishop was at least expected. The first extract is from a letter of Johnson: " It is a great satisfaction to us," he writes, " to understand that one of your Lordship's powerful interest and influence is engaged in so good a work as that of sending bishops into America, and that there is nothing you desire more or would be at greater pains to compass. This gives us the greater hopes that by your Lordship's pious endeavors, under the blessing of God and the benign influence of our most gracious King, it may at length be accomplished. And we humbly hope that the address and representation of the state of religion here which we have lately presumed to offer may, in Your Lordship's hands, be of some service in this affair. I pray God give it success " (Beardsley, *Life of Johnson*, 56–57). The second is a letter from the Reverend J. Berriman to Johnson, dated February 17, 1725, in which he says : " We hear of two Nonjuring Bishops (Dr. Welton for one) who are gone into America ; and it is said the Bishop of London will send one more of a different stamp as an antidote against them " (*Ibid*. 55).

[4] See Dr. Cutler to the secretary of the Society, January 4, 1723–24, in Perry, *Historical Collections*, iii. (Massachusetts) 142–144 ; Hawkins, *Missions of the Church of England*, 387–388.

The subject was discussed in a convention held at Newport, Rhode Island, July 21, 1725, and in another at Boston, July 20, 1727; and addresses were sent to the king and to the Society for Propagating the Gospel.[1] The congregations of King's Chapel and Christ Church also continued to interest themselves in the project. At a joint meeting of the ministers, wardens, vestries, and congregations of these two churches, held in King's Chapel, August 30, 1727, for the purpose of voting an address to George II. on the death of his father and his own accession, the following resolution was adopted: "That an Address be made to his Majesty for a Bishop, and that the said address be sent to the Bishop of London within twelve months, and that the persons who signed the address to his Majesty shall likewise sign the address for a Bishop, unless otherwise determined by the Bishop of London." This was signed by two hundred and nine members. It had been the intention of some of them to send an address at once to the king, but it was decided to wait and get the mind of their diocesan upon the matter. They also took care to make it plain that their desire to have a resident bishop arose from no dissatisfaction with Bishop Gibson.[2] A "Humble Address" of several of the clergymen of

---

[1] Hawkins, *Missions of the Church of England,* 387–388; the Society's *Digest,* 443; Perry, *Historical Collections,* iii. (Massachusetts) 175–178, where the whole address of the Rhode Island convention to Bishop Gibson is given, together with its letter to the secretary. Harris and Mossom refused to attend the convention, for reasons which they gave in a letter to their diocesan, December 17, 1725: "It arises from a sense of humble duty and modesty," said they among other things, "that we do not expressly pray a Bishop may be fixᵗ among us, because you, and not we, are the most competent judge of what will make most for the service of the Church in general, — our being at once cut off or still continued a part of the See of London" (Foote, *Annals of King's Chapel,* i. 338–339; Perry, *Historical Collections,* iii. 200). It is doubtful, however, whether this consideration influenced Harris so much as other reasons, chief among which was a personal quarrel in which he was then involved. For an account of the affair, in which John Checkley was the main figure, see Foote, *Annals,* i. ch. viii.; Perry, *American Episcopal Church,* i. ch. xv., and some documents in his *Historical Collections,* iii. *passim.* For the convention of July 20, 1727, see Perry, *Historical Collections,* iii. 224–227; Foote, *Annals,* i. 340.

[2] Foote, *Annals of King's Chapel,* i. 351–352.

New England, dated December 12, 1727 (probably the one in question) was later received by the Board of Trade, but was laid aside with the indorsement, "The Bishop of London desired that it might not be inserted in the Gazette." It has been thought that its suppression was due to the influence of Walpole.[1]

Meantime, although, as we have seen, the southern colonies were in general opposed to the introduction of bishops, some steps were taken in Maryland toward the attainment of that end. Among the few persons in that colony who desired a native episcopate were the commissaries, who in answer to Bishop Gibson's queries in 1724 suggested, among other things, the urgent need of a bishop.[2] Several other indications tend to show that the project was seriously thought of at this time.[3] Indeed, in 1727 the Bishop of London sought to make the Reverend Mr. Colbatch, a Maryland clergyman, his suffragan; but the courts of Maryland checked the attempt by issuing a writ of *non exeat regno.* This put an end to any attempts to establish a bishop in the southern colonies, for the next forty years.[4]

In the face of all manner of discouragements, Johnson, in New England, continued his efforts with unflagging energy. On April 5, 1732, after a conference with the dissenters, he submitted to Bishop Gibson a series of six proposals, the gist of which is as follows: since the attorney and solicitor generals have decided that the establishment does not extend to Amer-

[1] Palfrey, *New England,* iv. 479, citing *British Colonial Papers;* cf. Foote, *Annals of King's Chapel,* i. 353, with note 1. Evidently the Bishop was friendly to the cause; for in 1738 we find him "laboring much, but in vain, with the court and the ministry, and endeavouring to induce the archbishop, who had credit with both, to join him in trying what could be done to get a bishop sent into the plantations." His effort failed because Sir Robert Walpole was not favorable. See Wilberforce, *Protestant Episcopal Church,* 122.

[2] Perry, *Historical Collections,* iv. (Maryland) 231–232; Hawks, *Ecclesiastical Contributions,* ii. (Maryland) 172.

[3] See a reference to the subject in a letter from Commissary Wilkinson to Bishop Gibson, September 9, 1724, in Perry, *Historical Collections,* iv. (Maryland) 244–246. In the *Fulham MSS.* is a carefully elaborated plan for settling bishops in America which Dr. Bray, formerly commissary of Maryland, drew up and sent to Gibson, October 28, 1723.

[4] Hawks, *Ecclesiastical Contributions,* ii. (Maryland) 196.

ica, he would suggest some practical proposals for an episcopate; he ventures to do this for the reason that many are so
destitute that they will submit even to a Church of England
establishment; he would insist only upon essentials and would
advise the greatest leniency in the matter of non-essentials. In
spite of his assurances, some of the statements made by him
would very readily have excited suspicion among his brethren of
the Independent persuasions. Take, for example, the following
suggestion: "Is it impossible for the English Dominions in
America to be provided for with one or two Bishops, and those
subject to the Lord Bishop of London as Archbishop of the
Plantations abroad . . . and is it impossible that such a provision might be made without breaking in upon the interest of
the governors and governments as they now stand? Though,
indeed, it would be much happier for the Church, especially
unless we had a Bishop, if the charters were taken away; and
most people begin to think, since they have got into such a
wretched, mobbish way of management, that it would be best
for the people themselves."[1] A few expressions like this reach-
ing the ears of the inhabitants of New England might well have
made them tremble for the continuance not only of their ecclesiastical, but even of their political, independence.[2]

A most curious notion which gained currency about this time
was that the establishment of bishops in America would lead
to the independence of the colony. Moreover, it was maintained
that this consideration influenced the English government to
continue in its refusal to take any steps toward the furtherance
of the plan. There seems to be no contemporary evidence for
this view except in the writings of Dr. Johnson and in Archbishop Secker's refutation of the notion. Furthermore, such an
idea is absurd from the facts of the case. The Episcopalians
were, at least before the outbreak of the excitement which

[1] Hawks and Perry, *Connecticut Church Documents*, i. 153–154.

[2] But the ecclesiastical authorities were unable to prevail with the officers of
state; compare the following sentence from the Bishop of Gloucester to Johnson, March 9, 1735–36: "My own interest, to be sure, is inconsiderable; but
the united interest of the Bishops here is not powerful to effect so reasonable
and right a thing as the sending of some Bishops into America" (Beardsley,
Episcopal Church in Connecticut, i. 101–102).

culminated in the Revolution, among the most loyal subjects of the English government in the American colonies. If any danger of independence was to be feared as a result of episcopal establishment, it would come, not from the Episcopalians with their native episcopate, but from the Independents, roused to opposition by the apprehension of what they would regard as an attempt to impose upon them the burden of the Anglican ecclesiastical system. If any such reason as that noticed above was alleged by the home government for not granting an episcopate to its petitioners, it was only a pretext for a refusal resting upon quite different grounds.

Yet Dr. Johnson apparently believed that this notion was really fixed in the minds of the English government; for in his letters he repeatedly assured his diocesan and others that it was unreasonable to conclude that the attempt to obtain bishops for America proceeded from a desire for independence, since, indeed, the reverse was true.[1] Any one inclined to the view supposed to be held by the English government would have felt the untenability of any such idea after a perusal of Johnson's letters to his English correspondents. Take, for example, one written in 1742 to the Archbishop of Canterbury, in which he says: "An English Bishop would be the most effectual means to secure the people from that [the Moravian] and every other faction and delusion, as well as vastly to enlarge the Church. I have been informed that the chief pretense against sending Bishops has been an apprehension of these colonies effecting an independency on our mother-country. This is indeed a most groundless apprehension; but certainly a regular Episcopacy, even subordinate to the Bishop of London, would be so far from this that it would be one of the most effectual means to secure our dependency."[2] Or again: "It has always been a fact," he says, "& is obvious in the nature of the thing, that anti-Episcopal are of course anti-monarchical principles. So that the danger of our effecting Independency can never come from a regular Episcopacy, but would naturally flow from the want of it; — from that turbulent outrageous spirit which en-

[1] See letter cited, Beardsley, *Life of Johnson*, 94.
[2] Beardsley, *Episcopal Church in Connecticut*, i. 144.

thusiasm is apt to inspire men with. — To me therefore My Lord, there is nothing apparently more evident, than that a regular Episcopal Settlement would be so far from promoting a spirit of Independency, that it would be the most effectual means that could be devised to secure a Dependence on our Mother Country; especially at this Juncture when we are so puffed up with our late success at Cape Breton, that our Enthusiasts are almost apt to think themselves omnipotent. . . . But considering their Temper and Spirit, I should rather think a great Reason for it, as a necessary means to check their Impetuosity, & to prevent what I know will otherwise be the Effect of their Present Elevation which prompts them to think that they having so much merit, may persecute and tyrannize over the Church here as much as they please & none will say to them why do ye so? Instances which we have lately felt in this Colony, and more of them we expect every day." [1] Obviously, opinions such as these were calculated to stir up suspicions in the minds of the anti-prelatical New Englanders, and were certain forerunners of that great struggle concerning the establishment of native bishops which was soon to come.

Meantime, what was going on in England? From the time of their failure to secure the attention of King George I. and his ministers, the members of the Society for Propagating the Gospel appear to have done very little to further their plans for the introduction of native bishops. This inaction may have been due to their despair of accomplishing anything in that direction; or, what is less likely, they may have felt that under the capable administration of Bishop Gibson, the clergy and people of the Church of England in the colonies were being sufficiently cared for. At all events, from the death of Queen Anne until about 1740 we find among the Society's papers, whether abstracts or sermons, no record of the matter or allusion to it. It was on February 20, 1740–41, that Thomas Secker, then Bishop of Oxford, took occasion to reopen the subject in a sermon which he preached before the Society at its annual meeting in that year. In the opinion of at least one

---

[1] *Fulham MSS.* From a letter to Bishop Gibson, November 25, 1725, on hearing that he was again making an effort to secure an American episcopate.

contemporary, this sermon was extremely significant.[1] The bishop's main arguments are the same as those used by all the petitioners in favor of an American episcopate. He also considers the supposed fear of the English government, and seeks to allay it quite after the fashion of Johnson.[2]

Secker was answered by the Reverend Andrew Eliot, in a pamphlet entitled *Remarks upon the Bishop of Oxford's Sermon.* Eliot expresses the fear that if bishops were introduced, they would have to be supported out of the pockets of the colonists, by means of a tax levied by the provincial assemblies; failing this, the influence of the English episcopate would be brought to bear to obtain an act of Parliament to secure a general imposition, in which case there could be no exemption, since the establishment once acknowledged would perforce extend to all the colonies. "We have been told," continues Eliot, "that 'when any part of the English nation spread abroad into the colonies, as they continued a part of the nation, the law obliged them equally to the Church of England and to the Christian religion.'"[3] He rightly argues that, if such be the case, and if bishops be introduced, it would be unjust and impolitic to exempt New England from the support of an establishment which, if admitted to extend to one of the colonies, must extend to all of

---

[1] One who signs himself "A Man of Old England" says: "From the Sermon he preached February 20, 1741, it appears, the Bishop of Oxford, Dr. Secker furnished the disclaimers against the North American Colonies with the root ideas of deforming and episcopising them" (*London Chronicle,* August 18, 1768). This statement is overdrawn; but certainly Secker did much to revive in England an interest in the subject which had been on the wane for twenty years or more.

[2] "Nor would such an establishment," says Secker, "encroach at all on the Present rights of the Civil Government in our Colonies or bring their dependence to any degree of that Danger, which some persons profess to apprehend so strongly on this Occasion, who would make no manner of. scruple about doing other Things much more likely to destroy it; who are not terrified in the least that such numbers there reject the Episcopal Order entirely; nor would perhaps be greatly alarmed, were there ever so many to reject Religion itself: though evidently in Proportion as either is thrown off, all Dependence produced by it ceases of course" (the Society's *Abstract,* 1741, pp. 27–29).

[3] Massachusetts Historical Society, *Collections,* 2d Series, ii. 190–216.

them, and must come from a bishop whose jurisdiction would include them all. Such a partiality could not but excite jealousy in all the unexempted colonies. The force of this argument is evident from the known antipathy to episcopal control even in the colonies where the Church of England was established by provincial legislation.

Although Eliot is a bit unjust in his suspicion of the motives of all those who had hitherto lent their aid to the cause of the American episcopate, yet his fear of what might come to pass in case the proposed establishment were once attained was a perfectly natural one. It was quite reasonable to suppose that the bishops, once established, would hardly be content to confine themselves to purely spiritual affairs, and to remain deprived of all the accompaniments of office which their episcopal brethren in England enjoyed. Moreover, it would be most certain that the English bishops would support their claims, for fear of offering to the dissenters at home an example of an episcopate existing without temporal power or property. But even if this were not so, even if the bishops on both sides of the water would have been perfectly content with a purely spiritual episcopate, the scheme would still have been impracticable; for under an establishment of this sort the bishops would have had no more power to enforce their discipline than the commissaries had; and the latter, as was admitted on all sides, had lamentably failed to answer the needs of their office. Although certain expressions of Johnson, Secker, and others could hardly have been reassuring to the minds of those who stood for personal liberty and independence in the administration of their religious and political affairs, still, without questioning the motives of earnest missionaries, filled with a laudable ambition for the extension of that form of religious worship which to their minds best answered the spiritual needs of mankind, one can see that the thing which they desired could not but have led to a further tightening upon the colonists of that governmental system from which they were gradually coming to extricate themselves.

Probably to further the interest which Secker sought to revive, Bishop Gibson, in 1745, shortly before his death, offered the king and council £1000 toward the support of a bishop, in case one should be sent over in his time.[1] This was one of several gifts which from time to time during the century had been made in aid of the cause. As early as 1715 Archbishop Tennison left £1000 for the maintenance of such bishop or bishops as might be sent to America.[2] In the same year a like sum was bequeathed to the Society by an unknown benefactor. These gifts were followed in 1720 and 1741 by two bequests of £500 from Dugald Campbell, Esq., and Lady Elizabeth Hastings respectively.[3] Although these contributions show that there were, among the English clergy and laity, some who were willing to aid the project with their financial support, yet the sum total of them all would hardly have been sufficient to maintain even one bishop.

Looking back over the ground covered by this chapter, we may outline its broader features as follows: Laud, apparently as a step in the further development of his plan of extending the establishment to the American colonies, sought to settle a bishop in New England, but was prevented by a sudden turn of political affairs at home. During the Restoration period the English government made one or two abortive attempts with the same end in view. After the foundation of the Society for Propagating the Gospel, its missionaries took the matter earnestly in hand; but they struggled in vain to enlist the effective coöperation of the English government in their cause. The early movement for bishops was, at least in motive, void of all political connection, and was carried on almost exclusively from the northern and middle colonies, where the church was not established.[4] After the conversion of Cutler, Johnson, and their colleagues, the subject began to be more warmly and persistently agitated than ever before, and a political significance

---

[1] Protestant Episcopal Historical Society, *Collections*, i. 139, note.

[2] The interest on this bequest was later given to Talbot, as the oldest of the colonial missionaries; for, according to the will, such provision was to be made of the income until bishops should be introduced (*Ibid.* 79–80).

[3] See Hawkins, *Missions of the Church of England*, 383, 386; Protestant Episcopal Historical Society, *Collections*, i. 79–80; and Secker's Sermon, in the Society's *Abstract*, 1741, pp. 27–29.

[4] The case of Maryland (see above, p. 105) can hardly affect this generalization.

gradually crept into the discussions, particularly in the utterances of Samuel Johnson, and of Bishop Secker, who came to his aid in 1741. These two were, before many years, to be joined by a powerful ally in the person of Thomas Sherlock, who succeeded to the see of London in 1748. The course of events during the period of his administration will now be considered.

CHAPTER V.

EXPIRATION OF THE BISHOP OF LONDON'S COMMISSION:
SHERLOCK'S POLICY, 1748–1761.

THOMAS SHERLOCK, who succeeded Edmund Gibson in 1748 and held the see till his death in 1761, we have already come to know as a severe critic of the scope of the jurisdictionary powers of the Bishop of London over the American plantations. He was the inaugurator of a new policy, which consisted in withholding the ministrations of English bishops from the Episcopalians in the colonies for the purpose of forcing them to demand an episcopate of their own. In spite of his protestations to the contrary, there is good ground for believing that his action was influenced by political motives; but in justice to him it should be said that he probably had no intention of deliberately seeking to force upon the colonies ecclesiastical superiors, with accompanying civil powers which would encroach upon the independence which they had so long enjoyed. More likely he intended, by uniting the separate provinces under resident spiritual heads, to set a precedent for a political union which would gradually become more and more intertwined with the English church and state system. This was certainly the notion of many of his supporters on both sides of the water, some of whom went so far as to assert in after years that, had a colonial episcopate been established, the Revolution might have been averted.[1]

[1] See Hawkins, *Missions of the Church of England*, ch. xvii. Compare a letter from Chandler to the Society, January 15, 1766, in which, after speaking of the political situation that followed the passage of the Stamp Act, and of what he regards as the excesses of his countrymen, he says: "And yet this apology they are entitled to, y[t] the government has not taken much pains to instruct them better. If y[e] Interest of the Church of England in America had been made a National Concern from the beginning, by this time a general submission in y[e] Colonies to y[e] Mother Country in everything not sinful, might have been expected, not only for wrath, but for conscience' sake. And who can be certain but y[e] present rebellious disposition of y[e] Colonies is not

Whether we attach any weight to this theory or not, the fact is indisputable that, in the years from 1750 onward, as the chasm between the colonies and the mother country widened more and more, the establishment of an American episcopate was frequently suggested as an expedient for bridging it over.

Sherlock, whatever may have been the motives which actuated him, began his agitation as early as the first year of his accession, when he wrote to Edward Weston from Wallington on September 9, 1748: "The business of the diocese, and of the plantations (wch last article is immense, and to be carried on by foreign correspondence) sits heavy upon me."[1] Nor did he confine himself to mere expostulation; for, as we learn from a letter to the Lords of Trade, dated February 19, 1759, he went to the king soon after he became Bishop of London, and laid before his Majesty the state of religion in the colonies and the need of a resident bishop there. The king consented to allow him to refer the matter to his ministers. After a number of futile attempts to obtain an interview with them, Sherlock again applied to the king, who gave his sanction to the calling of a meeting in Newcastle House, at which, however, nothing was done; and finally the bishop brought the matter before the king in council, with a similar result.[2]

---

intended by Providence as a punishment for that Neglect? Indeed, many wise and good persons, at home, have had ye Cause of Religion and ye Church here sincerely at heart, and ye Nation, whether sensible of it or not, is under great obligations to that Worthy Society, who by their indefatigable endeavors to *propagate the Gospel* and assist the Church, have, at the same time, and thereby, secured to ye State, as far as their influence could be extended, ye Loyalty and Fidelity of her American Children" (A. H. Hoyt, *Thomas Bradbury Chandler*, in *New England Historical and Genealogical Register*, xxvii. 233, citing S. A. Clark, *History of St. John's Church*, 110–113, where the whole letter is given).

[1] Royal Historical Manuscripts Commission, *Tenth Report*, Appendix i. 320.

[2] Thus Sherlock made in all three applications to the government (cf. *North Carolina Records*, vi. 10–13). For his own account of the first stages of the proceedings, see his letter of 1749 to Dr. Johnson (Hawkins, *Missions of the Church of England*, 389–390, citing Chandler, *Life of Johnson*, Appendix, 131–132), and his letter of May 11, 1751, to Dr. Doddridge (Hawkins, *Missions*, 391–392, citing Doddridge's *Correspondence and Diary*, v. 201; Perry, *Historical Collections*, i. (Virginia) 371–374, citing *Fulham MSS.*). His final

Such is a bald outline of Sherlock's early movements. It will now be necessary to go into the question somewhat more in detail, in order to discover just what springs he set in motion for the accomplishment of his purpose. His activity in colonial questions began to attract attention very early; indeed, even in the first year of his translation there were rumors that bishops might soon be expected in America.[1] The plan seemed so certain of execution and so much to be feared in certain quarters, that in 1749 a deputation in England appointed a committee of two to wait upon those nearest in the counsels of the king, and to seek to convince them that such an establishment as that contemplated " would be very disagreeable to many of our friends in these parts and highly Prejudicial to the Interests of Several of the Colonies."[2] This intervention was well received and gratefully acknowledged abroad, the Massachusetts House of Representatives returning thanks to the committee in a letter signed by its speaker. In 1750 this committee renewed its activities, and it was perhaps to some extent owing to its efforts that the design of Sherlock was frustrated.

Simultaneously with his action in England, Sherlock had incited a similar movement in the colonies. Shortly before he presented his " Considerations " to the king, he sent an agent, one A. Spencer, to America to feel the pulse of the colonists on

application consisted in submitting to the council an elaborate memorial, entitled " Considerations relating to the Ecclesiastical Government in America," which he had drawn up February 21, 1750. It was first printed in the appendix to Chandler's *Free Examination of Secker's Letter to Walpole*, from a transcription by Dr. William Smith, provost of the College of Philadelphia, made from the original shown to him by "a great and excellent Prelate " (see editorial note to appendix of the *Free Examination*, 103). It is reprinted in *New York Documents*, vii. 360–369, from *Plantations General Entries* (Board of Trade), xvi. 9. Cf. Protestant Episcopal Historical Society, *Collections*, i. 145, with note, citing a letter from Sherlock to Johnson of September 19, 1750.

[1] See an abstract of a letter from the Reverend Clement Hall of North Carolina to the secretary of the Society, 1748, in Perry, *American Episcopal Church*, i. 406; also another letter, September 11, 1749, *North Carolina Records*, iv. 924.

[2] *Fulham MSS.*

the subject of the proposed establishment. According to his instructions, Spencer talked with several merchants and other prominent men in New York and Philadelphia. He found that their chief objection against such an establishment was the fear that it might infringe on the privileges of the people and the rights of the proprietaries. In answer to this objection, the agent pointed out that the proposed suffragan, without having any more power over the laity than that hitherto enjoyed by the commissaries, would have certain necessary advantages, such as the ability to choose suitable candidates for the ministry and to exercise an oversight over them. After this explanation, most of those interviewed declared, according to Spencer, that, if the case were as represented, they would rather concur in the plan than oppose it.[1] In reading Spencer's report, however, we must make some allowance for the enthusiasm of an agent seeking further employment, and must remember that the difficulty was in convincing the objectors that the plan was as represented.

In England Sherlock continued his exertions for the advancement of his cause. On February 21, 1749–50, he drew up his "Considerations relating to Ecclesiastical Government in his Majesty's Dominions in America";[2] but some months previously he had entered into correspondence with the chief officers of state on this subject.[3] Perhaps a short examination of some of the letters which passed back and forth will give the best

[1] Spencer to Sherlock, June 12, 1749, *Fulham MSS.*

[2] In his "Considerations" Sherlock emphasizes the need for an American Episcopate, and also seeks to refute the objections which might be urged against the plan. Chandler (*Free Examination,* 3, note 3) says that the "Considerations" were read in the council on February 21; but this is an error. They were drawn about that date, but were not submitted to the king until April 11 (see a transcription on the back of a manuscript at Fulham). Chandler's error is probably due to the fact that the document, though indorsed February 21, was before its final presentation submitted by Sherlock to some of the members of the government for their opinions upon it. In a letter to Newcastle, March 23, he says that he "intends" to submit it to the council.

[3] This correspondence, which I have extracted from the original letters among the *Newcastle Papers* in the British Museum, will be found below in Appendix A, No. xi.

insight into the opinions of the two parties concerned. On September 3, 1749, Sherlock, evidently angry, or at least disappointed, at the indifference with which his proposals had been received, wrote to the Duke of Newcastle expressing his unwillingness to take upon himself the burden which the episcopal oversight of the plantations would involve, and asked leave to confine himself to his "proper diocese of London."[1] The latter statement, and the implied threat which it conveyed, had the effect of nettling Newcastle, who answered rather sharply that "the appointing Bishops, in the West Indies, was a grave and national consideration; had long been under the Deliberation of great and wise men; and was, by them, laid aside;[2] and ought not to be resumed, for personal considerations; or at all to be looked upon in that Light."[3] Sherlock, in his reply, while admitting that his colonial charge was burdensome to him, nevertheless repudiated the thought that so important an affair could be settled on purely personal grounds. He insisted that the burden and expense of the jurisdiction beyond the seas belonged no more to the bishopric of London than to any of the other dioceses, and sought to prove that the shifting of the authority would not only benefit the see of London, but would be of inestimable service to the cause of the Episcopalians in America.[4]

[1] *Newcastle Papers*, Home Series, 32719, f. 97.

[2] Thus, according to Newcastle, the previous plans had received the serious consideration of the officers of state in the days of Sherlock's predecessor. Compare, however, the following passage : "The late Bishop Gibson was fond of the project of sending bishops to our plantations. The ministry of those days suffered him to play with his project till he had modelled it to his own liking; they then exposed the pernicious nature of it and left both the project and the projector to the contempt and derision of all wise and good men" (*London Chronicle*, January 17, 1764). This is an example of contemporaneous newspaper exaggeration.

[3] Newcastle to Sherlock, September 5, 1749, *Newcastle Papers*, Home Series, 32719, f. 105.

[4] " I reckoned (perhaps misreckoned)," he says, "that I was proposing a scheme for the *publick service*, to enable not only myself but every Bp. of London to execute with some tolerable degree of care the extensive commission he is to have in his Majesties foreign dominions, in the due of w^{ch}, the King's Honour is concerned; and on wch the Religion of the Country, the

Sherlock's next step, as has been said, was to draw up his " Considerations " ; these he sent to the Duke of Newcastle on March 23, 1749–50, together with a letter giving some account of his plans. He informs his correspondent that he intends to lay his representation before the king in council; that he has already submitted it to the lord chancellor, who, while finding " many difficulties as to the main point," admitted that there was nothing in the address to give offence. Sherlock hopes that, even should the king not agree with his plans, his representation may at least receive some consideration ; he is willing to put himself altogether out of the case, although he wishes for many reasons that he may succeed in his undertaking.[1] Two days later, on March 25, Newcastle replied to this communication. Though he expresses his agreement with the lord chancellor that the representation contains nothing which can offend, yet he is reluctant to lend his encouragement to the scheme. He strongly advises the renewal of the Gibson patent, suggesting that if it is defective in any way it may be extended. While professing the greatest unfitness to pass judgment on the merits of the question, he nevertheless places himself tentatively on the side of those who have hitherto regarded an establishment of American bishops as impracticable. Finally, he expresses a hope that, before presenting the scheme to the king in council, his Lordship will at least discuss it with his Majesty's principal servants.[2] But Sherlock was determined to press matters in the teeth of all advice, and submitted his representation at a meeting of the council on April 11. Owing, however, to the king's departure for Hanover, consideration of it was postponed.

But the subject was not dropped. On May 29, Horatio Walpole, brother of Sir Robert, and a member of the Privy Council, wrote to Sherlock for the facts of the case,[3] and

prosperity of the Ch. of England ; always esteemed the Bulwark agst Popery ; the members whereof are the only Set of Xtians in the King's dominions who own the Supremacy of the Crown, doe greatly depend " (Sherlock to Newcastle, September 7, 1749, *Newcastle Papers*, Home Series, f. 113).

[1] *Ibid.* 32720, f. 156.

[2] *Ibid.* f. 160.

[3] He was probably not present at the council meeting at which the memorial was read.

suggesting such objections to the project as occurred to him.[1] Sherlock probably made no other reply than to send him a copy of his "Considerations."[2] Bishop Secker, however, on January 9, 1750–51, wrote an elaborate reply, which was published after his death in 1769. This will be considered later. Now it may be well to give a short survey of the principal points of Walpole's letter. Refusing to admit that the colonies in general are desirous to have native bishops established in their midst, he goes on to show, in support of his position, that not only have they never hinted to the English officers of state any desire for such an establishment, but they have vested those powers requiring the oversight of a resident bishop in other hands, and have, in many cases, passed acts of assembly against ecclesiastical laws and jurisdictions for enforcing or establishing fines and other forms of punishment. He admits that they have never complained of the government by commissaries, but thinks that this fact argues rather that they are content with that system than that they desire a further extension of the exercise of ecclesiastical jurisdiction at the hands of a bishop, particularly since they have never objected to the commissaries' lack of power. He recalls the fact that the question of bishops was in agitation in 1725, shortly after Gibson came to the see, and points out that Lord Townshend was such a good friend to that "Orthodox Prelate" that he would have combined with him to bring the plan into execution, had it been thought advisable and not dangerous to the interests of the state.

What Walpole anticipated from an agitation of the scheme under the condition of things then existing may be best expressed in his own words: "I cou'd not forbear," he says, "letting your Lordship know that I apprehended as soon as a

---

[1] The letter was also sent to Secker, Bishop of Oxford, January 2, 1750–51 (*London Chronicle*, June 27, 1769, which wrongly puts the date of the letter May 9, 1750). The contents of Walpole's communication seem never to have been accurately known by any except those immediately concerned. Chandler says simply that it was friendly in tone, and cites the testimony " of a Person of the strictest Veracity, who saw his Letter soon after it was written, and remembers the Nature and Scope of it " (*Free Examination*, 3–4, with notes).

[2] Chandler, *Free Examination*, 4.

Scheme for sending Bishops to ye Colonys altho' with certain
restrictions shou'd under your Lordship's Authority & Influence be made publick it wou'd immediately become ye Topick
of all Conversation; a matter of Controversy in ye Pulpitts, as
well as by Pamphletts, & Libells, with a Spirit of bitterness &
acrimony that prevail more frequently in disputes about Religion
as ye Authors and Readers are differently affected than on any
other Subject. . . . The Dissenters of all Sorts whom I mention with no other regard or concern than as they are generally
well-affected, & indeed necessary supporters to ye present
establishment in State, & therefore shou'd not be provok'd or
alienated against it, will by the instigation and Complaints of
their bretthren in ye Colonys altho' with no solid reason be
loud in their discourses and writings upon this intended innovation in America, and those in ye Colonies will be exasperated
& animated to make warm representations against it to y^e
Government here, as a design to establish Ecclesiastical power
in its full extent among them by Degrees; altho' ye first step
seems to be moderate & measured, by conferring ye Authority
of ye Bishops to be planted amongst them to certain Colonys
and Functions." Nay, more, Walpole is inclined to believe
that the opposition would not be confined to the dissenters,
but that the high-church party, for the time quiet, would seize
such a plan as a handle for criticising the king and his ministers, and that the members of the low-church party, in general friends of the government, would be hostile to those who
furthered such a project for stirring up strife among the colonists, who were at that moment so quiet and satisfied with
both their civil and their ecclesiastical condition. In short, he
believes that, if the matter were brought before Parliament, the
step would offer a very good occasion for bringing out party
differences which had been latent since 1745.

Walpole then comes to consider a proposal which Sherlock
had made to the Society for Propagating the Gospel, namely,
that the various governors be asked to give their opinions on
the subject of the introduction of bishops into their respective
provinces. This step of the bishop he unhesitatingly condemns.
In the first place, he thinks that in the letter which Sherlock

and the Society purpose to send to the colonial governors they have given guarantees which they cannot carry out. "Can you undertake to promise," he asks, "that no coercive, or other Ecclesiastical power besides Ordination & Confirmation, shall ever be proposed & pressed upon ye Colonys when Bishops have been once settled amongst them, or beyond what is at present exercised by the Bishop of Londons Commissary. . . . Can ye Society undertake that ye maintenance of ye Bishops . . . shall be no Burthen to ye Colonys." In the face of these difficulties, he thinks there is every reason to believe that both governors and people would reject the scheme. But if nothing of this sort be apprehended, Sherlock's project seems to him still impracticable and blameworthy; for to what end or purpose should he consult the governors and people of America upon a matter which is still under the consideration of the council? Should the former be induced to return a favorable answer, and should the latter decide that for reasons of state the step is inadvisable, great confusion and strife would arise. For this reason, Walpole strongly advises the bishop to wait until the council has given its opinion in the matter, and urges him not to be impatient if it should delay, but to regard the fact as an indication that it is unwilling to move hastily in so important an undertaking.[1] Sherlock was induced, probably by this letter, to postpone his proposed queries to the several governors until some future date.

It is interesting to note the prophetic significance of Walpole's letter, for precisely what he foretold about the resistance which would arise from the colonies as soon as the plan became known came to pass. In support of the view that the refusal of the government to aid the bishop in the furtherance of his plans was influenced by such considerations as Walpole suggested, and did not, as some have maintained, arise purely from indifference, the correspondence which followed between Walpole and Newcastle may be cited.[2]

[1] For the whole letter, see Appendix A, No. xi., from *Newcastle Papers*, Home Series, 32721, f. 60.

[2] An opinion expressed in 1764 by Archbishop Drummond is as follows: "In the late reign, the fears of disturbing his majesty's governors, particularly

Soon after Walpole had written to Sherlock, he sent a copy of the letter to the Duke of Newcastle, with an explanation of how he came to write it.   With Newcastle he could have had no occasion for guarding or for concealing his real meaning; and what he says in his communication to him bears out in every particular what he had previously said in his letter to Sherlock.[1] Newcastle's reply to Walpole of July 5 is in the same tenor. "I think," he writes, "there is great weight, also in the consequences, You so judiciously suggest, that This Affair may have at Home, in reviving old Disputes, & Distinctions, which are at present, quiet; and, perhaps, creating new Divisions amongst Those, Who sincerely mean the good of His Majesty's Government and the Good of their Country.   For These Reasons, I am persuaded, The Lords of Council, will fully Consider all These Points, before any material Step is taken in this Affair."[2]   Walpole, in his acknowledgment of the receipt of Newcastle's letter, again alludes to the scheme, styling it "a matter of . . . much importance to Ye Peace and Quiet of his Majesty's Government."[3]   The hostile attitude of such men as Newcastle and Walpole proved too powerful to be overcome, and Sherlock's plan received no further consideration in the council.

About this time the efforts of Sherlock began to be reënforced by those of some of his brethren on the episcopal bench.   Chief among his new allies were Thomas Secker, Bishop of Oxford, and William Butler, Bishop of Durham, author of the celebrated *Analogy*.   The latter, in 1750, drew up a plan detailing the

---

in New England, so influenced the ministry, that they not only, perhaps very wisely, hesitated about the proposal of settling bishops in America, but *finally* postponed it" (Protestant Episcopal Historical Society, *Collections*, i. 142). This statement is true as far as it goes.

.[1] *Newcastle Papers*, Home Series, 32721, f. 158.   Compare the following statement: "Your Grace will be so good as to manage this Confidence, of an accidental, & private Correspondence between yᵉ Bishops, & me with your usual discretion, because if my apprehensions are at all well founded, the proposal of so great a man to settle Episcopacy in the Colonys should be as little known as possible to yᵉ Publick."

[2] *Newcastle Papers*, Home Series, 32721, f. 167.

[3] July 10, 1750, *Ibid*. f. 369.

limitations under which the proposed bishops would be sent. He explains :

" 1. That no coercive power is desired over the laity in any case, but only a power to regulate the clergy who are in Episcopal orders, and to correct and punish them according to the law of the Church of England, in case of misbehaviour or neglect of duty, with such powers as the commissaries abroad have exercised.

" 2. That nothing is desired for such bishops that may in the least interfere with the dignity, or authority, or interest of the governor, or any other officer of state. Probate of wills, licenses for marriages, &c., to be left in the hands where they are ; and no share in the temporal government is desired for bishops.

" 3. The maintenance of such bishops not to be at the charge of the colonies.

" 4. No bishops are intended to be settled in places where the government is in the hands of dissenters, as in New England, &c. ; but authority to be given only to ordain clergy for such Church of England congregations as are among them, and to inspect into the manners and behaviour of the said clergy, and to confirm the members thereof." [1]

This series of proposals, though not unlike many others of the period, is noteworthy as coming from so eminent a man ; for it justifies the assumption that, whatever would have been the results of the introduction of bishops, many of the advocates of the measure were actuated by purely spiritual motives. On

---

[1] A copy of Butler's plan of 1750, in his own handwriting, was formerly in the possession of William Vassal, of Boston. It was first published by the Reverend East Apthorp of Cambridge, Massachusetts. It was reprinted by a writer signing himself " The Anatomist " (Dr. William Smith, provost of the College of Philadelphia), in the *Pennsylvania Gazette*, December 8, 1768, from Butler's copy as revised and approved by Sherlock and published in the English edition of Johnson's *Ethics*, London, 1753 (see *Pennsylvania Gazette*, December 8, 1768, note). It may also be found in *An Address from the Clergy of New York and New Jersey to the Episcopalians in Virginia*, 21–22 ; Perry, *American Episcopal Church*, i. 408 ; Protestant Episcopal Historical Society, *Collections*, i. 142–144 (especially 143, explanatory note 2). It is here reprinted from the source last named.

the other hand, such a careful list of refutations shows that the apprehensions of the colonists had become sufficiently important to be worthy of consideration.[1]

The endeavor to allay any apprehension which might arise from the extension of the Church of England showed itself in a marked degree on all sides at this time. For example, the Society, in a series of instructions issued to its missionaries in 1753, enjoins them "that they take special care to give no offense to the Civil Government by intermeddling with affairs

---

[1] The proposals were introduced by the following preamble: "As the Chief obstruction to the settling Bishops in America arises from an apprehension here that the several Colonies abroad would be unwilling to have Bishops among them, from a jealousy that introducing ecclesiastical power among them may interfere with some rights which, by custom, or by acts of their respective assemblies, are now vested in other hands; it is become necessary, in order to know their sentiments, to inform them rightly in the case. Their objections (if they have any) must be, as is supposed, upon one or all of the following accounts.

" 1. With respect to the coercive power such Bishops may exercise over the people in causes Ecclesiastical.

" 2. With respect to the interest or authority of the Governors there.

" 3. With respect to the burthen that may be brought upon the people, of supporting and maintaining Bishops there.

" 4. With respect to such of the colonies where the government is in the hands of the Independents, or other dissenters, whose principles are inconsistent with episcopal government."

Conceiving that these objections were all founded on a misapprehension of the case, Butler advanced the considerations cited in the text. It was proposed to the Society "to recommend to such of their members as had correspondents abroad, to acquaint their friends with these particulars, in order to know the sense of the people there, when duly informed of the case; and to know what other objections they may have to the said proposals." The following testimony was made, November 28, 1750, by six Church of England clergymen resident in New England, — Timothy Cutler, Ebenezer Miller, Henry Caner, Charles Brockwell, William Hooper: "We, the subscribers, having read the foregoing objections, are not able to recollect any others made by the dissenters here against resident Bishops in America, but what are herein contained; and notwithstanding these objections, we are heartily desirous that bishops should be provided for the plantations, and are fully persuaded that our several congregations, and all other congregations of the Church of England in New England, are earnestly desirous of the same" (Chandler, *Life of Johnson*, Appendix, 169–171).

not relating to their calling or function.[1] Dr. Johnson, in a letter[2] appended to the English edition of his *Elements of Philosophy*, which appeared in this year, is equally deprecatory, although expressions in other parts of the same letter tend to counterbalance his assurances.[3]

Meanwhile, Sherlock continued his complaints to his correspondents, both within and without the Church of England.[4] Nor did he confine himself to expostulation ; he even sought to resort to coercion, for he went so far as to refuse to receive a commission for the exercise of the colonial jurisdiction. Since this action naturally threw the colonies into great confusion,[5] he finally relented, however, so far as to consent to act as diocesan provisionally until some other arrangement could be made. Although he would never consent to take out a commission, he was by 1752 obliged, much against his will, to reconcile himself to the idea of assuming the ecclesiastical charge of the colonies.[6]

---

[1] See the Society's *Abstract*, 1753, p. 35. But compare the following lines from the *Abstract* for 1756 (p. 43), in which the missionaries are instructed " to endeavor, with the utmost care and zeal in this juncture, to support his Majesty's Government, and to support the Welfare and Safety of his Majesty's American subjects, and for this good purpose, that they would upon all proper occasions, make the people sensible of the great blessing they enjoy, in the free exercise of their religion, and the advantages of lawful government under the benign reign of a Protestant prince."

[2] *A Letter containing some Impartial Thoughts concerning the Settlement of Bishops in America. By the Author and some of his Brethren.*"

[3] For example, he says (*Elements*, 262–271), that " in proportion as episcopal congregations have been settled among those called Independents. . . . their principles of government have become more unmonarchical and constitutional."

[4] For example, to Dr. Johnson, in 1749, to whom he gave an account of his efforts to obtain an episcopal establishment. Cf. Wilberforce, *Protestant Episcopal Church*, 139, note 1, and Hawkins, *Missions of the Church of England*, 390 ; both citing Chandler, *Life of Johnson*, 131–132.

[5] On October 6, 1749, Commissary Price of New England wrote to Bearcroft, secretary of the Society : " We are very unsettled here in our Ecclesiastical State, it is the current Report that the Bishop of London has refused to concern himself with the American Churches, and I suppose my Commissarial power is now extinct, I should be glad to have your thoughts upon it and to know what we are to expect " (Perry, *Historical Collections*, iii. (Massachusetts) 434 ; Foote, *Annals of King's Chapel*, i. 387).

[6] Bearcroft announced the Bishop's final determination in a letter to Dr. Miller, May 1, 1752 : " There are now," he said, " no farther hopes of obtain-

"I think myself, at present, in a very bad situation," he writes at this time. "Bishop of a vast country, without power or influence, or any means of promoting true religion, sequestered from the people over whom I have the care and must never hope to see, I should be tempted to throw off all this care quite, were it not for the sake of preserving even the appearance of an episcopal church in the plantation."[1] Truly an enviable state of things for the Church of England in America, always unpopular, but now, in consequence of the impending crisis, almost hated, with no authoritative guide save a man beyond the seas who performed his duty only in the most perfunctory way, because there was no escape for him, and who would not even take the necessary steps to legalize the small amount of jurisdiction which he consented to exercise!

As the middle of the century drew near, the authorities in Virginia began a systematic course of repressive measures against the dissenters, particularly the Methodists, who for some years had been organizing in the province.[2] One of the consequences of this persecution was the rise of an interesting correspondence between the Bishop of London and Dr. Joseph Doddridge, which gave the former another chance to express

ing a Bishop for you, and my Lord of London talks of taking out his patent for the ordinary Jurisdiction of the Plantations." (Perry, *Historical Collections*, iii. (Massachusetts) 444.) But if Sherlock ever seriously entertained this intention, he never carried it out.

[1] Abbey, *English Church and Bishops*, i. 363, citing John Stoughton, *Religion in England*, i. 325; Anderson, *Colonial Church*, iii. 433; Chandler, *Life of Johnson*, Appendix, 171–172.

[2] Dissent became prominent in Virginia with the "revival" of Whitefield, who visited the colony for the first time in 1740. Bibliography of the treatment of dissent in Virginia: Anderson, *Colonial Church*, iii. ch. xxiv.; Briggs, *Presbyterianism in America*, 86–90; Burk, *History of Virginia*, ii. 138, iii. 119, 125, iv. 377; Campbell, *Introduction to the History of Virginia*, 114–117; Foote, *Sketches of Virginia*, chs. i.–iii., vi., ix., xiv.; Hartwell, Blair, and Chilton, *Present State of Virginia*, 64–67; Hawks, *Ecclesiastical Contributions*, i. (Virginia) ch. vi. ff.; Hening, *Statutes*, v.–ix.; Howison, *History of Virginia*, ii. 31, 155, 160, 192; Jefferson, *Notes on Virginia*, 307–319; Jones, *Present State of Virginia*, 65–74, 95–112; Meade, *Old Churches, Ministers, and Families of Virginia*, i. 18, 94, 150–151, 162–163, 231, 250, 275, 283–284, 301, 387, 407, 470, ii. 179; Perry, *American Episcopal Church*, i. 604–614, and *Historical Collections*, i. (Virginia); Semple, *History of the Baptists*, chs. i.–iii.

his views on the general subject of episcopal control in the colonies. His first letter to Dr. Doddridge, dated May 11, 1751, was in answer to one from Doddridge on the subject of the famous Virginia Methodist preacher, the Rev. Samuel Davies. After disposing of the specific question in hand, Sherlock passes to his favorite theme of the folly of subjecting the Church of England in America to a non-resident diocesan.[1] The letter is interesting to us for two reasons: first, because it shows the determined insistence of Sherlock on what had grown to be the constant burden of his song — the total non-interference of the clergy, commissary, or bishop, except in matters of church administration, and the absence of any intention to press upon the colonists an episcopate which would in any way encroach on their vested rights in civil and ecclesiastical affairs; and, secondly, because it admits that the dissenters, unwilling to accept these constantly reiterated assurances, were prepared to resist to the utmost any attempts to introduce bishops into America.

Perhaps the very fact of Sherlock's attempt to show, as a first step in the accomplishment of his plans, that the Bishop of London had little basis either in law or in fact for the exercise of his authority, drew renewed attention to the subject in the colonies. At any rate, from the correspondence of this period we learn much concerning the light in which the bishop's jurisdiction was regarded both at home and abroad. There were ap-

---

[1] " Sundry of the people have been indicted and fin'd," he says, " and it is upon this information (I suppose) that you express yourself apprehensive that methods of severity, not to say of oppression, may be used. Of this I have heard nothing. But give me leave to right you in one thing, and to tell you that my name neither is nor can be used to any such purpose. The Bishop of London and his Commissarys have no such power in the plantations; and I believe they never desired to have it, so if there be any ground for such complaint, the Civil Government only is concerned. . . . The care of it . . . [the church of England there] is supposed to be in the Bishop of London. How he comes to be charged with this care I will not enquire now; but sure I am, that the care is improperly lodged, for a Bishop to live at one end of the world, and his church at the other, must make the office very uncomfortable to the Bishop, and in a great measure useless to the people " (Perry, *Historical Collections,* i. (Virginia) 371–374; Hawkins, *Missions of the Church of England,* 391–392; citing Doddridge, *Correspondence and Diary,* v. 201).

parently two views on the subject. These are well outlined in a report on the state of the church in Connecticut which the Reverend James Wetmore sent to Sherlock, August 11, 1752. The advocates of one view maintained that the colonies were part and possession of the English nation, and were therefore subject to that government in all things religious and civil; since, then, the mother country was of the Church of England, they were also theoretically subjects of that church. The authority for the establishment they drew from the declarations in the Act of Union, and from Gibson's patent empowering him to exercise ecclesiastical jurisdiction over the plantations.

Those who took the opposite view based their opinion on a passage in a letter from the lords chief justices to Governor Dummer of Massachusetts, in 1725, which declared that there was "no regular establishment of any national or provincial Church in these plantations" (meaning New England), and also in a passage in a letter of May 24, 1735, from Bishop Gibson to Dr. Colman, in which he says: "My opinion has always been, that the religious state of New England is founded on an equal liberty to all Protestants, none of which can claim the name of a national establishment, or any kind of superiority over the rest." Wetmore, who held the former of the opposing views, and who sent to the Bishop of London for his opinion on the subject, evidently had a high estimate of that prelate's colonial influence; for he remarks, "A short paragraph from your Lordship would be of equal authority with those alleged against us, and carry the same reverence and respect; and, for my own part, I shall most humbly submit to correction from your Lordship's hands if I have gone into mistakes." [1] Whether the bishop ever sent the "short paragraph" does not appear. Even if he had done so, it is, to say the least, extremely uncertain whether his words would have had the weight which his correspondent expected. It must, however, be remembered that the discussion took place in New England, where the authority of the Church of England and of the Bishop of London had a minimum of recognition.

After Sherlock's determination temporarily to assume his

[1] Hawks and Perry, *Connecticut Church Documents*, i. 292-295.

colonial jurisdiction was made public, apparently many of the clergymen beyond the seas began to regain courage. A sign of renewed interest is the fact that many accounts of the state of the church were sent at this time to the authorities in England.[1] Take as an example a letter of September 29, 1752, from the Reverend Alexander Adams of Maryland to Bishop Sherlock. It appears that Adams had sent to the bishop on the 5th of October in the previous year an appeal urging the necessity of bishops in America. He had written this earlier letter upon the news of Sherlock's refusal to undertake the care of the plantations. Now, hearing that his Lordship has reconsidered the matter, he writes again to lay before his diocesan the state of the churches in Maryland, the origin and basis of the establishment, and the various attempts which have been made to subvert it. Since the watchful care of the governor and the lack of a legally-appointed commissary make it impossible for the clergy to assemble and address their grievances to the home government, Mr. Adams has taken it upon himself to perform that duty. He begs his bishop to intercede with Lord Baltimore and his guardian, Mr. Onslow, speaker of the House of Commons, to prevent the assembly from encroaching any more upon the establishment. He regrets that for some years the clergy have had neither bishop nor commissary to call them together by authority, and expresses the hope that Sherlock will appoint two commissaries, one for the Eastern and one for the Western Shore.[2] As was said above, Sherlock was the recipient of many appeals of this sort; but when they concerned matters of purely church interest he gave them little or no attention. Except in Virginia, where the commissarial office went with the presidency of the college, he appointed no new commissaries; hence, after those serving at the time of his accession had died, there remained an authoritative representative of the Bishop of London in only one province in America.

[1 No doubt the circular letter asking for information concerning the state of the church, which Sherlock sent out, September 19, 1750, to those who had been commissaries under his predecessor, may have had considerable to do with increasing the volume of his colonial correspondence at this time.

[2] Perry, *Historical Collections*, iv. (Maryland) 327–329.

On questions concerning the political status of the colonies and the relation of the church thereto, Sherlock was more ready to express himself, and we find him constantly making decisions upon laws submitted to him by the Lords Commissioners for Trade and Plantations. The case of the Virginia Tobacco acts of 1753, 1755, and 1758 will serve as a good illustration. These acts were the basis of the celebrated " Parson's Cause," [1] which is treated of at length in every history of the period. They concern us here only so far as the Bishop of London was involved in the affair. His connection with it came about in this way. The Lords Commissioners, believing the subject to be one proper for his consideration, transmitted to him the successive acts, together with the memorial of the Virginia clergy directed against them.[2] Sherlock's reply reviewing the case is enclosed in the report of the Lords Commissioners to the crown, recommending the disallowance of the acts. He takes the ground that an act which has once received the royal assent — like that of 1748, against which the three acts in question are directed — can be repealed only by the same authority, and hence that it cannot be abrogated by any contrary act of assembly. For this reason he argues that the Virginia act of October 12, 1758, is *ipso facto* null and void. In the course of his letter he takes occasion to say that the rights of the clergy stand or fall with those of the crown, a significant utterance which may give a clue to the underlying motive of his agitation for an American episcopate. The Tobacco Act was disallowed by the crown in 1760.[3]

The next case to be taken up is that of the North Carolina Church Act of January, 1755, entitled " An Act for appointing Parishes and Vestries for the encouragement of an Orthodox

---

[1] For a full account of this subject, see Perry, *Historical Collections*, i. (Virginia) 434 ff. (where the correspondence and other original documents are printed) ; W. W. Henry, *Life of Patrick Henry*, i. 29 ff. ; William Wirt, *Life of Patrick Henry*, 19 ff. ; Mellen Chamberlain in Winsor, *Narrative and Critical History*, vi. 1–34 ; Foote, *Sketches of Virginia*, 310 ff. ; Campbell, *History of Virginia*, ch. lxv. ; Burk, *History of Virginia*, iii. ch. iv. The acts themselves, together with that of 1696, are printed in Hening, *Statutes*, iii., vi., vii.

[2] See Perry, *Historical Collections*, i. (Virginia) 458–460.

[3] *Ibid.* 461–463.

Clergy, etc." This was naturally referred to the lords in council for consideration, who, "it appearing to their Lordships that the Law . . . might operate to the prejudice of and interfere with the ecclesiastical jurisdiction of the Bishop of London," ordered their secretary to send his Lordship a copy, in order that he might express his opinion upon it.[1] The bishop's reply is interesting to us chiefly from the fact that it contains the fullest and latest exposition of his views on the subject of his jurisdiction. He considers one after the other the two questions referred to him: (1) How far the provisions of the act may "affect the right of the Crown to the Patronage and Presentation to ecclesiastical Benefices"; (2) How far they may "affect and interfere with the Bishop's ecclesiastical Jurisdiction in the Colonies." [2]

The first question he dismisses rather summarily as follows: The patronage and livings are rightfully in the control of the crown, and are delegated to the governor by virtue of his royal commission; the act of 1755 appropriates to the vestries the patronage of all livings in the province, sets up a new jurisdiction quite inconsistent with the Church of England form of government, excludes any bishop from the examination or correction of any misbehavior in the church, and takes from the crown the right of appeal; by these provisions, therefore, the king's supremacy and the bishop's jurisdiction are transferred from their proper lodgment to the vestries of the several parishes.

Having pronounced this rather general opinion upon the first of the two questions referred to him, Bishop Sherlock proceeds to a much fuller discussion of the question as to how far the act may trespass upon his own colonial jurisdiction. To this end he deems it necessary to show whether the Bishop of London really has any authority over the plantations, and if so what. As an answer to this question he encloses the report made by him upon his accession to the see, with a few appended remarks as to its history. We have so often had occasion to refer to and discuss various portions of this address, that we need here

[1] *North Carolina Records*, vi. 68
[2] *Ibid.* 10–13.

take time only to consider the supplementary remarks, so far as they concern our subject.

Among other things he seeks to explain the attitude which he has taken toward the Gibson commission. " It may be asked, perhaps," he says, " why the present Bishop of London could not go on with the Jurisdiction abroad, as his Predecessors had done, ever since the settling of the Colonies. My answer, is, that if the Jurisdiction had come to me upon the foot of customary usage, as it had done to my Predecessors, till Bishop Gibson's time, I should have made no difficulty of acting upon that foot, and I doubt not but those who come after me would have gone on in the same way; but when Bishop Gibson, for reasons best known to himself, applyed for a patent, and the consideration thereof was referred to the Attorney and Solicitor General, and they reported that the Jurisdiction was in the Crown, and that the Bishop of London had no right to meddle, it was time for me to consider the danger that attends the invasion of the Prerogative of the Crown, which could not be avoided but by accepting a Patent of like form with that which was granted before, which I judged not proper for me to do." [1]

This whole explanation is very unsatisfactory and unconvincing, and avoids the very point which one would wish to have elucidated; for just why his Lordship judged it not proper to renew the Gibson patént, he does not deign to inform us. Moreover, the statements made here do not accord with those made in other places, — for example, in his letters to the Duke of Newcastle, where the reason he ascribes for wishing to discontinue the colonial jurisdiction customarily exercised by the Bishop of London lies in the too great care and responsibility which it involves.[2]   In short, this letter leaves us as much in the dark as ever concerning Sherlock's motives.   Perhaps he was, for personal reasons, disinclined to assume the responsibility which such a charge, legally conferred, would carry with it. Perhaps he conscientiously believed that, from the nature of the case, a non-resident bishop ought not to undertake the charge. Or, finally, perhaps he was actuated by motives purely political,

[1] *North Carolina Records*, vi. 13.
[2] See above, p. 117 and note 4.

or at least, ecclesiastico-political. Assuming that a colonial episcopate was indispensable, he sought to secure it by starving the English government on the one side, and the colonial Episcopalians on the other, into acquiescence, by neglecting to perform, so far as his duties as a Christian shepherd would permit, even the few duties appertaining to the Bishop of London as colonial diocesan.

At any rate, whatever influenced him to act as he did, his policy of non-intervention in the concerns of the Church of England in the American colonies was rigidly adhered to. By this time all the commissaries appointed by Compton, Robinson, and Gibson were dead, and their places had been filled nowhere except in Virginia. This lack of oversight was so bitterly felt that even the most ardent advocates of an American episcopate were willing to prejudice their cause by a return to the old system.[1]

An interesting episode of this period is the correspondence carried on by Dr. Johnson of Connecticut and Bishop Secker on the subject of an American episcopate. The first important letter in the series is one from Secker, dated March 19, 1754, acknowledging the receipt of Johnson's *Elements of Philosophy*, published in London in the previous year. He expresses satisfaction with the arguments set forth in the letter appended to that work, and regrets that, since all their efforts have come to nothing, they must wait until a more favorable time for pushing the cause which they have so much at heart. Meantime, he suggests that the Episcopalians direct their attention to placating the dissenters, who, he says, will be heeded by the government so long as they have any objections to the plan. The ground of their aversion he attributes to their uneasiness caused by the rapid growth of the Church of England in the colonies.[2] Writing again some years later, Secker proclaims to Johnson the joyful news that he has found Lord Halifax " very earnest for Bishops in America," and expresses hopes that they are at last on the point of succeeding in their undertaking so soon as

---

[1] *New York Documents*, vii. 370–374.

[2] Beardsley, *Life of Johnson*, 177–179; Chandler, *Life of Johnson*, Appendix, 176–177.

the war then going on should cease.[1] But, aside from this single burst of enthusiasm, he was still biding his time; and most of his letters throughout the period were written to keep the over-zealous Johnson from taking any too precipitate step.[2] The continuation and conclusion of this correspondence will be considered in another connection.

During Sherlock's incumbency occurred a striking instance in which the authority of the Bishop of London to exercise one of his most recognized functions was for the first time seriously questioned by members of a congregation hitherto noted for its general loyalty to its diocesan. The case came up at Christ Church, Philadelphia, in connection with the Reverend William McClenaghan, a clergyman, originally a Presbyterian but afterward converted to Episcopacy, who came to Philadelphia in 1758.[3] Some of the congregation of Christ Church wanted to make him a third assistant to Dr. Robert Jenney, in spite of the latter's wishes. This attempt and the discussion which it involved drew forth some significant declarations. On the one hand, the second assistant minister at Christ Church, Jacob Duché, insisted that no one could be made an assistant without the consent of the rector and the license or the approbation of the Bishop of London. On the other hand, the members of the congregation who had first addressed the vestry in behalf of McClenaghan retorted as follows in a petition to Dr. Jenney and his vestry : —
" In Mr. McClenaghan's present state and settlement among us, we shall ever consider him invested with all the powers necessary for the discharge of any duties pertaining to his Office *as fully as if he had his Lordships License* . . .; his Lordship's *License means nothing here, as we humbly apprehend, without a*

---

[1] Beardsley, *Life of Johnson*, 253.

[2] On October 25, 1760, when George III. acceded to the throne, Johnson wrote to Secker as to the advisability of moving his Majesty to settle bishops in America at the conclusion of the war, and enclosed the draft of an " address to the king " which he had prepared. Secker, thinking the time not yet ripe, replied: " This is a matter of which you in America cannot judge ; and therefore I beg you will attempt nothing without the advice of the Society or of the Bishops " (*Ibid.* 256).

[3] For a fuller account of McClenaghan, see *New York Documents*, vii. 415, note 1 ; Protestant Episcopal Historical Society, *Collections*, ii. 250.

previous presentation from the people." They insisted on the validity of this assumption and asserted that it was acknowledged by the late Bishop of London.[1]

This attitude was rather extreme. It is true that the bishop was not accustomed to put a clergyman into any parish without a presentation from the people; but it is doubtful if any precedent could have justified a part, or even a majority, of the congregation in calling, settling, and inducting a minister in open disregard of the wishes of their diocesan. Certainly up to this time no such right had ever been claimed in Pennsylvania. The usual custom here, as in other colonies where nomination was not in the hands of the governor or of the Society for Propagating the Gospel, had been for the vestry to recommend and for the bishop to approve. The basis for this procedure — so far at least as it concerned Pennsylvania — may be found in a clause of the charter granted by Charles II. to William Penn: " Our further pleasure is . . . that if any of the inhabitants of the said Province, to the number of Twenty, shall . . . signify . . . their desire to the Bishop of *London* that any preacher or preachers, to be approved of by the said Bishop, may be sent unto them for their instruction, that then such preacher or preachers . . . may . . . reside within the said province."[2] In the opinion of Dr. Smith, provost of the College of Philadelphia, this clause made the approval of the Bishop of London for the time being necessary to the establishment of every Episcopal congregation and to the appointment of every Episcopal minister; nor was it likely that any laws made upon the authority of the charter would recognize any minister of the church " that had not his Lordship's license and approbation."[3] After

[1] They could point to precedents for this position in the cases of the two rectors who were appointed to King's Chapel, Boston, during the Gibson period, Roger Price in 1729, and Henry Caner in 1746 (see Foote, *Annals of King's Chapel*, 382). The case of Caner was clearly one in which the appointment was made by the congregation.

[2] Poore, *Charters and Constitutions*, ii. 1515. See also p. 36, note 1, above, where the clause is cited in full.

[3] Dr. Smith to Archbishop Secker, November 28, 1759, *New York Documents*, vii. 406–417. The sources of the case are printed in Perry, *Historical Collections*, ii. (Pennsylvania), 295–311, 320–323.

some discussion, the side of Dr. Jenney and the Bishop of London was sustained; McClenaghan, failing to get his appointment, removed to New Jersey, and this rather striking attempt of the congregation to appoint a minister in spite of the rector and the diocesan came to nothing.[1]

In Virginia there was still a commissary; but his authority was even more of a shadow than it had hitherto been. This is well illustrated by a case which came up for cognizance about the year 1757. One John Brunskill, minister of Hamilton parish, Prince William County, openly persisted in an irregular course of life, in spite of repeated reproof, advice, and exhortation. Finally, the church wardens and vestry made a complaint to the commissary and one of the representatives of the county. The latter, being in town during the session of the assembly, brought the matter to the attention of the governor, who advised the commissary to proceed against the offender in a judicial manner. The commissary replied that he had not sufficient authority to exercise any ecclesiastical jurisdiction, or, even in the most notorious cases, to proceed to either suspension or deprivation,[2] but promised that he would consult with the clergy and report to the Bishop of London, in order to find some means of removing the scandal. Meanwhile some of the council informed the governor that in the time of Blair irregular clergymen had been proceeded against by the governor and council; whereupon Governor Dinwiddie, in spite of the protest of Commissary Dawson, deemed it advisable to lay the matter before the council, which straightway removed the refractory clergyman and deprived him of his function as a preacher. This step was in accordance with Virginia law, which gave to the governor and council cognizance over all causes ecclesiastical and civil, and which had been recognized by the late commissary.[3] Neverthe-

---

[1] It is worth while to note that a convention of the Pennsylvania clergy, held in 1760, informed their bishop that, as the case was placed before him, his answer would be a "final determination."

[2] Thomas Dawson, who was commissary at this time, had been appointed in 1752, four years after the expiration of the Gibson patent, and had never received any commission.

[3] See Commissary William Dawson to Sherlock, July 15, 1751, *Fulham MSS*.

less, many persons, among them the commissary, objected to the proceeding as a violation of the one hundred twenty-second canon of the ecclesiastical law of the Church of England.[1] Thereupon Dawson wrote to his diocesan for advice, urgently soliciting a commission as an efficacious protection against such encroachments in the future, but adding, in justice to the governor and council, that they had been far from desirous of exercising any such power, and would much rather have seen it delegated to him as commissary.   The governor also wrote to the bishop to explain that he would not have interfered in the matter had the commissary been possessed of the proper authority; at the same time he expressed a hope that, since the commissary held no commission for erecting a spiritual court, his Lordship would approve the deprivation of Brunskill by the governor and council, for otherwise there would be no means of executing justice in such cases.   Moreover, he justified his act by a well-known precedent.[2]   The bishop evidently sustained the governor in his proceeding; at any rate, any future discipline of the clergy was undertaken, if at all, by the lay, not by the ecclesiastical authorities.

In summing up the events relating to the Bishop of London's colonial jurisdiction during the time of Sherlock's incumbency of that see, we strike the key-note of his policy by repeating what has been so often said already: that, except for a certain oversight in matters of political and constitutional significance, it was marked by an almost total disregard of American ecclesiastical affairs, and by a persistent endeavor to further the establishment of bishops in the colonies.[3]   His efforts, in con-

---

[1] It is also tolerably evident that they did not want such a precedent of lay control over the clergy to be established.

[2] Dawson wrote two letters to Sherlock, July 9, 1757 (Perry, *Historical Collections*, i. (Virginia) 451–454).   Dinwiddie's letter is dated September 12, 1757 (*Ibid.* 454–458); he had announced the decision of the governor and council to Brunskill's parish, May 20, 1757.

[3] In view of this fact, it is amusing to read the following extract from a funeral sermon on Sherlock, by Dr. Nicolls, master of the Temple: " He extended his care to the parts abroad," said the preacher, " and began a correspondence there, which would have been very usefull to the Church, if his health had permitted him to carry it on " (*London Chronicle*, January 20, 1762).

junction with those of his colleagues on the bench, notably of Bishop Secker, the later Archbishop of Canterbury, came into conflict with the increasing tendency toward independence in church and state which was growing more and more evident in the colonies, and led to those episcopal controversies which it will be the purpose of the next few chapters to examine.

CHAPTER VI.

THE MAYHEW CONTROVERSY, 1763-1765.

It was not long after Cutler, Johnson, and their companions passed over from the Presbyterian to the Episcopal communion, before discussions upon the relative merits of the two systems of government and worship began to agitate New England.[1] At first of a purely, or at least of a mainly, theological character, they soon assumed a more and more ecclesiastico-political tinge, until they finally culminated in the celebrated controversies of the decade 1760–1770.

The origin of these disputations seems to have been due to the apprehension and opposition which the New England clergy of the Independent persuasions manifested toward the introduction of the Episcopal church into the province. The position of the majority of the New Englanders toward the Church of England system is well expressed in the words of one of the best-known contemporaries: " Let all mankind know," he says, "that we came into the *wilderness*, because we would worship God without that *Episcopacy*, that *common prayer*, and those unwarrantable *ceremonies*, with which *the land of our fore fathers' sepulchres* has been defiled; we came hither because we would have our posterity settled under the pure and full *dispensations* of the gospel, defended by *rulers that should be of our selves*." [2] Starting out in such an attitude of mind, and with the history of the events of the first half of the seventeenth century deeply graven in their memories, it was natural that they should regard

---

[1] For a complete bibliography of the Episcopal controversy in New England, and the questions relating to it, see Foote, *Annals of King's Chapel*, ii. ch. xvii, particularly p. 274. Such of the pamphlets as are of a purely theological nature are not incorporated in the bibliography appended to the present work.

[2] Cotton Mather, *Magnalia* (Hartford, 1820), vol. i. book iii. pt. i. § vii. 219; Protestant Episcopal Historical Society, *Collections*, i. 143.

as a direct menace to the freedom and independence of their institutions, civil as well as ecclesiastical, every step which brought nearer to them that form of worship which represented the dreaded Anglican establishment.

As early as 1734 Dr. Colman wrote to Bishop Gibson in behalf of the associated ministers of Hampshire County, and enclosed a petition from them protesting against the practice of the Society for Propagating the Gospel in sending its missionaries to New England instead of to other places where they were more needed.[1] But the first really significant landmark in the always latent hostility between the two parties was an animated controversy concerning the validity of Presbyterian ordination, which came to a head in the years 1747–1751.[2] The immediate occasion for the outbreak seems to have been given by a sermon preached by the Reverend Noah Hobart at Stamford, Connecticut, December 13, 1746. Certain aspersions which the preacher made against the Episcopalians[3] brought forth early in the following year an answer from the Reverend James Wet-

[1] Colman's letter, dated September 13, 1734, is printed in Turell, *Life of Colman*, 141–143. The letter of the Hampshire ministers, dated September 10, 1734, is printed as the second number by the "Anatomist" in the *Pennsylvania Gazette*, September 15, 1768. David Humphreys answered this letter in behalf of the Society. The gist of his argument was (1) that the missionaries were sent to places where there were many people who did not care to worship with the dissenters; (2) that the places to which they were sent were published in the Society's annual *Abstracts*, and that, since large numbers of people continued their subscriptions, it was evident that the procedure of the Society was not regarded as a violation of the charter. The complaints begun by the Hampshire association of ministers in 1734 were taken up by the *Independent Reflector* and the *Watch Tower*, published in New York in 1752 and 1753 respectively.

[2] There is a good account of these controversies in Foote, *Annals of King's Chapel*, ii. 247 ff. The account given in the text is based on an actual examination of the original writings. References to the earlier Checkley controversy may be found above, pp. 66, 67. Though it is sometimes said that the Episcopal controversy originated in the discussion which Checkley stirred up, the evidence seems hardly to warrant the statement.

[3] Chiefly his assertion that it was unnecessary, and therefore a misappropriation of the charitable funds, for the Society to send missionaries into New England, where the Gospel was already sufficiently taught. This was precisely the contention of the Hampshire association of ministers.

more, rector of the parish of Rye, and missionary of the Society, in an open letter to a friend.[1] Thereupon Hobart replied with *A Serious Address to the Members of the Episcopal Separation in New England, occasioned by Mr. Wetmore's Vindication of the Church of England in Connecticut.*[2] The aim of this work was to "fix and settle" three points: (1) "Whether the Inhabitants of the *British Plantations* in *America*, those of *New-England* in particular, are OBLIGED, *in Point of Duty,* by the Laws of God or *Man,* to conform to the *Prelatic Church,* by Law established in the *South Part* of GREAT-BRITAIN;" (2) "Whether it be PROPER *in Point of Prudence* for those who are already settled in such Churches as have so long subsisted in *New-England,* to forsake them and go over to *that Communion;*" (3) "Whether it be LAWFUL for particular Members of *New-English Churches* to separate from them, and join in Communion with the *Episcopal Assemblies* in the Country."

These propositions give one a tolerably clear idea of the aim and scope of Hobart's pamphlet. Although it would be hardly worth while to consider in detail its one hundred and thirty odd pages of theological polemics, perhaps a brief summary of some of its main arguments will not be out of place. Under the first head the author discusses the question whether the Church of England establishment extends to America, and decides it in the negative.[3] Passing to the second point, he comes to the conclusion that the great number of "unnecessary ecclesiastical Officers" required by the Church of England system, and the great expense involved in supporting them, make it imprudent for those of his persuasion to submit to that system. The argument which he here employs is exceedingly utilitarian, and sounds strangely modern. For example, in one place he says: "A wise Man would chuse such a Constitution in *Church* or *State,* wherein the great Ends of Society are effectually an-

---

[1] It was published at Boston in 1747, under the title *A Vindication of the Professors of the Church of England in Connecticutt, against the Invectives contained in a Sermon preached at Stamford by Mr. Noah Hobart,* December 13, 1746.

[2] Boston, 1748.

[3] *Serious Address,* 5–44.

swered, with as little Burden and Charge as may be to the Community.[1] Another reason which he urges against the prudence of conforming to the Church of England, is that such a step would tend to bring the colonies into an "unnecessary and hurtful State of Dependence." By dependence, however, he means ecclesiastical dependence; for he says very decidedly that the colonies are, and of right ought to be, dependent upon the mother country in all civil affairs.[2] Besides, he argues, such a political relation is advantageous; but a state of ecclesiastical dependence, carrying with it no attendant advantages in the way of trade or civil privileges, would certainly not be beneficial to the colonies, and might be just the reverse. Evidently, the idea that civil independence is a necessary accompaniment of religious liberty, had not yet been developed. Without following Hobart's argument upon this head any farther, we may point out that he regards conformity to the Church of England to be imprudent for many reasons: first, on the ground of expense; secondly, because of the tyrannical discipline exercised by that church; thirdly, because of its arbitrary power in appointing and removing ministers; and, finally, because such conformity would lead to the destruction of practical religion.[3]

In the latter part of his book, Hobart touches on the subject of bishops. Apropos of the fact that the Church of England in America is suffering from an alarming lack of discipline, he considers the suggestion made by the Bishop of Oxford in his sermon before the Society[4] (a suggestion which had been taken up and repeated over and over by the pro-episcopal party on both sides of the water), namely, that this defect could be remedied by establishing bishops. His answer to this proposition is very sane, and quite to the point. "For my Part," he says, "I can't see that the Bishop himself has, according to the Practice of

[1] *Serious Address*, 49.

[2] "Whatever the Enemies of the Plantations may report at Home, of the Danger of their casting off their Dependence, I believe it may with Truth be affirmed," says he, "that there is not a Man of Sense in them all, but what is willing, nay, would chuse to continue in this State" (*Ibid.* 64–65).

[3] *Ibid.* 78.

[4] Printed in the Society's *Abstract*, 1741, p. 32. Cf. above, p. 109.

the Church of *England*, anything to do with the Discipline of the Church; this is managed in the spiritual Court, by a *Lay-Chancellor*, appointed, indeed, by the Bishop, and acting in his Name, but not under his Direction, nor liable to be controled by him." [1] This is very true; it is, indeed, hard to see how a bishop of the character advocated by Secker and those of his way of thinking could have exercised a discipline any more efficacious than that already exercised by the commissaries.

Such is a brief outline of Hobart's argument. From his standpoint the whole course of his reasoning is logical, and, for the time in which he lived, admirably calm and considerate of the feelings of his opponents.

The next step in the progress of the controversy was marked by the appearance, in the following year, of *A Calm and Dispassionate Vindication of the Professors of the Church of England*, purporting, as the title-page further informs the reader, to be directed "against the Abusive Misrepresentations and falacious Argumentations of Mr. Noah Hobart." The body of the work was written by John Beach, but was provided with a preface from the pen of Dr. Johnson, and with an appendix containing "Vindications" by Wetmore and Henry Caner. In reply to the charge that the Church of England has no discipline, Beach admits that its system is imperfect for want of a bishop, a lack which he hopes will soon be filled. Then, passing over, without any adequate refutation, the argument of Hobart cited above, he contends that the discipline of the Episcopal Church in America is, in spite of its imperfections, better than that of the Presbyterian bodies.[2] This view of the comparative merits of the respective systems of discipline of the two bodies is strangely optimistic, and hardly accords with

---

[1] *Serious Address*, 103.

[2] "Our Bishop," says he, "has a Patent from the King to exercise Jurisdiction in this Country: He appoints Commissaries in each Government; who can call any clergyman to account for misdemeanors, and, taking to his assistance the neighboring clergy, can suspend him. And if, after the Bishop has silenced him, he still persists to officiate as a member of the Church, the King's officers may be obliged to apprehend and imprison him. Because the Bishop is the King's minister as well as Christ's, whereas Yours is neither, I fear" (*Calm and Dispassionate Vindication*, 37–38).

the opinions on the same subject usually put forth in appeals for an American episcopate. Scattered through the book are several rather striking examples of the author's calmness and dispassionateness, as, for instance, the following sentence: " Mr. Hobart has raked together a large heap of vulgar trash, which he calls new, because nobody was ever so weak or childish as to put it in print before; so he tells us of the danger of tithes, if the Church should prevail in New England." [1]

Two years later, Hobart wrote in reply to the above vindication: *A Second Address to the Members of the Episcopal Separation in New-England occasioned by the Exceptions made to the former, by Dr. Johnson, Mr. Wetmore, Mr. Beach, and Mr. Caner,* to which was appended a letter from Moses Dickinson " in Answer to some Things *Mr. Wetmore* has charged him with." In this second address, which goes over much the same ground as its predecessor, one of the few new points which the author takes up is the question of the establishment, in opposition to the position held by Douglass in his *Summary.*[2] A reply which Beach wrote in the same year to Hobart's *Second Address* brought this particular controversy to a close; [3] but several things go to show that there was at least a measure of continuity between this and the later Mayhew controversy.[4] At all events, raising as it did many of the questions later brought up for consideration, it was certainly a forerunner of that stirring discussion.

Even as early as the time of the Hobart controversy, many of the New Englanders had awakened to what they considered

---

[1] *Calm and Dispassionate Vindication,* 38.

[2] William Douglass, *A Summary, Historical and Political, of the First Planting, Progressive Improvements, and Present State of the British Settlements in North-America* (see particularly the edition of 1755, ii. 120, note). Hobart bases his argument on citations from the letter of the lords justices to Governor Dummer, written in 1725, and from that of Bishop Gibson to Dr. Colman, May 24, 1735 (*Second Address,* 37–38). Cf. above, p. 128.

[3] Foote, *Annals of King's Chapel,* ii. 250–251.

[4] For example, a letter from Bishop Secker to Dr. Johnson, July 19, 1759 (Chandler, *Life of Johnson,* Appendix, 178–179), from which it appears that Johnson had been sending him the various contributions made by both sides to the discussion. Both were parties to the Mayhew controversy.

to be the dangers which might be apprehended from the introduction of an Episcopal hierarchy into their midst. A good
example of the most extravagant expressions of such fears may
be found in a sermon preached by Jonathan Mayhew, January
30, 1750, and afterward published. " People have no security,"
said the preacher, " against being unmercifully priest-ridden but
by keeping all imperious bishops, and other clergymen who
love to lord it over God's heritage, from getting their feet into
the stirrup at all." [1] Opinions of this stamp were, however,
probably not widely prevalent at this time; [2] it was only with
the outbreak of the Mayhew agitation in the early sixties that
the community at large became thoroughly roused.

Like all historical phenomena, the Mayhew controversy,
although it had an immediate and a specific occasion, was
really the outcome of causes slowly developing in an environ-
ment favorable to their growth. As has been noticed, there
had been for many years, among the Independents, evidences
of a strong hostility to the extension of the episcopal system
in the colonies, or at least to the introduction of bishops. This
opposition, dormant so long as there was nothing to call it forth,
would naturally spring up whenever there seemed to be any
indication that the hopes of their opponents were likely to be

---

[1] Mellen Chamberlain, *John Adams*, 30.

[2] Foote (*Annals of King's Chapel*, ii. 251) thinks that the following letter
from Secretary Willard to Governor Phips (Shirley was absent in England
from 1749 to 1753), written December 12, 1750, expressed the more sober
sentiment of the community: "As to the Project of sending Bishops into
America (the principal Subject of your Letter), I need say but little in that
Matter considering how fully and freely I express'd myself in a Letter I wrote
to your Excȳ. in June last, which lest it should have miscarried, I now send
you a Copy of. I can only add that the universal dissatisfaction to that
Scheme among Persons of our Communion is nothing lessened from the
Proposals your Excȳ. was pleased to send me with your Letter before mentioned, of the Restrictions therein contained as to the Exercise of the Episcopal Function here, those Persons expecting that if once Bishops should be
settled in America, it would be judged for some Reasons or other necessary to
extend their Jurisdiction equally to what that Order of Men are possessed of
in Great Britain: However, It is supposed our Sentiments in these Matters
will have but little Influence wth those Gentlemen in England who have the
Management of this Affair."

realized. Such an occasion came with the approach of the peace which was to end the Seven Years' War. Up to this time the English government had been too much occupied with its foreign relations to attend to anything else, but with the cessation of hostilities it would be likely to have time and opportunity to give attention to domestic and colonial concerns. Thomas Secker, now Archbishop of Canterbury, had, it was well known, long had at heart the matter of the American episcopate, and had often expressed the intention of taking the first favorable opportunity to press it upon the attention of the English government. The time now seemed ripe for the realization of his purpose; accordingly the apprehensions of the Independents and the hopes of the Episcopalians were proportionally excited.[1]

Such was the state of things when the death of the Reverend Ebenezer Miller, missionary at Braintree of the Society for Propagating the Gospel, occurred, February 11, 1763. Shortly after his decease there appeared a newspaper article attacking the policy of the Society in sending missionaries into New England, where they were not needed. In reply to this the Reverend East Apthorp, missionary at Cambridge, wrote a series of *Considerations on the Institution and Conduct of the Society for the Propagation of the Gospel in Foreign Parts.* Thereupon Jonathan Mayhew, a prominent Congregational minister in Boston, published his *Observations on the Charter and Conduct of the Society,* in the course of which he not only attacked the Society for sending missionaries into New England,[2] but also

---

[1] Cf. Chandler, *Life of Johnson,* 113–114. The same author (pp. 111–113) describes the origin and external history of the controversy. A good account written from the Puritan standpoint may be found in Alden Bradford, *Life of Mayhew,* 240–248. Porteus (*Life of Secker,* 60), describing the controversy from the point of view of a member of the Church of England, characterizes the opposition of the "Dissenters" in England and America as based upon "very unreasonable and groundless Jealousies of the Church of *England,* and its Governors." Cf. Bradford (*Life of Mayhew,* 242), who says that there was just cause to fear that the English wanted to "episcopize" New England, and that the "High-Tory" party in the mother country agreed to gain control of the colonies in ecclesiastical and civil affairs. For a modern account of the controversy, see Foote, *Annals of King's Chapel,* ii. ch. xvii.

[2] On the title-page of the *Observations* is a quotation from Paul to the Galatians, describing the Society's missionaries as "Brethren unawares brought

took occasion to censure the proposed scheme for the introduction of an American episcopate. It is at this point that the
agitation becomes of interest to us.[1]

This pamphlet of Mayhew's appeared in 1763. The author
sets out by attempting to prove that the Society for Propagating
the Gospel has long had " a formal design to root out Presbyterianism " and to establish episcopacy and bishops in the colonies, and that, in pursuance of this plan, it has in a great
measure neglected the important ends of its institution.[2]   In
support of his position he cites several selections from the publications of the Society.[3]   His conclusion is that New England,

in, who come in privily to spy out our LIBERTY which we have in Christ Jesus,
that they might bring us into BONDAGE : To whom we gave place by subjection, no, not for an hour; that the truth of the GOSPEL might CONTINUE WITH
YOU."

[1] There were in all four replies to Mayhew's *Observations*, three of which
came from America.   Two of these were short and unimportant, one of them
appearing at Portsmouth and the other at Newport.   The third, which Bradford (*Life of Mayhew*, 279–280) calls a " smart rather than an able performance," was published anonymously, under the title *A Candid Examination of
Dr. Mayhew's Observations.*   The authorship has been ascribed both to
Henry Caner and Dr. Johnson, but the weight of evidence seems to give it to
the former.   The English publication, an *Answer* to the *Observations*, which
also appeared anonymously, was later learned to have been written by a
person no less important than Archbishop Secker.   Other noteworthy contributions to the discussion were a *Defence* by Mayhew of his own *Observations*, and a final *Review* of the whole controversy by East Apthorp.   See
Protestant Episcopal Historical Society, *Collections*, i. 148 ff. ; Perry, *American
Episcopal Church*, i. 411 ff.

[2] *Observations*, 103.

[3] For example : " The want of a *Bishop* or suffragan in those parts was
often complained of.   And this matter has been carried as far as the difficulties in it would hitherto allow, and is under such farther solicitation and
advances, that we hope *shortly* to see a happy success of it " (*Ibid.* 105, citing
Account of the Society, 1706, p. 74).   And again : " It having been frequently
represented to the Society, that there is great want of a Bishop to govern
those missionaries, whom the Society has or shall, from time to time, send
over to New-England, — as well as the rest of the clergy in those and the
adjacent colonies ; and to ordain others, and to confirm . . . ; this matter
has been most seriously considered of, and is yet depending before the Society,
and in the mean time, and *till they can bring it to bear*, they are looking out
for the best and most commodious place, — to fix the *See* for the said Bishop "
(*Ibid.* citing the Society's *Abstract*, 1711, pp. 27–28).

and indeed all the colonies, have been from the beginning of the century in danger from the Society's episcopizing influence.[1]

Passing over the endless personalities and questions of purely theological import which abound in this as in all other controversial pamphlets of the period, let us consider for a moment the substance of Mayhew's argument. Of the truth of his assertion that the Society had from the very moment of its inception striven to push the cause of the episcopate, there can be no doubt; on the other hand, his further contention that such had been its only, or its chief, aim is open to question. That its missionary efforts had often been primarily directed toward the advancement of its own church is perhaps true, but it would be hard to find a church which has not proceeded along the same lines ever since missionary work began. Rightly or wrongly, the Episcopalians believed — and in this they were not alone among the religious bodies of that or of any other period before or since — that their own method of worship was the one most in accordance with the will of God. Conceiving, moreover, that a hierarchy was absolutely necessary for the existence of their system of doctrine and discipline, they sought to establish it in America, as they did in any other place or country where their church was represented. Whether it was wise to push the matter in the colonies at this time is another question; whether the Independents were justified in their suspicions of what might result from the rule of bishops once established is, in this connection, equally beside the point. The fact is that the earliest relations of the Independents with the Church of England had made them desirous, and justly so, to keep as far as possible from the sphere of her influence; and, whenever they had anything to do with the establishment, the memory of this early experience came into their minds and warped their judgments.

---

[1] "The affair of Bishops has lately been, and probably now is in agitation in England. . . . And it is supposed by many, that a certain *superb edifice* in a neighbouring town, was even from the foundation designed for the *Palace* of one of the *humble successors* of the apostles. . . . What other new world," he asks, "remains as a sanctuary for us from our oppressions, in case of need? Where is the COLUMBUS to explore one for, and pilot us to it, before we are consumed by the flames, or deluged in a flood of episcopacy?" (*Observations*, 107, 156.)

Jonathan Mayhew was a true Puritan; and it was the limitations that encompassed him *ipso facto* which caused him, although proceeding from premises that were in the main true, to draw conclusions concerning the mainspring and motives of the action of the Society which from the evidence before him were hardly tenable.

Mayhew's pamphlet called forth great applause from his fellow-believers, and contributed much to heighten the suspicions already latent in their minds. The effect extended to the mother country also. For example, Dr. Lardner of London, in a letter written July 18, 1763, in acknowledgment of the receipt of a copy of the *Observations*, commented on the strong probability that bishops would soon be sent to America, and echoed the suspicions of the Society which Mayhew had expressed.[1] "The present Archbishop of York, then bishop of St. Asaph's," he says, "at Bow Street church, in his sermon to the Society, . . . told his congregation without reserve, that the business of that society was not so much to increase the number of Christians by conversion of the Indians, as *to unite the subjects of Great Britain in one communion*."[2] This quotation, which, torn from the context, appears to mean more than it really does, hardly justifies the assertion made by the author of the *Annals of King's Chapel* that the Society for Propagating the Gospel "seemed to have been turned from the true objects of missionary work into a means for undermining and ultimately destroying the system of Independency itself."[3] As a matter of fact, whatever intentions the Society had as to the extension of episcopacy in the colonies were held at least as strongly in the first years of its existence as later, indeed one might almost say more strongly. The important thing was that the attitude of mind of the Independents had changed, and, as the breach with the mother country drew nearer and nearer, led them more and

---

[1] Bradford, *Life of Mayhew*, 269.

[2] Foote, *Annals of King's Chapel*, ii. 251, citing Bradford, *Life of Mayhew*, 271.

[3] Foote's whole account (*Annals*, ii. ch. xvii., "Episcopacy ard the Mayhew Controversy") relies too much on Dr. George E. Ellis to be strictly impartial. It is, to a considerable extent, made up of quotations from a manuscript lecture by Dr. Ellis on the "Episcopal controversy."

more to suspect the aims and to question the motives of the Society; whether justly or unjustly, the historical effect was the same.

Mayhew's *Observations* was answered in the same year by *A Candid Examination*, presumably written by Henry Caner, rector of King's Chapel, Boston. A detailed examination of this pamphlet is hardly necessary for the purposes of this study. It is taken up mainly with a discussion of Mayhew's character in general as shown in his works, of the motives actuating the conduct of the Society, and finally with an attempt to prove that the Independent churches of New England are not established, but that the Church of England is the established form of worship in the colonies.[1]

Another reply to Mayhew was that of the Reverend Arthur Browne of Portsmouth, published also in 1763 under the title *Remarks on Dr. Mayhew's Incidental Reflections relative to the Church of England, as contained in his Observations*, etc. This effusion is interesting upon two grounds: first, as an illustration of the methods of argumentation employed by a class of men of that time who, as Ruskin fitly says, mistook pugnacity for piety;[2] in the second place, for the charming frankness of the

---

[1] In support of his position the author cites several acts of Parliament — particularly the Act of Union, and also a letter to the Reverend Thomas Foxcroft, published in 1745, in which the following statement occurs: "The King (under God) is the supreme head of the church of England, and if he had not appointed an ordinary over New-England, it would have remained under his own immediate ecclesiastical jurisdiction as supreme head. But it is well known that his late Majesty in the first year of his reign, did impower the Bishop of London, under the great seal, to exercise jurisdiction over the clergy in the plantations, which were not in any Diocess, but remained under the immediate jurisdiction of the King" (*Candid Examination*, 39).

[2] See, for example, a passage in which Browne alludes to the "fanatic ravings of his [Mayhew's] predecessors the Oliverian holders-forth, whose spittle he hath lick'd up, and coughed it out again, with some addition of his own filth and phlegm" (*Remarks*, 24). Compare with this an "Advertisement" of "a Certain *Jonathan Mayhew*, an independent Holder-forth in *Boston*," a broadside that appeared at about the same time. Two extracts from it are especially markworthy: "And if he was treated according to his demerits, a strong-toed Shoe, or an Oaken Plant [plank?], well applied, would be quite gentle and seasonable. . . . And . . . if the said *Mayhew* should print any more such foul-mouthed anonymous Papers, tending to vilify Characters," concludes the

author. He readily admits the truth of the design charged to the Society, that it is seeking to settle bishops in North America, and justifies it on the ground that bishops are an indispensable limb of the Church of England system. Indeed, he adds, those who had been complaining of the irregularity and want of discipline among the Episcopalian clergy in the colonies ought to agree to the necessity of an episcopate to oversee their conduct. Regarding Mayhew's apprehension that episcopacy once firmly established would tend to drive out Presbyterianism, he says cheerfully: "If presbytarianism, as he calls the prevailing religion of the country, be disposed to go off, and make room for it's betters, let it go. But nobody has any thoughts of driving it away by force."[1] Moreover, supposing the Episcopalians come to a majority in America, what of it? In that case, if the colonists should be taxed for the support of bishops and for official tests, it would simply be by the wish of the majority, for the Episcopalians would be in the majority.[2] Such opinions as these could hardly be reassuring to a people jealous to the last degree of its liberties in church and state; but they were not sanctioned, or at least not openly, by the majority of those of Browne's persuasion.

The pamphlet on the episcopal side which attracted most attention was the so-called *Answer* to Dr. Mayhew's *Observations*. This appeared anonymously, but was later discovered to have been written by Archbishop Secker. The gist of the argument is that the Church of England is, in its constitution, episcopal; that it is already established in some of the colonies; that in others where it is not established there are many Episcopalians needing its ministrations; that, in a land where there is any pretence of toleration, the members of this church should enjoy that privilege in full — should have bishops and other necessary officers.[3] The author then proceeds to sketch a plan of what the proposed bishops would be allowed to do and what not to

advertiser, "I will advertise him again in such a Manner, as that his whole Character shall be known."

[1] *Remarks*, 26.
[2] *Ibid.* 28–29.
[3] *Answer*, 50–51.

do, a plan which corresponds in its essentials to that which Bishop Butler had drawn up in 1750.[1] This, he assures his readers, is the real and only scheme of episcopal establishment which has ever been proposed for America, "and whoever hath heard of any other, hath been misinformed through Mistake or Design."[2] Bishop Porteus, the biographer of Secker, remarks that "the Strength of the Argument, as well as Fairness and good Temper, with which this Answer was written, had a considerable Effect on all impartial Men, and even on the Doctor himself."[3] This statement is, in the main, correct. Secker was too politic and conciliatory, and indeed too refined and cultivated a gentleman, to descend to the low abuse and vulgar personalities which characterized many of the contributions to the discussion. While he said nothing particularly new, yet the moderation of tone which he almost habitually employed could not but have had some influence in allaying the fiery heat of the zealots of both parties.[4]

The many lesser pamphlets which appeared during the period will not be considered here, for they contain little that was not touched upon by the leading writers. Now and again, however, they bring out an interesting point. For example, the

[1] See above, pp. 122–124.

[2] *Answer*, 51.

[3] *Life of Secker*, 59.

[4] Yet Secker was far from receiving the reward which his moderation deserved. His biographer, Porteus, complains that " Posterity will stand amazed when they are told, that on this Account [his advocacy of an episcopate for America] his Memory has been pursued in Pamphlets and News-papers with such unrelenting Rancour, such unexampled Wantonness of Abuse, as he would scarce have deserved, had he attempted to eradicate *Christianity* out of *America*, and to introduce *Mahometanism* in its Room" (*Life of Secker*, 66). The following lines, written by an Episcopalian who happened to be opposed to the introduction of bishops, bear witness to the justness of Porteus's complaint: " As to Secker, he is laid in his grave: disturb not his slumber. His character no more than his body, can endure *the keen question of the searching air*. Unless you would give another specimen of your friendship, cause him not to stink to futurity " (Purdie and Dixon's *Virginia Gazette*, July 18, 1771). Nevertheless, Secker's reasonableness, ability, and courtesy were pleasantly acknowledged by his opponent Mayhew: see, for example, Protestant Episcopal Historical Society, *Collections*, i. 149, citing Mayhew's *Remarks*, 3 ; Perry, *American Episcopal Church*, i. 412.

author of a work entitled *The Claims of the Church of England seriously Examined* asks : " Is the *American* bishop to touch or affect no man's property ? is he to make no alteration in the civil condition of any of the people ? on what then must he maintain his episcopal port and dignity ? — on *American* air only ? " [1]

Dr. Mayhew replied to the *Candid Examination* and the *Answer* in two separate pamphlets. The title of the first is a bit belligerent; [2] but, since the ground gone over is much the same as that in his earlier argument, the details need not be considered. One point, however, may be touched upon with a word. In the course of his discussion, Mayhew takes occasion to answer an assertion made by his opponents, to the effect that the Episcopalians in Massachusetts are unreasonably taxed for the support of divine worship in the manner established by the laws of the province : he points out that, by a perpetual law passed by the government there, they are exempted from taxes for the support of ministers and churches not of their own denomination. [3] His manner of stating the case is rather strik-ing : " I have been informed," says he, " whether rightly or not, that his Excellency then in the chair, when the aforesaid act of exemption was passed, received the thanks of the then bishop of London for his service therein ; as having contributed his endeavours to relieve the members of the church of England from an *inconvenience* or *hardship,* not from an *illegal* oppression, which they had long labor'd under." [4] The act referred to, passed in 1742, did not emanate from the spontaneous will of the representatives of the people, but owed its passage to the efforts of the governor. Since, moreover, its provisions seem not to have been strictly enforced, and since it offered only a partial

---

[1] *Claims*, 17.

[2] *A Defence of the Observations on the Charter and Conduct of the Society for the Propagation of the Gospel in Foreign Parts, against an Anonymous Pamphlet falsly intitled, A Candid Examination of Dr. Mayhew's Observa-tions, &c., and also against the Letter to a Friend annexed Thereto, said to Contain a Short Vindication of said Society, by one of its Members* (Boston, 1763).

[3] See *Massachusetts Province Laws* (1742, ch. 8), iii. 25.

[4] *Defence*, 50. Cf. Foote, *Annals of King's Chapel*, ii. 265.

amelioration of existing conditions, the Episcopalians still labored under a substantial grievance.[1]

In Mayhew's reply to Secker's *Answer*, according to the
sub-title of the London edition,[2] "the Scheme of sending
Bishops to *America* is particularly considered; and the Inconveniences that might result from it to that country, if
put into Execution, both in *civil* and *religious* Respects, are
represented." It is significant that here for the first time,
from the Independent side at least, the question of establishing bishops in the colonies takes its place as the main topic of
the controversy. This was a result of the line of argument
adopted in the *Answer*. Mayhew begins by pointing out that
Secker's statement that his *Observations* was written partly
against the Church of England in general, partly against the
conduct of the Society, and partly against the project of appointing colonial bishops, is incorrect; for what Secker has said
about bishops is, he shows, incidental to what he has said about
the Church of England. With regard to the latter subject he
says, " It was by *no means* my design in this publication, to enter
into the controversy betwixt the church of England and us;"[3]
but, since the author of the *Answer* has dragged in the question of the episcopate, he professes his perfect readiness to
discuss it.[4]

He understands his opponent's reasons for advocating an
American episcopate to be, in substance, those more distinctly enumerated in the *Abstract* of the Society for 1715,
namely to provide the proper functionaries, (1) "to *rule* and
govern well those people who are desirous to be committed to
their charge," (2) " to *defend* and *protect* both the clergy and the

---

[1] In Foote's *Annals*, ii. 252, occurs this statement: " Their [the Independents'] toleration of episcopacy, under the new political conditions, may have
been compulsory, but it appears to have been sincere, so long as it was not
made the cover of unfriendly interference." The evidence which we have on
this point indicates quite the contrary view.

[2] *Remarks on an Anonymous Tract, entitled, An Answer to Dr. Mayhew's
Observations . . . Being a Second Defence of the Observations* (Boston, 1764;
reprinted London, 1765).

[3] *Remarks*, 4–5.   Cf. *Observations*, 151.

[4] *Remarks*, 56.

laity," (3) "to *unite* the clergy themselves, and *reduce them to order,"* and (4) "to *confirm* new converts from *schism* . . . in *ordaining* ministers from amongst themselves; in *confirming weak brethren,* and *blessing* all manner ·of people *susceptible* of *such holy impressions,* as are made by the *imposition of the bishop's* hand's." [1]

Recurring to the plan as sketched by the author of the *Answer,* he admits that the proposal is presented from " a more plausible and less exceptionable point of view " than he has ever seen it presented from before, for the reason that the bishops here suggested are, first, not to meddle with those not churchmen; secondly, not to have any power in matrimonial or testamentary cases, or to infringe on the functions of the governors and magistrates, or in any way diminish the powers of the laity, and, lastly, not to be settled in any but Episcopal colonies.[2] While Mayhew in this concession tries to do justice at least to the more reasonable demands of his opponents, he displays at the same time a rather curious ignorance of what had been really asked, for some time past, by the less extreme among the advocates for an American episcopate. The plans proposed by Sherlock and Butler,[3] for example, had called for not a whit more than that drawn up by Secker in the *Answer.* Sherlock's plan, designed only for the eyes of the king and the chief officers of state, was of course inaccessible; but that of Butler, expressly intended for the consideration of the colonists, had, as we have seen, actually been sent to New England.[4] In view of this fact, Mayhew's statement that the scheme as presented in the *Answer* is quite different from the one which he and others of his persuasion had supposed the Episcopalians to have in mind, and his allusions to a certain " superb house " which he had supposed to be the designed residence for a New England bishop,[5] carry

[1] *Remarks,* 56–57, citing the Society's *Abstract,* 1715, pp. 53–54.
[2] *Remarks,* 57–58.
[3] See above, pp. 122–124, and below, Appendix A, No. xii.
[4] See above, p. 124, note 1.
[5] Mayhew refers here to the house still standing in Cambridge, built (probably in 1761) by the Reverend East Apthorp. It is situated between Massachusetts Avenue and Mount Auburn Street, directly opposite Gore Hall, the Harvard University Library, and is popularly known as the " Bishop's Pal-

hardly the weight which they otherwise might. The same criticism applies to his objection that, although he regards the project as he now understands it to be very reasonable, he can hardly accept it as authoritative, since it comes from an unknown source.[1]

Mayhew believes, however, that, even though bishops should come to the colonies with the limited powers proposed, it is, from the nature of their relations with their English brethren, extremely unlikely that they would long be contented to maintain a position inferior to theirs, "without any of their temporal power and grandieur . . . and consequently wanting that authority and respect which, it might be pleaded, is needful. Ambition and avarice," he continues sententiously, "never want plausible pretexts, to accomplish their end."[2] At all events, the colonists, he thinks, are much safer without bishops; for, if they were once settled, pretexts might easily be found for increasing their power. For example, he adds, it is very natural to fear that by virtue of the establishment of bishops the number of Episcopalians might increase to such an extent as to attain a majority in the legislatures, and thereby secure, perhaps, not only an establishment of the Church of England, but also taxes for the support of bishops, test acts, ecclesiastical courts, and what not.[3] These matters are at this time, he thinks, all the more worthy of consideration, because the colonists have already got wind of the fact that "high-church tory-

ace" (cf. S. A. Drake, *Historic Fields and Mansions of Middlesex,* 196–197).

[1] *Remarks,* 59–60.

[2] *Ibid.* 60.

[3] *Ibid.* 62–64. In justice to Mayhew, it must be admitted that one of the most important concessions of Butler, Secker, and Sherlock, namely, that bishops should not be sent to New England, was not agreed to by the leading Episcopal clergymen of that province. Compare letters from Timothy Cutler and Henry Caner to Bishop Sherlock, April 24, 1751, and May 6, 1751, respectively (*Fulham MSS.,* reprinted below, Appendix A, No. x.). These letters were privately written to his Lordship. In view of the public testimony made by these gentlemen on the 28th of the previous November (see above, p. 124, with note), there seems to be pretty certain evidence of double-dealing on their part. Strangely enough, Perry omitted to print the letters in his papers relating to Massachusetts.

principles and maxims" have, under the new king, once more found favor since their overthrow in 1715 and 1745.[1]

It was here, indeed, that the strength of the Independents' position lay. Even admitting the single-mindedness and purity of motive of the pro-episcopal party, — a thing which, by the way, they seldom did, — they might still very correctly maintain that no one could answer for the future. Moreover, just at this moment, when the colonists were tending more and more toward a separation from the mother country as a result of their long independent growth, when their newly-attained freedom from the dangers of French attack made such a divergence, for the first time, possible, and when certain specific encroachments on the part of the English government made it for their interest to stand on their own bottom,[2] they were hardly in a position to accept any innovation which would offer the least menace to their liberties. Hence the efforts of the Episcopalians to push their plan at this time was at least one of the causes tending to accentuate that growing alienation between Great Britain and her colonial subjects beyond the seas which prepared the ground for the Revolution soon to follow.

Though the calmness of temper which Secker manifested in his *Answer* had a soothing effect on Mayhew, causing him, in his last contribution to the discussion, to moderate his tone and modify the violence of his expressions, it had no effect whatever in shaking his fundamental convictions on the point at issue. Such concessions as he seems to make are merely apparent yieldings. When he says, for example, "I think it but justice to him [the author of the *Answer*] to acknowledge, that if such a scheme as he has proposed were to be put in execution, and *only* such consequences were to follow, as he *professedly* has in view, as the ends aimed at, I could not object against it; except only upon the same principle, that I object against the church of England *in general*, and should be sorry, from a regard to what I suppose a more scriptural way of worship, to see that church prevail here;" and when, agreeing with his opponent

---

[1] *Remarks*, 63–67.

[2] For the last two points, compare Lecky, *England in the Eighteenth Century*, iii. ch. xii.

that every man has a right to enjoy the full benefit of his religion so long as the machinery he requires to secure it does not
menace the interests of the community, he assures him that he
would not prevent, even were it in his power, what would be
merely religious toleration,[1] — when he says these things, he is
in reality yielding nothing whatever. Since his qualifications
rob his apparent concession of all practical weight, his position is, and remains, aside from a certain polite recognition
of the courtesy of his opponent, essentially uncompromising.
Of this attitude his closing remarks are a convincing proof.
While acknowledging the author of the *Answer* to be a man of
moderation and good sense, he nevertheless continues to think
that he himself has not been wrong on any material point; and
he refuses, in case anything more should be written, to reply
simply "for the sake of having the last word" on the subject.[2]

To this last work of Mayhew's the Reverend East Apthorp
replied in a pamphlet entitled *A Review of Dr. Mayhew's
Remarks*, etc. Since the *Review* contains little that is new, it
may be passed without detailed consideration. The author takes
Mayhew to task for his statement that he has been misinformed
as to the grounds for the establishment of an American bishop,
and quotes from Butler's plan of 1750, which he assumes that
Mayhew must have seen. The burden of his argument is to
prove that there is no basis in fact for the apprehensions which
Mayhew has expressed. As to the question of maintenance,
for example, — one of the greatest obstacles from the colonial
point of view, — he assures his readers that if no money should
be found for the support of bishops, no bishops would be sent.[3]
Mayhew, on reading Apthorp's work, said that he should not
answer it. He died in the following year.[4]

Although Apthorp's *Review* was the last contribution made
to the controversy by either side, the matter continued to be
discussed in private correspondence for at least a year longer,
Thomas Hollis, writing from London to Mayhew in 1765,
expressed the wish that "Mr. Otis could be induced, in his bold
and able manner," to write something against the scheme of

---

[1] *Remarks*, 77–78.   [3] *Review*, 54–55, 60–61.
[2] *Ibid.* 85–86.   [4] Porteus, *Life of Secker*, 60.

episcopizing the colonies. According to Hollis, the advocates for bishops were more active and sanguine than ever ; and he feared, from the fact that they had won over some of the English statesmen to their side, that their cause was in danger of triumphing.[1] But Hollis's wish remained unfulfilled, and the Mayhew controversy, as such, was at an end.

A word as to the results of the discussion may be added. Naturally, both sides claimed a victory. Chandler says that it was the opinion of Dr. Johnson that the church had gained ground in the controversy, rather than lost it ;[2] but his statement has no basis in fact. It is most likely that the agitation had the effect of uniting the forces of those who were in favor of episcopacy, and, indeed, of inducing many who had hitherto been lukewarm to take a decided stand beside the leaders of their cause. On the other hand, it had precisely the same effect on the members of the opposing party, awakening large numbers for the first time to the realization of the danger which the leading Independents had for some time apprehended. As to the influence of the question on the history of the time, we have a decided opinion from an authority no less important than John Adams, who, writing of the causes of the Revolution, says : " If any gentleman supposes this controversy to be nothing to the present purpose, he is grossly mistaken. It [the plan of episcopizing the colonies, especially New England] spread an universal alarm against the authority of Parliament. It excited a general and just apprehension, that bishops, and dioceses, and churches, and priests, and tithes, were to be imposed on us by Parliament. It was known that neither king, nor ministry, nor archbishops, could appoint bishops in America, without an act of Parliament ; and if Parliament could tax us, they could establish the Church of England, with all its creeds, articles, tests, ceremonies, and tithes, and prohibit all other churches, as conventicles and schism shops." [3]

---

[1] Bradford, *Life of Mayhew*, 375-376.

[2] " As indeed it had always done in similar cases," adds Chandler (*Life of Johnson*, 111-113).

[3] Letter to H. Niles, February 13, 1818, in John Adams, *Works*, x. 288 ; also cited in Foote, *Annals of King's Chapel*, ii. 267, and in Bradford, *Life of*

Whether one agrees with this statement or not, is of no consequence; its significance lies in the fact that it shows how much importance was attached to the episcopal controversy by a great political leader of the period, a leader who expressed and influenced the people of his day and generation. At least this much is certain: the controversy brought to a head apprehensions which were at once a sign and a further cause of the political events of the period; it sharpened the point at issue between the two great church parties, caused them to organize for the first time into two great opposing camps, and left them in this situation to face what was to come.

Mayhew, 276.   Bradford adds: " How then can it ever be said, the writings of Mayhew, against introducing and establishing episcopacy, were not important in support of the cause of civil and religious liberty, and against the claims of arbitrary power in the British parliament ? "

CHAPTER VII.

THE CHANDLER-CHAUNCY CONTROVERSY, 1767-1771.

THIS disputation originated in some remarks made by John Ewer, Bishop of Llandaff, in a sermon which he preached before the Society for Propagating the Gospel at its annual meeting in February, 1767. In the course of his discourse, he animadverted upon the meagreness of the provisions for religious instruction in the colonies; and, after pointing out what the Society had done toward supplying that need, he went on to bewail the fact that there was still a dearth of native ministers in the country, a fact which he attributed to the absence of resident bishops. He waxed especially eloquent in detailing the hardships to which the candidates were subjected in being forced to come to England for orders. "What encouragement," he asked, "have the inhabitants of these regions to qualify themselves for holy orders, while, to obtain them, they lie under the necessity of crossing an immense Ocean, with much inconvenience, danger and expence; which those who come hither on that errand can but ill bear. And if they have the fortune to arrive safe, being here without friends, and without acquaintances, they have the sad business to undergo, of presenting themselves unknown to persons unknown, without any recommendation or introduction, except certain papers in their pocket. Are there not circumstances in this case, sufficient to deter every ordinary courage, and to dampt the most adventurous spirit." [1] Such is the burden of Ewer's claim. Dr. Charles Chauncy, a well-known Boston clergyman, in an open letter "to a friend," [2] undertook to answer Ewer's assertions. He quotes the statements noticed above, and declares that they are very much exaggerated as to both fact and implication. He says that the candidates do not go

[1] Chauncy, *Letter to a Friend*, 43, citing the Society's *Abstract*, 1767, p. 21. Cf. also *Letter*, 45, citing *Abstract*, 22.

[2] Dated December 10, 1767, and published at Boston.

at their own expense and unknown, or if they do happen to be unknown they are always in a position to make themselves easily acquainted.[1] The want of ministers he attributes to quite other causes than that assigned by the Bishop of Llandaff, — namely, to lack of sufficient opportunity for exercising their functions, and to inadequate provision for their support. The real point aimed at in the introduction of bishops is, he asserts, not so much to increase the missionary force for spreading the Gospel among the heathen as to make the colonists turn Episcopalians, in order that the Church of England may obtain a majority over the other denominations, an exigency which, however, is not to be so much feared as the possibility that the bishops, once settled, would "make use of their superiority" to force the establishment willy-nilly on the inhabitants.[2] He goes on to say that in all the colonies only eight or nine Episcopal churches are self-supporting, the rest (some sixty) being to a considerable extent dependent on the Society. In view of this fact, the conclusion is unavoidable that any further extension of the Episcopal system would incur a grave expense, a consideration in which, he thinks, lies the chief objection to the plan.[3]

Passing on to Ewer's assertion that if the settlement of bishops be once secured, "the American Church will soon go out of its infant state; be able to stand upon its own legs; and without foreign help support and spread itself. THEN THE BUSINESS OF THIS SOCIETY WILL HAVE BEEN BROUGHT TO THE HAPPY ISSUE INTENDED." Chauncy concludes triumphantly; "The conduct of the Society has, for many years, given us reason to suspect their MAIN VIEW was to EPISCOPIZE the colonies; but we were never before, that I know of, told so in direct terms."[4] This conclusion was hardly the one to be drawn from the Bishop of Llandaff's statement, for it might very well have been the purpose of the Society to build up its church and make it self-supporting in order that its sphere of usefulness might be as broad as possible. The results apprehended by Chauncy might, of course, have followed; but he certainly

---

[1] *Letter to a Friend*, 43–44.
[2] *Ibid*. 46–47.
[3] *Ibid*. 48 ff.
[4] *Letter to a Friend*, 51.

finds no warrant for them in any statements which he quotes from the sermon of his opponent.

Chauncy's letter was supplemented by *A Letter to the Bishop of Llandaff* from William Livingston, who was induced to take part in the discussion after a perusal of Chauncy's pamphlet, to which his attention had been drawn by seeing a long quotation from it in Chandler's *Appeal to the Public.* Livingston's argument contains little that is new, and in arrangement and phrasing is so similar to that of Chauncy that hostile critics have denounced it as a plagiarism. This charge, however, is rather too severe. Original the work certainly is not; but the author is perfectly honest, for he not only at the outset refers to Dr. Chauncy as one to whom he has been indebted for several facts and observations, but frequently in the course of his work gives his predecessor in the field credit for many of the remarks which he quotes in regard to certain passages in the Bishop of Llandaff's sermon.

The last word on the subject was said by Charles Inglis,[1] in *A vindication of the Bishop of Llandaff's Sermon from the Gross Misrepresentations, and Abusive Reflections, contained in Mr. Wm. Livingston's Letter to his Lordship with some additional Observations on certain Passages in Dr. Chauncy's Remarks, &c.* This pamphlet, which appeared anonymously, was signed by "A Lover of Truth and Decency." After devoting some sixty-two of his eighty-two pages to justifying the Bishop of Llandaff's assertions concerning the lack of sufficient missionary provision for America, he comes to closer quarters with his opponent. To Livingston's assertion that the "grand burden" of Ewer's sermon appeared to be an attempt to persuade the English people of the necessity of an American episcopate, he retorts that "the grand burden of Livingston's paper is to prejudice the public against the plan, and thus to deprive colonial Episcopalians of the common rights and privileges of all Christians."[2] It is in his postscript that the charge of plagiarism against Livingston first occurs.[3] Whether Inglis's argument

---

[1] At that time an Episcopal clergyman in New York.
[2] Inglis, *Vindication*, 64. Cf. Livingston, *Letter*, 21.
[3] *Vindication*, 70–82.

silenced his opposers, whether they thought it not worth while to answer, or whether, as is most likely, interest in the discussion was lost in a far more important and significant controversy which had already opened, may be left to the reader to answer for himself. We now pass on to consider the origin, progress, and result of that stirring pamphlet war between Thomas Bradbury Chandler[1] and Charles Chauncy which agitated the colonies during the years 1767–1771.[2]

Chandler, in his biography of Dr. Johnson,[3] tells us how his *Appeal to the Public*, which opened the controversy, came to be written. Johnson, it seems, thought that Secker's *Answer* and Apthorp's *Remarks*, which explained the sort of episcopate desired, had not been sufficiently circulated, and that the disaffection of opponents was due chiefly to their ignorance of the true nature of the scheme. For this reason he desired to have further explained or reiterated the fact that no encroachment on the civil or religious liberties of any denomination was intended. Since, owing to a paralysis of the hand, he could not write himself, he chose Chandler as a person suitable to undertake the task. Johnson's plan and selection were confirmed by a convention of the clergy of New York and New Jersey, which met in 1767.[4] This was an organization of comparatively recent origin, the first meeting having been held May 21, 1766, at the house of the Reverend Dr. Auchmuty, rector of Trinity Church, New York. The purpose of the association is best explained in the words of the following resolution then adopted : " The Clergy of the Province of New York taking into their serious consideration the present state of the Church of England in the Colonies,

---

[1] Chandler was rector of St. John's Church, Elizabethtown, New Jersey, from 1751–1790 (cf. title-page of A. H. Hoyt's *Life of Chandler*).

[2] Good accounts of the external history of the controversy may be found in Protestant Episcopal Historical Society, *Collections*, i. 151–153; and Perry, *American Episcopal Church*, i. 416–418.

[3] Pages 114–116. See also his advertisement to the *Appeal*, ix–xi.

[4] It resolved " that fairly to explain the plan on which American bishops had been requested, to lay before the public the reasons of this request, to answer the objections that had been made, and to obviate those that might be otherwise conceived against it, was not only proper and expedient, but a matter of necessity and duty." (Perry, *American Episcopal Church*, i. 415, from the original manuscript of the convention.)

where it is obliged to struggle against the opposition of sectaries of various denominations, and labours under the want of the Episcopal Order, and all the advantages and blessings resulting therefrom; agreed upon holding voluntary conventions, at least once in the year and oftener if necessity required, as the most likely means to serve the interests of the Church of England; as they could then not only confer together upon the most likely methods, but use their joint influence and endeavours to obtain the happiness of Bishops, to support the Church against the unreasonable opposition given to it in the Colonies, and to cultivate and improve a good understanding and union with each other."[1] On the 22d they sent a letter to the Society stating what they had done and outlining the purpose of their action.[2] They continued their meetings from year to year until the eve of the Revolution.[3]

In the course of the year 1767, Chandler finished his *Appeal to the Public in behalf of the Church of England in America*.[4] There is, among the manuscripts at Fulham, a letter which he sent to the Bishop of London, with a copy of his book. Perhaps an examination of this letter will serve to give an idea of the opinion which he held of his own work. What he has written, he informs his diocesan, expresses the opinions of the clergy in most of the colonies, and names some of the facts and reasons upon which these opinions are based. But, and this is markworthy, only *some* of these reasons are considered; the rest are kept in the background, for, says Chandler, " There are some Facts and Reasons, which could not be prudently mentioned in a Work of this Nature, as the least Intimation of them would be of ill Consequence in this irritable Age and Country: but were they known, they would have a far greater Tendency to engage such of our Superiors, if there be any such as are governed by Political motives, to espouse the Cause of the Church of England in America, than any contained in the

---

[1] Perry, *American Episcopal Church*, i, 415, from the original manuscripts of the convention.

[2] *Ibid.* 416.

[3] The work of this convention will be considered in more detail in a later chapter.

[4] It was sent to the press on the 24th of June.

Pamphlet. But I must content myself with having proposed those only which could be mentioned safely, and leave the event to Divine Providence." [1]

This confession is of the utmost significance in forming an ultimate judgment of the ensuing controversy, for it shows that Chandler could hardly have been perfectly open and straightforward in his advocacy of the cause of an American episcopate.[2] Moreover, various indications — as, for example, some expressions used by Johnson in his correspondence with the leading ecclesiastics in England,[3] and the conflicting assertions of Cutler and Caner already noted[4] — go to show that Chandler was not the only one involved. The fact that these leaders of the Church of England in America thought and acted in concert, and, furthermore, that many of them held well-known loyalist sympathies, makes the supposition possible that they had some ulterior motives in the introduction of bishops, which boded no good to the religious liberties of their fellow-colonists. Accordingly, while one must appreciate the deplorable position of the Church of England in America, and acknowledge the justice of the attempts of its members to free themselves from the hard conditions restricting them in the maintenance and propagation of their form of worship, one is forced to admit that the suspicions of their opponents had some foundation.

To be sure, the condition of things following the passage and the repeal of the Stamp Act made it most unlikely that the English government would lend its aid to the machinations of the extremists among the pro-episcopal party;[5] but, even

---

[1] Chandler to Bishop Terrick, October 21, 1767, *Fulham MSS*. The whole letter is printed below in Appendix A, No. xiii.

[2] Chandler was an ardent loyalist, and either at this time or subsequently entered into a compact with Samuel Seabury and Charles Inglis "to watch and confute all publications in pamphlets or newspapers that threatened mischief to the Church of England and the British Government in America " (Beardsley, *Life of Seabury*, 30).

[3] Cf. above, pp. 106–110, *passim*, and below, ch. xi. *passim*.

[4] See above, p. 156, note 3.

[5] Chauncy, in his *Appeal Answered*, 110, points out that the time for bringing up the matter was not favorable, since harmony had not been restored, as Chandler had assumed that it was.

if it had before that time had any such intention, the determined attitude of the Independents had had the effect of checking, in its very conception, a plan likely to have been very dangerous in its ulterior consequences.[1] No one realized the situation in England better than Chandler; hence, the wish with which he concludes his letter, that some one there would take up the cause and push it energetically, or, as he expresses it, "set it forth to advantage." With his letter and these preliminary considerations in mind, we may now proceed to consider Chandler's first contribution.

He prefaces his work with the words of Justin Martyr: "We desire a fair Trial — if we are guilty, punish us; if we are innocent, protect us." Then follows an advertisement to the reader, in which he draws attention to the fact that the Church of England is the only religious body in America not fully tolerated; that, while even the Romish church is allowed bishops, the Anglican church is "left in a maimed state, lopt of Episcopacy, . . . And whence this disgraceful distinction?" he asks, "whence this mark of distrust? what is the fear? what the danger? A few persons vested with authority to ordain ministers, to confirm youth, and to visit their own clergy. Can two or three persons, restrained to these spiritual functions, be dangerous to any in any matter? in what? or to whom? Can they possibly, so limited, on any pretence whatever, attempt to molest any in their religious concerns? Can they invade the rights and jurisdiction of magistrates? Can they infringe the liberties of the people? Can they weaken, or be thought disposed to weaken, the fidelity of the colonies to his Majesty, or their dependence on this country?"[2] Certainly, from a religious point of view, it was unjust to deprive the members of the Church of England in America of so necessary a part of

---

[1] If the advocates of an American episcopate had ever had any chance of prevailing with the home government, it was in the interval between the close of the Seven Years' War and the passage of the Stamp Act; hence, if there was need of the stand so firmly taken by Mayhew, the time which he chose was most opportune. The attitude of the English officers of state toward the question after 1750 will be considered in a later chapter.

[2] *Appeal to the Public*, xi., quoting from the Bishop of Llandaff's *Sermon*, 22–24.

their system as bishops.   Yet, if the case was so simple, and the intention so innocent, as Chandler here professes, why did he consider certain arguments in favor of the plan as unsafe to be put before the public, when avowedly his only motive in writing his book was to show the people in the colonies that the suspicions which impelled them to oppose the plan were unfounded and unjust?

His argument is arranged under four heads: (1) the origin and nature of the episcopal office; (2) reasons for sending bishops to America; (3) a plan by which they are to be sent; (4) a refutation of objections against the plan.   Since the first point (which he considers in the first two of the eleven sections into which his work is divided) has no connection with the subject in hand, we may pass at once to sections iii.–vii. inclusive, in which he takes up his second point, namely, the need of an American episcopate.   The functions of the desired bishops, he says, would be governing, confirming, and ordaining ministers. For the first of these offices there is a crying need, since the Church of England is practically without any form of government; for, though the Bishop of London has taken some cognizance of those under his charge, he has been able to effect little, living, as he does, at a distance of three thousand miles.[1] The offices of a bishop, he continues, are needed by two sorts of clergy, the good, who need his advice and encouragement, the bad, who need his coercive hand;[2] moreover, the laws and canons enjoin a strict episcopal discipline and oversight of the clergy,[3] which in the present state of things is impossible.

With regard to ordination, Chandler thinks that under the existing conditions the difficulties are almost insurmountable, owing to the expense and hardship involved in crossing the Atlantic.   The trip, he says, can hardly be made for less than £100; and, further than that, out of fifty-two candidates who have gone to England for orders only forty-two have returned in safety.   This state of affairs is, he thinks, responsible for an appalling lack of clergy, and can be remedied only by settling

---

[1] *Appeal to the Public*, 28–29.   [2] *Ibid.* 33.
[3] *Ibid.* 31.

bishops in the colonies.[1] Still another evil lies in the fact that, since the candidates are often unknown to the Bishop of London, unworthy men often obtain ordination from him.[2]

He gives three main reasons why bishops have not hitherto been sent: first, because, since the country was originally settled by private adventurers chiefly of a dissenting faith, bishops of the Church of England have been little needed; secondly, because, though they have since come to be necessary, the troublous times abroad have kept the home government too much occupied to attend to the spiritual wants of the clergy; finally, because, though the officers of state have now time to consider the question, they will of their own accord take no steps for fear of infringing on the religious liberties of the dissenters.[3] He thinks the present juncture favorable for the advancement of the plan, because Great Britain is at peace and the government has no other distracting occupation, and also because, from the recent large acquisition of Episcopalians, the need is more urgent than ever.[4] Hence, since the first two conditions which have operated against the realization of the project exist no longer, it is time to do away with the remaining one, and thereby bring the plan to fruition. This is the purpose of the *Appeal to the Public*.

His next step is to define the plan upon which bishops are to be sent, for the enlightenment of such as oppose the project. These opposers he divides into three classes: (1) the enemies

[1] We have already met this argument in the consideration of the Bishop of Llandaff's sermon. Chandler gives some statistics for February, 1767: in New Jersey there were twenty-one parishes, of which eleven were without clergymen; in Pennsylvania and the three lower counties outside of Philadelphia, twenty-six churches and only seven clergymen; in North Carolina (according to a letter from Governor Dobbs to the Society, March 29, 1764), twenty-nine parishes, *i.e.* one for each county, and only six ministers. See *Appeal to the Public*, 34–35.

[2] *Ibid.* 36.

[3] *Ibid.* 47–48.

[4] He estimates that at this time there were 3,000,000 British subjects in America, of whom 1,000,000 were Episcopalians (*Ibid.* 54–55). These figures are disputed: Chauncy, for example, says that there were only 26,000 Episcopalians north of Maryland, and only upward of 300,000 in the whole country (*Appeal Answered*, 114, 133–134).

of all religions; (2) the enemies, secret or open, to the Protestant religion in particular; (3) those who, while friendly to religion in general, fear that the extension of episcopacy may be prejudicial to the integrity of their property or religious liberty.[1] It is mainly for the third class that the *Appeal* is intended; for their benefit, therefore, are enumerated — in spite of the fact that the explanation has been so often made before — the proposed functions of an American episcopate, namely, " That the Bishops to be sent to America, shall have no Authority, but purely of a Spiritual and Ecclesiastical Nature, such as is derived altogether from the Church and not from the State — That this Authority shall operate only upon the Clergy of the Church, and nct upon the Laiety nor Dissenters of any Denomination — That the Bishops shall not interfere with the Property or Privileges, whether civil or religious, of Churchmen or Dissenters — That in particular, they shall have no Concern with the Probate of Wills, Letters of Guardianship, and Administration, or Marriage-Licences, nor be Judges of any Cases relating thereto — But, that they shall only exercise the original Powers of their Office as before stated, *i.e.*, ordain and govern the Clergy, and administer Confirmation to those who shall desire it."[2]

Having outlined the functions and limitations of the proposed episcopate, Chandler next proceeds to answer such objections as have been or may be urged against it.[3] He counts among the most serious of these one which was brought up by some of the London papers at the time of the Stamp Act agitation, to the effect that the discontent and uneasiness manifested by the colonists on that occasion were due in a great measure to the fear that bishops would be settled among them.   This notion Chandler strenuously repudiates, challenging any one to find a trace of such an idea in any of the remonstrances of the time, and asserting most emphatically that the discontent then manifested was wholly due to what the colonists regarded as 'an *unconstitutional oppressive Act.*"[4]

After considering and replying to the more general objections,[5] he proceeds to a refutation of those of a more special nature.

---

[1] *Appeal to the Public*, § viii.   [2] *Ibid.* 79.   [3] *Ibid.* §§ ix.–xi.
[4] *Ibid.* 89.   [5] They have been considered in chapter vi. above.

For example, he assures his readers that there is no design of establishing ecclesiastical courts in America;[1] that any apprehension concerning tithes is wholly ungrounded ; that the colonists will not be taxed for the support of bishops, and, even if they should be, the amount would be very small, for there already existed in the hands of the Society a fund for the maintenance of bishops, and if it should prove insufficient for the purpose, more could easily be raised.[2] Assurances as these were too vague to satisfy the class of opponents with whom Chandler had to deal. He utterly failed to answer satisfactorily the question of the likelihood of a possible augmentation of the powers of bishops if once settled, and he even expressed opinions which, to say the least, would hardly tend to allay the suspicions which were growing stronger every day in the minds of the colonists.[3]

In general it may be said of Chandler's book that, from a religious point of view, it presented the case of the Episcopalians in a most convincing light. For a complete enjoyment of their form of worship, bishops were absolutely necessary both to maintain the system where it already existed and to propagate it where it did not exist. This fact was already admitted by the more reasonable among the anti-episcopal party ; but, unfortunately, the granting of the request for bishops was bound up with certain political consequences which an eminently practical people must perforce take cognizance of. The attempt to cope with this difficulty led Chandler to ground upon which he was not so sure-footed as in other parts of his *Appeal.* To be

[1] *Appeal to the Public*, 96.

[2] *Ibid.* 107–108.

[3] For example, a writer in the *Boston Gazette*, May 28, 1768, says : " The Appeal to the Public in favor of an American Episcopate is so flagrant an attempt to introduce the Canon Law, or at least some of the worst fruits of it, into the Colonies, hitherto unstained with such pollution, uninfected with such poison, that every friend of America ought to take the Alarm — Power, in any forms, and under any limitations, when directed only by human wisdom and benevolence, is dangerous ; the most terrible of all power that can be entrusted to man is the Spiritual." This paragraph was quoted by the *London Chronicle*, July 19, 1768. Chandler's admission concerning taxing was at once made capital of : see, for example, two articles by " Atlanticus," in the *London Chronicle*, June 27 and July 26, 1768.

sure, he satisfied himself by reiterating the very plausible and innocent-appearing plan which had often been sketched by his predecessors; but such reasoning satisfied his opponents not a whit.   Indeed, in view of what he wrote in his letter to the Bishop of London, it is hard to be sure that he himself was wholly sincere in the plan he here set forth.   As a result, his book, instead of smothering the agitation, stirred it up to even greater heat.   Proof of this fact is to be found both in particular pamphlets written in reply to his, and in the violent newspaper controversy which his book called forth.[1]

The *Appeal* was answered in the following year by Charles Chauncy, who, considering the four points of Chandler's argument one after another, sought to show that the reasons alleged for an American episcopate were insufficient to justify its establishment, and that, notwithstanding the recent apologetic, the objections against it remained in full force.   His reasons for writing the *Appeal Answered* he declares in the advertisement to be, first, the solicitations of " private friends," [2] and secondly, Chandler's statement that, if no further objections were offered against an American episcopate, it would be taken for granted that all parties were satisfied with the plan as set forth by him.[3]

Taking up first [4] the question of the necessity of bishops for purposes of discipline,[5] Chauncy points out that the Anglican bishops are not the real governors of the church, but are mere creatures of the state ; and that the Church of England, at least so far as its government is concerned, is a parliamentary church.

---

[1] Two newspaper writers at once took sides against the *Appeal*, the " American Whig" and the "Centinel."   This controversy in its many ramifications will be made the subject of a later chapter, in which numerous other contributors will be mentioned and their main arguments considered.

[2] This is a sarcasm on Chandler, who said in his advertisement that he had been commissioned by the convention to write his *Appeal*.

[3] Chauncy's accusation, that the Episcopalians had kept secret their arguments for bishops until they were on the eve of accomplishing their purpose (*Introduction to the Appeal Answered*, 5–6), is manifestly contrary to fact.

[4] That is, first in respect to what concerns the present study.   Chauncy's preliminary discussion is theological.

[5] In the course of his argument, he incidentally takes Chandler to task for advocating discipline for the clergy and not for the laity, a position which he considers to be illogical.   See *Appeal Answered*, 69–70.

Such being the case, his conclusion is that a bishop of the proposed sort could do nothing in the way of enforcing discipline which a commissary might not equally well do, that is, unless he employed the accessories in use in England, such as spiritual courts, institutions which, as the *Appeal* emphatically assures the public, it is not proposed to introduce into the colonies.

Passing from the subject of discipline to that of ordination, the *Answer* devotes some pages to showing that Chandler's picture of the danger and hardship involved in the necessity of going to England for orders is very much overdrawn.[1] He also points out, what seems very true, that a commissary's testimonial to a candidate would be as good a safeguard against unworthy ministers as a bishop's immediate oversight.[2] Another point which, he says, seems to have been generally overlooked in the contemporaneous discussion, is that a large number of the unworthy clergymen consecrated for America are not those who go from the colonies to England for orders, but those sent from there; for, since as a rule the most talented and capable clergymen prefer to remain in England, the colonies usually get only those who, from unfitness, either moral or intellectual, are unable to maintain their positions at home.

In answer to an assertion often made, among others, by Chandler, that the proposed bishops would not be settled in the dissenting colonies, he answers that they would, nevertheless, have power there, and would, moreover, be settled there as opportunity should arise.[3]

Another objection to the scheme for American bishops Chauncy finds in the fact that the question has been agitated almost wholly by the clergy, and by the laity scarcely at all. "It is to me," he says, "as well as to many I have conversed with upon this head, Episcopalians among others, very ques-

---

[1] In this respect Chauncy shows himself erroneous, unjust, and uncharitable.

[2] *Appeal Answered*, 87.

[3] *Ibid.* 101–102. It has already been shown that many of the prominent Episcopalian clergymen in New England, notably Timothy Cutler, rector of Christ Church, and Henry Caner of King's Chapel, were not in favor of excluding the proposed bishops from New England (see above, p. 156, note 3).

tionable, whether, if the members of the Church of England, in these northern Colonies, were to give in their votes, and to do it without previous Clerical influence, they would be found to be on the side of an American Episcopate." [1]

In spite of Chandler's assurance to the contrary,[2] Chauncy expresses the fear that tithes might come with the bishops, and, in this connection, pounces on Chandler's incautious admission that, if taxes should be laid on the colonists, the amount would be very small, perhaps fourpence on one hundred pounds, or about one six-thousandth of a man's income, a refusal to pay which would show that one was neither a " good subject " nor a good " member of society." Upon this Chauncy remarks, and with justice, although his language is a little extravagant, that he and those of his persuasion ought not to pay for that which their ancestors left England to escape — " the Episcopal yoke of bondage." [3] Nor does he allow to pass unnoticed another incautious admission of Chandler: that, " Should the government see fit hereafter to invest them (the proposed bishops) with some degree of civil power, worthy of their acceptance, which it is impossible to say they will not, yet it is inconceivable that any would thereby be injured." [4]

After seeking to meet Chandler's arguments point by point, Chauncy proceeds to treat of his main objections under five heads, as follows: (1) The government and discipline of the Church of England, under the proposed American episcopate, would not conduce to the best interests of the church itself, since the bishops would not have any power over the laity; or to the interests of the bishops who should be sent, since their authority in a matter most essential would be thus restricted. (2) It would be inconsistent to have colonial bishops without ecclesiastical courts, if these institutions were to be continued

[1] *Appeal Answered*, 135–136.

[2] He is continually, either explicitly or implicitly, questioning Chandler's good faith. For example, he says that the plan of an episcopate as proposed by him, being without royal consent, can have no validity (*Ibid.* 137–140).

[3] *Ibid.* 192–194.

[4] *Ibid.* 195–196. What Chandler says on this head, together with Chauncy's answer, is quoted by Foote, *Annals of King's Chapel*, ii. 276–277.

in the mother church. (3) The project is on its face doomed to failure, for there are no such bishops known to the Church of England as Chandler describes; his proposed bishop is to have no authority at all as an officer of state, whereas a Church of England bishop could not exist divorced from the state;[1] hence any such plan could not but be rejected by the king and Parliament. (4) The plan would meet with no support from the Independents, who, since they seek no establishment for themselves, would not feel justified in seeking it for others. (5) Since, according to his reasoning, the proposed episcopate would be of no practical value, even to the Church of England itself, the money required for the support of bishops might better be applied to missionary work.[2] How far these arguments are cogent must be left to each reader to determine for himself.

The rest of Chauncy's objections are professedly a reaffirmation and confirmation of those of Mayhew.[3] Summed up in a single phrase, they are what had been, was, and ever would be, the kernel of the whole opposing argument, namely, that bishops once settled would be apt to extend their powers. Chauncy, however, goes a bit farther than his predecessor in accusing the advocates for bishops of a wilful suppression of facts. His opinion is that "they have much more in design than they have been pleased to openly declare. . . . We are as fully persuaded," he adds, "as if they had openly said it, that they have in view nothing short of a COMPLETE CHURCH HIE-RARCHY, after the pattern of that at home, with like officers, in all their various degrees of dignity, with a like large revenue for their grand support, and with the allowance of no other privilege to dissenters but that of a bare toleration."[4] It has been shown that the first part of his statement had some basis

---

[1] "Did Bishops of the Church of England," he says, "no more depend on the STATE, and no more derive their authority from it, than our ministers do, the Episcopal Churches here might as well be supplied with Bishops as our's are with Pastors" (*Appeal Answered*, 151).

[2] *Ibid.* 141–157.

[3] After citing Mayhew at length, he states that he regards the objections advanced by him as reasonable (*Ibid.* 178).

[4] *Ibid.* 201–202.

in fact. The second part, although possibly an exaggeration, is interesting as a fairly typical expression of the fear prevailing not only in New England, but elsewhere,[1] and as an illustration of the guiding principle in the action of a large number of earnest and serious-thinking men.

Chandler's defence was published in the following year.[2] On the title-page he prints the following quotation from *A Letter to the Author of the Confessional:*[3] "There are some spirits in the world who, unless they are in actual Possession of Despotism themselves, are daily haunted with the Apprehension of being subject to it in others, and who seem to speak and act under the strange Persuasion that every Thing short of Persecution against what they dislike must terminate in the Persecution of themselves." These words sum up the conception which Chandler and those of his party had of the attitude of the Independent bodies toward forms of religion other than their own. Although, like all generalities, it is subject to some qualification, it is a fairly accurate, though somewhat harsh, representation of the actual state of things; for even yet the idea of toleration as such was only slowly beginning to make itself felt in the colonies and in Christendom.

While lamenting the virulent and unfair way in which his proposition has been received, and his arguments — which he intended to be serious — have been ridiculed in the public prints of Boston, New York, and Philadelphia, Chandler is still full of a naïve optimism, for, in spite of the opposition which his publication has called forth, he sees no evidence of any objection to the settlement of bishops, provided they be not invested with temporal powers, or, as Chauncy chose to put it, "under a state establishment."[4]

Among his numerous opponents he singles out Chauncy for his chief attention, and passes over as unworthy an answer two

---

[1] See, for example, a favorable review of the *Appeal Answered*, by "A Quaker," in the *London Chronicle*, June 14, 1768.

[2] *The Appeal Defended: or, The Proposed American Episcopate Vindicated*, etc. (New York, 1769).

[3] By Dr. Ridley and Thomas Secker, published at London in 1768.

[4] *Appeal Defended*, Introduction, 4, 9.

pamphlets written by "An Antiepiscopalian" and by "A Presbyter in Old England."[1]

In replying to Chauncy, he goes over the ground already covered in the *Appeal*. His opponents, he says, have more than once asserted that the taxation of the colonies and the proposal to send bishops to America are parts of one general scheme, the former menacing the political, the latter the religious liberties of the country; but he denies that there is any ground for this supposition. So far as the definite purpose of the English government came into the question, he was perfectly right, for there is no evidence whatever that the two things were connected in its thought, and he was equally successful in showing that his opponents were both uncharitable and unconvincing in their attempts to make light of the disadvantages under which the Episcopalians suffered in being forced to get on without bishops. Where he failed was in his efforts to show that the settlement desired would be, in its logical consequences, no menace to the religious and political independence of the country.

So much for the general trend of Chandler's argument; now let us consider a few of the specific questions which he handles. In answer to Chauncy's suggestion, that commissaries might be sufficient for purposes of church government, he points out that "Reason and Experience teach the contrary."[2] In seeking to

[1] Of these, the latter is the more important. The title is, *A Supplement to a Letter to a Friend, containing an Answer to the Plea of T. B. Chandler for American Bishops, wherein his Reasonings are shown to be Fallacious and his Claims Indefensible.* The argument of the "Presbyter" contains little more than a restatement of the opinions to be found in any of the better-known publications. The points on which he lays most stress are the following: that, if bishops are to exercise discipline over none but the laity, the need of them is very much diminished (p. 63); that the time for introducing them is inopportune; that, since the amount of money already in the hands of the Society for their settlement and maintenance (some £4700) is obviously inadequate, the burden of the expense would probably fall upon the colonists; that the bishops once in position would gradually usurp power. He sees a particularly dangerous tendency in Chandler's statement that "Episcopacy can never thrive in a Republican government, nor Republican principles in an Episcopal Church" (p. 78).

[2] *Appeal Defended*, 117.

show that bishops would be able to do what the commissaries had proved themselves unequal to do, he is forced to admit that there might be need of spiritual courts for the trial of the Episcopal clergy only.[1]   But these courts had already existed under the commissarial régime, and "reason and experience" had shown that they too were not practicable without some coercive power to back their decrees.   However, if that power had been added, even for necessity's sake, the episcopal form of government thus created would hardly have been that professedly advocated by Chandler.

Chandler next proceeds to consider the five objections urged by Chauncy;[2] and, considering the fact that the burden of proof lies with him, he holds his own in this part of the argument very well.[3]   The rest of his refutation is rather weak, or at least unsatisfactory.   He endeavors to meet his opponent's objections to what he had said about the possibility of taxation, and a future augmentation of episcopal powers, with the lame plea that he had considered these questions only as possible extreme suppositions for the sake of illustration.[4]   Nevertheless, they were, after all has been said, extremely unfortunate admissions ; and it would be hardly too much to assume that they had the effect of counteracting whatever favorable effect his book might otherwise have had on the hostile or the indifferent.   His challenge to his opponents to produce evidence that the motives of the advocates for bishops are not what they appear on the surface,[5] has a touch of insincerity, after what he has been shown to have said on this matter in his letter to Bishop Terrick. The same may be said of his assumption that the scheme would obtain the assistance of the government if desired ; for he must have known that certain scruples — the dissenting interest, combined with several other considerations — had always been strong enough to defeat any support from that quarter.

His conclusion may be summed up somewhat as follows : Since an American episcopate is greatly desired, the objections to it have been foreseen and regarded in drawing up the plan on which it is to be settled.   In accordance with this plan, the

---

[1] *Appeal Defended*, 118.
[2] See above, p. 174.
[3] *Appeal Defended*, 206–207.
[4] *Ibid.* 248–253.
[5] *Ibid.* 258–260.

proposed bishops are to be supported only by private dona-
tions, and to have no jurisdiction over any but their own clergy.
To save themselves from being outflanked by these concessions, the irreconcilable opponents to the plan have been
forced to bring up new objections, which may be classed under
two heads: first, that the episcopate in the modified form
advocated would not be desired by the Episcopalians themselves; and secondly, that such a system, harmless in the
beginning, would tend to grow oppressive. In regard to the
first point, he asserts that the publications of the Society for
Propagating the Gospel, as well as the vouchers of its leading
members, prove just the contrary. As to the second point, he
maintains that there is not only no intention, but also no probability, of such an exigency. As no valid objection stands in the
way, the Church of England demands the settlement of bishops
in the colonies as an indisputable right, grounded both on the
sacred claims of toleration and on the freedom due under the
English constitution.[1]

How much effect these arguments of Chandler had on his
opponents is shown by the wording of the title of Chauncy's
answer (1770), which announced itself to be *A Reply to Dr.
Chandler's "Appeal Defended": wherein his Mistakes are rectified, his false Arguing refuted, and the Objections against the
planned American Episcopate shown to remain in full Force notwithstanding all he has offered to render them invalid.*[2] Over a
third of the pamphlet is devoted to a discussion of the origin
and nature of the episcopal office. Since that matter does not

---

[1] *Appeal Defended*, 264–268.

[2] The quotation from Baxter's *Treatise of Episcopacy*, which he takes as
a motto for his title-page, is very amusing: "When such as our Diocesans
sprang up, the Church was presently broke into pieces, and by odious Contentions and Divisions became a Scandal and Scorn to Unbelievers. To read
but the Acts of Councils, and the History of the Church, and there find the
horrid Contentions of Prelates against each other; the Parties which they
made, their running up and down the World to Princes, and Rulers, and
Synods, to bear down one another; it will do as much to grieve and amaze
the Soul of a sober Christian, as almost any History in the world he can
peruse." It should be remarked that, on the score of courtesy, Chandler was
throughout the controversy a shining contrast to his opponents.

concern us here, we may proceed at once to examine what the author has to say in particular on the subject of the introduction of bishops into America.

As in his previous publication, he takes up the question of ordination, and remarks that this purely spiritual office can be satisfactorily performed by the two bishops already in America, the Roman Catholic bishop in the North and the Moravian bishop in the South.[1] Like all his predecessors and associates, Chauncy fails to do justice to the fair claims of his opponents in matters of purely spiritual concern: all that he says on this head is either trivial or unsatisfactory.

To proceed to another step in his argument; he says that the plans hitherto proposed for an American episcopate have been formulated by the clergy with no authority from their laity and no official sanction from the king of England;[2] hence any plan established by the "proper authority" would very probably differ from those of Secker, Butler, and others, whatever the pro-episcopal agitators may "intend or pretend." Moreover, the fact that, when Dr. Stiles made a formal application to the clerk of the New York convention for copies of its petitions, especially of those to the king, his request was denied, furnishes good ground for supposing that the arguments put forth in the public prints were not the same as those used in the petitions. Another indication of the dubiousness of the motives of those advocating the settlement of bishops he finds in the fact that the applications have come from the colonies in which the Church of England is weakest, namely, the seven colonies north of Virginia and Maryland. This shows that the main point aimed at is to episcopize the colonies.[3]

In a recapitulation of the arguments contained in his five specific points against the introduction of bishops, he says little that is new.[4] He does, however, succeed in presenting in clearer form the inconsistency of settling bishops on the plan advocated by Chandler, contending that such bishops as the latter proposes could not be sent consistently with the constitution of the Church of England. This consideration he regards

---

[1] *Reply to " Appeal Defended,"* 91–93.
[2] *Ibid.* 110–116.   [3] *Ibid.* 152–153.   [4] *Ibid.* 121–153.

as the chief obstacle to their introduction; for, were it not for the fact that they are by the nature of their office inextricably bound up with the state and its functions, they could without more ado be settled in American dioceses as simply as the independent pastors are settled over the parishes.

Chauncy devotes the remainder of his argument to showing, mainly from antecedent probability, the dangers inevitably consequent upon an Episcopal establishment. In support of his case, he cites the well-known example of the New York synod. The Presbyterians of New York had made several attempts to obtain a charter of incorporation for their body, and to that end had applied successively to Colonel Schuyler in 1721, to Governor Burnet in 1734, and to Lieutenant Governor Delancey in 1759; but, in spite of the fact that on August 20, 1724, Counsellor West had given it as his opinion that such a request could be legally granted, the cause had made no progress. In March, 1767, a fourth petition was hazarded, this time to the king. After being considered in the Privy Council, it was referred to the Board of Trade, before which the Bishop of London appeared twice and spoke against it. Owing probably to his efforts, the report made to the council was unfavorable, and in consequence the king rejected the petition.[1] From the evidence that we have it is hard to say whether the bishop's action was based on the legal ground alleged, namely, that it would have been a breach of the Coronation Oath for the king to grant the petition, or whether he proceeded on the principle that, as diocesan of the colonies and as a leading prelate of the Church of England, he must perforce oppose anything that would tend to advance the interests of any other form of worship than that which he represented. Whatever the truth of the matter may have been, Chauncy draws the inference that Bishop Terrick's action was dictated by his own intolerance and the pressure of the New York Episcopalians.[2] He argues that this instance goes to show what may be expected from bishops, if once they are settled in the colonies.

He adduces as collateral evidence the connection between the episcopal question and the recent course of political events, a

[1] *Reply to "Appeal Defended,"* Appendix, i.–vi.　　　[2] *Ibid.* ix.

point already touched upon in his previous pamphlet. "If Bishops," he quotes approvingly from Mayhew, "were speedily to be sent to America, it seems not wholly improbable from what we hear of the unusual tenor of some late parliamentary acts and bills, for raising money on the poor colonies *without their consent*, that provision might be made for the support of these Bishops, if not of all the church clergy also, in the same way."[1] This idea, like all the other attempts of Chauncy to join the two issues, was strenuously resisted by Chandler. Whether it was a shrewd device of the leaders among the Independent clergy to frustrate the plan by coupling it with one which the colonists would fight to the last ditch, or whether they sincerely believed the two matters to be really connected, is a question difficult to decide. It will be unnecessary to follow the argument of the *Reply to the "Appeal Defended"* any farther, for its central position is sufficiently clear, that there could be no colonial episcopate except upon the basis of a state establishment, and this would involve tendencies and consequences dangerous to the integrity of the civil and religious institutions of the colonists.

Chandler, in his *Appeal Farther Defended*, which appeared in answer to the *Reply* in 1771, probes the heart of the question at issue and seeks to grapple with this main point. Chauncy has conceded that those of his party do not wish to oppose the Episcopalians in the exercise of their religion, even under bishops, provided the latter be purely spiritual shepherds.[2] By this concession, Chandler maintains, his opponents have given up the point in dispute. On closer examination, however, a nonpartisan eye would discover that this concession was fully as hollow as that made by Mayhew at a previous stage of the controversy. Chandler's assumption cheerfully presupposes that he and his colleagues have explained away all that would tend

---

[1] *Reply to "Appeal Defended,"* 166.

[2] Chandler (*Appeal Farther Defended*, 10) quotes the passage in which Chauncy has best summed up this matter: "It is not SIMPLY the exercise of any of their religious principles that would give the least uneasiness, nor yet the exercise of them under as many PURELY SPIRITUAL Bishops as they could wish to have; but their having Bishops under a STATE-ESTABLISHMENT" (Chauncy, *Appeal Answered*, 189).

to indicate that the form of episcopate introduced would neither be under the Church of England establishment nor bring in its train the apprehended political effects. As a matter of fact, however, neither he nor any of his party had ever succeeded in proving the harmlessness of the design to the satisfaction of its critics; hence his victory was not so assured as he would have led his readers to think.

As in the *Appeal* and the *Appeal Defended*, he is, to be sure, full of assurances: the proposed bishops are to have " 'no Authority, but such as is derived altogether from the Church.' . . . The Government is not expected or desired to give them any Support or peculiar Protection; and consequently they are not to be on the Footing of a STATE ESTABLISHMENT."[1] But these were merely assurances, which the colonists, considering the dangerous times in which they were living, neither could nor would accept without some further guarantee. On one point in this connection, however, Chandler succeeded in confuting Chauncy, and in a negative way, at least, added strength to his own assurances: he printed in his book the petitions for American bishops sent, October 2, 1765, by the convention held at Perth Amboy, New Jersey, to the king and the Archbishop of Canterbury, and they proved to contain nothing new or secret.[2]

He devotes some space to a consideration and refutation of the suggestion that the candidates for orders in the Church of England can very well be consecrated by the bishops already in America. To this plan he enumerates five main objections: that the Episcopalians are neither Moravians nor Papists, and therefore would not like to have their spiritual offices performed by members of those bodies; that such a procedure would offend the temporal and spiritual authorities of the Church of England; that it would be schismatical according to the canons of the church;[3] that there are only two bishops in the colonies, whereas

---

[1] *Appeal Farther Defended,* 12.

[2] *Ibid.* 21–27.

[3] "We look upon Schism in the Church," says Chandler, "to have much of the same Nature with Rebellion in the State; and the Guilt of both is so flagrant in our Opinion, that we constantly pray in our Litany to be preserved

the Episcopalians prefer to follow the canonical custom of having three bishops for the imposition of hands;[1] that since the
home government would undoubtedly be unwilling to lend its
consent to the plan, the Roman Catholic bishop of Canada and
the Moravian bishop of Pennsylvania would very probably
refuse to do anything in the matter for fear of offending the
authority which tolerated them.   In this line of reasoning we
see Chandler at his best: his tone is moderate, and his arguments logical and convincing.   Surely, from the spiritual point
of view, the members of the Church of England in America
had the strongest of cases; and, had no other considerations
entered into the question, nothing but the most narrow bigotry
and the most unjustifiable intolerance could have induced any
one to resist their entreaties.

Chandler, however, overlooked these "other considerations."
In the teeth of the most contrary evidence he seeks to show
that the tendency toward a favorable consideration of the plan
is much more marked than formerly.   "There were many
Members of the Church," he says, "that were, upon the
whole, averse to an Episcopate in this country, imagining it
would either expose them to considerable Expence for its
Support, or put them to some other Inconveniences.[2]   But

from it — 'from all false Doctrine, Heresy, and *Schism*,' as well as 'from all
Sedition, privy Conspiracy, and *Rebellion*.' Were the British Colonies independent of their Parent-Kingdom, the Episcopalians in this Country would be
a Society independent of the national Church; and in that Case they might
seek for an Episcopate from any Part of the Globe, from which they could
expect most easily to obtain it.   But such an Independency they do not affect
— they wish not to see; they desire no more than the common Rights of
British *Subjects*, and the common Privileges of their Fellow-Christians; or, in
other Words, such a *Toleration* as the Government allows to the Dissenters
from its own religious Establishment " (*Appeal Farther Defended*, 113–114).
Although this passage plainly betrays the author's loyalist sympathies, it contains nothing open to disparaging criticism.

[1] This of course applies to consecration of bishops.   According to the
canon law only one bishop was needed to confer ordination.

[2] He says in another place that before the publication of the *Appeal* men
had had two objections to a native episcopate, namely, the payment of tithes
and the power of spiritual courts (*Appeal Farther Defended*, 235).   It has been
shown that certain assertions in Chandler's publication had tended rather to
confirm than to remove these apprehensions.

when they came to see that every Thing of this Kind had been carefully guarded against, and that from its Design and Tendency it would be mild and beneficial in its Operation, which appeared as soon as it was explained to them, their Aversion immediately ceased, and from that Time they have generally viewed it in the same Light with that wherein it is seen by the Clergy."[1] This statement, even as regarded the members of his own communion, was hardly in accordance with the facts of the case; for, as later events showed, a considerable body of Episcopalians in Virginia came out squarely against the scheme of superseding the authority of the Bishop of London by that of native bishops, and in some of the other colonies they showed hardly any enthusiasm, to say the least.[2]

In this connection Chandler points out a consideration or two of considerable interest; namely, that the Quakers of Pennsylvania and New Jersey show no aversion to the proposed American episcopate,[3] and furthermore that the Baptists stand on the side of the Episcopalians against the enemies of both, the Congregationalists and Presbyterians.[4] Among the evidences cited as proof of the latter assertion is the following extract from an author writing in favor of the Baptists: "The Fraternity," says this writer, alluding to that recently formed between the Presbyterians and Congregationalists, "last Year have sent Letters to Baptist Ministers in New England, requesting their Aid against the Church of England. But truly it is the Interest of the Baptists that the Church of England should multiply in Massachusetts and Connecticut, so far as to form

[1] *Appeal Farther Defended*, 144.

[2] See below, ch. x.

[3] *Appeal Farther Defended*, 145.

[4] A later passage by Chandler states facts hard to reconcile with the optimism of these utterances. Referring to the effect of the *Appeal*, he says: "What shortly after ensued on the Occasion, what inflammatory periodical, Papers, and Pamphlets from different Quarters, were issued in Answer to it, is well known. An Alarm was sounded throughout the Colonies, that a general Invasion of their religious Liberty was projected, — the Minds of the Populace were inflamed by Arts that were wicked and infamous, — the Church of England, the whole Order of Bishops, and the Clergy of our Convention were shamefully abused in the Common News-Papers" (*Ibid.* 234).

a Ballance of ecclesiastical Power there, as in other Colonies.
And as for *Bishops*, they are welcome there; their coming
thither is an Object *worthy of* PETITIONS; we cannot be worse
off; we may be better; *they* are Gentlemen at least, and have
some Generosity for vanquished Enemies.   But the New-England People (of a certain Denomination) are supercilious in
Power and mean in Conquest.   I will venture to say that all
the Bishops in Old England have not done the Baptists there
so much Despite for 80 Years past as the Presbyterians
have done *this Year* to the Baptists of New-England."[1]   Yet,
while it was a notorious fact that the Presbyterians and Congregationalists, particularly in New England, where they were in
power, had been strenuously unrelenting against those who
professed beliefs contrary to their own, and while this fact
might deprive them of some support in their efforts to combat
the introduction of bishops, this quotation is significant rather
as an indication of hatred to the Orthodox Church of New
England than as an evidence of friendship to the cause of an
American episcopate.   Moreover, although a New England
Baptist, in a fit of rebellion against measures of oppression
directed against him in that particular province, might, as a
means of securing an ally, have been induced to write such lines
as the above, it is doubtful how far the opinions which he
expressed concerning the Church of England were general.
Certainly Semple's *History of the Baptists*, which details the
rigors which the sect suffered under the establishment, has little
good to say about the ecclesiastical rule of the Episcopal Church.

The *Appeal Farther Defended* was the last contribution to
what may be specifically termed the "Chandler-Chauncy controversy."   Meantime, however, the episcopal question had
been reopened in England, leading to a discussion which, from
the fact that Chandler took part in it, may be considered in
this connection.   The occasion for this new outbreak was the
publication, in 1769, of a letter by Archbishop Secker in answer
to Walpole's letter of May 29, 1750.[2]   Although written Janu-

---

[1] *Appeal Farther Defended*, 145–146, citing *Pennsylvania Chronicle*,
November 26, 1770.

[2] See above, p. 119.

ary 9, 1750–51, its contents, in deference to an expressed wish of the late archbishop, had not been made public until after his death.[1] Secker's argument, having been composed so early in the discussion, will naturally strike one who has followed the controversy through its various stages as stale and unprofitable both in form and in matter. It is necessary, however, even at the risk of tediousness, to outline its main points, in order to appreciate the later publications attacking and defending it.

The writer's purpose is to consider whether the proposition to send two or three bishops to America, to perform the episcopal offices and to exercise such jurisdiction as has been formerly, or may be in future, exercised by the Bishop of London's commissaries, would be reasonable and practicable; and whether, as Walpole seems to apprehend, the power acquired by such bishops, once established, would, in the nature of things, be stretched to the extent of introducing exorbitant ecclesiastico-political innovations, thereby causing uneasiness both in England and in the colonies.[2]

Of the "reasonableness of the proposal abstractedly considered" Secker thinks there can be no doubt. Walpole himself, he says, admits that much, and there has been scarcely a bishop of the Church of England from the revolution to this day who has not desired such an establishment. Archbishop Tennison, for example, who was certainly no high churchman, left a provision in his will for the advancement of the cause. It may indeed be argued, he continued, that bishops are naturally partial to the plan; but to such objectors he points out that the Society for Propagating the Gospel, consisting, as it does, partly of inferior clergy and partly of laymen, can hardly be suspected of designing to advance episcopal authority for its own sake, and yet this body, almost from its incorporation, has been eager for the plan.[3] Any fair-minded man, he goes on, must see that for the necessary purposes of ordination, confirmation, and discipline,

---

[1] See the advertisement to the published letter.

[2] Secker, *Works*, vi. 492.

[3] *Ibid.* 496–497. But it has been seen (above, p. 101) that the Society, after its defeat in 1714, had practically ceased to agitate the question until Secker himself revived it by his sermon in 1740.

bishops are indispensable to the very existence of the Church of England in the colonies.[1]

Having shown that the demand for American bishops is both just and reasonable, Secker next faces the objection that such an establishment may be attended with a dangerous increase of the church's power in the colonies. He sees no likelihood or possibility of such an event. The commissaries have neither attempted nor been able to extend their authority beyond its original limits, and " Bishops will be still more narrowly watched by the Governors, by other Sects, by the Laity, and even the Clergy of their own Communion."   In other words, even if the bishops should seek to extend their authority, which is unlikely, checks exist adequate to defeat any such attempt.   As a matter of fact, however, there is nothing in the plan to excite any apprehension either at home or abroad.   There neither is nor ever has been any design to tax the colonists or burden the crown for the support of the bishops to be settled under it. Indeed, an earlier attempt to establish a bishopric in Virginia failed, for the very reason that the endowment was to be out of the customs.[2]   The present plan has nothing of the character of a state establishment ; it need not go to Parliament, since the law permits the ordination of suffragan bishops solely with the royal approbation.   The Bishop of London can send the suffragans thus created as his commissaries, but with power to ordain, confirm, and exercise ecclesiastical jurisdiction.[3]

---

[1] It had been argued that no petitions had been received from the laity or from the clergy in certain quarters, a fact which showed that practically all the former, and at least a portion of the latter, were very cool toward the scheme. But, according to Secker, the lack of petitions, far from indicating such a state of things, might be explained on quite other grounds ; namely, by the general neglect of mankind for spiritual concerns, by the fact that the clergy where the church was established enjoyed more liberty and power without the episcopal oversight, and by a disposition to leave the matter in the hands of the Bishop of London and the Society.

[2] Secker refers to the occasion when the Reverend Alexander Murray was to be sent, and cites as his authority some papers of Bishop Gibson. It has been seen (above, p. 90) that another equally possible reason was assigned for the failure of this plan.

[3] Compare with the plan of Bishop Compton in 1707 (above, pp. 97–98, and below, Appendix A, No. iii.).

Finally, not only is the demand for such an establishment reasonable, not only is it in its aims and motives independent of any political design, and therefore unlikely to be opposed by the majority of the colonists, but it is advisable as a matter of public policy, since the refusal of the request will hurt the government more in the eyes of the Church of England than the amount of favor which the policy will secure from the dissenters will benefit. The time at which these words were written must be borne in mind, for, as has been seen, later events prove Walpole to have been far more correct than Secker in his forecast concerning the attitude of public opinion on the question at issue.

Such is an outline of the main arguments of Secker's letter. The year after its publication Francis Blackburne, archdeacon of Cleveland, replied with *A Critical Commentary*. He begins by hazarding a conjecture that Walpole did not begin the discussion, since the ministers of state were not then anxious to offend the colonists. The cause of the trouble should, he thinks, be laid rather to the Bishop of London, who, as diocesan of the colonial members of the Church of England, would naturally seek by all means in his power to raise their condition.[1] But whoever was to blame for starting the agitation for an American episcopate, Blackburne thinks that all must lament the publication of Secker's letter at the present juncture, when the colonists ought not to be unnecessarily irritated.[2]

The *Critical Commentary* need not here be considered in detail. It is made up partly of a rebuttal of the arguments advanced in Secker's letter, partly of expressions of apprehension as to the probable outcome of an episcopal establishment, and partly of charges against the sincerity of its advocates. The writer's remarks under the last two heads are characteristic. He regards the fact that the bishops are to be appointed purely on the approval of the crown as far from quieting ; for such an arrangement would give the crown all the more chance to enlarge its powers, should it find them insufficient for its political purposes.[3] Moreover, he refuses to trust Secker's assurances as to the limitation of the authority of the bishops to be sent. For his own part, he regards the whole scheme as an outcome of the

[1] *Critical Commentary*, 6.   [2] *Ibid*. 8.   [3] *Ibid*. 28.

machinations of the Society for Propagating the Gospel, for it is that body which has instructed its missionaries to stir up the colonists to petition for bishops: Apthorp, Chandler, and the others were only instruments in its hands;[1] and indeed, so ardent and powerful an advocate as Bishop Sherlock, to whom the matter owes much of the attention which it has attracted in recent years, proceeded not so much on his own initiative as at the incitement of the Society.[2]

Blackburne pointed out, more clearly than any one else had done, the motives which influenced the dissenters in England to take the side of their colonial brethren. "They knew," he said, "the hardship of these legal disabilities under which they themselves lay at home. They had good reason to believe that the influence of the established Hierarchy contributed to continue this grievance." Their brethren in America were as yet free from the incubus of episcopacy, and their safety lay in remaining so. "If Bishops were let in among them, and particularly under the notion of presiding in *established* Episcopal Churches, there was the highest probability they would take their precedents of Government and Discipline from the Establishment in the Mother Country, and would probably never be at rest" till they had themselves secured an establishment based on an exclusive test. English dissenters, then, knowing that their brethren across the water were of their mind, had determined to coöperate with them.[3]

Chandler, who had some time ago said the last word in the disputation with Chauncy, now entered the lists against this new opponent of his cause. In 1774 he published a reply to Blackburne under the title of *A Free Examination of the Critical Commentary.* He begins by citing some extracts from recent sermons before the Society for Propagating the Gospel, as

---

[1] *Critical Commentary*, 65.

[2] He informs us that in May, 1749, Bishop Sherlock, while in conversation with Mr. Hooper, one of the council of Barbadoes, said, "It is not I that send Bishops to America, it is the Society for Propagating the Gospel in foreign Parts, who are the movers of this matter" (*Ibid.* note). One would like the authority for this statement.

[3] *Critical Commentary*, 82–83. Cf. Mellen Chamberlain, *John Adams*, 32, with note, citing Blackburne.

evidence of the purity of motive of responsible persons who desire an American episcopate.[1] In almost every annual sermon since the outbreak of the Mayhew controversy, the preacher before the Society had made some allusion to the episcopal question which was agitating the colonial mind. Their general line of reasoning is already familiar to us, but it may be well to give a word to each of the more important utterances. Dr. Terrick, Bishop of London, pointed out the need of an establishment for promoting "order and discipline," and rejected the imputation of an intention to infringe on the religious liberties of other denominations.[2] Dr. Ewer, Bishop of Llandoff, confined himself to a discussion of the need of Episcopal clergymen in America, the lack of whom with its attendant disadvantages he attributed to the want of bishops.[3] Dr. Green, Bishop of Lincoln, merely emphasized what others had laid stress on; namely, the injustice of that condition of things which made the Church of England the only church in America to which toleration for its complete system was not allowed.[4] Dr. Newton, Bishop of Bristol, pointed out that "the greatest Want of all is that of an American Bishop for the Purposes of Confirmation, Ordination, Visitation of the Clergy, and other ecclesiastical Offices, without the least Share of civil Power or Jurisdiction whatever." He too exclaimed at the injustice of "depriving," as he termed it, one-third of the ecclesiastical population of their just rights.[5] Dr. Keppel, Bishop of Exeter, desired "not to ingros Authority, or give a Check to Liberty of any Sort," but simply hoped "for equal Indulgence with others."[6] Dr. Lowth, Bishop of Oxford, advocated the appointment of "one or more resident Bishops" solely as a remedy for the needs of the church in the colonies.[7] Dr. Moss, Bishop of St. David's, went a bit farther than his predecessors in hazarding the statement that the government must have had some motives for

[1] *Free Examination*, Introduction, v.–xii.
[2] *Ibid.* v., citing the Society's *Abstract*, 1764, p. 34.
[3] *Ibid.* vi., citing *Abstract*, 1767, p. 22.
[4] *Ibid.* vii., citing *Abstract*, 1768, p. 22.
[5] *Ibid.* viii., citing *Abstract*, 1769, p. 26.
[6] *Ibid.* ix., citing *Abstract*, 1770, p. 11.
[7] *Ibid.* x., citing *Abstract*, 1771, p. 14.

" withholding this Indulgence [of an American Episcopate] " ; but whether these motives arose from negligence or from some other cause, he would not venture to say.[1] This attempt to demonstrate, from the professions of the leaders of the church, that political interests played no part in their endeavors to secure bishops for America is the most important part of Chandler's pamphlet. The rest of it goes over old ground.

The anti-episcopal writers for the *London Chronicle*, a newspaper concerning which more will be said later, attacked Secker's *Letter*, with the asperity with which they were accustomed to treat anything coming from the pens of the advocates or the defenders of the American episcopal scheme. One contributor says that the writing of the archbishop indicates an attempt of the church power to claim an alliance with the state, under the cover of seeming to work for the propagation of the gospel; and that such an alliance, under which English nonconformists have suffered in times past, fills the present generation with dread and foreboding.[2] Another contributor asserts that it has been proved to a demonstration by Hobart, Mayhew, and Chauncy, in their respective controversies with the Society, that the main purpose of the several leaders of that body, and especially of the late Archbishop Secker, has been and is, not so much to spread the gospel among the heathen, as to episcopize the colonists, to convert Presbyterians and Congregationalists, to " persuade Christians to become Christians," a proceeding totally inconsistent with the Society's charter and the expectations of the public, its contributors. It is all a farce, he maintains, to pretend that they want a bishop in America for the sake of the few souls of the Episcopal persuasion there, to convey to them "the means of sacramental grace," as the Bishop of Exeter expressed it in his recent sermon before the Society ; it is, rather, " to reduce the Sectaries, to extend the dominion of the Church, and to bring all to bow their knees to them, that the late primate and others have been so eager to carry their point." Otherwise, he says, "they might have been provided with a bishop, either from

---

[1] *Free Examination*, Introduction, xi., citing *Abstract*, 1772, p. 28.
[2] *London Chronicle*, March 22, 1770.

among themselves or one privately sent hence. But nothing but a State Bishop, with lordly titles, unknown in New Testament Code, will go down. And then they will boast, indeed, that the Church established in the Colonies, and of Consequence all the civil offices of the country belong to them alone, or to such as go through their turnpike."

These statements are not only unreasonable, but in one respect they are a palpable misrepresentation of facts. Any one not blind with partisan frenzy would have seen and admitted that it was impossible for Episcopalians, under the system to which they professed adherence, to choose bishops from their own midst. As to accepting a bishop privately sent from England, provided he were properly consecrated, no churchman on either side of the water had advanced any objection; on the contrary, more than one advocate for the American episcopate had suggested such an arrangement. This, indeed, was the gist of the project for bishops, more than once alluded to in these pages; and the majority of the opponents of the plan, fearing the consequences which the step would involve, had objected to even this. Such apprehensions may or may not have been well grounded; but certainly it was the opponents, and not the favorers, of bishops who had contended against a trial of the experiment.

The same correspondent of the *Chronicle* alludes also to the old Laudian project, and sarcastically laments that the prelate who had the chief hand in driving the ancestors of the colonists into the deserts of America could not have lived to witness the present efforts of his followers in continuation of his scheme, which was interrupted by the outbreak in Scotland. The archbishop's plan, he thinks, had it not "been strangled in its first conception," might have altered the whole course of English colonial history.[1]

[1] "I apprehend," he says, "that if Laud had not had other work cut out for him, in consequence of pushing his beloved prelacy too vehemently upon the Scotch, but had pursued his plan in New England, he would soon have unpeopled that infant colony, and we should now have heard no disturbance from that quarter, which some people might have been pleased with. Though I own myself, I think it for our honour, that our fellow-citizens on the other side of the Atlantic make such a noble stand for their civil and religious liber-

Such endeavors as Archbishop Secker's, writes another, "administer fresh fuel to a flame too ready to break out, and too alarming not to give every well-wisher of his country very serious thoughts." The "passion and vehemence" with which the project has been espoused and advocated by many of the Church of England missionaries is, he says, "one great ingredient in the jealousy entertained by the Colonists for some time of the designs of the Mother Country." For this reason he regards it as particularly unfortunate that the matter should be stirred up again, when councils of peace and reconciliation between the mother country and her American children have become so necessary and desirable.[1]

Such was the controversy occasioned by the publication of Secker's letter. It was but a ramification, or perhaps one might say an echo, of those stirring discussions which had gone before. From this time the near approach of the Revolution, bringing with it questions of more immediate and pressing interest, crowded the matter of the introduction of bishops into the background; and yet, during a certain period in the struggle, the ecclesiastical question was as hotly agitated as any other then current. To appreciate the extent to which public opinion was stirred up over the episcopal issue, it will be necessary to turn now to a consideration of the virulent newspaper battle which raged during the years 1768–1769.

ties, and New England may contribute to save Old England. . . . Our churchmen have not taken warning by Laud's fate," he continues, ". . . for these last ten years they have pursued their episcopizing plan more vehemently than ever, and have also joined in the cry against the Americans if they have not taken the lead in it, and blacken'd and abus'd them in all their publications, and have perhaps contributed not a little to the virulence that some men show against them. But, avert it, Heaven! that Heylyn's military forces should be adopted or continued to carry Episcopacy, or any other measure in our colonies. AMYNTOR AMERICANUS" (Letter iii. to the *London Chronicle*, July 6, 1770).

[1] "Phormio," in the *London Chronicle*, September 8, 1770.

CHAPTER VIII.

THE NEWSPAPER CONTROVERSY,[1] 1768–1769.

DISCUSSION on the subject of introducing American bishops first became general in the newspapers in 1768, and reached its height during the course of this and the following year. It was ushered in by two series of articles: one in the *New York Gazette*, under the signature of "The American Whig"; the other in the *Pennsylvania Journal*, under the signature of "The Centinel" (or "Sentinel"). Though the several numbers of each series were evidently written by different hands, the chief contributors under these respective names seem to have been William Livingston and Francis Alison. The latter, vice-provost of the College of Philadelphia, was assisted by some of his Presbyterian brethren, particularly John Dickinson, the celebrated author of *The Farmer's Letters*.[1] The ostensible purpose of these earlier articles was to answer Chandler's *Appeal to the*

[1] Though various single sets of newspapers have been used, particularly a complete file of the *London Chronicle*, the main source has been a contemporaneous reprint entitled *A Collection of Tracts from the late Newspapers, &c., containing particularly The American Whig, A Whip for the American Whig, with some other Pieces, on the Subject of the Residence of Protestant Bishops in the American Colonies, and in Answer to the Writers who opposed it, &c.* (2 vols., New York, 1768–1769; "printed by John Holt, at the Exchange"). This book is now extremely rare. The articles by the "American Whig" and the "Kick for the Whipper" originally appeared in Parker's *New-York Gazette*, those by the "Whip for the American Whig" in Gaine's *New York Gazette*, those by the "Centinel" and "Anti-Centinel" in the *Pennsylvania Journal*, those by the "Anatomist" in the *Pennsylvania Gazette* (founded by Benjamin Franklin). Other articles on the subject appeared in the *New York Journal*, the *Pennsylvania Chronicle*, the *Boston Gazette*, and the *Connecticut Journal*, the latter published in New Haven. Throughout the chapter the extracts, whether taken from the *Collection* or not, are ascribed to the newspapers in which they first appeared.

[1] Protestant Episcopal Historical Society, *Collections*, i. 153 ff. Compare a letter from Chandler to the secretary of the Society, June 24, 1768, printed in S. A. Clark, *History of St. John's Church*, 135–138.

Public, though it has been conjectured that the disappointment occasioned by the failure of the New York Presbyterians in 1767 to obtain their charter of incorporation, a defeat which they attributed to the Bishop of London, may have had some influence in the matter.[1] The "American Whig" was answered by "Timothy Tickle" in "A Whip for the American Whig," who was in turn called to account by "Sir Isaac Foot" in "A Kick for the Whipper." The chief opponent of the "Centinel" was Dr. William Smith, provost of the College of Philadelphia, who wrote a series of essays under the pseudonym of "The Anatomist."

The "American Whig" made his first bow to the public March 14, 1768. He announced the appearance of Chandler's first book, and after a satirical characterization of its contents concluded as follows: "Considering the encroachments that have lately been made on our civil liberties, and that we can scarcely obtain redress against one injurious project but another is forming against us — considering the poverty and distress of the colonies by the restrictions on our trade, and how peculiarly necessary it is, in these times of common calamity, to be united amongst ourselves, one could scarcely have imagined that the most ambitious ecclesiastic should be so indifferent about the true interest of his native country as to sow, at this critical juncture, the seeds of universal discord; and besides the deprivation of our civil liberties, lend his helping hand to involve us in ecclesiastical bondage into the bargain. Is this a time to think of episcopal palaces, of pontifical revenues, of spiritual courts, and all the pomp, grandeur, luxury, and regalia of an American Lambeth? 'Tis true the pamphlet is specious, and appears to ask nothing but what is highly reasonable; and could any man, above the capacity of an Ideot, really persuade himself, the *Doctor* and the *Convention* would content themselves with a Bishop, so limited and curtailed as he is pleased to represent his future Lordship; it were manifest injustice to deny them what in their opinion their eternal salvation so greatly depends upon. But it is not the *primitive Christian* Bishop

---

[1] Protestant Episcopal Historical Society, *Collections,* i. 153. Cf. above, p. 181.

they want. It is the *modern, splendid, opulent, court favoured, law-dignified, superb, magnificent, powerful* prelate, on which their hearts are so intent. And that such a Bishop would be one of the worst commodities that can possibly be imported into a new country, and must inevitably prove absolute desolation and ruin to this, I shall abundantly evince in the course of these speculations."[1]

This utterance marks a new development in the discussion. Hitherto, though the apprehension of an ecclesiastico-political tyranny had been the essential underlying cause of the opposition to bishops, particularly in New England, the issue had been obscured by a network of theological polemics. During the period from Hobart to Chauncy, however, the political element was steadily pushing its way to the front, and now for the first time it presented itself squarely and unequivocally as the chief topic of consideration. In spite of the efforts of the Episcopalians, the Independents had at last succeeded in shifting the basis of the argument.

Not only had the controversy undergone a change of character; it had also become a matter of more general interest. The earlier discussions had been confined almost solely to pamphlets, and hence, it is safe to say, had claimed the attention of not more than a very narrow circle of readers. With the entrance of the newspapers into the lists, however, the public eye was arrested. For the first time people began to discuss the question in their homes, in the coffee-houses, on the street corners. Once a subject of purely spiritual concern, it now assumed a prominent place among the burning questions of the hour, to influence them or to be influenced by them, as the case might be.

Some four numbers of the " American Whig" series had already appeared when " Timothy Tickle " began to wield his " Whip for the American Whig." His appearance on the scene gave the "Whig " occasion to reiterate, this time in language more stirring than before, his warning cry against the danger which menaced the country. " You are yet to be chastised *only* with *whips*," he says, *à propos* of the name chosen by his

---

[1] "American Whig," No. i., Parker's *New York Gazette*, March 14, 1768.

antagonist; "but depend upon it, when the *apostolical monarchs*
are come over, and well established in their American dominions,
you, and such as you, will be chastised with *scorpions*. But this
is not all: the *bellum episcopale* will doubtless be declared with
every circumstance of awful pomp; and this extensive continent may soon be alarmed with the thund'ring signal, *the
sword of the Lord, and of the Bishop.* Then, O dreadful!
The torrent of episcopal vengeance! Then all who will not
be so senseless as to adore the *mitre* and *surplice*, and dedicate
both their consciences and their purses to his *episcopal Majesty*,
may lay their account with — with what? with something I
will not yet particularly name, but what one may easily discover,
by turning over a Church history or two. This may be the fate
of many, unless indulgent heaven interpose, by not suffering the
right reverend and holy tyrants to plunge their spiritual swords
in the souls of their fellow creatures; or, if this is permitted, by
determining the secular powers, not to suffer their *anathemas* to
be executed to the utmost limits of their severity. I know what
I am saying, Americans shall feel the truth of what I have now
surmised, at least in part, if they do not now bestir themselves,
and unite as one man to oppose the erection of spiritual
monarchies, with all the heroism they would display in opposing a formidable array of *dons* and *monsieurs.*"[1] Here is

[1] "Remarks on the title of 'A Whip for the American Whig,'" Parker's
New York Gazette, April 4, 1768. Hawks, who quotes the extract and gives
the above reference (see Protestant Episcopal Historical Society, *Collections,*
i. 144, note 1), has taken it, not from the *Gazette*, but from a garbled version
in Inglis's *Vindication*, Introduction, vi. In the *Gazette* for April 18 the
"Whig" gives another sample of his eloquence in the same strain: "Let my
lords the bishops," he says, "be once landed and fortified in their palaces,
guarded by their dependents, and supported by their courts, and instead of this
coaxing and trimming we shall soon hear the thunder of excommunication
uttered with all the confidence and pride of security. The soft bleatings of
the lamb will be changed into the terrible howling of the wolf; and every
poor parson whose head never felt the weight of a bishop's hand will soon
know the power of his pastoral staff, and the arm of the magistrate into the
bargain. . . . Without the knowledge of mankind it is impossible to govern
them well. This necessary accomplishment seldom falls to the lot of specu-
lative mortals immured in a study. Hence their conceit, contradiction, and
obstinacy. Give the reins to one of these book-worms, and he will attempt

another of his tocsins : " A bishop and his officers, independent of the people!" he cries; "I tremble at the thought of such a powerful spy, in a country just forming a state of soundness and stability. Rouse then, Americans! You have as much to fear from such a minister of the Church as you had lately from a minister of state; and whether this project is not a device of the latter, by dividing us to favour his designs, tho' he is now in disgrace, is submitted to your wisdom, to discern and prevent." [1]

Strange as it may seem, such utterances as these were not the aberrations of a solitary disordered fancy. In one form or another they were made again and again, and they were considered, discussed, and repeated seriously, if not soberly, by earnest and patriotic men. We know now that this conjunction of ecclesiastical and political motives in the English colonial policy was a pure figment of the imagination. But, though it is certain that there was no basis in fact for the suspicion that the English state authorities as such were in any way concerned in the episcopal project, it is equally certain that their complicity was suspected by a large proportion of the American public; and it is a historical fact that, however unfounded this mistrust may have been, it had no small influence in alienating the colonists from the mother country at this critical juncture.

If any doubt the importance which the ecclesiastical side of the question had assumed in contemporary politics, let them examine the motives which led the " American Whig " to undertake his task. His aim, as he informs his readers, is to advocate " the general liberties " of his fellow-subjects in North America. To this end he has chosen the particular subject of the American episcopate and a consideration of Dr. Chandler's *Appeal to the Public* in favor of it, since he esteems the question to be one of greater importance in its consequences to his native country " than the imposition of any customs, or commercial restrictions,

to drive the chariot of the sun: let him be an ecclesiastic besides, and impelled by the two irresistible momentums of the *glory of God and the salvation of souls*, and how can he refrain from adopting the Popish comment upon the text, *compel them to come in !* "

[1] " American Whig," No. v., Parker's *New York Gazette*, April 11, 1768.

which affect not the right of conscience."[1]   It is possible that the intention of many, perhaps of the author of these words, was precisely the opposite of that here stated; it may be that, actuated primarily by an uncompromising hostility to the introduction of bishops, they artfully coupled the episcopal question with the political in order to secure its certain defeat.   The question is hard to answer.   However one looks at the matter, whether he gives the priority to the one or the other impulse, the main conclusion must remain the same, — that the ecclesiastical element was playing a large part in contemporary politics.

Dr. Chandler had asserted that there was little opposition to the project among the people at large.   This statement was strenuously contradicted by the " American Whig."   He admits that, before the public was informed of the seven famous petitions and of the united attempts of the clergy to introduce bishops into the country, the Doctor had not heard of, or perhaps foreseen, "any clamor on this account"; but now, after these events and since the publication of the *Appeal*, he appeals to him whether "a very general uneasiness is not visible among the people," and "a general popular opposition expressed against his episcopal project, among all ranks of men, as they become daily more diffusively acquainted with the reality of the design."   He is sure that the Doctor will find himself grossly mistaken in his estimate of the tame acquiescence of the inhabitants, and moreover, "that if the zealous opponents of his American episcopate merit the genteel appellation of ' noisy hot-heads and pragmatical enthusiasts,' he will hear of not a few such among the lay members of his own communion."   Not only are the laity of the Church of England in Virginia[2] "warmly and almost universally opposed to it," he says, but there is an extreme likelihood that a majority of the American Episcopalians throughout the colonies are equally hostile.   "Should any British ministry therefore be found so weak, or so corrupt, as to betray the true interest, and disregard the tranquility of the provinces by the establishment of spiritual lordships," concludes the "Whig," "for my part I should conceive no scene more

---

[1] " American Whig," No. x., *Ibid.* May 16, 1768.
[2] For Virginia, see below, ch. x.

likely to open than such a one as we have recently seen; I mean the conduct of the populace with respect to the officers appointed under the late unpopular statute.[1] Nor would I be answerable for the safety of the ablest prelate that ever wore a mitre, was he to arrive in this country, under the character of a *Protestant American Bishop*."[2] It must be borne in mind that these are the utterances of a bitter partisan; but, in spite of their extravagance of expression, they must not be relegated to the realm of ungrounded supposition and surmise. What is said about the probable attitude of the majority of the Church of England laity was no doubt true, assuredly so in the case of Virginia. The most interesting point about the passage, however, is the threat conveyed in the concluding sentences.

Meanwhile, as has been said, the "Whip for the American Whig" had entered the fray. This author did not confine himself to the "Whig," but included the "Centinel" also in his chastisement. He begins to write, he announces, because " it is high time for the members of the Church of England, whose lenity has been much and often abused by them, to vindicate themselves from the false aspersions of these enemies to peace, and administer some wholesome discipline to the author, or authors of the *American Whig* — which paper is to be the future vehicle of their malice." The following is a good sample of the "Whip's" method of criticism: " No. I. [of the " American Whig "] is," he says, " stuffed with low, spurious witticisms, misrepresentations, scurrility, buffoonery, falshood, abuse, and slander. But to pass by all these, the author deserves flagellation for his blunders with which this piece is plentifully begrimed. . . . It is more than probable," he continues, "that the same motives set some Philadelphia engineers to work, in writing a paper called the *Centinel*. . . . No. I. . . . has somewhat more of the appearance of reasoning than the *Whig;* but breaths the same rancorous, insolent spirit; and plentifully abounds in misrepresentations, impertinence, nonsense, &c. &c."[3]

[1] The Stamp Act.

[2] " American Whig," No. x., Parker's *New York Gazette*, May 16, 1768.

[3] "Whip for the American Whig," No. i., Gaine's *New York Gazette*, April 4, 1768.

Thus began the duel of words between the two chief opponents, the "American Whig" and the "Whip for the American Whig." None of the arguments advanced on either side contain much that is new ; indeed, the whole newspaper discussion is in no way striking for the cogency or the logic of its reasoning. Its chief interest and value consists in the picture which it gives of contemporaneous methods of discussion, and the light which it flashes upon the popular attitude toward the episcopal question.

The most logical specimen of argumentation — in fact, one of the few contributions which can be dignified by the name of argument at all — is an article which appeared under the title "A Short Way to End Strife now it is Meddled with." The author presents his case under the form of ten propositions, as follows : —

" 1. That the convention[1] desire an *American Bishop*, is certain.

" 2. That they declare, that they only want a *primitive Bishop*, is certain.

" 3. That they *really mean* what they declare, is uncertain.

"4. That a *modern English Bishop* would be dangerous to the religious rights and privileges of all the Non-Episcopalians in America, is certain.

" 5. That they ought, therefore, in justice to themselves and their posterity, and according to the rules of common prudence, to be alarmed about their religious liberty, and oppose the project of introducing a Bishop into America ; till they have sufficient security that he will be only a *primitive Bishop*, is certain.

"6. That the Tory scribblers, for representing them as disloyal subjects, for taking such alarm, and as a faction against religion, the church, and the clergy, are extremely abusive, and rather exasperate than allay the ferment, is certain.

" 7. That the convention, as honest men, ought to give such security before they can expect our acquiescence in their project, is certain.

" 8. That they have not hitherto done it, is certain.

---

[1] "The Convention of the Clergy of New York and New Jersey." See above, pp. 164–165, and below, pp. 215–216.

" 9. That until it is done, the opposition will proceed; and may be attended with very disagreeable consequences, is highly probable.

" 10. That when it is done, the controversy ought to cease, is certain." [1]

This stands out from the midst of the confused and abusive utterances of the period as a coherent and rational presentation of the question at issue. Nevertheless, it is plain that it offered no solution of the difficulty; for the fears of those opposed to the episcopal project, real as they might have seemed to their possessors, were vague and indefinite; hence no conceivable guarantee which the episcopal party could have given them would have been regarded as satisfactory.

It will be hardly worth while to examine the effusions of those who ranged themselves on the side of the "Whig" and the "Whip" respectively, for they present practically no new arguments, and are distinguished from their predecessors only in being more trivial and abusive in their remarks. The "Whip" characterized "Sir Isaac Foot," who had taken it upon himself to administer sundry "kicks" to his opponent, as "that lowest and most despicable of all low and despicable scribblers." [2] But no one of the participants in this war of words was in a position to criticise the others fairly: foulness, scurrility, and persiflage dominated the utterances of each and all.

Meanwhile, the controversy was raging with equal violence in another quarter. A few days after the "Whig" opened the subject in the *New York Gazette*, the " Centinel" published his first piece in a Philadelphia newspaper. His professed purpose was to put several questions so that the people might be better able to judge " whether the apprehensions on account of our civil Liberties, which this avowed application has raised in the minds of many people, be well or ill founded." The "Centinel" shows himself more frankly uncompromising than any of his predecessors, declaring that he and those of his way of thinking will under no considerations listen to the plan for bishops, be the arguments and assurances what they may. · Let the

---

[1] Parker's *New York Gazette*, May 23, 1768.
[2] Gaine's *New York Gazette*, August 22, 1768.

Doctor[1] flatter as much as he pleases," he says, "if ever the attempt be made, he will find that the prejudices and objections of most of our Colonies are too deeply rooted and too well founded for them ever to submit quietly to an American Episcopate, established over them, even by act of Parliament; this would be to destroy their charters, laws, and their very constitutions; and it will be well if the Doctor and his associates are not considered as abettors of Mr. Greenville and those Enemies of America who are exerting their utmost endeavours to strip us of our most sacred, invaluable, and inherent Rights; to reduce us to the state of slaves; and to tax us by laws, to which we never have assented, nor can assent."[2]

The whole argument of the "Centinel" is, to an even greater degree than that of the "Whig," based upon an assumption of the close connection between the two questions, the religious and the political. From the general principles of liberty, he maintains, Parliament ought not to interfere in the civil freedom of the colonies, and any application to that "august body," not only to make laws for them but also to establish among them any form of church discipline, deserves to be treated as an attack upon their civil liberties.[3] His aim, he professes again and again, is not to combat any religious denomination or to oppugn the theological opinions of any man or set of men, but to defend the liberties of his country. The point in dispute, as he views it, is not concerning a bishop or concerning episcopal discipline as such, but as to the manner of introducing the bishop and establishing the discipline in America; and he hopes that "the friends and lovers of America" will consider themselves no further concerned in the controversy than as it relates to civil liberty.[4] Though some of the distinctions which he formulates are a bit too fine to be appreciated, the main trend of his argument shows clearly enough that the theological aspect of the question had become thoroughly absorbed in the political.

[1] Dr. Chandler.

[2] "Centinel," No. i., *Pennsylvania Journal*, March 24, 1768.

[3] "Centinel," No. vii., *Ibid.* May 5, 1768.

[4] "Centinel," No. viii., *Ibid.* May 12, 1768.

The "Centinel" furthermore sees not only a present but a historical connection between religion and politics in the relations between the colonies and the mother country. His language is striking : " Every attempt upon American liberty," he says, " has always been accompanied with endeavours to settle bishops among us. Thus in the reign of Charles I., when Laud attempted to subjugate the colonies, then in their infancy, he was not content with contriving to cramp their trade by foolish proclamations ; [1] but to complete their mortification and effect their ruin was upon the point of sending them a bishop,[2] with a military force to back his authority. The same attempt was revived in the latter end of Queen Anne's reign ; and had not God in his Providence interposed, and blasted the designs of the enemies of Britain, the same year might have been remarkable for the downfall of protestantism, the introduction of the Pretender, and the revival of Popery in England, and for the establishment of bishops in America. The unsettled state of the nation after the accession of George I. gave the enemies of that prince and of their country some faint hopes of accomplishing their design ; and, therefore, in the year 1714, while the spirit of rebellion was kindling into a flame, and the friends of Popery and the Pretender were forming their party and preparing to overturn the government and the religion of their country, the same restless spirits, who in the last reign had laboured to get bishops established in America, ' renewed their attempt and made one vigorous effort to accomplish ' what they called their ' grand affair.' But (thanks to the great overruler of events) the designs of both ' proved abortive.' The rebellion was quashed, and the scheme of an American Episcopate dropt of course: some persons, however, still continued to keep sight of the great object; and as they are always watching for seasonable opportunities of exerting themselves to obtain it, we find it resumed with great warmth not long before the rebellion in 1745." [3]

In the course of all the episcopal controversies, this is the first

[1] He cites as authority Rushworth, *Historical Collections*, ii. 718.
[2] He cites Heylyn, *Cyprianus Anglicus*, 369.
[3] " Centinel," No. xvi., *Pennsylvania Journal*, July 7, 1768.

instance that I have found of an attempt to trace closely and exhaustively a connection of this sort.[1]   So far as the case of Laud is concerned, the connection certainly holds, for not only is it attested by contemporaries,[2] but it is, indeed, self-evident. In the other instances the connection is more open to question, though two indications give some color to the "Centinel's" assumption.   The first is the fact that John Talbot, one of the most enthusiastic advocates of an American episcopate during the Queen Anne period, was a notorious Jacobite, and was himself supposed to have received consecration from the hands of the non-juring bishops.[3]   The second is a passage in Horatio Walpole's letter to Sherlock,[4] in which he says that in his opinion one of the chief objections to the plan is that the English people look upon any attempt to extend the episcopate as a Tory scheme.   It should be noted, however, that the cases in the eighteenth century were not parallel with those in Laud's time; for Laud's efforts were sanctioned by the government, while those of the later period were put forth by a faction that was unsupported by the authority of the state.

[1] A fitting continuation of this historical survey is to be found in one of the later numbers of the "American Whig."   The writer says: "Scarce had we concluded our exultation on the repeal of the Stamp Act before we heard of the execrable scheme for enslaving the whole continent under the dominion of spiritual courts.   The Bishop of Llandaff assures us, that the introduction of Prelates into this country was the main design of erecting the society for propagating the gospel in the reign of King William.   Ever since that period they have had their eye upon us; and now when the conquest of Canada bids fair for such an increase of wealth, as to enable us to support the hierarchy, every exertion is made on both sides of the water to accomplish the project. Bishops preach it up, legacies are given for it.   Our own clergy petition the King, the Universities, and others in its favor.   Private letters are written to solicit the men in power.   Pamphlets and papers are published to wheedle and deceive the Americans; and the late Archbishop of Canterbury himself undertook to defend the scheme, and in his answer to Dr. Mayhew, who gave the first alarm, boldly presumes without the royal leave to intimate that if any colony will signify the request for a Bishop, a bishop will be sent" ("American Whig," No. xlvi., Parker's *New York Gazette,* January 23, 1769).

[2] See above, p. 21, note 2.

[3] Governor Hunter called him a "sower Jacobite."   For Hunter, see above, p. 92.

[4] See above, p. 118 ff.; also below, Appendix A, No. xi.

The "Centinel's" arguments were answered by the "Anato-mist" in a series of letters published in the *Philadelphia Gazette.* This writer considers the various charges made by his opponent, both general and particular, that the Church of England is an enemy to the liberties of America, that the Episcopal clergy in the colonies are endeavoring in conjunction with Grenville to enslave their fellow-countrymen, that applications for American bishops have ever been preludes to attacks upon American lib-erty, that the attempts to introduce the Pretender, to revive popery, and to establish a colonial episcopate are parts of one great movement, and he denies them all.[1] He is particularly strenuous in disclaiming any connection between the Stamp Act and the attempt to introduce bishops.[2] Episcopalians will, he says, both from interest and duty join the other denominations

[1] "Anatomist," No. i., *Pennsylvania Gazette,* September 8, 1768.

[2] The following letter to Bishop Terrick, written by Dr. Smith in conjunc-tion with the clergy of Christ Church, Philadelphia, June 30, 1775, after mat-ters had reached a crisis, testifies to his sincerity on this point: "All that we can do," say the memorialists, "is to pray for such a settlement and to pursue those principles of moderation and reason which your Lordship has always recommended to us. We have neither interest nor consequence sufficient to take any great lead in the affairs of this great country. The people will feel and judge for themselves in matters affecting their own civil happiness, and were we capable of any attempt which might have the appearance of drawing them to what they think would be a slavish resignation of their rights, it would be destructive to ourselves as well as to the Church of which we are ministers. But it is but justice to our superiors, and to your Lordship in par-ticular, to declare that such conduct has never been required of us. Indeed, could it possibly be required, we are not backward to say that our consciences would not permit us to injure the rights of the country. We are to leave our families in it, and cannot but consider its inhabitants entitled, as well as their brethren in England, to the right of granting their own money; and that every attempt to deprive them of this right will either be found abortive in the end or attended with evils which would infinitely outweigh all the benefits to be obtained by it. Such being our persuasion, we must again declare it to be our constant prayer, in which we are sure that your Lordship joins, that the hearts of good and benevolent men in both countries may be directed towards a plan of reconciliation worthy of being offered by a great nation that have long been the patrons of freedom throughout the world, and not unworthy of being accepted by a people sprung from them and by birth claiming a partici-pation in their rights" (quoted by Stillé, *Historical Relations of Christ Church,* 23–24).

in the defence of their country and their liberties ;[1] but in nothing short of this can they, after the treatment which they have received at the hands of the various independent sects, properly have anything in common with them.[2] The blame for this unhappy state of affairs he lays at the door of his opponents. Dr. Chandler, he asserts, far from being the aggressor, is only a defendant in a dispute which was commenced by the antagonists of the church in New England as early as 1734, from which time their attacks may, he declares, be traced down in unbroken sequence to the date of the Doctor's pamphlet.[3]

The "Anatomist" denies that the settling of bishops in America will by common law necessarily involve the establishment of diocesan episcopacy, ecclesiastical courts, and the whole Church of England system. He farther denies that certain of the statutes already made will tend to produce such an establishment, or that some act of Parliament may be passed or some judge intimidated "to wrest both common and statute law in favor of this establishment."[4] Another writer who contributed to the " Anatomist " series under the name of " Horatio," not content with mere refutation, carried the war into the enemies' own country, and met their charges by counter charges. " To obtain an exclusive dominion," he says, " founded on true Oliverian principles, and with it a power of tyrannizing over the consciences and religious sentiments of all who should presume to differ from

---

[1] Compare the following statement from another member of the same communion : " All the members of the Church, to a man, are far from desiring . . . they are extremely averse to a Bishop vested with Temporal Powers, and those appendages before mentioned. They are convinced that such a measure would injure the Church . . . besides their being as fast Friends to every species of Liberty, religious or civil, as any Dissenter that exists " (" Whip for the American Whig," No. xxxi., Gaine's *New York Gazette,* November 9, 1768).

[2] His exact words are: " In defence of their country and their *liberties,* whenever they shall be in danger, it will undoubtedly be the interest as well as the duty of all denominations among us to unite ; but in nothing less than this have Presbyterians any right to expect the attachment of *Churchmen,* whom they have so cruelly and ungratefully treated " (" Anatomist," No. i., note, *Pennsylvania Gazette,* September 8, 1768).

[3] *Ibid.*

[4] " Anatomist," No. xii., *Pennsylvania Gazette,* November 24, 1768.

them, has, ever since the days of KNOX, been the constant aim of those people.[1] The *Church of England*," he continues, " ever friendly to our present glorious constitution, and to the religious rights of every protestant denomination, hath constantly opposed them in these pursuits ; and for this reason they hate the *Church of England* and 'have so ill an opinion of her'— They look upon her as the grand obstacle in their way, which if they could once remove, their wished for superiority over the rest of their fellow-subjects might, they think, be easily effected. Is it not then equally the duty, and the interest too, of every religious society in the new world, as well as of the *Church of England*, to make head against this aspiring party, and to join unanimously in crushing the *Cockatrice* in the egg, which otherwise may, and assuredly will, one day become a *fiery flying serpent ?* "[2]

It would have been difficult for the Independents or the Presbyterians to frame a successful defence against this indictment. It cannot be too often insisted upon that a general charge of intoleration and of an attempt to further a particular form of discipline and worship at the expense of all others would have touched a weak spot in the armor of most of the religious bodies of the period. But, while it would have been reasonable to accuse the non-Episcopalians of encroaching upon the liberties of the established church of the mother country because that system did not jibe with their own, it is most amusing to hear their action charged to the fact that the Church of England was the advocate of religious freedom in general.

The " Anatomist" in his twelfth letter formulates two conclusions to be drawn from the recent controversy, which sum up the matter very well : —

" 1st, That the advocates for an American *Episcopacy* do steadfastly declare they have no farther nor other view in this

---

[1] A similar charge had been made some fifteen years before by Dr. Johnson in his "Letter containing some Impartial Thoughts on an American Bishop," appended to the London edition of his *Elements of Philosophy*.

[2] "Anatomist," No. iii., by "Horatio," *Pennsylvania Gazette*, September 22, 1768.

measure than that the Episcopal Churches in the colonies may have the same opportunities of keeping up a succession of Ministers and Ecclesiastical order in their body, and agreeable to their principles, which all other religious bodies in *America* do enjoy.

" 2dly, That the opponents of this measure strive to alarm all *America* against it, contending, that although the above may be the specious plea of the Episcopal Clergy, yet their true design (notwithstanding any assertions to the contrary) is to introduce that yoke of spiritual bondage and jurisdiction over the laity, which neither they nor their fathers could bear." [1]

In this as in the other ramifications of the discussion, the two leaders were supported by contributions from their respective followers,[2] but, since their arguments bring out nothing of sufficient importance to warrant an examination,[3] we may pass them by, and, leaving the colonies for a time, see how the controversy was regarded by the English newspapers.

In the spring of 1768 the *London Chronicle* notes that "the controversy relating to the fitness of sending bishops to America rages strongly in the provinces of North America at this time." [4] During the next few years this paper followed the controversy with the closest attention, and printed in its col-

---

[1] "Anatomist," No. xii., *Pennsylvania Gazette*, November 24, 1768.

[2] For example, "Anti-Centinel," "Remonstrant," and "Irenicus."

[3] The following extract from a contemporaneous poetaster ("Veridicus's Verses to the Whig Writer," *Pennsylvania Chronicle*, April 11, 1768) will serve to illustrate the character of some of the more trivial and abusive contributions : —

> ". . . if in the present debate you shou'd find
> We reply with some warmth, do, for once, be so kind,
> Ye grave *Centinels, Whigs, and all other abettors,*
> Of the *scurrilous writers of scandalous letters,*
> *Once for all,* be assur'd what we tell you is true,
> It is not at Dissenters, *as such,* but at *you,*
> At you *only* we level our aim, and determine
> No such insolent, meddling, *anonymous* vermin
> Shall be suffered among us to sculk, *with impunity,*
> To disturb our repose, and infest the community
> By sowing the seeds of dissention and strife
> Among those who wou'd fain lead a peaceable life."

[4] June 21, 1768.

umns many communications, most of which supported the anti-episcopal position. Like their brethren across the water, the contributors to the English sheets regarded the religious and political questions as closely allied. Their opinion was that the religious grievances of the colonists, though not up to that time carried to so great a height as those of a civil nature, were nevertheless as real, and, if allowed to continue and to operate to their full extent, might perhaps in time become more intolerable.[1] Commenting upon two schemes then in contemplation, which were to be offered for consideration on the meeting of an "august assembly particularly formed on purpose to remove those frequent jealousies and heart-burnings between our colonies and the mother country," a writer in the *London Chronicle* remarks that these relate to such jealousies of the colonies as concern what they conceive to be encroachments on their civil rights and liberties. "But to what good purpose of theirs or ours," he asks, "will these jealousies and heart-burnings be removed, if there are among them the seeds sown of a religious war, ready to break out with the utmost fury, which has attended all ecclesiastical contests when fomented to the extremity?" Since this is likely to be the event of the controversy about an American episcopate, he advises that the first duty of the "benevolent healers of civil feuds in America" shall be to inquire after and properly censure the authors or the instruments of the religious animosities. He accuses the state authorities of a criminal negligence in having allowed the affair to go so far without making an effort to check it.[2]

Among the articles published in the English newspapers we find some arguments that are new, but more that are old. One of the most interesting is that in which a writer, who signs himself "A Country Clergyman," elaborates a proposition which had to some extent been utilized by Chauncy. It is, in sub-

[1] *North Briton*, No. lxi., quoted by "American Whig," No. xxxiii., Parker's *New York Gazette*, October 24, 1768.

[2] "No regard," he complains, "has been paid by our drowsy watchmen of state to . . . warnings, and now behold the beginnings of those sorrows, in the wildfire thrown among our colonists by fomenting their idle, wretched, wicked controversy about an American Episcopate" ("William Prynne," in *London Chronicle*, July 1, 1768).

stance, that bishops in the Church of England are no more than presbyters set apart by act of Parliament to perform certain offices in the said church; that all the separate episcopal powers enjoyed by them are derived from the authority of the state, and by no means belong to them as clergymen of the Church of England: hence that there is no need of settling bishops in the colonies, since the Bishop of London's commissaries have with the approbation of their superior as much right to confer orders as his lordship himself.[1] The statements upon which this argument is based are obviously contrary to fact; for there are now, were then, and had always been three totally distinct orders in the Church of England, the highest of which, the episcopal, alone possessed the peculiar function of ordination and confirmation.

The English writers were generally agreed that there was little likelihood that bishops would be sent to America. One "Atlanticus," who sent many communications to the *London Chronicle*, quotes from a public paper, the name of which he omits to mention, a statement to the effect that it is absolutely determined not to establish an episcopate in the colonies, and for two reasons: first, because it is not necessary; secondly, because the Americans would probably not submit to it. He says that he personally has never heard the purpose asserted on any sufficient grounds, and that he never could bring himself to believe that "our excellent Sovereign and Legislature ever intended to lay such a burden on our American brethren"; that he has ever regarded it as the "device of a very few bigot-headed Churchmen," and is firmly persuaded that the majority of Episcopalians both in Old and New England have no real inclination to the plan.[2] The occasion for "Atlanticus's" article was a rumor, widely circulated in some of the public prints at the time, that the project for sending bishops had been revived.

As has been said, very few contributors to the English newspapers wrote in favor of the plan. Those who did, however, like the pro-episcopal writers in the colonies, often gave expression to opinions concerning the necessary connection between the episcopal and the monarchical system which were well calculated to arouse apprehension in the minds of Independents in

[1] *London Chronicle*, September 21, 1768.   [2] *Ibid*. September 18, 1768.

church and state.[1]   On the other hand, we find among the English as well as the American opponents of the scheme the same suspicions, the same insistence on knowing what authority the episcopal apologists had for asserting that the bishops desired would confine themselves to their purely spiritual functions, and what security they could give that in due time claims to temporal power would not be advanced.[2]

Such was the newspaper controversy of 1768–1769. In reviewing the arguments of the two parties concerned, we find that those who contended for the introduction of bishops sought to prove that no temporal authority was expected or desired for the proposed episcopate, and hence that the matter concerned the Episcopal communion as a purely religious body, and that all other persons or persuasions were unjust, intolerant, and meddlesome in interfering. Their opponents, on the other hand, insisted that they had all the reason in the world for concerning themselves in the question; that, in spite of all assurances to the contrary, they had good cause to fear that the proposed establishment would involve in time many innovations, such as spiritual courts, the assumption of secular functions by the bishops, the taxation of the inhabitants for the maintenance of the episcopate, and the introduction of tithes — a measure which would be a dangerous menace to the integrity of their institutions political and civil. They went even farther, and included the attempt to foist an episcopate upon them among the oppressive measures recently directed against them by the English government. These arguments, as such, are not new;[3] but the weight of emphasis laid upon them, as compared with that attached to questions of a theological complexion, is new, and the popular interest is also new.

[1] For example, "Crito" (*Ibid.* September 26, 1768) says, "I cannot conclude without observing that some late alarming transactions, and the republican spirit which prevails in some of our Colonies, give too much reason to apprehend that what has happened in England [the Puritan Revolution] may happen in America, and that this rage against Episcopacy may be a prelude to downfall of monarchy."

[2] Cf. *London Chronicle*, September 19, 1768.

[3] The one last named of course played no part in the Mayhew and pre-Mayhew controversies.

Hence the significance of the newspaper utterances lies in phases of public opinion which they both moulded and reflected, and in the sure evidence which they furnish, that the episcopal question, in its political aspect, had become important in the minds of the people. One certain indication of the widespread interest which the subject had aroused is the fact that a New York publisher found it a profitable investment to collect all the articles which contributed to the discussion, and to reprint them in the form of pamphlets. Certainly, if the question of the establishment of bishops did not contribute a lion's share in causing that enmity to the mother country, which was manifested mainly in a political direction, it was involved in the struggle and deserves to be regarded as an important part of it.

One more point in regard to the significance of the newspaper controversy deserves notice. It is generally admitted that, while the majority of the Puritans advocated the principle of forcible resistance to the oppressive measures of the home government, many influential members of the Church of England preached the doctrine of non-resistance and passive obedience.[1] Upon closer examination it will be seen that most of these persons were in the Middle and Northern colonies, particularly in the latter, where the Puritan element predominated, and that almost to a man those who sought the introduction of bishops adopted this attitude. In view of these facts it is at least a tenable hypothesis that the bitterness of the controversy brought out so sharply the latent hostility between Episcopalian and Puritan, that many churchmen who might otherwise have taken the side of their country were, by the force of their injured religious convictions, driven over to the loyalist ranks.

[1] One should, of course, be careful not to go too far on this point. Large numbers of prominent Episcopalians, even among the clergy, particularly in the Southern colonies, were ardent patriots. See Perry, *American Episcopal Church*, i. ch. xxiv., " The Position of the Clergy at the Opening of the War for Independence." Cf. also Dr. George E. Ellis, in his article " The Sentiment of Independence," in Winsor, *Narrative and Critical History*, vi. ch. iii. 240–244. The letter from the clergy of Christ Church, Philadelphia (cited above, p. 207, note 2), shows that the leaders of at least one important congregation were not without patriotic sympathies.

CHAPTER IX.

THE CONVENTIONS AND THE EPISCOPAL QUESTION, 1766-1775.

In the preceding chapters we have followed the course of the struggle for and against the establishment of an American episcopate as it was carried on in various contemporaneous publications; we have examined the arguments advanced by both parties in letters, public and private, in pamphlets, broadsides, and newspaper articles, and have, in this way, sought to make clear the attitude of the officers and members of the various churches, and of the public at large so far as it interested itself in the question. Up to this point, however, we have been almost exclusively concerned with the opinions, utterances, and actions of individuals as such. It is now time to consider what had been done, and was to be done, by the opposing religious bodies as organizations.

It will be remembered that the pamphlets of Dr. Chandler did not proceed from his own initiative, but were undertaken at the united request of his episcopal brethren expressed in a convention assembled primarily to deliberate and act upon this very matter.[1] The origin of this convention may be traced to an agreement, entered into by the Episcopal clergy of the provinces of New York, New Jersey, and Connecticut, to hold voluntary annual conventions "for the sake of conferring together upon the most proper methods of Promoting the welfare of the Church of England, and the interest of religion and virtue, and also to keep up as a body an exact correspondence with the Honorable Society."[2] This preliminary action

[1] The suggestion had originally come from Dr. Johnson. See above, p. 164.
[2] See a letter from the assembled clergy to the secretary of the Society, dated May 22, 1766, quoted by Beardsley; *Life of Seabury*, Appendix A, and by Perry, *American Episcopal Church*, i. 416. Their purpose is more specifically stated in a resolution which has been noticed in another connection (above, pp. 164-165). By the "Honorable Society" is meant the Society for Propagating the Gospel.

was taken at a meeting opened May 21, 1766, at the house of the Reverend Samuel Auchmuty, rector of Trinity Church, New York.[1] The first convention of the new organization was held at Elizabethtown, New Jersey, November 1, 1766.[2] Here a "plan of union" was formulated, consisting of several articles, which declared that the "design" of the association was to defend "the religious liberties of our Churches, to diffuse union and harmony, and to keep up a correspondence throughout this united body, *and with our friends abroad.*" At this meeting a letter containing the plans of the organization and soliciting encouragement and aid in the advancement of them was composed and sent to the brethren resident in Massachusetts Bay, New Hampshire, and Rhode Island, and to the members of the Dutch churches.[3] The main work of the convention, so long as it continued, consisted in drawing up numerous petitions to the king, the archbishops, the bishops, the Society, and the universities of Oxford and Cambridge, in behalf of its cause, in commissioning Chandler to write his pamphlets, and in taking a lively part in the newspaper controversy of 1768–1769.

Meanwhile, the synods of the New York and New Jersey Presbyterians had joined forces with the several Congregationalist associations of Connecticut, and by means of annual conventions composed of delegates from these various bodies, and of correspondence with a committee of the dissenting sects in London, were bending all their energies toward frustrating the endeavors of the rival Episcopal organization, so far as it was concerned with the introduction of American bishops.[4]

---

[1] Fourteen clergymen were present.   See Perry, *American Episcopal Church*, i. 415, citing *Minutes of the Proceedings of the Convention*, of which the original folio, in Seabury's handwriting, is in the possession of Professor William J. Seabury, D.D., of New York City.

[2] It was attended by nine clergymen from Connecticut and twenty-two from New York and Philadelphia.

[3] S. A. Clark, *History of St. John's Church*, 128–129, citing *Church Review*, iv. 572 (article entitled "American Episcopate before the Revolution").

[4] Protestant Episcopal Historical Society, *Collections*, i. 146.   Cf. Samuel Miller, *Memoirs of John Rodgers*, 186–187: "Among the measures which were taken for defeating the plan of an American Episcopate, and for keeping the non-episcopal churches awake to their interests and dangers, was the

The work of the association was supplemented by the organized efforts of a company of prominent Congregationalists and Presbyterians, chief among whom were the Reverend John Rodgers, the Reverend Archibald Laidlie, the Reverend John Mason, William Livingston, William Smith, and John Morin Scott, who published a number of articles and pamphlets on the "impolicy and danger of an American episcopate" and kindred matters.[1]

The main purpose of the convention of the New York and New Jersey Presbyterian synods and the Connecticut Congregationalist associations, as expressed in its public declarations, was, like the purpose of the Episcopalian convention, guarded and disguised under indefinite generalities. Although the professed object in uniting was "the promotion of Christian friendship between the members of their respective bodies, the spread of the Gospel, the preservation of the religious liberties of their churches, &c.," the first and second conventions "were occupied mainly in forming and completing their plan of union and effort," and the subsequent conventions in "prosecuting measures for preserving the liberties of their churches, threatened at the time by the attempts made by the friends of Episcopacy in the colonies and in Great Britain, for the establishment of Diocesan Bishops in America."[2] The association, while protesting that it had no objection to bishops who should confine themselves to overseeing the affairs of the Episcopal churches, expressed the apprehension that those intended to be introduced would come invested with the powers ordinarily possessed by Church of England bishops, or else would soon acquire them; and that in the exercise of these functions they would necessarily encroach

appointment of a general Convention, to compare opinions and concert plans for the promotion of these objects."

[1] Miller (*Memoirs of John Rodgers,* 192–193) characterizes these men as "vigilant observers of the course of public affairs . . . who did much to awaken and direct the public mind at that interesting period."

[2] See Convention of Delegates from the Synod of New York and Philadelphia, and from the Associations of Connecticut, *Minutes* (published at Hartford, 1843, from the material collected by a committee of the "General Association" appointed in 1842), 3. Perry, *American Episcopal Church,* i. 422 ff.) gives a good account of the work of this convention, based on the *Minutes.*

upon the colonial charters, and would prejudice the liberties of other Christian denominations. For the purpose of averting such dangers, which were in its opinion inextricably interwoven with the episcopal system, the association made arrangements for holding annual meetings, for entering into correspondence with the English "Committee of Dissenters" in London, for collecting all charters, laws, and customs in force in North America which related to religious liberty, and for ascertaining the number of non-Episcopalians resident in the colonies, in order to prove to how great an extent they outnumbered the members of the Church of England.[1]

The convention held its first sitting at Elizabethtown, New Jersey, November 5, 1766. To the printed minutes of the regular proceedings of this meeting was appended a letter which is worth considering as a fair expression of the opinions of a majority of the less violent among the assembled delegates. The letter, as there published, bears no signature; it seems to have been inserted as a sample letter from a typical American dissenter to his correspondent in London. There is, however, at least a possibility that the author was no less important a person than Roger Sherman, and that the communication was addressed to the son of Dr. Samuel Johnson, William Samuel Johnson, who was in England as agent for the colony of Connecticut during the years 1766–1771.[2]

This letter professes much anxiety on account of sundry petitions that have been sent to England in behalf of an American episcopate, and this not because the sects for whom the writer speaks are intolerant, or because they envy the Episcopal churches the privileges of a bishop for ordination, confirmation, and discipline, provided that he have no power over the other denominations and no share in the civil affairs of the colonists. It is the lack of any authoritative provision in the pending

[1] *Minutes*, 3.

[2] A copy of this letter was found among the papers of Sherman, and was in his handwriting. His biographer conjectures that it was written about 1768 (see L. H. Boutell, *Life of Sherman*, 64–68). Since it was annexed to the Minutes for 1766, and not incorporated in them, this hypothesis is not precluded. Johnson assumed his duties as agent, December 24, 1766 (Beardsley, *Episcopal Church in Connecticut*, i. 263).

scheme which, he says, makes non-Episcopalians uneasy. In order, therefore, to insure a proper limitation of the powers intrusted to the proposed episcopate, he recommends that the question be settled under an act of Parliament providing by legal enactment that in the colonies the episcopal office shall be divested of all functions that are annexed to it by the common law of England. Without such a guarantee, he says, the good-will of the other religious bodies cannot be secured, since to their minds it is all too probable that an unlimited episcopate cannot but tend to prejudice their best interests, temporal and spiritual. Their reasons for so thinking are, in his opinion, easy to explain. For example, a bishop of the Church of England is a public minister of state, versed in the common law, authorized to erect courts for taking cognizance of all matrimonial and testamentary causes, and to inquire into and punish "all offences of scandal." Such being the case, he may very properly claim the same functions in the colonies. Moreover, he continues, there is nothing to hinder a bishop, once settled, from enjoying the powers formerly exercised by Laud and his ecclesiastical courts; for the laws in force in England at the time when America was first settled are still valid in the colonies, while the later enactments limiting the exorbitant powers of the bishops at home do not extend to the colonies, since in no case has such an extension been especially mentioned.[1] In view of these facts, what might not be expected under an episcopal régime? he asks; might not the registrar's office, the care of orphans, and similar duties be transferred from the present officers to such as the bishop might appoint? might not the legality of marriage and divorce cases be tried in an ecclesiastical court? And this would not be all; for a "covetous, tyrannical, and domineering prelate," or his chancellor, would have it in his power to harass the country, to impose fines, and imprisonments, and in general to act with "lawless severity." Still farther, not only civil danger, but also religious oppressions might be apprehended from the undue exaggeration of the power of a single denomination. In short, under an episcopal

---

[1] The rule was that a law passed in England should have no force in the colonies unless an express provision to that effect was made.

establishment, left to itself, the worst abuses are all too likely to appear, the event of which would be either to force the present inhabitants of North America "to seek new habitations among the heathen, where England could not claim a jurisdiction, or excite riots, rebellion, and wild disorder." The writer, while pointing out what he considers would be, under certain conditions, the inevitable result of the project in question, preserves, nevertheless, an extremely moderate tone. He concludes what he has to say with professions of loyalty to "our most gracious King and the British Constitution," and assures his correspondent that "we dread the consequences as oft as we think of this danger," that is, the danger which might result from the introduction of an episcopate under no legal guarantee. All he asks is that, if bishops must be sent, an event which he fears will in any case be attended with bad consequences, "they may be under such restraints as are consistent with our present state of peace and liberty" (in other words, be confined by law to the care of the people and clergy of their own church), and that other denominations may be secured against encroachments of their power and against the burden of their support.[1]

The writer seemingly makes a very natural and moderate demand, and yet the parliamentary guarantee for which he asks is the very last thing which the colonists would have accepted. From long-established principle they were averse to any parliamentary legislation in their affairs, whether it were favorable or unfavorable. A striking illustration of this feeling occurred in the first half of the seventeenth century: when, in 1645, the Long Parliament offered to guarantee the Massachusetts Body of Liberties, the representatives of the province, fearing the precedent, refused without hesitation the well-meant proposal. As a matter of fact, the suggestion for a parliamentary guarantee made in this first convention was repudiated by a later one.[2]

There is in the *Minutes* another letter of the same style as that just noticed. It is an answer by the Reverend Francis

---

[1] This letter is annexed to the Minutes for November 5, 1766, in the Registry of the New Haven East Association; it is printed in *Minutes* (1843), 13–14, and in Boutell's *Life of Sherman*, 64–65.

[2] See below, p. 225.

Alison to a communication from the Reverend Mr. Sproat asking why the people of Philadelphia [1] are so firmly persuaded that there is, at this time, a determination to send bishops to America. Alison cites the usual evidence: a written declaration of Chandler that Archbishop Secker, in a conversation with him, has stated such an intention; a statement of Dr. Smith that the Quakers of Pennsylvania have expressed a willingness to sign a certificate of their consent to admit a moderate episcopate; the petitions of the clergy of New York and New Jersey to the authorities in England; [2] and, finally, the fact that in Philadelphia it is the topic of conversation in the coffee-houses and in public companies " as an affair that must take place, and as an affair that it would be disloyal and intolerant to oppose." Alison makes this letter to Sproat, who was one of the officers in the convention, an occasion for discussing the dangers of the expected establishment. [3]

At a meeting held October 5, 1768, also at Elizabethtown, the convention drafted and sent its first letter to the " Dissenting Committee " in London. This letter informs the committee that " the Pastors of the Consociated Churches of Connecticut have agreed with the Synod of New York and Philadelphia to meet annually by Delegates in Convention on the most catholic foundation; to give information of the public state of our united interests; to join our counsels and endeavors together for spreading and preserving the civil and religious liberties of our Churches; to recommend, cultivate, and preserve loyalty and allegiance to the King's Majesty, and to keep up a correspondence through this united body and with our friends abroad." It says that the aim of the convention is twofold: first, to "strengthen our interest in suppressing and discouraging any measures that might be fallen upon by the

---

[1] Dr. Alison was vice-provost of the College of Philadelphia. See above, p. 195.

[2] October 2, 1765. There were seven in all: one each to the king, the Archbishop of Canterbury, the Archbishop of York, the Bishop of London, the University of Oxford, the University of Cambridge, and the Society for Propagating the Gospel.

[3] It is dated November 15, 1766, and is printed in the *Minutes*, 14-16, from the files in the Registry of the New Haven East Association.

people committed to our care that would be inconsistent with our character as peaceable and loyal subjects, or detrimental to the public peace and tranquillity"; and secondly, "that we might as faithful officers in the Church of Christ watch over her rights and privileges, to endeavor more effectually to prevent any attempts of any other denomination of Christians to oppose us."

Having outlined the policy of the association, the letter proceeds to explain the reason for forming it, which is in substance the "very general alarm" which the recent attempts to secure an American episcopate have caused. Upon this particular issue the convention expresses itself substantially as its individual members had done in the letters noted above, except that it is much more uncompromising. Although it is filled with "an utter abhorrence of every species of ecclesiastical tyranny and persecution," which it regards as the inseparable accompaniment of an episcopal régime, it does not wish to oppose bishops as such, but only to avert the consequences inevitable upon the settlement of the only kind of an episcopate known to it. It will gladly acquiesce in any plan by which the safety and integrity of present conditions may be assured; but it is only too certain that such assurance is not possible except under an episcopate so mutilated as to satisfy no Episcopalian, either at home or abroad. In a word, the convention involves its possible agreement in such a multitude of impossible conditions as to make of it a practical refusal. "Nothing," it remarks *à propos* of the proposed episcopate (under whatever form it might be established, be it noted), "seems to have such a direct tendency to weaken the dependence of the Colonies upon Great Britain and to separate them from her — an event which would be ruinous and destructive to both, and which we, therefore, pray God long to avert." Such a combination of apparent compliance and essential irreconcilability can be matched only in the address of the earlier Stuart parliaments to the crown.

The profession here made concerning the origin and purpose of the convention differs in two marked particulars from that first given to the public. In the first place, it lays greater emphasis on the matter of loyalty to the English crown, probably for the purpose of propitiating the English dissenting brethren, particularly Jasper Mauduit, who was friendly to the crown.[1] In the second place, it confesses with greater distinctness what was really the primary and sole purpose of the dissenters in uniting ; namely, their opposition to the introduction of bishops.

The convention, after explaining its policy and justifying it by arguments already familiar, next states, as its reason for writing to the London committee, its wish to solicit the coöperation of that body in the effort to keep bishops out of the colonies. Although it apprehends no immediate danger, it has reason, it says, to believe that the prelates in England, who have the cause so much at heart, are constantly on the alert for a favorable chance of pushing it ; accordingly, it behooves anti-Episcopalians to be constantly on their guard. Since, however, the great distance from England would prevent the colonists in case of a sudden move on the part of their opponents from doing anything until too late, they are " obliged to depend on the vigilance and interest of . . . friends in Great Britain who are engaged in the same common cause." Therefore the convention, as a representative of the colonial anti-episcopal interests, urges its English brethren to unite with it in a common effort, and suggests a correspondence by which the colonists may be kept continually informed of such things as it would be advantageous for them to know.[2]

Besides preparing the foregoing letter, the convention, during this session, appointed a standing committee to take charge of future correspondence with the friends in London, with the brethren in Massachusetts, Rhode Island, and New Hampshire, and with the presbytery in Boston. It also appointed local committees in New York, New Jersey, and Pennsylvania.

The first reply of the London committee of which there is a record was written August 4, 1770, not, however, in answer to the letter just noticed, but to a later letter of the convention, sent September 14, 1769. In this communication the London

[1] Mauduit, who had been agent for Massachusetts from 1762 to 1766, was at this time chairman of the committee for managing the civil affairs of the dissenters.

[2] *Minutes*, 22–24.

committee explains its delay in replying as due to the fact that the letter from the colonial brethren did not come to the hand of its chairman until nine months after it was written. The chairman immediately summoned a meeting of the committee, which took the letter into consideration, and, as a result of the deliberations, its secretary is now authorized to assure the convention that the committee is "fully sensible of the many civil and religious inconveniences that would arise from the introduction of Diocesan Bishops into America," and will do its utmost to "oppose and frustrate any such design." At the same time it has the pleasure of stating, from information based upon the strictest inquiries from the best authorities, that there is no immediate cause for apprehension. Moreover, it hopes that the government is "so sensible of the confusion such a step would make among our American brethren" as to block the design, "however warmly some of our Bishops may wish for it, and express their desires in their sermons on public occasions." Should any new danger of a revival of the project arise, however, the committee is ready to lend its efforts to defeat it. The letter concludes with a profession of willingness to continue the correspondence, and with the assurance that the committee will promptly impart to the convention any information relative to the matter [1] which it can obtain.

A second letter from the London committee is dated January 22, 1771. It is interesting from the fact that it contains a consideration of a proposal made by the convention for securing an agent to look after its interests in London. The committee opposes this scheme as impracticable and impolitic: in the first place, because it would be difficult to find a person for the position endowed with the qualities specified by the convention; in the second place, because, even if such a one could be found, he would not answer the end, since he would not have the "weight with administration as this committee would; for, whatever he might at any time say, they would look upon him as an agent for the colonies and under their influence, whereas no such bias could be imputed to this Committee." [2] Evidently no means were to be left unemployed to prevent the hated

---

[1] *Minutes*, Appendix, 65.   [2] *Ibid.* 67–68.

establishment. It was at this time, according to a letter from the convention to the committee, that the colonies of Connecticut and Massachusetts gave instructions to their agents to oppose any movement toward the introduction of an American episcopate of which they could get wind.[1]

It is interesting to note that now for the first time the convention declares emphatically that nothing, not even a parliamentary, act limiting the episcopal powers, could induce it to accept bishops; for "no act of Parliament," it says, "can secure us from the tyranny of their jurisdiction."

Without further study it is possible to form a sufficiently clear idea of the policy and methods of the " Convention of Delegates from the Synod of New York and Philadelphia and from the Associations of Connecticut." It held annual meetings and continued to correspond with the " Dissenting Committee " in London till 1775, when its sittings were interrupted by the outbreak of the Revolution. Since the outcome of the war removed all possibility of an episcopal establishment in America by action of the English government,[2] the convention had no occasion to meet again. Its work was done.[3]

[1] September 5, 1771. See *Minutes*, Appendix, 32–34.

[2] The part which the convention, through its connection with the London committee, had in averting such a possibility will be considered in a later chapter.

[3] Cf. *Minutes*, 48, editorial note.

CHAPTER X.

THE OPPOSITION IN VIRGINIA.

THE opposition of Virginia to the introduction of bishops is of peculiar interest, for in that colony the Church of England was established, and Episcopalians were stronger than they were in any other part of the country.

Before the episcopal question came to the front, the most significant feature of Virginian ecclesiastical history after the death of Sherlock, and the one with which his successors in the see of London had most to do, was that concerning the tobacco troubles and the events leading out of them.[1] It is important to note that in these disputes the Bishop of London had taken the side of the crown, — a fact which contributed not a little to hurt the popularity of the Church of England in the public estimation.[2] It needed but a few such acts as this on the part of the bishop to convince even Episcopalians that their safety lay on the patriotic side.

So much for the bishop's personal activity; now let us see how his representatives were faring in the province. Though commissaries continued to be appointed up to the Revolution,[3] no holder of the office received a commission for the exercise of his functions after the expiration of Gibson's patent. Up to the time of William Robinson, however, who became commissary in 1761, each new appointee had been granted a royal warrant and a salary. Robinson was unsuccessful in obtaining

---

[1] More familiarly known as the "Parson's Cause" (see above, p. 130, note, where a brief bibliography is given). A letter from Commissary Robinson to Bishop Terrick, August 17, 1764, rehearses the history of the question at length. See Perry, *Historical Collections*, i. (Virginia) 489-501.

[2] Cf. Richard Bland, *Letter to the Clergy of Virginia, passim.*

[3] The commissarial office and the presidency of William and Mary College usually went to the same person. The commissary as such was a member of the council and a judge of the Supreme Bench. See Robinson to Sherlock, November 20, 1760, in Perry, *Historical Collections*, i. (Virginia) 463-470.

even a warrant, and for that reason did not feel authorized to call conventions of the clergy, as his predecessors had done.[1]

But although the bishops who succeeded Gibson showed very little interest in maintaining any discipline in Virginia, cases came up from time to time which indicated that their authority was still regarded in the colony. For example, in 1767 the inhabitants of Albemarle County, taking offence at the conduct of their minister, the Reverend Mr. Ramsay, applied to a lawyer to redress their grievances. At a loss to know how to proceed, he referred the matter to the General Court. The court, considering that it had jurisdiction over all causes, criminal, civil, and ecclesiastical, and hence that it could legally take cognizance of a case of this nature, ordered the issue of citations, that the affair might be inquired into and justice be done between the parties.[2] As soon as the matter came to the attention of Governor Fauquier, he at once sent a report of it to Bishop Terrick, with the assurance that he would keep him informed of every step in the process.[3] There is an entry on the back of the original letter among the Fulham manuscripts stating that his lordship replied to Fauquier, September 7, 1767. It would be interesting to know what position he took on the question, but unfortunately his letter has disappeared. Moreover, even the issue of this case is not certainly known, although there is some ground for believing that proceedings were stopped

[1] See Robinson to Terrick, May 23, 1765, *Ibid.* 503–505.

[2] Richard Bland, writing August 1, 1771, to Thomas Adams, said: " The King has assented to the Act of Assembly which declares that the general court shall take cognizance of and ' have Power & jurisdiction to hear & Determine all causes, matters, or things whatsoever relating to or concerning any Person or Persons ecclesiastical or civil ; or to any Persons or Things of what nature soever, the same shall be ' " (*William and Mary College Quarterly*, January, 1897, v. 150 ff.). But Bland does not mention the date of the act, and I can find no record of it. It is doubtful if it was in force at this time. Certainly the custom had hitherto been for the governor and council to proceed against irregular clergymen (see the Brunskill case, above, pp. 136-137). According to the *Methodus Procedendi* issued by Gibson in 1728, the commissary was empowered to take cognizance in such cases ; but any authority which that instrument carried (and it seems to have been little observed) ceased at the expiration of Gibson's commission.

[3] Fauquier to Terrick, April 27, 1767, *Fulham MSS.*

by the death of the accused minister. There is a possible allusion to this outcome in an interesting discussion, dating from about this time, concerning the theoretical extent of the authority of the Bishop of London in regard to clerical offences. The discussion is contained in two letters, dated respectively November 11, 1770, and April 17, 1771, from President Nelson [1] of Virginia to Lord Hillsborough, at that time secretary of state for the colonies.[2] The occasion of Nelson's first communication was the perusal of the sixty-seventh article of his instructions, which directed him to use "the proper and usual means for the removal" of any minister, already preferred to a benefice, who should appear to him "to give scandal either by his doctrines or his manners." Nelson states that there are few irregular clergymen in the colony, but expresses his doubts whether, if any should be found, there are any "proper & regular means in this country to remove such for want . . . of the Bishop of London having any power in this respect from his Majesty." [3] He is of opinion, however, that, were his lordship possessed of any such power, he might delegate it to his commissaries, to enable them to hold jurisdiction and "to enquire into the Orthodoxy, Morals, or neglect of Duty of the Clergy or to suspend or deprive on proper occasions." [4] After pointing out that the king, as constitutional head of the church, had formerly by a special commission to the Bishop of London given such power to the commissaries, who with the assistance of two assessors held courts, Nelson continues, "but I cannot find that any Bishop of London hath had such a Commission since the time of Dr. Edmund Gibson, of that See, and consequently

---

[1] William Nelson (1771–1772) was president of the Council of Virginia, and during the interval between Lord Botetourt and Lord Dunmore, 1770–1771, he acted as governor. He also presided over the General or Supreme Court of law and equity of the province, being regarded as one of the ablest lawyers of his time.

[2] These letters are printed in Perry, *Historical Collections*, i. (Virginia) 532–534.

[3] This power Gibson had, of course, given to his commissaries while his commission was in force.

[4] Gibson had done this by the issue of commissions and sets of instructions. For examples of these see below, Appendix A, No. vi.

no such courts have been held here since that era." [1] In view of these facts, since a court is needed for taking cognizance of spiritual causes, and since there exists in Virginia no court for the purpose, Nelson wishes to submit the case to the attorney and solicitor generals, to know whether the General Court, which claims the right, and has already attempted to exercise it in two cases, both abated by death,[2] can properly exercise that function.[3]

Meanwhile, before sending his second letter, Nelson read the Gibson commission a second time more carefully, but found no reason for changing his opinion; for, as he reminds Lord Hillsborough, with the death of Gibson the powers granted to him had expired, and the commissaries since that time had received no other appointment than letters from the succeeding bishops of London, which they regarded as insufficient to authorize their taking any official action in ecclesiastical concerns. Nelson complains that, for want of such commissarial authority to set up an ecclesiastical court, the prestige of the crown is suffering;[4] and requests again that, if an adequate commission cannot be sent to the commissary, the attorney and solicitor generals be moved to deliver an opinion on the jurisdiction of the General Court in spiritual causes, particularly since the case of an immoral clergyman is pending, which, in the ensuing October, is going to be used by both parties as a test case to determine the extent of the jurisdiction of the General Court.[5] But at this time the political issues directly preceding the Revolution were beginning to absorb the attention

---

[1] Such courts had almost never been held in Virginia. Commissary Garden held several in South Carolina, his most celebrated case being the trial of George Whitefield.

[2] Without doubt one of these was Ramsay's case. See above, pp. 227–228.

[3] Perry, *Historical Collections,* i. (Virginia) 532–533.

[4] The Independents and Congregationalists, particularly in New England, liked to get hold of such statements as this.

[5] Perry, *Historical Collections,* i. (Virginia) 533–534. It is strange that Nelson makes no mention of the act to which, according to Bland's letter of August, 1771, the king had given his assent. Possibly it was ratified between April and August, in consequence, it may be, of Nelson's inquiry; but the fact that it is not recorded among the Virginia statutes inclines one to doubt whether it was passed in the form of a regular legislative act.

of the colonists, and there appears to be no record of any test trial, or of any opinion of the attorney and solicitor generals. If any opinion was given, it must have favored the General Court, particularly if the crown had assented to an act of assembly by which ecclesiastical jurisdiction was either granted or confirmed to this court.[1]

Though in general the clergy and laity of the Church of England in Maryland and Virginia had taken very little share in the agitation for an American episcopate,[2] at least one earnest attempt to secure the desired bishops was made in each of these colonies. Only the Virginia case will be noticed here.[3] All the

---

[1] See above, p. 227, note 2, and p. 229, note 5.

[2] This fact was noticed at the time. The "American Whig," in his thirteenth article, says: "From the best information I have been able to obtain, the clergy of Maryland, Virginia, North Carolina, South Carolina, Georgia, and the West India Islands had no concern in the late petitions transmitted on this subject; they seem to have been hatched by a few warm missionaries in the provinces of New York, New Jersey, Pennsylvania; and propagated to the Eastern colonies by the help of the frequent unconstitutional assemblies, latterly convoked under the name of the convention" (Parker's *New York Gazette*, June 6, 1768). President Nelson, in a letter to Edward Hunt, May 11, 1771, says: "The Virginians, tho' almost all of the Episcopal Church, have as yet taken no part in the Dispute, the reason I believe is, that it is a matter of more indifference to us than to the other Provinces which are full of every kind of Dissenters inimical to Episcopacy. We do not want Bishops; yet from our Principles I hardly think we should oppose such an establishment; nor will the laity apply for them" (*William and Mary College Quarterly*, January, 1897, v. 149–150; from Nelson's letter-book in the Episcopal seminary at Alexandria, Virginia). It is interesting to note in this connection what Hawks thought on the subject. "*A faithful bishop*," he says, "would have been a blessing to the colony, and this was plainly perceived by the worthy part of the clergy in Virginia [in support of this statement he cites Jones, *Present State of Virginia*, 99]; nor did they hesitate to ask that one might be sent, with powers so limited in certain particulars as to allay the suspicious fears of the people, who dreaded nothing more than ecclesiastical tyranny" (*Ecclesiastical Contributions*, i. (Virginia) 95). Hawks's assertion conveys an utterly false impression. Apparently there never was an appreciable number of either clergy or laity in Virginia who desired anything of the sort; indeed, most indications show that they were not only indifferent, but hostile to the plan. In preceding pages of this work an attempt has been made to account for their attitude.

[3] For general accounts of this affair, see Perry, *American Episcopal Church*, i. 419 ff.; Hawks, *Ecclesiastical Contributions*, i. (Virginia) 126–131, citing

evidence goes to show that the original moving cause of the application from this province came from the " United Convention of New York and New Jersey," which deputed Dr. Myles Cooper, president of King's (now Columbia) College, and the Reverend Robert McKean, missionary at Amboy, New Jersey, " to visit the southern part of the continent, for the purpose of securing the coöperation of their brethren in that region in procuring an American episcopate." [1]

Probably, owing to the efforts of this committee, Commissary Horrocks [2] issued in April, 1771, by means of an advertisement in the Virginia papers, a summons for the clergy of the province to meet on the 4th of May at the College of William and Mary. Since only a small number answered the call, it was voted, in the informal meeting which was held, that the commissary insert a second advertisement, stating the business to be taken up in the proposed convention. In consequence of this second summons, twelve clergymen presented themselves, and the convention was opened on the 4th of June. The question as to whether the number present was sufficient to

Burk, *Virginia*, iii. 364–365 ; Protestant Episcopal Historical Society, *Collections*, i. 155–156.

[1] Hawks, *Ecclesiastical Contributions*, i. (Virginia) 126, citing the *Journals of the United Convention of* 1767, pp. 32–35, from the *Seabury MSS.*

[2] James Horrocks, sixth president of William and Mary College, succeeded William Robinson as commissary in 1771. On account of failing health he was forced to resign his duties, and to go to England early·in the summer of the same year. He left, to represent him in his various duties, the Reverend John Camm as president of the college, the Reverend Mr. Willie as commissary, and the Reverend Samuel Henley as minister of Bruton parish, of which Horrocks was rector. Horrocks died in England, March 22, 1772. He was succeeded as president and commissary by Camm. Burk, Hawks, and Perry name Camm as the one who called the convention and presided at it ; but this statement is erroneous. They may have taken the notion from the fact that Camm was the leader, on the Episcopal side, of the disputes which arose from the action taken by the meeting. Gwatkin, a member of the convention, in his *Letter to the Clergy of New York and New Jersey* (p. 4), says simply that it was called by the "commissary." The two letters of Nelson and Bland, which have been already mentioned, and which Burk, Hawks, and Perry probably never had an opportunity to peruse, seem to settle the question beyond a reasonable doubt. See *William and Mary College Quarterly* (January, 1897), v. 149–156 *passim*.

constitute a convention was first debated, and was decided in the affirmative. Having settled this point, the convention passed to a consideration of the business for which it was assembled; namely, the advisability of addressing the king on the subject of an American episcopate, and, after some discussion, voted in the negative, though it decided unanimously to refer the matter to the Bishop of London for his opinion and advice. Later the question of addressing the king was reconsidered, in spite of a strong opposition, the movers of which argued, first, that such a proceeding would indicate ingratitude to their diocesan, the Bishop of London; secondly, that it would be impolitic, in view of the state of the country, particularly after the late Carolina disturbances;[1] and, finally, that if such an address were sent, it should be first referred to the assembly for its approval. But these arguments were disregarded by the majority; Camm, indeed, refused even to consider the request to refer the proposition to the assembly, because he was " sure it would not succeed."[2]

The exact form of the resolution adopted by the convention was as follows: " That a Committee be appointed to draw up an Address to the King for an American Episcopate, and that the Committee shall apply for the Hand of the Majority of the Clergy of this Colony, in which, if they succeed, the Bishop of London is to be addressed for his Concurrence, and requested to present their Address to his Majesty, but without a Concurrence of a Majority of the Clergy the Address not to be transmitted, and that the Reverend Messieurs Camm, Willie, Skyring, White, and Fontaine, or any three of them, are appointed a committee to prepare the said Address."[3]

Two leading clergymen of the colony — the Reverend Thomas Gwatkin, professor of mathematics, and the Reverend Samuel

[1] An allusion to the Mecklenburg convention and resolves.

[2] See Gwatkin, *Letter to the Clergy of New York and New Jersey*, 4–5. From now on Camm figures as the leader of the pro-episcopal party. He had led the clergy of Virginia in the " Parson's Cause," and had gone to England to advocate their claims. He represents the Tory element in the Revolution.

[3] Of the twelve members present, eight, including Horrocks, voted for the resolution, and four against it. See Bland to Adams, August 1, 1771, *William and Mary College Quarterly*, v. 153.

Henley, professor of moral philosophy, in William and Mary College — registered a formal protest against the vote of the meeting. They assigned seven reasons for their opposition, which are in substance as follows : —

First, because the clergy present at the convention insufficiently represent the clergy of the province, who number over a hundred.

Secondly, because the resolution contradicts one previously made by the same convention, to the effect that the king shall not be addressed on the subject of an American episcopate.

Thirdly, because the jurisdiction of the American episcopate desired would probably include the other colonies as well as Virginia, and therefore it would be improper for the clergy of Virginia to " petition for a Measure which, for ought that appears to the contrary, will materially affect the Natural Rights and fundamental Laws of the said Colonies without their Consent and Approbation."

Fourthly, " because the establishment of an American Episcopate at this time would tend greatly to weaken the connexion between the Mother Country and her Colonies, to continue their present unhappy Disputes, to infuse Jealousies and Fears into the Minds of the Protestant Dissenters, and to give ill-disposed Persons Occasion to raise such Disturbances as may endanger the very Existence of the British Empire in America."

Fifthly, because it is " extremely indecent . . . to make such an Application without the concurrence of the President, Council, and Representatives of this Province."

Sixthly, because, since the colony has always hitherto been under the jurisdiction of the Bishops of London, and the rule of the present diocesan is perfectly satisfactory, they think " a Petition to the Crown to strip his Lordship of any Part of his Jurisdiction but an ill Return for his past Labors, and contrary to our Oath of Canonical Obedience." Moreover, since the convention has already determined to consult his lordship in the matter, they think it should wait to hear from him before proceeding farther " in an Affair of such vast Importance."

Seventhly, because they regard the method to be employed for ascertaining the wishes of the majority of the clergy of the province as not only undignified but even "contrary to the universal Practice of the Christian Church."[1]

Of these seven reasons on which Gwatkin and Henley based their objections to the action of the convention, that concerning the unaptness of the occasion chosen for making the application is the only one of any cogency.[2] Two of them, the first and the sixth, display a total misunderstanding of the resolution quoted in their own preamble.[3] Although it is true that the convention was so small as to be hardly a representative body, it will be noticed that it planned to take no action until assured of the support of a majority of the brethren present. In petitioning the crown, the intention was not to circumvent their diocesan, but rather to coöperate with him in a cause which he had as much at heart as they. The address was first to be referred to him for his concurrence, and was to be by him presented to the king. It was certainly no evidence of ingratitude to the Bishop of London to seek to relieve his see of a burden which its successive holders had been striving to throw off ever since the days of Sherlock. Richard Terrick, who held the office at this time, was just as anxious as any of his predecessors to transfer to a native episcopate the functions which custom had fastened on him. He had many times said so in no uncertain terms.[4]

---

[1] Gwatkin, *Letter*, 6–8. The protest was also printed in the *London Chronicle*, August 30, 1771, and has been reprinted by Hawks, Perry, and others in their accounts of the episode.

[2] This is the fourth. The third, and perhaps the fifth, were, however, not without weight.

[3] Perry, Hawks, and the *Collections* do not print the preamble; Burk does.

[4] Writing to the clergy of Connecticut, February 18, 1765, a few months after his accession, he said: "I am very sensible (and in this I speak the sentiments of my brethren) that nothing can more effectually contribute to the happy and prosperous state of the colonies, in a civil as well as a religious view, than the appointment of resident bishops. A bishop of London, however inclined to do his duty, is too sensible of the importance of the charge which long usage and custom has committed to him, and too conscious of the little service he can do to a clergy at this distance from him, not to feel very anxiously the necessity of a more immediate inspection and government" (Protestant Episcopal Historical Society, *Collections*, i. 138, note 1). In the very year in which the protest appeared (1771), he wrote to Dr. Johnson,

The last objection advanced by Gwatkin and Henley is based on a technicality of procedure, and therefore need not concern us.

Soon afterward the matter was brought before the House of Burgesses. As a token of their approval and appreciation of the action of the protestants, the burgesses, on July 12, passed, "*nemine contradicente*," the following resolution: "That the Thanks of this House be given to the Reverend Mr. *Henley*, the Reverend Mr. *Gwatkin*, the Reverend Mr. *Hewitt*, and the Reverend Mr. *Bland* for the wise and well-timed Opposition they have made to the pernicious Project of a few mistaken Clergymen, for introducing an American Bishop: A Measure by which much Disturbance, great Anxiety, and Apprehension would certainly take place among his Majesty's faithful American Subjects: And that Mr. Richard Henry Lee and Mr. Bland do acquaint them therewith."[1] It is interesting to see the representative assembly of Episcopalian Virginia taking the same stand against the introduction of bishops as that of Puritan Massachusetts.[2] This decided expression of opinion on the part

July 22: "I feel as sensibly as you can wish me to do the distress of the Americans in being obliged, at so much hazard and expense, to come to this country for orders. But I own I see no prospect of a speedy remedy to it. They who are enemies to the measure of an Episcopacy, whether on your part of the globe or ours, have hitherto found means to prevent its taking place. Though no measure can be better suited to every principle of true policy, none can be more consistent with every idea I have formed of truly religious liberty. . . . But whatever are our sentiments or wishes, we must leave it to the discretion and wisdom of Government to choose the time for adopting that measure. Whether we shall live to see that day, is in the hands of God alone. We wish only that we could look forward with pleasure and enjoy the thought" (Beardsley, *Life of Johnson*, 345–346; Chandler, *Life of Johnson*, 200–201; Hawkins, *Missions of the Church of England*, 395, citing Chandler).

[1] *Address from the Clergy of New York and New Jersey to the Episcopalians in Virginia*, 7, note, citing Rind's *Virginia Gazette*, July 12, 1771. See also Perry, *American Episcopal Church*, i. 420.

[2] On January 12, 1768, the Massachusetts House of Representatives had commissioned Samuel Adams to write a letter on the subject to Dennis de Berdt, its agent in London. It ran as follows: "The establishment of a protestant episcopate in America is . . . zealously contended for: And it is very alarming to a people whose fathers, from the hardships they suffered under such an establishment, were obliged to fly their native country into a

of the House of Burgesses put a stop to any further proceedings on the subject of the proposed address to the king.

The matter, however, was not allowed to drop. The hostile attitude of some, and the indifferent attitude of a majority, of the Virginia Episcopalians caused the "Convention of the Clergy of New York and New Jersey" to address them a letter,[1] which requires a brief consideration.

The authors of the *Address* profess the same motives which actuated Chandler in writing his *Appeal*, that is, a wish to expound the true plan on which it is desired to establish bishops, thinking that if their brethren in Virginia understand its true character they will lend it their support.[2] Among other things they point out a fact which, as has been shown, was disregarded, either intentionally or unintentionally, by Gwatkin and Henley in the sixth article of their protest; namely, that since the time of Gibson the Bishops of London have properly possessed no jurisdiction over the colonies, although "according to former Usage," they add, "our Candidates apply to the Bishop of London for Ordination, and he is generally allowed to have a more immediate Connection with the Colonies than

---

wilderness, in order peaceably to enjoy their privileges, civil and religious: Their being threatened with the loss of both at once, must throw them into a very disagreeable situation. We hope in God such an establishment will never take place in America, and we desire you would strenuously oppose it. The revenue raised in America, for ought we can tell, may be as constitutionally applied towards the support of prelacy as of soldiers and pensioners: If the property of the subject is taken from him without his consent, it is immaterial, whether it be done by one man or five hundred; or whether it be applied for the support of ecclesiastical or military power, or both. It may be well worth the consideration of the best politician in Great Britain or America, what the natural tendency is of a vigorous pursuit of these measures" (*Collection of Tracts from the Late Newspapers*, i. 67; W. V. Wells, *Samuel Adams*, i. 157; Mellen Chamberlain, *John Adams*, 30–31; Protestant Episcopal Historical Society, *Collections*, i. 154–155; Perry, *American Episcopal Church*, i. 418). This was not the only time Massachusetts had taken legislative action on the matter (see above, p. 225).

[1] Entitled, *An Address from the Clergy of New York and New Jersey to the Episcopalians in Virginia; occasioned by some late Transactions in that Colony relating to an American Episcopate* (New York, 1771).

[2] *Address*, 9.

any other Bishop." [1]   Then, by a citation from Bishop Terrick's sermon before the Society for Propagating the Gospel, in 1764, they easily refute the assertion that an appeal for a resident episcopate would either be disagreeable to him or be regarded by him in the light of a reflection upon his conduct as diocesan.[2]

The remainder of their paper is conceived in an apologetic tone, and, since it differs but little from most of the publications on the subject, it needs only a word or two here.   One point they insist on is that the Society has been consistent from its foundation, having always sought to secure for the colonies bishops with a jurisdiction purely spiritual.[3]   They also scout the aspersion that it has ever had any design which did not appear on the surface,[4] and indignantly deny the charge that the petitions which it has drawn up from time to time were a result of direction from England, or that Chandler's *Appeal* was written at the instigation of the Archbishop of Canterbury.[5]

To convince the Virginia public at large of what is wanted, and what a part of the clergy of their own colony have actually asked for, they quote from a public print[6] a sample of the proposed address from the Virginia clergy to the king.   It runs as follows: " We make it our humble Request, that the Bishop appointed may come over with no Authority, no Expectation of acquiring any in Respect to the Laity; that he may be empowered to interfere with no Privileges, civil or religious, at present enjoyed by any Society professing Christianity, but dissenting from the national Church; that he may not be

---

[1] *Address,* 27, note.

[2] He "hopes that a Provision will be made for a more regular Exercise of Discipline" in the colonies, and cannot "apprehend that this Provision, confined merely to Purposes of Order and Decency, without affecting any Privilege or Distinction, which might seem to interfere with the Rights of Civil Government, or give any just Occasion to those of a different persuasion, with whom we wish to live as Friends, and Servants of the same common Master, can reasonably admit of Objection from any quarter" (*Ibid.* 27–28).   For other utterances of Bishop Terrick on this head, see above, p. 234, note 4.

[3] *Address,* 30–32.

[4] *Ibid.* 32.

[5] *Ibid.* 34–35.   For these charges, see Blackburne, *Critical Commentary,* 65, 71, note.

[6] Purdie and Dixon's *Virginia Gazette,* July 4, 1771.

suffered to think of taking out of the Hands of Your Majesty's
Courts, already fixed by Law, any of the Business which they
have been used to transact, and which, it must be acknowledged,
they have hitherto transacted with universal Acquiescence and
Approbation; that he may be confined, within the Limits of his
pastoral Charge, to Offices purely episcopal; and that he may
owe a Maintenance suiting his Station and Dignity (as our
Commissary does at present)[1] to the Bounty and Benefaction
of Your Majesty, or to any other Mode of Support not burthen-
some or disagreeable to your American Subjects."[2] Such is a
brief outline of the address of the Northern clergy to their
Southern brethren.[3]

Gwatkin replied to the *Address* in the following year.[4] His
main justification for the position which he takes on the question is based on grounds of political expediency. "I have not,"
he says, "any aversion to Episcopacy in general, to the mode
of it established in England, or even to an American Episcopate,
introduced, *at a proper time, by proper authority, and in a proper
manner*"; but he protests against an "immediate establishment,"
from a prudential regard to the *practicable*, a desire to preserve
peace, heal divisions, and calm the angry divisions of an en-
raged people."[5] According to the existing Virginian laws, the
General Court is, he says, an "Ecclesiastical Court," and claims

---

[1] Through the good offices of his diocesan, Commissary Robinson had
finally obtained his salary, with a warrant for arrears. See a letter to Bishop
Terrick, June 6, 1766, in Perry, *Historical Collections*, i. (Virginia) 519–524.

[2] *Address*, 35.

[3] Besides quoting from the proposed address to the king, the authors cite
the words of Camm, in an answer which he had written to the protest of one
of the opposing clergymen. Camm said, in effect, that he would not have had
anything to do with the application to the king, had he not believed "that
such an American Episcopate, as is at present desired, by any of its Favorers,
as far as he could judge, . . . can affect, in the least Degree, neither the natural Rights, nor the fundamental Laws, nor the Property, nor the legal Privileges, civil or religious, of any Body of Men, or of any Individual whatever"
(*Address*, 36).

[4] His pamphlet is entitled *A Letter to the Clergy of New York and New
Jersey, Occasioned by an Address to the Episcopalians in Virginia* (Williamsburg, 1772).

[5] *Ibid.* 8.

"an entire and complete jurisdiction over the clergy of the Province."[1] In his opinion, bishops settled in Virginia ought to enjoy all the powers of English bishops; for otherwise a precedent, dangerous to the integrity of the establishment in the mother country, would be set for curtailing the powers legally appertaining to the episcopal office.[2] He shows that in Virginia this episcopal power would involve, in the first place, a seat in the council; in the second place, the authority to set up ecclesiastical courts; thirdly, jurisdiction over the laity, as well as over the clergy, of its own communion; and, finally, at least a negative on the choice of the vestries in the matter of presentation.[3] Obviously all this would have clashed with ideas and institutions that were, by both law and custom, firmly rooted in Virginia.

A unique contribution to the episcopal discussion is Gwatkin's attempt to prove that the powers of a bishop, in their fulness, are involved not only in the English state system, but in the very structure of the church. In order to show this, he quotes the following extracts from the canons: "Priests and Deacons must do nothing without the knowledge and consent of the Bishop" (Apostolical Canons); "Priests are not allowed to proceed to business without the license of their Bishop" (Canons of Ancyra); "If any priest go to the Emperor without the Consent and Letters of the Bishop of the Province, and especially of the Metropolitan, he shall not only be ejected from the communion, but also be deprived of his dignity; but if Business require him to make any application, he shall do it with the Advice and Consent of the said Metropolitan and Bishop, and leave their Letters" (Antiochian Canon).[4] This argument, reënforced though it is by a formidable array of quotations, really amounts to nothing, since it only proves the necessary subjection of priests to their bishops; and this was something which every advocate for an American episcopate desired and provided for, even in his most limited plans.

---

[1] *A Letter to the Clergy of New York and New Jersey, Occasioned by an Address to the Episcopalians in Virginia* (Williamsburg, 1772), 11.

[2] This argument had been often used before.

[3] *Ibid.* 12–15.

[4] *Ibid.* Postscript.

Such is the general character of the reasoning of Gwatkin, who apparently had the last word to say in the discussion. Many of his arguments are either technical or faulty, or at best of mere antiquarian interest. An attempt to estimate them at their true worth has shown that the root of his objection, and probably of that held by those who actively supported his protests, is the old one which we have so often had occasion to consider, that bishops would of necessity come over vested with state powers, which, involving encroachments on the existing colonial system, would tend to increase the opposition to the home government, already strained to the danger point.[1]

[1] This is well voiced in an earlier protest written by Hewitt and Bland. "As the Right of appointing them [bishops] is vested in the Crown," they say, "and will, at present, be delegated to a Ministry, whose Sentiments have ever appeared extremely hostile and inimical to the common Rights of Mankind, it can never be thought for the Interests of Religion, in the present Situation of political Affairs, to extend the Power of the Crown, and the Influence of such Ministers . . . Such Ministers in the Appointment of an American Bishop could never think of chusing a Man the most proper and fitting to discharge the Functions of so important an Office. They would only be solicitous to meet with a Person of blind Submission and unlimited Obedience who should never feel any Remorse in executing what they, in their Omnipotence, should command him" (cited in the *Address*, 38–39).

CHAPTER XI.

FROM SHERLOCK'S DEATH TO THE REVOLUTION, 1761–1775.

It remains to consider the history of the episcopal question in the colonies from the death of Sherlock to the beginning of the Revolution. Sherlock's successor was Thomas Hayter. He was consecrated October 5, 1761, but died January 9, 1762,[1] before he had time to identify himself in any way with the colonies. Hayter was succeeded by Richard Osbaldeston, who continued in office till his death in 1764.[2] He seems to have possessed the esteem and confidence of the Lords of Trade, for they consulted him frequently on colonial church matters.[3] Although always willing to give an opinion on such occasions, he was extremely careful not to meddle with any cases except those relating to the maintenance of the clergy or the status of the Church of England in those colonies where it was established. For this reason he refused to decide upon the legality of an "Act for Propagating Christian Knowledge," of which Henry Caner, rector of King's Chapel, Boston, had complained to the Archbishop of Canterbury, who in turn had handed the matter over to Osbaldeston.[4]

On the other hand, the question of the North Carolina vestry acts,[5] which was still unsettled,[6] gave the bishop an opportunity to make several declarations of interest. The act of 1755 having been annulled by the crown, the assembly of North Carolina

---

[1] For Hayter, see *Dictionary of National Biography*, xxv. 305–307.

[2] *Ibid.* xlii. 275–276.

[3] From long-established custom, for he was no longer by law diocesan of the Church of England in the colonies. Cf. Archbishop Secker to Dr. Caner, October 6, 1762, in Perry, *Historical Collections*, iii. (Massachusetts) 474–476.

[4] Osbaldeston to Secker, October 11, 1762, *Ibid.* 476–477.

[5] The Church of England was at least partially established in North Carolina during this period; its regular establishment was first secured by an act of assembly of May, 1765. See *North Carolina Records*, vii. 472–491.

[6] See above, p. 130 ff.

in 1760 passed two other laws, which reached the hands of Bishop Hayter for consideration November 25, 1761. After his death they were returned to the province by his executors. Nothing farther was done until the following spring, when, on March 18, 1762, the Board of Trade ordered its secretary, Mr. Pownal, to transmit the two acts to the new bishop, in order that he might pass an opinion on them, "so far as they regard the establishment of the Church of England in that Colony the right of patronage to livings and the method established for the suspension or removal of Ministers guilty of immorality." [1]

On the 3d of May, Bishop Osbaldeston sent his reply. His objections were directed mainly against a provision in the last part of one of the laws, in regard to the punishing of irregular clergymen. The act proposed to set up a new jurisdiction for prosecuting offenders, by lodging the articles of complaint against them in the temporal courts, "which," according to the bishop, "have an undoubted Right to judge in temporal Matters; but Immoralities being spiritual Crimes whether in the Minister or people, wherever the Church of England has been established these have always been censured in the Ecclesiastical Courts by the Bishop or his Commissaries. To set up any other authority for this purpose is taking away the little Remains of Ecclesiastical Jurisdiction if any is left in that province and reducing the Bishop of London by the Act only to certify as a public Notary that the Minister is duly ordained. This part of the Act is contrary to the common principles of Justice, to punish spiritual Crimes in temporal Courts. It is likewise contrary to an express Law in North Carolina, which enacts that all Statutes made in England for the Establishment of the Church shall be in force there." [2] He should have said that such offences had been tried in the ecclesiastical courts during the time of Gibson; but that, after his commission had lapsed with his death, such courts ceased to have any legal status.[3] According to the letter of the law, therefore, Osbaldeston's contention was unsound.

---

[1] *North Carolina Records*, vi. 751.

[2] *North Carolina Records*, vi. 714-716.

[3] As a matter of fact, there were at this time no spiritual courts in the province (*Ibid.* vii. 483).

Nevertheless, his objections seem to have had weight with the Lords of Trade; for soon afterward, they presented the two acts, entitled respectively " An Act for establishing Vestries " and " an Act for making Provision for an Orthodox Clergy," to the king, with a recommendation that he reject them. This was done by his Majesty in a sitting of the Privy Council held at the court of St. James on June 3, 1762.[1] So long as Bishop Osbaldeston occupied the see of London, he saw to it that his functions, or what he regarded as such, were not infringed upon.

His successor, Richard Terrick (1764–1777), did not take such high ground.[2] More than one of his utterances show that he had come to recognize, as fully as Sherlock did, the impotence of the colonial authority formerly appertaining to the see of London, and the necessity of substituting for it a system of control by resident bishops;[3] but either from want of energy or because of the more unfavorable circumstances which had arisen, he made no efforts to alter the existing conditions.

Meanwhile, the North Carolina assembly had passed a new vestry act, which gave less authority to the people and more to the crown, and, in cases of clerical immorality, allowed an appeal from the sentence of the provincial governor to the Bishop of London.[4] Bishop Terrick, to whom it was referred, wrote to the Board of Trade, January 13, 1766, approving the act.[5] He gives it as his opinion that the new law is free from the objectionable features of the acts of 1755 and 1760, namely, the provisions relating to powers claimed by the vestries with regard to the right of presentation, and those affecting the prerogative of the crown. He holds that, since it is silent concerning any claims to such rights, it impliedly leaves them vested in the crown, to be exercised by the governor by virtue of his patent from the king. Many subterfuges, however, remained open

---

[1] *North Carolina Records*, vi. 723.

[2] For Terrick, see *Dictionary of National Biography*, lvi. 78–79.

[3] For examples, see above, p. 234, note 4.

[4] The right of presentation was transferred from the vestries to the crown (see pamphlet in *Fulham MSS.*). It was by this act that the first regular establishment of the Church of England in North Carolina was secured.

[5] *North Carolina Records*, vii. 150–153.

to the vestries which the governor could neither foresee nor prevent.

In his letter the bishop also makes incidentally some interesting comments on his conception of his own jurisdiction. Under the new act he sees no need of any certificate from the Bishop of London as a prerequisite to candidacy for induction; for this restriction formerly acted, he says, only as a check on the vestries. Since the right is now vested in the governor, security from any one of the bishops of the Church of England would, in his opinion, be sufficient.[1]

He notes, further, that the act provides "that if any Incumbent shall be guilty of any gross Crime or Immorality, it shall be lawful for the Governor with the advice of His Majesty's Council to *suspend* him; and that such *suspension* shall remain until such time as the Bishop of London shall either restore or pass sentence of Deprivation upon him by notifying the same to the Governor."[2] Concerning this provision he asks: "But by what authority can the Bishop of London (who has no Commiss^n from the Crown) proceed judicially to restore or to pass Sentence of Deprivat^n? As the case stands at present the Bishop cannot deprive him, however guilty, or if the Governor suspends the Clergyman, however innocent, he must remain suspended if it depends on the Bishop to restore him."[3]

---

[1] Terrick's recommendation on this matter was not adopted, and the Bishop of London continued to enjoy the sole right of issuing certificates (see Governor Tryon to the Reverend D. Burton, secretary of the Society, April 30, 1767 (*North Carolina Records*, vii. 457–458).

[2] This seems to have been the only act passed by any colonial assembly making any such provision.

[3] Terrick got out of the difficulty by granting the governor " full power and authority over the clergy" (Reverend James Reed to the secretary of the Society, July 2, 1771, *North Carolina Records*, ix. 5). I find no record that the act was either confirmed or rejected by the crown. On March 20, 1767, " their Lordships took [it] into consideration . . . together with the Bishop of London's Observations thereupon in his letter to the Board dated 13th January 1766, and it was Ordered, that the Draught of a Representation to His Majesty thereupon should be prepared — which was approved, transcribed, and signed 30th March " (*Ibid.* vii. 546). Since the Bishop's recommendation was favorable, and since the attitude of his predecessors had been the main cause of the rejection of former acts, it is to be presumed that at least the crown did not

Led up to the subject by a consideration of these questions, Terrick next takes occasion to observe "not only how defective the Bishop of London's Jurisdict^n is in the plantations, but what Inconveniences arise from that defect. It is far from being clear," he says, "that a Commiss^n granted to the Bishop of London as it was to Bishop Gibson wo^d be an adequate remedy to those Inconveniences: Bishop Sherlock, who certainly co^d Judge as well as any man how far the powers given by that Commiss^n wo^d enable him to go, and who it is to be supposed had no object^n to the exercise of any Jurisdict^n which wo^d answer the purposes for which it was intended, stated his object^n to such a Commission to his late Majesty in Council as defective in many parts of it and giving Powers which no Bishop at this distance from the Plantat^{ns} co^d exercise effectually."[1] The supposition that Bishop Sherlock would have been willing to undertake the charge of the colonies under a commission arming him with adequate powers has been shown to be erroneous. He was totally opposed to the exercise of any such powers, and was bent upon shifting the seat of episcopal power from the mother country to the colonies.

After reviewing the reasons of his predecessor for wishing a colonial episcopate, and the history of his attempts to secure it, Terrick adds: "And whoever considers the superior Abilities of Bishop Sherlock, as well as the more enlarged extent of our dominions in America since his time, will readily allow that the same objections may be urged with additional strength by one who by experience feels the force of them & sees too much reason to lament that with the best inclinat^{ns} to do his duty He feels himself unequal to that important part of it—the care and superintendency of Religion in the Plantations."[2]

annul the new act. Moreover, several indications go to show that it was accepted by the home government. For example, Governor Tryon, in a letter to the Reverend T. S. Drage, July 9, 1770, speaks of the Church of England as "a Religion that was . . . by Act of the Legislature in 1765 established upon the most solid foundation" (*Ibid.* viii. 217). At any rate, until Tryon was transferred to New York in 1771, he always acted upon this assumption; and the act was practically in force in the province for some years, and seems to have materially strengthened the position of the Church of England there.

[1] *North Carolina Records*, vii. 153. [2] *Ibid.*

Manifestly, Sherlock had fixed his policy on his successors. Following in the footsteps of their zealous predecessor, they desired bishops for the colonies; they refused to take out commissions for the legal exercise of an authority which appertained to them from immemorial custom; and, except in rare instances, they declined to interfere actively in colonial ecclesiastical affairs. As has been said before, just what motives actuated the initiator of this policy it is hard to tell. If Sherlock's own assertions be accepted, the diocese was growing beyond the control of a single man, and a non-resident at that; or, if we go beyond his own statement, perhaps he was influenced by a personal disinclination to undertake an onerous task which he felt did not properly belong to him; or, finally, he may have refused to perform the functions of a colonial diocesan that he might make the need of a resident episcopate more imperative and more apparent, and so force its establishment. But why did he desire bishops for the colonies? Here again, three conjectures at least are possible. It may have been that he was moved by an honorable desire to further the spiritual interests of his fellow-believers beyond the seas; it may have been that he had a selfish wish to shift the burden of the charge from his own hands into others'; or, in accordance with the Jacobian maxim of "no bishop no king," he may have been following the Laudian policy of extending the authority of the Church of England establishment for the purpose of rehabilitating the steadily crumbling political structure in the colonies. Perhaps all these considerations had a share in influencing his action. But whatever object he had in mind, he regarded it necessary, as the first step in its attainment, to show that the Bishop of London was incapable, not only *de facto*, but also *de jure*, of exercising any ecclesiastical authority over the colonial dependencies of Great Britain. In his efforts to secure his end, he struck a blow at the Bishop of London's power in the colonies from which it never recovered, and he succeeded in stamping his policy indelibly upon those who came after him. From his time on, we never again find any incumbent of the see conscious of the rights, or active in the exercise, of his colonial jurisdiction.

Such was the state of things during the period between the

death of Sherlock and the Revolution. The authority of the Bishop of London had faded to such a pale tradition that, in spite of the laws establishing the Church of England, which still remained on the statute books of some of the colonies, a contemporaneous historian was justified in stating broadly that there was really no provincial church government.[1] Naturally, many remedies were suggested, of which, as has been seen, that most frequently urged was the settlement of resident bishops. But other plans were also put forward. For example, the author just alluded to remarks that perhaps a superintendent from the "Society of 1701 might have a good effect, with a power and instructions to remove missionaries from one station to another, as the interest of propagating the gospel might require."[2] Dr. William Smith, provost of the College of Philadelphia, later a stanch supporter of the plan of introducing bishops,[3] advocated, in 1762, the restoration of commissaries, who should have more power than they had hitherto possessed and should be distributed as follows : one for the district of New Hampshire, Massachusetts, and Rhode Island, with a residence at Boston ; one for the district of Connecticut and New York, with a residence at New York ; one for the district of Pennsylvania and New Jersey, with a residence at Philadelphia ; one for Maryland, if Lord Baltimore would give his countenance and authority to support him in his duty ; one for Virginia, to reside at the College of William and Mary ; one for the district of North and South Carolina, with a residence probably at Charleston.[4]

These suggestions, however, met with scant consideration,[5]

[1] Meaning, of course, according to the Church of England system. See Douglass, *Summary*, i. 230.

[2] *Ibid.*

[3] See above, ch. viii. *passim.*

[4] The seat of the commissary for Maryland was evidently not determined ; perhaps it was meant to be left to the proprietary. Delaware was, of course, intended to be included in the district of Pennsylvania and New Jersey, and Georgia probably in that of North and South Carolina. See Dr. Smith's "General Account," in *Fulham MSS.*

[5] Nevertheless, February 3, 1763, the clergy of Pennsylvania sent an address to Bishop Osbaldeston, praying that he would make Dr. Smith their commissary (*Fulham MSS.*).

for the episcopal question was the leading topic of the hour. Having already described the various controversies waged on the subject, and the arguments urged for and against the plan, we shall now examine the correspondence between the leading Episcopal clergymen in the colonies and the bishops in England. In this way we can supplement the public by the private utterances of the pro-episcopal party, in order to make sure whether its real and its assigned motives always agreed.

The accession of King George III.,[1] and the prospect of a speedy termination of the war which had been for some years engaging the attention and taxing all the energies of the English nation, gave a glimmer of hope to those earnest in the cause of American bishops. Accordingly, Dr. Johnson sent a letter to Archbishop Secker to sound him on the advisability of moving the new sovereign to settle bishops in the colonies at the conclusion of the peace, and enclosed the draft of a proposed address to his Majesty.[2] Secker, however, thinking that the time was not yet ripe, and fearing that any rash step might ruin the whole cause, at once replied, " This is a matter of which you in America cannot judge; and therefore I beg you will attempt nothing without the advice of the Society, or of the Bishops." [3] Indeed, Secker's whole energy at this time was bent toward checking the rather unbridled zeal of his colonial correspondent. This attitude is best seen in an undated answer to a letter from Johnson of July 13, 1760. Johnson had prepared a paper for the *London Magazine,* and also letters for Lord Halifax and William Pitt, and had sent them to Secker for his approval. The Archbishop, while acknowledging the truth and justice of the statements contained in the article submitted to him, was nevertheless opposed to publishing them unseasonably to the world, and thought that even when the right time should come, the preferable method would be a private application to such persons as had the ear of the king. To flaunt the matter in a public magazine, the character and reputation of which his

[1] October 25, 1760.

[2] See Beardsley, *Life of Johnson,* 256; Chandler, *Life of Johnson,* Appendix, 184–188 (Secker to Johnson, December 10, 1761).

[3] *Ibid.*

Grace justly held in low esteem, would be the surest way to draw down upon their cause the contempt of those men in high positions whose good opinion it was necessary to secure.[1] After this reproof he rewards his correspondent with a crumb of comfort by way of assuring him that he has not been idle in their common cause. " I have spoken," he says, "concerning a new Lieutenant-governor, in the manner which you desired, to the Duke of Newcastle and Mr. Pitt, and also to Lord Halifax, in whom the choice is. They all admit the request to be a very reasonable and important one, and promise that care shall be taken about it. The last of them is very earnest for bishops in America. I hope we may have a chance to succeed in that great point, when it shall please God to bless us with a peace." Owing to the fall of the Newcastle ministry, which followed hard upon the writing of this letter, the sincerity of its promises was never put to the test, and the subject was again left hanging.

It will be unnecessary to follow in detail the correspondence of this period, abounding as it does in expressions of alternate hope and fear. If it ever happened, as it did in a few cases, that some member of the ministry promised to bring the matter up for consideration, adverse circumstances invariably occurred to prevent him from keeping his word.[2] Johnson and his

---

[1] For the letter, see Beardsley, *Life of Johnson*, 252–253; Chandler, *Life of Johnson*, Appendix, 179–182.

[2] See, for example, a letter from Secker to Johnson, March 30, 1763, in Chandler, *Life of Johnson*, Appendix, 191–195. On September 28, 1763, he wrote again to Johnson: "What will be done about Bishops, I cannot guess. Application for them was made to Lord Egremont, who promised to consult with the other ministers, but died without making any report from them. His successor, Lord Halifax, is a friend to the scheme; but I doubt whether in the present weak state of the ministry he will dare to meddle with what will certainly raise opposition" (Beardsley, *Life of Johnson*, 276–278). Compare also Secker to the Reverend Jacob Duché, September 16, 1763, in Perry, *Historical Collections*, ii. (Pennsylvania) 389–391. Writing again to Dr. Johnson, May 22, 1764, he says: "The affair of American Bishops continues in suspense. Lord Willoughby of Parham, the only English Dissenting Peer, and Dr. Chandler have declared, after our scheme was fully laid before them, that they saw no objection against it. The Duke of Bedford, Lord President, hath given a calm and favorable hearing to it, hath desired it may be reduced into writing, and promised to consult about it with the other ministers at his

adherents, in their letters written at this period, suggest one expedient after another, only to find themselves checkmated at every move. One result of these successive disappointments was to alienate what little sympathy this coterie of prominent Episcopal clergymen in America had ever had for free colonial institutions, and it had always been dubious enough. This fact crops out from time to time in the correspondence. " Is there then nothing more that can be done," writes Johnson to Secker, December 20, 1763, " either for obtaining bishops or demolishing these pernicious charter governments, and reducing them all to one form in immediate dependence on the king? I cannot help calling them pernicious, for they are indeed so as well for the best good of the people themselves as for the interests of true religion." [1] Apparently oblivious of the fact that the home government, which had never, since the end of the previous century, taken any steps toward setting up a colonial episcopate, had as a government shown no indications of changing its policy, the pro-episcopal leaders attributed to it a disposition in their favor which was only restrained by the powerful political influence of the dissenters. Hence such utterances as those of Johnson, should they by any chance

first leisure. Indeed," he continues, " I see not how Protestant Bishops can decently be refused us, as in all probability a Popish one will be allowed, by connivance at least, in Canada " (Beardsley, *Life of Johnson,* 280–283 ; Chandler, *Life of Johnson,* Appendix, 195–198 ; Hawkins, *Missions of the Church of England,* 393).

[1] The whole letter is printed in Beardsley *Life of Johnson,* 278–280. Writing again, September 20, 1764, he says: " With regard to the settling Episcopacy in these countries . . . I know that all the Church people (except a few luke-warm persons and free-thinking pretenders to it, and sometimes attendants on it, but are really enemies to any establishment) are very desirous of it ; and that all moderate Dissenters, who, I believe, are the most numerous in the whole, and who know what is really designed, have little or no objection to it ; and that the number of such bitter zealots against it is comparatively few, and chiefly in these two governments [Massachusetts Bay and Connecticut], either such loose thinkers as Mayhew, who can scarcely be accounted better Christians than the Turks, or such furious bitter Calvinistical enthusiasts as are really no more friends to monarchy than Episcopacy ; and against people of both these sorts Episcopacy is really necessary towards the better securing our dependence, as well as many other good political purposes ' (*Ibid.* 294–297).

have become public, could have had no other effect than to prejudice their own prospects, as well as the cause of peace between the colonies and the mother country.

Since the consideration of the subject thus far has shown how potent a factor the episcopal question was in forcing apart the two great branches of the English race, it seems almost incredible that persons could have been found in those days who maintained that the timely establishment of an American episcopate would have been one of the surest means of cementing them and of averting the separation which followed. Yet such was the fact. The view is most clearly set forth in a letter of Chandler to the secretary of the Society, January 15, 1766. Having pictured the political situation after the repeal of the Stamp Act, and commented on what he regards as the excesses of his countrymen, Chandler adds that "if the interest of the Church of England in America had been made a National Concern from the beginning, by this time a general submission in the Colonies to the Mother Country in everything not sinful might have been expected"; and he goes on to say that the home government is under great obligation to the Society for Propagating the Gospel for its efforts in assisting the church, and thus indirectly in securing the loyalty and fidelity of the colonists.[1] And this was no isolated or ephemeral notion. The same idea was expressed by the clergy of Massachusetts and Rhode Island in a convention opened at Boston, June 6, 1767,[2] and as late as 1775, by Bishop Lowth, in a letter to Dr. Chandler.[3] But any careful study of the Puritan mind and

[1] This letter is cited more fully above, p. 113, note 1.

[2] They say: "We flattered ourselves that such an extensive territory as was heretofore possessed, and hath since been added to the British dominions by the late war, would certainly have been followed by some provision of this kind; but especially the late popular tumults in these colonies, we imagined, would have strongly pointed out the necessity of such a step towards the uniting and attaching the colonies to the mother country, and have silenced every objection that could be raised against it" (Hawkins, *Missions of the Church of England*, 396–397, quoting from a report to the Society).

[3] He says: "If it shall please God that these unhappy tumults be quieted, and peace and order restored (which event I am sanguine enough to think is not far distant), we may reasonably hope that our governors will be taught, by experience, to have some regard to the Church of England in

of previous colonial history makes it evident that such a step would probably have had the result of precipitating, rather than of retarding, the struggle which other circumstances made inevitable sooner or later.

The Stamp Act, however, spoiled what little chance the Episcopalians had ever had of securing their long-cherished wish. The question was agitated, indeed, long afterward, till the near approach of the war and the accompanying excitement crowded it to one side; but it is certain that, from this time on, though they did not publicly admit it, two of the prominent leaders in England and America began to despair.[1]

America " (the Society's *Digest*, Appendix, 748). See also Chandler, *Life of Johnson*, Appendix, 205–208 ; Hawkins, *Missions of the Church of England*, 401.

[1] In 1765 Johnson wrote to Secker: "These people will stick at nothing to gain their point. It seems they make gentlemen believe that nineteen twentieths of America are wholly against it [the introduction of bishops] themselves, and that it would make a more dangerous clamor and discontent than the Stamp Act itself, than which nothing can be more false. Had it been done last spring (when the dissenters themselves expected nothing else), and the Stamp-Act postponed till the next, it would have been but a nine-days' wonder, nor do I believe one-half of the people of America would have been much, if at all, uneasy about it" (Beardsley, *Episcopal Church in Connecticut*, i. 243). Secker, in a letter to Johnson, July 31, 1776, gives additional testimony on this point. " It is very probable," he says, " that a Bishop or Bishops would have been quietly received in America before the Stamp-act was passed here. But it is certain that we could get no permission here to send one. Earnest and continued endeavors have been used with our successive ministers, but without obtaining more than promises to consider and confer about the matter, which promises have never been fulfilled. . . . Of late indeed it hath not been prudent to do anything unless at Quebec. And therefore the Address from the clergy of Connecticut, which arrived here in December last, and that from the clergy of New York and New Jersey, which arrived in January, have not been presented to the King. But he hath been acquainted with the prospect of them, and directed them to be postponed to a fitter time. In the mean while I wish the Bishop of London would take out a patent like Bishop Gibson's, only somewhat improved. For then he might appoint commissaries, and we might set up corresponding societies, as we have for some time intended, with those commissaries at their head. He appears unwilling, but I hope may be at length persuaded to it. . . . I have mentioned our late and former losses of missionaries to the King," says Secker in his concluding paragraph, "as one argument for

William Samuel Johnson, at this time agent for the colony of Connecticut in England,[1] wrote to his father in the summer of 1769 expressing his pleasure that the episcopal controversy was nearing its close, and adding that little attention was paid to it abroad.[2] But the publication of Secker's *Letter* in this year, and the discussion which it stirred up, together with the contributions in the *London Chronicle* relative to this and the " American Whig " controversy, contradict Johnson's assertion.[3] Moreover, the continual pleas of the Anglican bishops in the annual sermons before the Society tended to keep alive an interest in the subject.[4]

Bishops. He is thoroughly sensible that the Episcopalians are his best friends in America. . . . Nor do I think there is any considerable increase of vehemence against Episcopacy here. Declaimers in newspapers are not much to be minded; nor a few hot-headed men of higher rank." (For the full letter, see Beardsley, *Life of Johnson*, 302–304, and Chandler, *Life of Johnson*, Appendix, 198–200; for extracts, Hawkins, *Missions*, 393–394). Secker's closing burst of optimism does not, however, relieve the current of pessimism which pervades the letter. Bishop Lowth, in a letter to Johnson, May 3, 1768, is equally discouraging: " As to the great and important design of an American Episcopate," he writes, " I see no immediate prospect of its being carried into execution. While the state of affairs, both with us and with you, continues just as it now is, I am afraid we may not expect much to be done in it " (Chandler, *Life of Johnson*, Appendix, 201–203; extracts in Beardsley, *Life of Johnson*, 326).

[1] He held this office from 1766 to 1771.

[2] Beardsley, *Life of Johnson*, 326. Johnson was continually writing letters with a view to dampen his father's enthusiasm. See, for example, his reply to a letter from his father, dated June 8, 1767, in which he says: " I doubt not Lord Shelburne said as you have been told. [Shelburne was then secretary of state for the southern department, and was in control of the entire colonial administration; he is reported to have said that there was no need of an American episcopate.] I wish he was the only one amongst the ministers of that opinion. I fear it is universal, and the common sentiment of all the leaders of all parties, and that, perhaps, of all others in which they are most agreed. The 'appeal' you mention [Chandler's *Appeal to the Public*, which Johnson's father had proposed sending him as soon as it was printed, in the hope that it might convince Shelburne of his error], however well drawn up, will, I fear, have very little effect. Perhaps the more you stir about this matter at present, the worse it will be " (Beardsley, *Life of Johnson*, 315–316).

[3] The subject is treated in detail in chapter viii. above.

[4] Some of them are enumerated above, pp. 191–192.

In spite of the discouragements under which the clergy in America labored, and in spite of the fact that the hostility of the dissenters and the indifference of the home government were becoming more and more marked, they continued with unabated zeal their petitions to the authorities in England, both civil and ecclesiastical.[1] As the purpose of the colonists to separate from the mother country became more and more evident, the American Episcopal clergy sought to make use of the situation to secure the great end at which they had been so long aiming. We have already noted, in the correspondence of Johnson and the polemical writings of Chandler, how the monarchical tendency of the episcopal system was emphasized and contrasted with the republican character of independency. Going a step farther, some of the later petitions, which were directed to the English officers of state, strove to prove that the settlement of bishops in the colonies would be one way, if not the only way, to save them from revolt.[2] For example, in

---

[1] For example, May 29, 1771, the "voluntary convention" of the clergy of the Church of England in Connecticut petitioned to the Bishop of London and to the king through the Archbishop of Canterbury. They also asked the support of the Archbishop of York, the Board of Trade and Plantations, Lord Hillsborough, Lord North, the Bishop of Oxford, and the Bishop of Lichfield (Hawks and Perry, *Connecticut Church Documents*, ii. 176-177; Beardsley, *Episcopal Church in Connecticut*, i. 282-283). One extract from the petition to the Bishop of London is interesting for the curious threat which it conveys. The words are as follows: "Must it not be surprising, and really unaccountable, that this Church should be denied the Episcopate she asks, which is so necessary to her well being . . . ? Must not such a disregard of the Church here be a great discouragement to her sons ? Will it not prevent the growth of the Church, and thereby operate to the disadvantage of religion and loyalty? These, may it please your Lordship, not to mention the burthens we feel, are the evils we fear, should our request be denied. Should our application be judged unreasonable, we doubt not it will be remembered that necessity has no law" (Hawks and Perry, *Connecticut Church Documents*, ii. 177). These utterances are in striking contrast to all the other professions of the pro-episcopal party, and indeed to its acts ; for its members were among the king's most loyal subjects, both before and after the date of this writing.

[2] Compare also the following paragraph, written in 1764, probably by Archbishop Drummond (see Protestant Episcopal Historical Society, *Collections*, i. 136, note 1): "It must be owned that the probable consequence [of the establishment of a colonial episcopate] will be the increase of the Church

an " Address of a Committee of the Clergy of the Church of England in New York and New Jersey " to the colonial secretary, Lord Hillsborough, we find the following view: "The members of the national Church are from Principle and Inclination, firmly attached to the Constitution. From them it must ever derive its surest support. We need not enter into a formal Proof of this, as the Reasons are sufficiently obvious. Omitting all other Arguments, that might be adduced, let past Experience decide. Independency in Religion will naturally produce Republicans in the State; and from their Principles, too prevalent already, the greatest Evils may justly be apprehended. The Church must inevitably decrease in the Colonies, if bishops are not sent to relieve its Necessities; and the Dissenters will in Time gain an entire Ascendancy. How far it may be consistent with good Policy and the Safety of the State to permit this, we are willing that your Lordship should determine."[1] But the English officers of state, if they considered this argument at all, saw the fallacy of it, saw that in the situation in which they were placed further to disregard the will of the majority of the colonists was not the way to hold them in submission. Unwise in other respects, they were wise in this.[2]

This seems to be at least a plausible explanation of the disinclination on the part of the home government to meddle in the affair of an American episcopate. Many will say that its apathy was due to indifference. But in 1750 (the only date on which, so far as we have found, there was any complete expres-

of England in America when the present disorder of it is removed; but it should be considered that the Civil Government here [in England] may receive great support there from such increase, and that it is no less important, even as a matter of State, that Ecclesiastics should be able to do good, than that they should not be able to do harm " (" Thoughts upon the Present State of the Church of England in America," *Ibid.* 162).

[1] New York, October 12, 1771, *New Jersey Archives,* x. 309–313. " By order of the clergy " it was signed by the following committee of four: Samuel Auchmuty, Thomas Bradbury Chandler, John Ogilvie, and Charles Inglis, and was taken to England by Dr. Myles Cooper, president of King's College, New York City.

[2] As a public newspaper writer truly said, " There are dissentions enough already in America. Our governors want not to increase, but to pacify them " (*London Chronicle,* February 6, 1769).

sion of opinion from the ministry on the subject) the government was far from indifferent; on the contrary, it entertained grave apprehensions of the consequences which such a step would involve, and made strenuous efforts to keep the question out of public politics.[1] In this it was, for the time being, successful. When the question came up again, more than a decade later, new circumstances had arisen to complicate the situation. The ministers must then have considered the matter, even if only in a cursory way; in fact, we have some slight evidence that they did;[2] and in letting it drop they were probably actuated by reasons of policy. Undoubtedly the great pressure brought to bear on them by the influential dissenters contributed not a little to this result; for enough has already been said about the storm which the bare apprehension of an American episcopate raised both in the colonies and in England,[3] to show that the opponents of the plan did not confine themselves to mere idle raging, but made systematic efforts through such of the English dissenters as had the ear of the government, to prevent the latter from giving any aid or countenance to the project.[4] It was to this interference that the leaders among the pro-episcopal party attributed their defeat.[5]

[1] See above, p. 116 ff. For the correspondence in full, see below, Appendix A, No. xi.

[2] For example, March 30, 1767, in reply to an invitation from the Duke of Newcastle to call at Newcastle House, Archbishop Secker writes, "I am engaged by Appointment to talk with Lord Shelburne about the wonderful State of our ecclesiastical Affairs in America, at half an Hour after Eleven on Wednesday" (*Newcastle Papers*, Home Series, 32980, f. 444).

[3] See above, chs. vi. vii. viii. One other striking instance, coming from an extreme Southern colony, may be added. Mr. Martyn, writing to the Bishop of London from South Carolina, October 20, 1765, says, "If I may form a Judgment from that present prevailing turbulent Spirit which like an epidemick disorder seems everywhere to diffuse itself through this and the other Colonies, I can venture to affirm that it would be as unsafe for an American Bishop (if such should be appointed) to come hither, as it is at present for a Distributor of the Stamps" (*Fulham MSS.*).

[4] See above, ch. x. Cf. Bishop William White, *Memoirs of the Protestant Episcopal Church*, 50.

[5] See, for example, Johnson to Camm: "We have been informed from home that our adversaries, who seem to have much influence with the ministry, endeavor, and with too much success, to make it believed that nineteen twen-

In view of these facts, English statesmen saw that they had nothing to gain and everything to lose by involving themselves in the episcopal question. They knew that bishops with purely spiritual functions settled here would avail them little, and would arouse fully as much odium as an out-and-out state establishment; and, moreover, that the dreaded state establishment would be resisted in the colonies, not only by the Puritans, but by the major part of the Episcopalians themselves.[1] Some writers, as

tieths of America are utterly against receiving Bishops, and that sending them, though only with spiritual powers, would cause more dangerous disturbances than the Stamp-act itself; insomuch that our most excellent Archbishop, who has been much engaged in this great affair, . . . has lately informed me that he has not been able to gain the attention of the ministry to it, though his Majesty is very kindly disposed to favor and promote it" (Beardsley, *Life of Johnson*, 324–325). In one of his many letters to Johnson, Secker said: "We must wait for more favorable times, which I think it will contribute not a little to bring in, if the ministers of our Church in America, by friendly converse with the principal dissenters, can satisfy them that nothing more is intended or desired than that our church may enjoy the full benefit of its own institutions, as all others do. For so long as they are uneasy and remonstrate, regard will be paid to them and their friends here by our ministers of state" (Protestant Episcopal Historical Society, *Collections*, i. 146, note 3). The following testimony is from one of the leading advocates for an American episcopate: "From him I first learned the true reason of the Bishop of London being opposed and defeated in his scheme of sending us bishops. It seems that the Duke of Newcastle, Mr. Pelham, and Mr. Onslow can have the interest and votes of the whole body of the dissenters upon condition of their befriending them, and by their influence on those persons the ministry was brought to oppose it" (Chandler to Johnson, *Ibid.*). May 19, 1766, the Reverend Hugh Neill of Oxford wrote an interesting letter on the same subject (see the Society's *Digest*, 35).

[1] William Samuel Johnson, in reply to a letter from Governor Trumbull asking what had been done in England as to American bishops, expresses the sentiments of many of his fellow-believers. "It is not intended, at present," he says, "to send any Bishops into the American colonies; had it been, I certainly should have acquainted you with it. And should it be done at all, you may be assured it will be done in such a manner as in no degree to prejudice, nor, if possible, even give the least offence to any denomination of Protestants. It has indeed been merely a religious, in no respect a political, scheme. . . . More than this would be thought rather disadvantageous than beneficial, and *I assure you would be opposed by no man with more zeal than myself, even as a friend to the Church of England.* Nay, I have the strongest grounds to assure you that more would not be accepted by those who under-

we have seen, maintained that native bishops would have created a bond of union between the colonies and the mother country which might have averted the war for independence; but such a theory is untenable, and was so regarded by those in authority at that time. Though episcopacy, once established, might have strengthened the arm of the English executive here, yet the advantages did not seem alluring enough to tempt it. Hence, owing to the cautiousness of the Englishmen who had control of affairs, the introduction of bishops was not one of the final causes of separation from the mother country, though the apprehension that such a danger excited in the colonies formed a striking, and not unimportant, phase of the struggle which led to that consummation.

Before concluding this chapter it may not be amiss to notice a few scattered facts concerning the relations of the Bishop of London, or his representatives, with particular colonies.[1]

The little authority which Roger Price exercised as commissary of New England ceased with the expiration of his commission at the death of Bishop Gibson, and from this time the Episcopal churches of the province remained without any resident authoritative head. In spite of the efforts of the clergy,[2] no attempt was made to supply the vacancy.

Finally, the clergy, realizing that they could obtain no help from the authorities at home, determined to take the matter into their own hands. Accordingly, while assembled at Dr. Cutler's funeral in 1765, they agreed to have "an annual convention in Boston, to promote mutual love and harmony amongst ourselves, and to assist each other with advice in difficult cases." Their

stand and wish well to the design, were it even offered" (Beardsley, *Episcopal Church in Connecticut*, i. 265–266).

[1] Owing to the points of more general interest involved, the relations with North Carolina were considered at the beginning of the chapter.

[2] See, for example, Henry Caner to Archbishop Secker, January 7, 1763, "We are a Rope of Sand," he says; "there is no union, no authority among us; we cannot even summon a Convention for united Counsell and advice, while the Dissenting Ministers have their Monthly, Quarterly, and Annual Associations, Conventions, &c., to advise, assist, and support each other in many Measures which they shall think proper to enter into" (Perry, *Historical Collections*, iii. Massachusetts, 489–491).

first meeting took place June 1, 1766. Dr. Caner, who was chosen moderator and secretary, delivered an address in King's Chapel, in which, among other things, he informed his assembled brethren that their convention had the approval of the Bishop of London. Following the service was a dinner, at which the governor was present. "We . . . made something of an appearance for this Country," says Dr. William McGilchrist in his account, "when we walked together in our Gowns and Cassocks."[1] These meetings, which were held annually for some years, served to make the clergy acquainted with one another, if they did nothing more.

The rest of the history of ecclesiastical affairs in Massachusetts during this period has to do mainly with the opposition to the establishment of an American episcopate. Indications of this resistance are found not only in the share which the people of the province took in the pamphlet and newspaper wars already described, but also in the action of the public authorities. One example of such official action has been seen in the letter sent, January 12, 1768, by the Massachusetts House of Representatives to its agent in London, Dennis de Berdt, requesting that he would "strenuously oppose" the introduction of bishops.[2] Throughout these years there were many evidences of such forebodings, expressed both officially and unofficially.[3] When the British evacuated Boston, March 17, 1776, most of the Episcopal clergy in Massachusetts left the colony, and those who remained were forced, at least seemingly, to go over to the

---

[1] Letter to the secretary of the Society, June 27, 1766 (Perry, *Historical Collections*, iii. (Massachusetts) 524).

[2] See above, p. 235, note 2, where an extract from the letter is cited.

[3] For example, Dr. Andrew Eliot wrote to Thomas Hollis in London, January 5, 1768, "The people of New England are greatly alarmed; the arrival of a Bishop would raise them as much as any one thing" (Massachusetts Historical Society, *Collections*, 4th Series, iv. 422; Mellen Chamberlain, *John Adams*, 31). Again, in 1772, the Boston Committee of Correspondence, in a report made in Faneuil Hall on the rights of the colonists, said, "Various attempts . . . have been made, and are now made, to establish an American Episcopate," adding as its opinion that "no power on earth can justly give either temporal or spiritual jurisdiction within this province, except the great and general court" (J. W. Thornton, *Pulpit of the American Revolution*, 192; Chamberlain, *John Adams*, 31).

patriotic side. In the following year an act was passed "forbidding all expressions in preaching and praying that may discountenance the people's support of the independency of these colonies on the British Empire on the Penalty of £50."[1] From this time to the close of the Revolution, the Episcopal Church plays no important rôle in New England history.

At the time when the opposition to an American episcopate was at its height, an interesting project was devised by the royal governor of New Hampshire for establishing the Church of England in his province. His scheme is thus outlined in a letter to a friend: "My dear Sir, I cordially venerate the Church of England and hope to see it universal in this Province, whose lasting welfare I have much and sincerely at heart. Whatever is done in this proposed Plan must be without parade or Show and under powerful Direction, or the whole Matter will be injured rather than served; and I should think that if the Bishop of London should wish well to this Scheme, from being convinced of its utility and speedy practibility, His Lordship could represent it to His Majesty so effectually as to obtain the Chaplainship,[2] which would be so eminently advantageous to the cause of our Religion, and exceedingly dignify and facilitate the Political Administration of the Government, both of them you are sensible, Sir, at this Time requiring all the care and prudence they can have."[3] Although this plan was never carried out, it is interesting as another indication of the close connection which existed in the minds of many people at that time between episcopal and monarchical forms of government.

In the various colonies, many questions of ordinary church administration, as they came up for solution, were, as heretofore, referred to the Archbishop of Canterbury, the Bishop of London, and the Society for Propagating the Gospel; but throughout the country the clergy were complaining of the lack

---

[1] From an address by the Reverend William Clark to his congregation at Dedham, March, 1777. See Perry, *Historical Collections*, iii. (Massachusetts) 591–592.

[2] The governor regarded a royal chaplain as necessary for the furtherance of his project.

[3] Governor John Wentworth to Joseph Harrison, September 24, 1769, *Fulham MSS.*

of efficient organization of ecclesiastical government. Most of these complaints, however, came from the Northern and Middle colonies, where the remedy almost invariably suggested was the settlement of resident bishops. In the Southern colonies, on the other hand, at least in Virginia and Maryland, there was, if not a general, at least a very decided, opposition to such an establishment. The course of events in Virginia has been described at some length in a previous chapter. An attempt to introduce bishops into Maryland called up a like resistance. When eight of the clergy drew up a petition to be presented to the governor, the Archbishop of Canterbury, the Bishop of London, and Lord Baltimore, the governor intervened, refusing to accept the petition as the act of the whole body of clergy in the province. He informed the petitioners, however, that in view of the many and important considerations involved, he would lay the matter before the House of Representatives. This was hardly welcome news to the authors of the petition, for the reason that they had alluded to the legislative body in rather unflattering terms. After some deliberation the governor and assembly refused to consent to the sending of the petition to England; but in spite of this prohibition it was sent,[1] and as a result Lord Baltimore instructed Governor Eden to prevent the clergy from assembling thenceforth on any occasion whatever.[2]

As heretofore in this province, there continued to be many complaints of the bad character of the clergy and of the encroachments and tyranny of the proprietary, who claimed the sole right of patronage and often caused clergymen unpleasant to the people to be inducted.[3] With a view to amending and regulating the conduct of the clergy, the assembly drafted an

---

[1] Compare a letter from the "Convention of Delegates from the Synod of New York and Philadelphia and from the Associations of Connecticut" to the "Dissenting committee" of London, *Minutes of the Convention*, 32–34.

[2] Hawks (*Ecclesiastical Contributions*, ii. Maryland, 256) gives the date of their petition as 1770; but either the petition was earlier or the prohibition of Lord Baltimore was not, as Hawks conjectures, in consequence thereof, for the Reverend T. J. Claggett, writing September 20, 1769, speaks of the prohibition as already issued (see Perry, *Historical Collections*, iv. Maryland, 340–341).

[3] See Chandler to Bishop Terrick, October 21, 1767, *Ibid.* 334–335.

act providing "That after such a day the Governor, 3 Clergymen, & 3 Laymen should be constituted a spiritual court. That any Clergy man that was guilty of any acts or act of immorality, or should be 30 days absent from his Parish at one time, should be suspended from preaching and be deprived of his living." Though no one disputed the need of some means of regulating the lives of irregular clergymen, the clerical order, as a whole, become alarmed at the prospect of such a presbyterian form of government with lay elders, and, moreover, considered it subversive of the canons of the church, which gave to the bishop alone power to pass sentence in such cases. Hence they raised a strong opposition to the measure, and, though the bill passed the upper and lower house of assembly, Governor Sharpe refused to sign it, alleging that he had no instructions authorizing him in such a case.[1] This was apparently the last attempt on the part of the Maryland assembly, before the Revolution, to assume the authority of the Bishop of London in ecclesiastical concerns.

Little more remains to be said. Ecclesiastical questions lost their significance as those of a civil nature became more pressing. The agitation kept growing, till the colonists secured what for a period of more than one hundred and fifty years they had been striving to attain, independence in all relations, religious as well as secular. The treaty of 1783, which acknowledged the United States as a sovereign and independent nation, put an end to all official connection between the Church of England establishment and her trans-Atlantic offspring. If the Episcopal Church was to continue to exist in the new nation, it must, like all other institutions of the land, be self-governing. If it was to have bishops, it must have them independent of all foreign control.

---

[1] See the Reverend Hugh Neill to Bishop Terrick, September 20, 1768, in Perry, *Historical Collections*, iv. (Maryland) 337–338. Neill urges the bishop to obtain some instruction to prevent in the future any such encroachment on the integrity of the establishment. The story is told also in an anonymous letter, and in one from the Reverend T. J. Claggett to Bishop Terrick, September 20, 1769 (*Ibid.* 339–341).

CHAPTER XII.

AFTER THE REVOLUTION: THE ESTABLISHMENT OF AN AMERICAN EPISCOPATE.[1]

ONE result of the American Revolution was to break off all authoritative connection between the Church of England establishment and the Episcopal Church in this country, to abolish the colonial jurisdiction of the Bishop of London, and to put an end to any further prospect of obtaining from the English government the settlement of an American colonial episcopate as a branch of the Anglican hierarchy. Apparently, the last instance in which the Bishop of London, as such, was identified with the Episcopal Church here was an act, passed in 1784, "to impower the Bishop of London for the time being, or any other bishop to be by him appointed, to admit to the order of deacon or priest, persons being subjects or citizens of countries out of his Majesty's dominions, without requiring them to take the oath of allegiance as appointed by law."[2] This act was passed as an expedient to get over a very obvious difficulty brought about by the changed relations between the two countries. Early in the year two candidates from the United States had gone to England for holy orders, and had been refused because, as American citizens, they could not take the oath of allegiance to the British crown. In their perplexity they appealed to their influential countryman, Benjamin Franklin, then in Paris. Although willing, he hardly knew how to help them, as he showed by going first to the French bishops,

---

[1] The account of the events treated of in this chapter is drawn chiefly from the unpublished letter books of Bishops Seabury, White, and Parker, most of which are either printed or cited in Hawks and Perry, *Connecticut Church Documents*, ii. 210 ff. The story is also told in Beardsley, *Life of Seabury*, chs. xi.–xxi. and in his *Episcopal Church in Connecticut*, i. ch. xxvi. ff.

[2] Statute 24 George III. c. 35.

and finally to the pope's nuncio.[1] As a temporary shift, the passage of the above-named act was secured, but it was of necessity only an expedient for the time being until a more satisfactory plan could be devised. Its chief defect was that it made no provision for the consecration of American bishops; and plainly, if the American Episcopal Church was to grow, there must be resident bishops vested with authority to ordain, confirm, and administer ecclesiastical affairs. The United States of America could have no place for a church which was not essentially American in its government and tendencies. How to continue the traditions of the Church of England, and at the same time to meet this end, was the problem upon the settlement of which the church's future here was dependent. Meanwhile, a plan had been set on foot which aimed to solve the difficulty, and it will be the purpose of this chapter to trace the inception, progress, and final success of that plan.

The first step toward obtaining bishops for America was taken in 1783, when the ten missionaries of the Society for Propagating the Gospel, still remaining in Connecticut, assembled, and chose the Reverend Samuel Seabury to go to England for episcopal consecration.[2] Into all the negotiations concerning Seabury, which went on between the New York and Connecticut clergy on the one hand and the Archbishop of York[3] on the other, and into all Seabury's conferences with the Archbishops of York and Canterbury, and the Bishop of London, it will not be necessary to enter here.[4] Suffice it to say that, failing to accomplish anything in England, Seabury

---

[1] Hawkins, *Missions of the Church of England,* 402–403, citing Hoare, *Memoirs of Granville Sharp,* 215.

[2] Hawks and Perry, *Connecticut Church Documents,* ii. 211. The details of the proceedings may be found in the letters of the Reverend Daniel Fogg, rector of Pomfret, Connecticut, to the Reverend Samuel Parker of Boston, *Ibid.* 212–213, citing Bishop Parker's correspondence.

[3] Who acted as primate during a brief vacancy of the see of Canterbury.

[4] They are considered at length in the *Churchman's Magazine* (1806), iii. and in Hawks and Perry, *Journals of the General Conventions of the Protestant Episcopal Church,* 1785–1853, i.; also in Bishop White's *Memoirs* (Appendix and illustrative documents). For a fuller discussion of the sources, see Hawks and Perry, *Connecticut Church Documents,* ii.

turned at last to the Scotch non-juring bishops for aid.[1] This
idea did not originate with him, or, indeed, with any American,
but with an Englishman; for the subject was first broached by
Dr. George Berkeley, son of the famous Bishop of Cloyne, in
a letter to the Reverend John Skinner, later coadjutor to the
non-juring primus of Scotland. Skinner finally gave his approval to the plan, and soon after gained the acquiescence of
his superior. With the ice thus broken, Seabury's request for
consecration was readily granted, and on November 14, 1784,
the ceremony was performed by Robert Kilgour, primus and
Bishop of Aberdeen, John Skinner, his coadjutor, and Arthur
Petrie, Bishop of Ross and Moray.[2]

Seabury's reasons for applying for the Scottish consecration
are stated at length by him in a letter of February 27, 1785, to
the Reverend Dr. William Morice, secretary of the Society.
" Finding," he says, " at the end of the last Session of Parliament that no permission was given for consecrating a Bishop
for Connecticutt or any of the American States, in the Act
enabling the Lord Bishop of London to ordain foreign candidates for Deacon's or Priest's orders; and understanding that a
requisition or at least a formal acquiescence of Congress, or
of the supreme authority in some particular State, would be
expected before such permission would be granted; and that a
diocese must be formed, and a stated revenue appointed for the
Bishop, previously to his consecration, I absolutely despaired
of ever seeing such a measure succeed in England. . . . The
reasons why this step [his consecration] should be taken immediately," he continues, " appeared . . . to me to be very strong.

[1] An account of the negotiations with the Scottish bishops may be found
in Hawks and Perry, *Connecticut Church Documents*, ii. 239–240, and Wilberforce, *Protestant Episcopal Church*, 199–212.

[2] See Hawks and Perry, *Connecticut Church Documents*, ii. 247–252, citing
Scottish Ecclesiastical Journal, October 16, 1851, which quotes from the
" Minute Book of the College of Bishops in Scotland," where may be found
the original records of the consecration, together with the concordat between
the Episcopal churches of Scotland and Connecticut, and the letter from the
Scottish bishops to the Connecticut clergy. For Seabury's own account of
the consecration, see in his letter book a letter of December 3, 1784, to the
Reverend Jonathan Boucher.

Before I left America a disposition to run into irregular practices had showed itself; for some had proposed to apply to the Moravian, some to the Swedish Bishops, for ordination; and a pamphlet had been published at Philadelphia urging the appointment of a number of Presbyters and Laymen to ordain Ministers for the Episcopal Church.   Necessity was pleaded as the foundation of all these schemes; and this plea could be effectually silenced only by having a resident Bishop in America." [1]

There is no need to consider all the opposition which Bishop Seabury had to encounter on his return to his native land.   It will be sufficient to point out that, owing to the influence of the Reverend Samuel Provoost of New York, who, as an ardent patriot, could not but oppose by every means in his power the loyalist Seabury, an alienation had grown up between the Episcopal clergy of New England and those of the Middle and Southern states.   The former recognized Seabury as bishop, and hence the validity of the Scottish succession; [2] the latter, rejecting both, sought to obtain a bishop through the English line, as well as a revision of the Book of Common Prayer. [3]   Finally the English government was prevailed upon to grant to its American brethren in the faith the Anglican Episcopal succession.   To this end an act was passed by Parliament authorizing either of the two archbishops, together with such of the bishops as they might desire to call as their assistants, to consecrate bishops for America. [4]

As soon as the news reached this country, Dr. Samuel Provoost of New York and Dr. William White of Pennsylvania

---

[1] Hawks and Perry, *Connecticut Church Documents*, ii. 256–259.

[2] This matter of orders was regarded as a crucial question on both sides of the water.   October 29, 1785, nearly a year after Seabury's consecration, Granville Sharp, in a letter to Benjamin Franklin, expressed his doubts as to the validity of orders derived through non-juring bishops, and his preference for a consecration by English bishops.   This, he thought, might be secured if the candidates would bring the proper testimonials.   See Massachusetts Historical Society, *Collections*, 1st Series, iii. 162–164.

[3] Hawks and Perry, *Connecticut Church Documents*, ii. 292–293.

[4] Statute 26 George III. (1786), c. 84.   See Makower, *Constitutional History and Constitution of the Church of England*, 142.   Cf. the Reverend Benjamin Moore to the Reverend Samuel Parker, New York, November 4, 1786, in Hawks and Perry, *Connecticut Church Documents*, ii. 305.

went to England,[1] where they were consecrated, February 4, 1787, by John Moore, Archbishop of Canterbury, William Markham, Archbishop of York, Charles Moss, Bishop of Bath and Wells, and John Hinchcliffe, Bishop of Peterborough.[2] Some two years after their return to America the differences existing between them and Bishop Seabury, and hence those of their respective followings in the churches of the Middle and Southern States, and of New England were amicably adjusted; and Bishop Seabury was invited to attend the " General Convention of the Protestant Episcopal Church of the United States," which opened at Philadelphia, September 29, 1789. Three bishops, the number required by the canons of the Anglican church for the perpetuation of its holy orders, had now been obtained; and the House of Bishops was finally organized, with Bishop Seabury as its first president.[3]

With the establishment of the Protestant Episcopal Church in the United States of America, under the supervision of its own

---

[1] See Hawks and Perry, *Connecticut Church Documents*, ii. 305.

[2] Perceval, *Apostolical Succession*, Appendix, 121. For an account of the consecration of Provoost and White, see the fourth in a series of articles from the *Episcopal Magazine*, printed in the *Pennsylvania Register* (June 27, 1829), iii. 405–406. The series is entitled " A Narrative of the Organization and of the Early Measures of the Protestant Episcopal Church in the United States."

[3] Hawks and Perry, *Connecticut Church Documents*, ii. 359. On September 19, 1790, James Madison was consecrated Bishop of Virginia by John Moore, Archbishop of Canterbury, Beilby Porteus, Bishop of London, and John Thomas, Bishop of Rochester (Perceval, *Apostolic Succession*, 121). This gave the United States three bishops according to the English succession, a sufficient number to consecrate any one who should question the validity of the Scottish line. About this time, however, the English church restored the Scottish non-juring bishops to their position as an integral part of the Anglican hierarchy.

One cause of regret in the formation of the Protestant Episcopal Church in the United States was the refusal of the Methodists to join in its organization. Their secession from the Church of England system began in 1784, when Lowth, then Bishop of London, refused Wesley's request to ordain at least two priests to administer the sacrament to the American Methodists. Coke and Asbury, whom Wesley, in spite of Lowth, sent out as " superintendents," assumed the functions of bishops, and laid the foundations upon which the structure now known as the American Methodist Episcopal Church was reared. See McConnell, *American Episcopal Church*, 170–171, citing Abel Stevens, *History of American Methodism*.

bishops, the connection of the Bishop of London with this country ceased. Likewise, all attempts to establish resident bishops subject to the authority of the Church of England came to an end. It may not be out of place to say a word or two, by way of conclusion, concerning these two lines of development as treated in the preceding chapters. The first may be dismissed with a brief summary. Originating, probably, with a step instigated by Laud in the rounding out of the Stuart-Laudian policy of uniting church and state, the Bishop of London's colonial authority, in America at least, faded into oblivion during the Commonwealth and the Protectorate. Reviving again with the Restoration, under the energetic administration of Henry Compton, it obtained a direct legal recognition during the lifetime of Bishop Gibson, under whom it reached its highest development. Receiving a blow from Bishop Sherlock from which it never recovered, it nevertheless did not become completely extinct until the close of the Revolution.

As regards the second point, almost from the time when the authority of the Bishop of London was extended to include the plantations, efforts were made to introduce a native episcopate to take over his American jurisdiction. This plan was pushed with more or less constancy from its inception in the days of Laud to the outbreak of the War of Independence. At first it was a matter of purely spiritual concern, but with the beginning of the second half of the eighteenth century it became almost inextricably involved in the political history of the period. There are innumerable evidences of the public interest which the question excited during the years just preceding the Revolution. One may point, for example, to the newspaper controversy of 1768–1769; to the active part which such prominent men as William Livingston, John Dickinson, and Roger Sherman took in the agitation; and, finally, to the fact that John Adams, while not concerned in the affair at the time, expressed, later in life, a firm conviction of the importance of the episcopal question in the final epoch of our colonial history.

In view of these facts, some writers have gone so far as to argue that the attempt to impose Anglican bishops on the colonies had an important effect in bringing about the separation

from Great Britain. This theory has been most strongly advocated by Mellen Chamberlain, in an address on John Adams
delivered before the Webster Historical Society.[1] One or two
of the extracts which he cites in support of his opinion are
worthy of consideration. The first is from the Reverend Jonathan Boucher's *View of the Causes and Consequences of the
American Revolution*, published in London in 1797. Boucher
says: "That the American opposition to episcopacy was at all
connected with that still more serious one so soon afterwards
set up against civil government was not indeed generally apparent at the time [in Virginia]; but it is now [1797] indisputable,
as it also is that the former contributed not a little to render the
latter successful. As therefore this controversy was clearly one
great cause that led to the revolution, the view of it here given,
it is hoped, will not be deemed wholly uninteresting."[2] Another
significant quotation is from the letter of John Adams to Dr.
Jedidiah Morse, written December 2, 1815. "Where," he asks,
"is the man to be found at this day, when we see Methodistical
bishops, bishops of the Church of England, and bishops, archbishops, and Jesuits of the church of Rome, with indifference,
who will believe that the apprehension of Episcopacy contributed
fifty years ago as much as any other cause, to arouse the attention, not only of the inquiring mind, but of the common people,
and urge them to close thinking on the constitutional authority
of parliament over the colonies? This, nevertheless, was a fact
as certain as any in the history of North America. The objection was not merely to the office of a bishop, though even that
was dreaded, but to the authority of parliament, on which it
must be founded . . . if parliament can erect dioceses and
appoint bishops, they may introduce the whole hierarchy, establish tithes, forbid marriages and funerals, establish religions, forbid dissenters."[3] These references, supplemented by additional

---

[1] Afterward reprinted in his *John Adams and Other Essays* (1898).

[2] *View*, 150; quoted by Chamberlain (*John Adams*) 37, and, among others,
by Perry, *American Episcopal Church*. i. 425, note 4.

[3] John Adams, *Works*, x. 185; quoted by Chamberlain, *John Adams*, 25,
note. In the same note, Chamberlain quotes an earlier utterance of Adams
from *Novanglus*, February 13, 1775: "It is true that the people of this country

citations, have also been made use of by at least two other writers,[1] neither of whom, however, has drawn such definite and far-reaching conclusions from them as Chamberlain has. Another writer, without giving any authority for his statement, says : " The necessities of the Church, no less than those of the State, demanded the Declaration of Independence and freedom from the Mother Country. Religious freedom was to come as the result of political independence. Its progress was slow before the Revolution . . . But had the New England colonies granted entire toleration, the Church of England would have been fastened upon them. To prevent this was one of the underlying reasons for the Declaration of July 4, 1776." [2]

Undoubtedly, there is something to be said in favor of the argument that the attempt to introduce bishops, and the opposition thereby excited, formed one of the causes of the Revolution. There can be no doubt that the opposition to bishops was based mainly on political grounds : this fact is indicated by the absence of any resistance to the establishment of an episcopate after the Revolution.[3] Moreover, fear and hatred of the Church

in general, and of this province in special, have an hereditary apprehension of and aversion to lordships, temporal and spiritual. Their ancestors fled to this wilderness to avoid them ; they suffered sufficiently under them in England. And there are few of the present generation who have not been warned of the danger of them by their fathers or grandfathers, and enjoined to oppose them."

[1] See Perry, *American Episcopal Church*, i. 425, where he cites the extract from Boucher, and also that from Adams, taking it from Morse's *Annals*, 197–203. These references are also used in the " General Remarks " of the editors of the *Minutes of the Convention of Delegates* (Hartford, 1843), Appendix, 64. The Society for Propagating the Gospel, in its *Digest*, 747, advocates the same view as the authors mentioned above, and refers for authority to Perry, *American Episcopal Church*, i. 408, 410, 425, and to Chandler, *Life of Johnson*, 177. An interesting citation may be found in Perry, *American Episcopal Church*, i. 412, from a speech by Lord Chatham. " Divided as they are," he says, " into a thousand forms of policy and religion, there is one point on which they all agree : they equally detest the pageantry of a king, and the supercilious hypocracy of a bishop."

[2] H. B. Smith, *History of the Church of Christ, in Chronological Tables*, 70.

[3] " The sudden collapse of all such opposition after the Revolution had dissevered the colonies from the motherland shows that the popular objection to

of England and all its appendages were existent in the colonies from their first foundation; and the fact that the majority of the colonists professed a religion hostile, or at least alien, to the Anglican establishment offered good ground for nourishing the seeds of political discontent. But, admitting all this, it must be apparent to one who has followed carefully the course of events, religious and political, during the eighteenth century, that the strained relations which heralded the approach of the War of Independence strengthened the opposition to episcopacy, rather than that religious differences were a prime moving cause of political alienation. The religious controversies, accentuated and drawn into more public prominence, though not first called into being, by the existing political situation, had a reactionary effect, in that, once in full swing, they contributed, in combination with other causes, to embitter the minds of the patriots and thus to accelerate the impending crisis.[1]

Those, then, who argue that the episcopal question was a cause of the Revolution, if they mean an impelling cause, are exposed to the criticism of misconstruing evidence and of con-

the introduction of bishops was chiefly political " (Tiffany, *Protestant Episcopal Church*, 277). Or, to quote one who lived almost in the midst of the events which he described, and who was hostile to the Church of England: " The friends of the Episcopate, notwithstanding all the zeal and exertions which they employed in its behalf, were continually disappointed by difficulties and delay, until the Revolution; which, by establishing the Independence of the United States, effectually precluded the dangers apprehended from their scheme, removed the fears of their opponents, and terminated the controversy " (Miller, *Memoirs of John Rodgers*, 186).

[1] Sir William Johnson, writing to the Society, December 10, 1768, doubts the reality of the fear concerning the introduction of bishops. "We cannot have a clergy here," he says, "without an Episcopate; and this want has occasioned many to embrace other persuasions, and will oblige greater numbers to follow their example, of which the dissenters are very sensible; and by pretended fears of an episcopal power, as well as by magnifying their own numbers and lessening ours, give it all possible opposition " (cited in Perry, *American Episcopal Church*, i. 418). This view, even if true, does not change the aspect of the question in the least; for the important and essential thing is, not so much what actuated the dissenters in their opposition to episcopacy, but the fact that they were really opposed to it.

fusing cause and effect.　　Nevertheless, religious affairs were closely involved in the political questions of the time, and if the ecclesiastical causes of the Revolution were secondary and contributory rather than primary and impelling, certainly there was an ecclesiastical phase of pre-Revolutionary history of no little interest and importance.

APPENDICES.

———◆———

APPENDIX A.

ILLUSTRATIVE DOCUMENTS.

The majority of these documents are transcripts of manuscripts in the Fulham Library, the British Museum, and the Public Record Office, London. The remainder have already been printed, but are included here for the purpose of supplementing and elucidating the text.

I. ORDER OF THE KING IN COUNCIL VESTING THE JURISDICTION OF THE CHURCHES OF DELPH AND HAMBURGH IN THE BISHOP OF LONDON.

P. R. O., *State Papers, Domestic Series,* Charles I., No. 247 for October 1-15, 1633.

At Whitehall ye first of October 1633.

Present.

The King Most Excellent Matie

Lo Arch Bpp of Cant.	Ea of Dorset
Lo Keeper	Ea of Bridgewater
Lo Tresor	Ea of Holland
Lo Privy Seal	Ea of Kelley
Lo Marq^s Hamilton	Lo Cottington
Lo Chamblain	Mr Jus. Mr Sec. Coke

Mr Sec. Windebank

This day his Matie being present in Councell the pticuls following concerning ye Company of Merchant Adventurers and their Government in forreigne parts were fully debated at ye Board vizt

1. The Scandell and prejudice arising by supporting & using a form of discipline in their Church at Delph ; — different from that of their mother Church here, of which they are members.

2. Their opposing and rejecting of Mr. Misselden their Deputy Governor there.

3. The removing and translating of ye principall power and Government of ye said Trade from those forreigne parts and establishing ye same here.

For·ye first which concerns their Church Government. It was agreed upon ye voluntary Assent and Submission of said Company, not only of those here but of some authorized on ye behalf of those at Delph and Hamburgh now present before ye Board and upon other important reasons and considerations resolved & ordered that they should not hereafter receive or admit of any Minister into the said Churches in forreigne parts without his Maties knowledge and approbation of the person : And that ye Liturgy and Discipline now used in ye Church of England should be receaved and established there, And that in all things concerning their Church Government they should be under ye Jurisdiction of ye Lord Bpp of London as their Diocesan. For ye orderly doing whereof Mr Attorney General is hereby prayed and required to advise and direct such a cours as may be most essentiall. . .

II. COMMISSION FOR REGULATING PLANTATIONS. — 1634.

Bradford, *History of Plymouth Plantation* (Massachusetts Historical Society, *Collections*, 4th Series, iii. 456–460). For an account of the various texts of this commission, see above, p. 19, note 1.

Charles by ye grace of God king of England, Scotland, France, and Ireland, Defender of ye Faith, &c.

To the most Reve^d father in Christ, our wellbeloved & faithful counsellour, William, by devine providence Archbishop of Counterbery, of all England Primate & Metropolitan ; Thomas Lord Coventry, Keeper of our Great Seale of England ; the most Reverente father in Christ our wellbeloved and most faithful Counselour, Richard, by devine providence Archbishop of Yorke, Primate & Metropolitan ; our wellbeloved and most faithfull coussens & Counselours, Richard, Earle of Portland, our High Treasurer of England ; Henery, Earle of Manchester, Keeper of our Privie Seale ; Thomas, Earle of Arundalle & Surry, Earle Marshall of England ; Edward, Earle of Dorsett, Chamberline of our most dear Consorte, the Queene ; and our beloved & faithfull Counselours, Francis Lord Cottington, Counseler, [Chancellor?] and Undertreasurour of our Eschequour ; S^r : Thomas Edmonds, knight, Treasourer of our household ; S^r : Henery Vane, Knight, Controuler of ye same household ; S^r : John Cooke, Knight, one of our Privie Secretaries ; and Francis Windebanck, Knight, another of our Privie Secretaries, Greeting.

Whereas very many of our subjects, & of our late fathers of beloved memory, our sovereigne lord James, late King of England, by means of license royall, not only with desire of inlarging yᵉ teritories of our empire, but cheefly out of a pius & religious affection, & desire of propagating yᵉ gospell of our Lord Jesus Christ, with great industrie & expences have caused to be planted large Collonies of yᵉ English nation, in diverse parts of yᵉ world alltogether unmanured, and voyd of inhabitants, or occupied of yᵉ barbarous people that have no knowledg of divine worship. We being willing to provid a remedy for yᵉ tranquillity & quietness of those people, and being very confidente of your faith & wisdom, justice & providente circomspection, have constituted you yᵉ aforesaid Archbishop of Counterberíe, Lord Keeper of yᵉ Great Seale of England, yᵉ Archbishop of Yorke, &c. and any 5. or more, of you, our Commissioners ; and to you, and any 5. or more of you, we doe give and comīte power for yᵉ govemente & saftie of yᵉ said collonies, drawen or which, out of yᵉ English nation into those parts hereafter, shall be drawne, to make lawes, constitutions, & ordinances, pertaining ether to yᵉ publick state of these collonies, or yᵉ private profite of them ; and concerning yᵉ lands, goods, debts, & succession in those parts, and how they shall demaine themselves, towards foraigne princes, and their people, or how they shall bear them selves towards us, and our subjects, as well in any foraine parts whatsoever, or on yᵉ seas in those parts, or in their returne sayling home ; or which may pertaine to yᵉ clergie governmente, or to yᵉ cure of soules, among yᵉ people ther living, and exercising trad in those parts ; by designing out congruente porcions arising in tithes, oblations, & other things ther, according to your sound discretions, in politicall & civill causes ; and by haveing yᵉ advise of 2. or 3. bishops, for yᵉ setling, making, & ordering of yᵉ bussines, for yᵇ designeing of necessary ecclesiasticall, and clargie porcions, which you shall cause to be called, and taken to you. And to make provision against yᵉ violation of those laws, constitutions, and ordinances, by imposing penealties & mulcts, imprisonmente if ther be cause, and yᵗ yᵉ quality of yᵉ offense doe require it, by deprivation of member, or life to be inflicted. With power allso (our assente·being had) to remove, & displace yᵉ governours or rulers of those collonies, for causes which shall seeme to you lawfull, and others in their stead to constitute ; and require an accounte of their rule & governement, and whom you shall finde culpable, either by deprivation from their place, or by imposition of a mulcte upon yᵉ goods of them in those parts to be levied, or banishmente from those provinces in wᶜʰ they have been goveʳ or otherwise to cashier according to yᵉ quantity of y⁰ offense. And to constitute judges & magistrats politicall & civill, for civill causes and under y⁰ power and forme, which to you 5. or more of you shall seeme expediente. And judges & magistrats & dignities, to causes Ecclesiasticall, and under y⁰ power & forme, whiche to you 5. or more of you, with the bishops viceregents (provided by y⁰ Archbishop of Counterbure for y⁰ time being), shall seeme expediente ; and to ordaine courts, pretoriane and tribunall, as well ecclesiasticall, as civill, of judgementes ; to detirmine of y⁰ formes and maner of proceedings in y⁰ same ; and of appealing from them in matters & causes as well criminall, as civill, personall, reale, and mixte, and to the seats of justice, what may be equall & well ordered, and what crimes, faults, or exesses, of contracts or injuries ought to belonge to y⁰ Ecclesiasticall courte, and what to y⁰ civill courte, and seate of justice.

Provided never y⁰ less, yᵗ the laws, ordinances, & constitutions of this kinde, shall not be put in execution, before our assent be had therunto in writing under our signet, signed at least, and this assente being had, and y⁰ same publikly proclaimed in y⁰ provinces in which they are to be executed, we will & comand yᵗ those lawes, ordinances, and constitutions more fully to obtaine strength and be observed shall be inviolably of all men whom they shall concerne.

Notwithstanding it shall be for you, or any 5. or more of you, (as is afforesaid,) allthough those lawes, constitutions, and ordinances shalbe proclaimed with our royall assente, to chainge, revocke, & abrogate them, and other new ones, in forme afforesaid, from time to time frame and make as afforesaid ; and to new evills arissing, or new dangers, to apply new remedyes as is fitting, so often as to you shalle seem expediente. Furthermore you shall understand that we have constituted you, and every 5. or more of you, the afforesaid Archbishop of Counterburie, Thomas Lord Coventrie, Keeper of y⁰ Great Seale of England, Richard, Bishop of Yorke, Richard, Earle of Portland, Henery, Earle of Manchester, Thomas, Earle of Arundale & Surry, Edward, Earell of Dorsett, Francis Lord Cottinton, Sʳ Thomas Edmonds, [Edwards in the manuscript] knighte, Sʳ Henry Vane, knight, Sʳ Francis Windebanke, knight, our comissioners to hear, & determine, according to your sound discretions, all maner of complaints either against those collonies, or their rulers, or govenours, at y⁰ instance of y⁰ parties greeved, or at their accusation brought concerning injuries from hence, or from thence, betweene them, & their members to be moved, and to call y⁰ parties before you ; and to the parties or to their procurators, from hence, or from thence being heard y⁰ full complemente of justice to be exhibited.

Giving unto you, or any 5. or more of you power, y^t if you shall find any of ye collonies afforesaid, or any of ye cheefe rulers upon ye jurisdictions of others by unjust possession, or usurpation, or one against another making greevance, or in rebelion against us, or withdrawing from our alegance, our own comandments, not obeying, consultation first with us in y^t case had, to cause those colonies, or ye rulers of them, for ye causes afforesaid, or for other just causes either to returne to England, or to comand them to other places designed, even as according to your sounde discretions it shall seeme to stand with equitie, & justice, or necessitie. Moreover we doe give unto you, & any 5. or more of you, power & spetiall comand over all ye charters, leters patents, and rescripts royall, of ye regions, provinces, ilands, or lands in foraigne parts, granted for raising colonies, to cause them to be brought before you, & ye same being received, if any thing surrepticiously or unduly have been obtained, or y^t by the same priviledges, liberties, & prerogatives hurtfull to us, or to our crowne, or to foraigne princes, have been prejudicially suffered, or granted; the same being better made knowne unto you 5. or more of you, to comand them according to ye laws and customs of England to be revoked, and to doe such other things, which to ye profite & safgard of ye afforesaid collonies, and of our subjects residente in ye same, shall be necessary. And therfore we doe comand you that aboute ye premisses at days & times, which for these things you shall make provission, that you be diligente in attendance, as it becometh you; giving in precepte also, & firmly injoyning, we doe give comand to all and singuler cheefe rulers of provinces into which ye colonies afforesaid have been drawne, or shall be drawne, give atendance upon you, and be observante and obediente unto your warrants in perill. In testimony wherof, we have caused these our letters to be made patente. Wittness our selfe at Westminster the 28. day of Aprill, in ye tenth year of our Raigne.

By write from ye privie seale,

WILLIES.

Anno Dom: 1634.

III. OBSERVATIONS OF THE BISHOP OF LONDON REGARD-
ING A SUFFRAGAN FOR AMERICA.

Printed in the *New York Colonial Documents*, V. 29, 30, from the *Lambeth MSS.*, No. 711, p. 118.

[Dec. 1707]

The present disorders now arising in some of ye Plantations, and likely to increase to an entire discouragement of the Clergy already there Established, doe, I presume, fully convince the necessity of having a Bishop Established in those parts.

The only question therefore is, what sort of Bishop will be most proper first to settle there. An absolute Bishop, as that of the Isle of Man, will not be so proper, at least to begin with, for these reasons.

1. It will give a great alarm to the several colonies, as it did in K. Charles ye 2^{ds} time, when there came over Petitions and addresses with all violence imaginable.

2. Because the grounds of that opposition are generally still the same.

3. For the true reason of their averseness to a Bishop, is the great apprehension they have of being restrained from that Licentiousness they now too often put in practice.

4. As in Virginia they seldom present a Minister to the Governor to be inducted, but keep him as a probationer all the while he stays with them, that they may make what Composition they please with him for his allowance, and it may be give him leave to make up the rest by taking care of a Neighboring Parish.

5. Besides, all over the Plantations they frequently take other men's wives, are guilty of Bigamy and Incest, which they are apprehensive would be more strictly inquired into, had they a Bishop to inspect over them.

Now a Suffragan would cóme among them with all necessary power to restrain vice and keep good order, without any noise or clamor.

1. They having already been used to a Commissary, a Bishop will come upon them then more insensibly, if he comes over by the same authority, and under ye same Jurisdiction as the others did.

2. Confirmation, Consecration of Churches and conferring Holy Orders are powers they desire to have among them ; and when they come in only by the change of a Title, it will be cheerfully received as a thing of their own seeking.

3. It will be the safest way to take at first for a proof how it will take amongst them, and all faults and defects may more Easily be corrected and amended : because it will not be neer so troublesome to question and remove a Suffragan Bishop as another ; nor will his being put out of office be neer so inconvenient.

4. Besides, the beginning of any new Establishment ought to be carried on gradually, which will make all steps Easier and in case of disappointment the matter will not be so grievous.

This is what occurs to me at present of such observations as I apprehend proper to be laid down.

IV. CORRESPONDENCE OF COMMISSARY GORDON OF BARBA-
DOES CONCERNING THE JURISDICTION OF THE BISHOP
OF LONDON IN THE COLONIES.

From the Manuscripts in the Fulham Library.

I.

Rev. Wm. Gordon to Gov. H. Worsley of the Barbadoes, February
10, 1723/24.

I beg leave to acquaint your Excellency that altho' I never did myself the Honour of writing or applying to the present Bishop of London,
yet his L : ship has thought fit to send me some circular Letters, with some
General Queries, to be answered by the Clergy of this Island ; as also a
Letter, and some particular Queries to myself, and as I shall ever study
to avoid all Appearance of doing anything, in your Excellency's Government ; without your Approbation, so I thought it my Duty to Communicate these Papers to your Excellency, and humbly pray your Excelly
to peruse them, and let me know, whether it be your Excellency's pleasure, that I should forward them as his Lordship desires, being deter-
min'd to take no step without your Excellency's Approbation.

2.

Gov. H. Worsley of Barbadoes in reply to Rev. Wm. Gordon.
February 15, 1723/24.

From the perusal of the R! Reverend Lord Bishop of London's Letter to you, I find his Lordship is of Opinion that there is a great uncertainty in the ground and Extent of his Jurisdiction in the Plantations, and
as I can't authorize any Jurisdiction the Bishop of London may have till
I know what it is, I must consider his Lordships Letters and Queries to
you and the rest of the Clergy of this Island, as private Letters and
Queries to you and them, to which I think you ought all to pay in your
private Capacity, all the honour and respect, that is due to so learned, so
good, so wise, and so great a Prelate. Your prudent Conduct in this
Affair is very Commendable and praiseworthy.

3.

Rev. Commissary Gordon to the Bishop of London.
November 3, 1725.

[Gordon understands that the successive Bishops of London] by ancient right and prescription claimed Jurisdiction of all the foreign plan-

tations. [He also understands that Laud got a declaration of this right by an order in Council; but though he has "searched the Council Books from Queen Elizabeth to King Charles" he has been unable to find any trace of such an order.

After these prefatory remarks he continues as follows :]

If the Bishop of London's authority over the Colonies should not be so very Ancient, It is I think pretty certain that they were put under his Care by an Order in Council in the Latter End of King Charles, or at least in the Beginning of King James 2ᵈ Reign; And, notwithstanding the Original Order is not now to be found in the Council Books, Yet about the time the Order is said to be made there is a Blank to be seen in the Council Books left for Inserting Something which the Clerks have still neglected to insert, and which was probably the very Order wanting; and I am of opinion that whoever has Mr. Blathwaite's Papers, who was at that time Chief Acting Clerk of Council, may find the said Original Order among them —

That there was such an Order I am strongly induc'd to believe from the following Reasons.

1ˢᵗ — Because about that time there was an Order of Council made for adding the Bishop of London to the Lords Commissioners for Trade and Plantations who were then all Lords of the Privy Council.

2ᵈˡʸ Because, about the same time, Several Clauses were added to every Governors Instructions and Authorities, and have ever since continued, some of which are in the Words following. . .[1]

This last Instruction [i.e. that reserving to the Governor the three functions of licenses for marriages, probate of wills, and collation to benefices] or Authority, having these Words, which we have *Reserved* &c, seems to refer to Something done before; for every Reservation necessarily implies some previous Grant out of which the Reservation is made.

3ᵈˡʸ From the annexed Copy of a Letter from Bp. Compton to Lord Howard Governor of Virginia, Septr 1685. Wherein the Order is expressly mentioned, and the Reason why the Power was Vested in the Bishop.

4ᵗʰˡʸ From two Orders of Council, Oct 1686 One Suspending the Bp of London from his Diocese, and Vesting the Exercise of his authority in Commissioners; The other, in about a week after, Suspend-

---

[1] The two clauses about the exercise of ecclesiastical jurisdiction and licensing clergymen; see above, p. 30.

ing him with the same fformality from his Authority in the Plantations, & vesting it in the same Commissioners.

These Reasons, in my Opinion, are Sufficient to Shew that there was a Standing Order of Council Vesting the Ecclesiastical Jurisdiction of the Colonies, in the Bishop of London; tho' not to be found in the Council Books; But even Supposing there never was any such Order, it will make but little alteration in the Case, whilst the Temporary Orders of Council in every Governor's Instructions and Authorities Subsist and continue; ffor as long as they do, they are of as much, nay of more, force than any standing Order of Council, as being themselves not only Solemn Orders of Council pass'd and establish'd but also referred to and expressly enforc'd by Letters Patents under the Broad Seal. The Instructions, which His Majesty in his Patent calls also by the more proper Name of *Authorities* are (in all Matters relating to Government, and not otherwise settled by the English Common or Statute Law before the Year 1626, nor by any Law made in the Barbadoes since) standing Laws, of the same force with Acts of Parliament and equally Obligatory.

'Tis only by Virtue of these Instructions & Authorities that we enjoy the Liberty of being admitted to Bail for all Crimes Bailable by the Laws of England; and by these the Judges think themselves well warranted to proceed accordingly. 'Tis by this we have a Court of Errors, and Liberty of appeal to his Majesty in Council; And Since, by these, the King orders that the Govern.' give all Countenance & Encouragement as far as conveniently may be to the Exercise of the Ecclesiastical Jurisdiction of the Bishop of London excepting as before excepted, the Exercise thereof is well warranted by the Instructions & Authorities and by the Commission under the Great Seal, by which these are expressly enforc'd.

It has been urged that the Words, as far as conveniently may be leave it to the Governor's Discretion whether he will Suffer a Commissary to Act at all; but even in that Sense of the Instruction; it will Surely be Granted that where he not only permits but desires a Commissary to Exercise his Power, there the Instruction is Sufficient Warrant for every Legal Act of his.

This Power only labours under the Defect of being Alterable and Determinable at the King's Pleasure, as the Commissions and Instructions are; But til the King actually Determines Alters or Revokes his Commission & Instructions, they are (with all Deference to Superior Judgments) in my humble Opinion, very Sufficient to Warrant the appointment of a Commissary to proceed in a *Judicial* manner, the Leave & Countenance of a Governor, and so it was always judged in Barbadoes, and ever since the foregoing Authorities were inserted in the Governor's Commission & Instructions, til Mr. Lowther [a clergyman tried in Barbadoes] questioned the Validity of the Bishops Authority. . .

4.

COPY OF A LETTER FROM HENRY L.P BP. OF LONDON TO THE LORD HOWARD OF EFFINGHAM, GOVERNOR OF VIRGINIA.

From the Manuscripts in the Fulham Library.[1]

My Lord,

" I read your Commands for the Books and hope to get an order for them Suddenly, that I may send them by Some Ship of this Season. I do most humbly thank your Ldp for the great Care you have taken in Settling the Church under your Government. There is a Constant Order of Council remaining with Mr. Blaithwaite that no Man shall continue in any Parish without Orders, nor any be received without a License under the hand of the Bishop of London for the time being, and that the Minister shall be always one of the Vestry. This Order was made four or five years since, and I make no doubt, among others, you have it in your Instructions. This King has likewise made one lately that except Licenses for marriages, Probat of wills, & disposing of the Parishes, all other Ecclesiastical Jurisdiction shall be in the Bishop of London. By Virtue of which you shall have a Commission to appoint M.ʳ Clayton, or whom else you think most proper to execute that Authority. One chief Reason why this power is put into me is because unless it comes originally from an Ecclesiastical Person it cannot be legally executed; And I beseech Do not think I would proceed in this or anything else without putting it into Your Ldp's hands and leaving it wholly to your Disposal. I would likewise beg of you to let M.ʳ Clayton know that to go farther would be very unreasonable at this time which may serve for an Answer to his Letter, But as soon as it shall be proper to move in that Business be sure to hear from [me.]

[1] The copy in the *Fulham MSS.* is undated. Gordon, in his letter to Gibson, see above, p. 280, puts it September, 1685.

5.

ORDER IN COUNCIL SUSPENDING BISHOP COMPTON FROM THE EXERCISE OF HIS JURISDICTION IN THE COLONIES.[1]

"AT THE COURT, WHITEHALL, October 27 1686.

"THE KING IN COUNCIL.

Whereas His Majesty has thought fitt to appoint Commissioners for exercising the Episcopal Jurisdiction within the City & Diocese of London, His Majesty in Council does this Day Declare his pleasure that the Ecclesiastical Jurisdiction in the Plantations shall be exercised by the said Commissioners; and did order & it is hereby ordered that the R! Honble the Lords of the Comm̄n for Trade & Plantations do prepare Instructions for the Several Governors in the Plantations accordingly.

V. GIBSON'S COMMISSION AND RELATIVE PAPERS.

I.

EXTRACTS FROM THE WEEKLY MISCELLANY.[2]

Of the Jurisdiction of the Bishop of London in the Foreign Plantations.

[Bishop Gibson applied for a Commission from the King because the ecclesiastical jurisdiction over the colonies was] beyond the limits of his own Diocese; the Plantations being no part of the Diocese of London, nor the Ecclesiastical Affairs thereof under his Care, any otherwise than by special Authority from the King, who, if he please, may as well authorize any other Bishop for that Purpose. . .

To satisfy himself in this Point, he examined all the Council-Books of the Reign of King Charles the Second, Page by Page, but did not find any such Order of Council, either enter'd there, or remaining in the Council-Office. And he was moreover informed by very able Lawyers,

---

[1] Referred to by Commissary Gordon in his letter to Bp. Gibson, see above, pp. 280–281.

[2] This periodical is very rare, the only file I have seen being that in the British Museum. These extracts, from Vol. I, No. 11, pp. 79–86, are valuable as giving a practically contemporary account of the opinions concerning the scope of the Bishop of London's colonial jurisdiction and of Gibson's efforts to place it on a definite footing. The full title is *Weekly Miscellany, Giving an Account of the Religion, Morality, and learning of the Present Times.* Ed. Richard Hooker, Esq. London, 2 vols. 1736–1738.

that such an Order, though it should be found, would not warrant the Bishop to grant Commissions to others, unless he himself should be first empowered so to do by a Commission from the King under the great seal, the Plantations being not part of any Diocese, but remaining under the sole and immediate Jurisdiction of the King; and that Jurisdiction not to be legally delegated, but under the Great Seal. . .

And because the Bishop forsaw, and was inform'd, That the exercise of an Ecclesiastical Jurisdiction over the whole *Body* of the *Laity* in the Plantations, might occasion great Uneasiness, and perhaps publick Disturbance, he humbly proposed to his Majesty in Council, that the Commission under the Great Seal, if thought proper to be granted, might extend only to the Clergy, and to such other Persons and Matters as Concern'd the Repair of Churches, and the decent Performance of Divine service therein: Which was approv'd, and Commission accordingly ordered and issued.

After this, the Bishop presented a second Petition to his late Majesty, relating to the Correction and Reformation of the Lives and Manners of the Laity, in the several Governments of the Plantations. According to the Prayer of which Petition, his Majesty was graciously pleased to order in Council, That an additional Instruction should be sent to the several Governors, of the following Tenor:

' His Majesty having had under his Royal Consideration, a Petition from the Right Reverend Father in God Edmund Lord Bishop of London, humbly beseeching him to send İnstructions to the Governors of all the several Plantations in America, that they cause all Laws already made against Blasphemy, Prophaneness, Adultery, Fornication, Polygamy, Incest, Prophanation of the Lord's Day, Swearing and Drunkenness, in their respective Governments, to be vigorously executed; and his Majesty thinking it highly just, that all Persons who shall offend in any of the Particulars aforesaid, should be prosecuted and punished for their said Offenses; it is therefore his Majesty's Will and Pleasure, That you take due Care for the Punishment of the aforementioned Vices, and that you earnestly recommend it to the Assembly of his Majesty's Province of —— to provide effectual Laws for the Restraint and Punishment of all such aforementioned Vices, against which no Laws are as yet provided; and also you are to use your Endeavors to render the Laws being more effectual, by providing for the Punishment of the aforementioned Vices, by Presentment upon Oath, to be made to the Temporal Courts by the Church-wardens of the several Parishes, at proper Times of the Year, to be appointed for that Purpose, And for the further Discouragement of Vice, and the Encouragement of Virtue and good Living (that by such Example the Infidels may be invited, and desire to embrace the Christian Religion) you are not to admit any Person to publick Trusts and Employments in the Province under your Government, whose ill Fame and Conversation may occassion Scandal. And it is his Majesty's further Will and Pleasure, that you recommend to the Assembly to enter upon proper Methods for the erecting and Maintaining of Schools, in order to the training up of Youth to leading, and to a necessary knowledge of the Principles of Religion.'

The Commission above-mention'd expired upon the Death of his late Majesty; and before a new one could pass the Great Seal, it was represented to the Bishop, 'That insomuch as the Laws of the Several Governments have already provided for the Repair of Churches, and the furnishing of such things as are necessary for the decent Performance of Divine Service; the taking that care out of the Hands of the Vestries who are chiefly intrusted with it, would probably give Uneasiness, and be the Occasion of having the Fabricks and Furniture of Churches not so well taken Care of as they are at present': Whereupon the Bishop, desiring as much as possible to avoid the giving Offense, and the raising any Uneasiness, was content that the new Commission should be confined to a Jurisdiction of the CLERGY alone; and so it stands.

2.

PETITION OF BISHOP GIBSON TO HAVE HIS JURISDICTION PLACED UPON A MORE DEFINITE BASIS.

From the Manuscripts in the Fulham Library.

To the King's Most Excellent Majesty The humble Representation of Edmund Bishop of London.

Sheweth

That from the time that Churches have been regularly established in the Plantations abroad, it has been generally understood that the Spiritual Jurisdiction over those Churches was vested in the Bishop of London by an Order of Councill in the Reign of King Charles the Second. And tho' no Such Order appears upon the Councill Books, nor has the present Bishop been able to discover it after the Strictest Search, yet he finds evident Testimonies of such a Jurisdiction claimed and exercised so early as that Reign...

[After a short historical survey which he concludes by alluding to the appointment of commissaries by Compton and Robinson, Gibson continues :]

That the Commissaries being thus Empowered by the Bishops of London, have attempted to proceed in the Exercise of Jurisdiction ; but thô they have been very careful not to intermeddle in Collations, Wills or Licenses, yet have they been absolutely forbidden and hindered to hold any Courts at all, or to proceed judicially in any matters whatsoever ; and great Disturbances have been occassioned thereby, particularly, the Prohibition was carried so far by Mr. Lowther, late Governor of Barbadoes, as to procure an Act of Assembly and Councill to forbid the issuing any Citation or Process whatsoever, under a Penalty of £500.

That by this and the like Restraints and Prohibitions, the Jurisdiction of the Bishop of London in the Plantations is become merely nominal ; and the Commissaries appointed as above have been deterr'd from proceeding judicially against any Persons for Immoralities or Irregularities of any Kind. And it hath been inserted in some Instructions to Governors as follows, *If any Person already preferr'd to a Benefice, shall appear to you to give Scandal, either by his Doctrine or Manners, you are to use the best means for the Removal of him.* By which Clause in the Instructions, the Jurisdiction of the Bishop even over the Clergy, seems to be transferred to the Governor.

That upon account of the Uncertainties in the Jurisdiction of the Bishop of London, and the Difficulties attending the exercise of it ; the present Bishop, to prevent the like Disorder and Confusion that hath formerly happened between the Governors and Commissaries, hath forebore to appoint a Commissary in any one of the Governments, till your Majesty's Royal Pleasure shall be known, and the Extent of his Jurisdiction shall be explained and ascertained, in such manner as may best answer the Ends of Spiritual Jurisdiction, and at the same time may be Consistent with the Temporal Peace and Welfare of the Several Governments.

EDM'. LONDON.'

3.

ORDER IN COUNCIL RELATING TO ECCLESIASTICAL JURISDICTION IN THE PLANTATIONS.

P. R. O., B. T., Plantations General, Vol. X. [8] 70.   Printed in *New Jersey Archives*, V. 126–128.

AT THE COURT AT KENSINGTON THE 9ᵗʰ DAY OF AUGˢᵗ 1726.

PRESENT

THE KINGS MOST EXCELLᵗ MAJESTY IN COUNCIL.

Whereas the Right Reverend the Lord Bishop of London did some time since humbly represent unto his Majesty at this Board the Uncertaintys in his Spiritual Jurisdiction over the Churches in his Majestys Plantations and the Difficultys attending the Exercise of the Same, and prayed that the Extent of his said Jurisdiction might be explained and Ascertained — His Majesty was thereupon pleased to referr the Consideration thereof to a Committee of the Privy Council — And Whereas the said Lords of the Committee did this day Report to his Majesty that having considered the several Points, wherein it might be proper for the Lord Bishop of London or his Commissaries to exercise such Ecclesiastical Jurisdiction, they had thereupon caused a Draught of a Commission to be prepared for putting the same into Execution — Which Draught the said Lords of the Committee humbly offered as proper to be forthwith past under the Great Seal of Great Britain.   His Majesty in Council taking the same into Consideration was pleased to approve the said Draught of a Commission which is hereunto annexed[1] and to order that the same to be forthwith past, under the Great Seal of Great Britain — And his Majesty is hereby pleased to Order, that the Blanks, left in the Draught for the names of the persons to compose a Court, for hearing Appeales from any Sentences that shall be given in the Plantations by Virtue of the Said Commission, shall be filled up with the names of the following Lords Vizᵗ —

William Lord Arch Bishop of Canterbury and the Lord Arch Bishop of Canterbury for the time being.

Peter Lord King Lord High Chancellor and Lord High Chancellor or Lord Keeper for the time being.

---

[1] This commission expired with the death of George I., June 12, 1727; the one under which Gibson exercised his jurisdiction was issued by George II., April 29, 1728, and is printed below, pp. 289–293.

Lancelot Lord Arch Bishop of York and the Lord Arch Bishop of York for the time being.

The Lord High Treasurer for the time being.

William Duke of Devonshire Lord President of his Majestys Most Honble Privy Council and the Lord President of the Council for the time being.

Thomas Lord Trevor Lord Keeper of the Privy Seal and the Lord Privy Seal for the time being.

Lionel Duke of Dorset Lord Steward of his Majesty's Household and the Lord Steward for the time being.

Charles Duke of Grafton Lord Chamberlain of his Majesty's Household and the Lord Chamberlain for the time being.

Thomas Holles Duke of Newcastle — One of his Majesty's Principal Secretarys of State and the Principal Secretary of State for the time being.

Thomas Earl of Westmoreland

James Earl of Berkley First Commiss^r of the Admirality and the Lord High Admiral and First Commissioner of the Admirality for the time being.

Charles Lord Visco^t Townshend One of his Majestys Principal Secretaries of State and the Principal Secretary of State for the time being.

Edmund Lord Bishop of London and the Lord Bishop of London for the time being.

Sr Spencer Compton Kn^t of the Bath Speaker of the House of Commons and the Speaker of the House of Commons for the time being.

Sr Robert Walpole Kn^t of the Garter Chancellor of the Exchequer and First Commiss^r of the Treasury and the Chancellor of the Exchequer and first Commiss^r of the Treasury for the time being.

Sr Robert Raymond Kn^t Lord Chief Justice of his Majestys Court of Kings Bench and the Lord Chief Justice of the Kings Bench for the time being.

Sir Joseph Jekyll Kn^t Master of the Rolls and the Master of the Rolls for the time being.

Sr Robert Eyre Kn^t Lord Chief Justice of the Court of Common Pleas and the Lord Chief Justice of the Common Pleas for the time being.

being members of his Majesty's most Honble Privy Council, And that any three of the said Lords do make a Quorum. And one of his Majesty's Principal Secretaries of State is to prepare a Warrant for his Majesty's Royal Signature in order to pass the said Commission under the Great Seal Accordingly.

Copy of an Order in Council of the 19ᵗʰ of August 1726 directing a Commission to pass under yᵉ Great Seal relating to yᵉ Ecclesiastical Jurisdiction in yᵉ Planˢ & appointing a Court for Hearing Appeals pursuant to yᵉ Sᵈ Com'ission.

4.

COMMISSION TO THE BISHOP OF LONDON FOR EXERCISING JURISDICTION IN THE AMERICAN COLONIES.

New York Colonial Documents, V. 849–854, from Plantations General Papers, XI. 10.

Royal Commission for exercising Spiritual and Ecclesiastical Jurisdiction in the American Plantations.

GEORGE THE SECOND, by the Grace of GOD, King of Great Britain France and Ireland, Defender of the Faith &c, To the Reverend father in Christ, Edmund, by Divine permission, Bishop of London, Greeting :

Whereas the Colonies, Plantations, and other our dominions in America, are not yet divided into, constituted as, neither annexed to, any Diocese within our Kingdom of Great Britain ; by reason whereof Jurisdiction in Ecclesiastical causes arising in them, or in any one of them, belongeth to Us only, as the Supreme Head of the Church on earth ; And whereas it seemeth to Us necessary that henceforth Spiritual and Ecclesiastical Jurisdiction should, in the cases hereinafter mentioned, be established, and exercised in those parts, by virtue of our Royal Authority, according to the Laws and Canons of the Church of England, in England lawfully received and sanctioned, to the better promoting of the sincere worship of God, and the pure profession of the Christian Religion ; and whereas our Royal Father, George the First, late King of Great Britain, &c., did, by letters patent, under the great seal of Great Britain, bearing date at Westminster, the ninth of February, in the thirteenth year of his reign, give and grant unto you, the Bishop of London aforesaid, full power and authority, by yourself, or by your sufficient commissary, or commissaries to be by you substituted and named, to exercise Spiritual and Ecclesiastical Jurisdiction in his several Colonies, Plantations, and other dominions in America, during the good pleasure of the said late King, as by the said letters patent doth, upon examination, more fully appear ; KNOW YE, that We have revoked, and determined, and do, by these presents, revoke, and determine the above mentioned letters patent, with all and singular the things therein contained. And further know ye, that We, reposing especial confidence in your sound religion, learning and probity, and in your prudence and industry in the management of affairs, have, of our special favor, certain knowledge and mere motion, given and granted, and do by these presents, give and grant to you, the Bishop of London aforesaid, full power and authority, by yourself, or by your sufficient commissary, or commissaries to be by you substituted and named, to exercise Spiritual and Ecclesiastical Jurisdiction in the special causes and matters hereinafter expressed and specified, within our several Colonies, Plantations, and other dominions in America, according to the laws and canons of the Church of England, in England lawfully received and sanctioned. And for declaration of our Royal Pleasure as to the special causes and matters in which we will that the Jurisdiction above named be, by virtue of this our commission, exercised, we have further given and granted, and do, by these presents, give and grant to you, the Bishop of London aforesaid, full power and authority, by yourself, or by your sufficient commissary, or commissaries to be by you substituted and named, to visit all churches in our aforesaid Colonies, Plantations, and other dominions in America, in which Divine Service according to the Rites and Liturgy of the Church of England shall have been celebrated, and the Rectors, Curates Ministers and Incumbents, by whatever name called belonging to said Churches, and all Presbyters and Deacons admitted into the Holy Orders of the Church of England, with all and every Sort of Jurisdiction, power, and Ecclesiastical coercion, requisite in the premises ; and to Summon the aforesaid Rectors, Curates, Ministers, Incumbents, Presbyters or Deacons admitted into the Holy Orders of the Church of England, or any of them, and no person else, before yourself or your commissary, or commissaries aforesaid, upon whatever days and hours, and at whatever suitable places, as often as, and whensoever, to yourself or to your commissary, or commissaries aforesaid, shall seem most fit and convenient, and by means of witnesses, to be sworn in due form of law by yourself, or your commissary, or commissaries aforesaid, and by such other proper ways and methods, as can with right be more advantageously and effectually used, to examine concerning the manners of the same, according to the laws and canons of the Church of England ; and also to administer all oaths lawful and customary in Ecclesiastical Courts, and to correct and punish the aforesaid Rectors, Curates, Ministers, Incumbents, Presbyters and Deacons in the Holy Orders of the Church of England, according to their demerits, whether by amotion, suspension, excommunication, or by any sort of Ecclesiastical censure, or due correction, according to the canons and Laws Ecclesiastical aforesaid. And further, of our superabundant favor, we have given and granted, and do, by these presents, give and grant to you, the Bishop of London aforesaid, full power and authority, from time to time, to nominate and substitute under your hand and Episcopal seal, sufficient Commissaries to exercise and effectually execute all and singular the premises, in each and every of the Colonies, Plantations, and Dominions aforesaid, in America, according to the tenor and true intent of this our Commission, and from time to time, to remove and change such Commissaries, as to you shall seem fit. You, the Bishop of London aforesaid having and enjoying all and singular, the powers and authorities above recited, during our good pleasure. We will, nevertheless, and do by these presents, declare and ordain, that it may and shall be lawful for any person, or persons whatsoever, against whom any judgment, decree, or sentence, shall have been given or pronounced, by virtue of this our Commission, to appeal from such judgment, decree, or sentence, to our Right trusty and Well-beloved Councillors, the most Reverend Father in Christ William, Archbishop of Canterbury, and to the Archbishop of Canterbury for the time being; Peter, Lord King, Baron of Ockham, our Chancellor of Great Britain, and to our Chancellor of Great Britain, or Keeper of our Great Seal of Great Britain for the time being; the Most Reverend Father in Christ, Lancelot, Archbishop of York, and to the Archbishop of York for the time being; our High Treasurer of Great Britain for the time being; William, Duke of Devonshire, President of our Privy Council, and to the President of our Privy Council for the time being; Thomas, Lord Trevor, Keeper of our Privy Seal, and to the Keeper of our Privy Seal for the time being; Lionel Cranfield, Duke of Dorset, Steward of our Palace, and to the Steward of our Palace for the time being; Charles, Duke of Grafton, Chamberlain of our Palace, and to the Chamberlain of our Palace for the time being; Thomas, Duke of Newcastle, one of our Principal Secretaries of State; Thomas, Earl of Westmoreland, Charles, Viscount Townshend, another of our Principal Secretaries of State, and to our Principal Secretaries of State for the time being; George, Viscount Torrington, First Lord Commissioner of our Admiralty, and to our Lord High Admiral, and first Lord Commissioner of the Admiralty for the time being; Arthur Onslow, our Speaker of our House of Commons, and to the Speaker of our House of Commons for the time being; Robert Walpole, Knight of the most Noble Order of the Garter, Chancellor of our Exchequer, and First Lord of our Treasury, and to the Chancellor of the Exchequer, and first Lord of the Treasury for the time being; Robert Raymond, Knight, our Chief Justice of Pleas before Us, and to our Chief Justice of Pleas before us for the time being; Joseph Jekyll, Knight, Master of the Rolls of our Chancery, and to the

Master of the Rolls of our Chancery for the time being, and Robert Eyre, Knight, our Chief Justice of Common Pleas, and to our Chief Justice of Common Pleas for the time being, To whom, that is to say, to William, Archbishop of Canterbury, and to the Archbishop of Canterbury for the time being; Peter, Lord King, Chancellor of Great Britain, or the Keeper of our Great Seal of Great Britain for the time being; Lancelot, Archbishop of York, and to the Archbishop of York for the time being; our High Treasurer of Great Britain for the time being; William, Duke of Devonshire, and to the President of our Privy Council for the time being; Thomas, Lord Trevor, and to the Keeper of our Privy Seal for the time being; Lionel Cranfield, Duke of Dorset, and to the Steward of our Palace for the time being; Charles, Duke of Grafton, and to the Chamberlain of our Palace for the time being; Thomas, Duke of New-castle, Thomas Earl of Westmoreland, Charles Viscount Townshend, and to the Principal Secretaries of State for the time being; George Viscount Torrington, and to our Lord High Admiral and First Lord Commissioner of our Admiralty for the time being; Arthur Onslow, and to the Speaker of our House of Commons for the time being; Robert Walpole, and to the Chancellor of our Exchequer, and First Lord of our Treasury, for the time being; Robert Raymond, and to our Chief Justice of Pleas before Us for the time being; Joseph Jekyll, and to the Master of the Rolls of our Chancery for the time being; and to Robert Eyre, and to our Chief Justice of Common Pleas for the time being, being of our Privy Council, or to any three or more of them, being of our Privy Council; We do by these presents give and grant, full power and Authority, from time to time, to hear and determine, all and singular, such appeals; and, such judgments, decrees, and sentences, to confirm, change, or revoke, and final judgment or sentence thereupon, to give and pronounce, in manner and form as full as the Commissioners constituted and appointed under our Great Seal of Great Britain by virtue of the Statute of the twenty fifth year of Henry Eighth late King of England entituled, "An Act for the submission of the Clergy and the restraint of Appeals," can or ought to proceed, in appeals subject to their decision, by the Statute aforesaid; anything in these presents contained, to the contrary, notwithstanding. Commanding, moreover, and by these presents strictly enjoining, all and singular, our Governor-Generals, Judges, and Magistrates, together with all and singular, our Rectors, Incumbents, Ministers, Officers, and Subjects of what sort soever, within our Colonies, Plantations, and other dominions aforesaid, in America, that they and each of them, shall be to you, the Bishop of London aforesaid, and to your commissary, or commissaries aforesaid, in all things, aiding and assisting, as is fit, in the due execution of the premises. In testimony whereof, We have caused these Our Letters to be made patent. Witness Ourself, at Westminster, the twenty ninth day of April, in the first year of our Reign.

By writ of Privy Seal

BISSE and BRAY.

5.

ADDITIONAL INSTRUCTIONS TO THE GOVERNORS OF THE PLANTATIONS — TO SUPPORT THE BISHOP OF LONDON AND HIS COMMISSARIES.

From P. R. O., B. T. Plantations General, No. 35, Entry Book F, 165. Also printed in *New Jersey Archives*, V. 264.

To the King's Most Excell.^t Majesty.

May it please your Majesty,

In Obedience to Your Majesty's Commands Signify'd to Us by his Grace ye Duke of Newcastle's Letter of the 21st of the last Month, we have prepar'd the inclos'd Draughts of Instructions to all Your Majesty's Governors in America, (except as undermention'd) directing them to support the Bishop of London & his Commissaries in the Exercise of Such Jurisdiction as is granted to his Lordship by Your Majesty's Commission to him.

We have not inclos'd the Draughts of the Instruction to the Governors of the Leeward Islands, Massachusetts Bay & New Hampshire, North & South Carolina, as we intend to incorporate it in the General Instructions we are now preparing for the Governors of those Places :

All which is most humbly Submitted.

EDW.^D ASHE.   WESTMORELAND.
ORL. BRIDGEMAN.   P. DOEMINIQUE.
W. CARY.   T. PELHAM.
M. BLADEN.

WHITEHALL 17th March 17$\frac{29}{30}$.

6.

DRAUGHT OF AN ADDITIONAL INSTRUCTION RELATING TO THE BISHOP OF LONDON'S ECCLESIASTICAL JURISDICTION IN AMERICA.

From P. R. O., B. T. Plantations General, No. 35, Entry Book F, 165. Also printed in *New Jersey Archives*, V. 265.

Having been graciously pleas'd to grant unto the Right Revd Father in God Edmund Lord Bishop of London, a Commission under Our Great Seal of Great Britain, whereby he is impower'd to Exercise

Ecclesiastical Jurisdiction by himself or by such Commissaries as he shall appoint, in Our Several Plantations in America; It is Our Will & Pleasure, That you give all Countenance & due Encouragement to the Said Bishop of London or his Commissaries in the Legal Exercise of Such Ecclesiastical Jurisdiction, according to the Laws of *the Island* [Province] *Colony* under your Government, & to the Tenor of the Said Commission, a Copy whereof is hereunto annex'd, & that you do cause the Said Commission to be forthwith Register'd in the Publick Records of that *Our Island* (Province) *Colony:*

Draughts of the foregoing Additional Instruction, were prepar'd for

Robert Hunter, Esq!	Gov! of Jamaica.
Henry Worsley	Barbadoes.
John Pitt	Bermuda.
Woodes Rogers	Bahama's.
Rich! Philips	Nova Scotia.
J^no Montgomerie	New York & N. Jersey.
Earl of Orkney	Virginia.
Ben! Leonard Calvert, ...	Maryland.
Patrick Gordon, ...	Pennsylvania.

VI. METHODUS PROCEDENDI CONTRA CLERICOS IRREGU- LARES IN PLANTATIONIBUS AMERICANIS.[1]

From a copy in the Fulham Library.

I.

APPOINTMENT OF A COMMISSARY.

Edmundus, Permissione Divinâ London' Episcopus, Dilecto Nobis in Christo,

Salutem, Gratiam & Benedictionem. Ad exercendam Jurisdictionem Spiritualem & Ecclesiasticam infra Provinciam —— in Americâ sitam, secundum tenorem Commissionis Serenissimi nostri Regis Georgii Secundi sub magno Sigillo gerentis dat' vicesimo nono die Aprilis,

---

[1] A quarto pamphlet of 16 pages. The copy among the *Fulham MSS.* is the only one known to be in existence. There is no date or place of publication; but the instructions were issued by Bishop Gibson on the 28th of September, 1728, and were probably printed privately.

anno Regni sui primo, præsentibusq*ue;* annexæ, & non aliter neque alio modo, Tibi de cujus Scientiâ, Circumspectione, Fidelitate, & Industriâ plurimum Confidimus, Vices nostras tenore præsentium Comittimus, Teque Commissarium nostrum ad omnia in dictis Literis Commissionalibus contenta, & non alio, Commissarium nostrum Facimus & Constituimus per Præsentes, durante bene placito nostro.　In cujus rei testimonium, Sigillum nostrum Episcopale præsentibus opponi fecimus.

N. B.　The Commissary, before he enters upon his Office, is to take the Oaths, and make the Subscription required by the 127th Canon.

2.

DIRECTIONS TO THE COMMISSARY.

Good Brother,

His Majesty having been pleased to empower me, under the Great Seal, to exercise Jurisdiction over the Clergy in the Plantations abroad, which are as yet within no Diocese, but remain under the immediate Jurisdiction of the King as Supreme Head ; I have thought proper to appoint you my *Commissary,* and do accordingly transmit to you a Commission under my Episcopal Seal, together with a Copy of his Majesty's Commission to me ; by which you will see the Manner and Extent of the Jurisdiction that is to be Exercis'd by you as my Commissary within the Government of ——.

As to the Method of your Procedings, and the Things which I would more particularly recommend to your Care ; I have judg'd it proper to set them down distinctly under the following Heads.

I. That when any Clergyman shall be found irregular in his Life, or negligent in the Duties of his Station, you give him a *private* Admonition ; and acquaint me, by the first Opportunity, with the Occasions you found to give him such Admonition : Only, if the Crimes charg'd upon him be of a flagrant Nature, and also publick and notorious, it will be fit, either that the Admonition be more *publick,* in the presence of such of the Clergy as you shall think proper, or that he be immediately proceded against in a *judicial* manner.

II. That the Process be in a *short* and *summary* Way, according to the Order and Method laid out, and Contain'd in a Paper of *Directions* herewith transmitted to you ; entitled the *Method of Proceding against irregular Clergymen.*

III. That when the Cause comes to the Hearing, you take to your Assistance at least Two Clergymen, whom you shall think most proper ;

and that you confer with them, and that you desire their Opinions in Relation to the Nature of the Crime, and the Circumstances of the Proofs, and the Sentence proper to be given.

IV. That if the Crime be not flagrant, and notorious, you rather chuse the Sentence of *Suspension ab Officio & Beneficio,* for such time as shall be judg'd convenient, than immediate *Deprivation,* tho' the case in Strictness might bear the latter; To the End the Party may have an Opportunity, in that Space, to give Proof of his Repentence and Reformation, or if he do not, that he may be prosecuted a-new in order to Deprivation.

V. That once every year you hold a Visitation of the Clergy, in some Place or Places which may be most convenient for that Purpose; and that you take that Opportunity to Communicate to them any Directions or Notices which you shall receive from hence; and to give such Things in Charge, as either the General State of the Church, or any particular Occasions, may require; and to confer with them about the State of Religion, and the best Methods of promoting it, in your several Parishes. More particularly, to put them in mind that one necessary means of promoting and propagating it within the [Parish], is, the exemplary Lives of themselves and their Families, and the Care they take to instruct their own Negro and Indian Servants in the Christian Faith. . . Of all which Proceedings, you are to give me an Account, as soon as you conveniently can, after the Visitation is finished.

VI. That you make proper Enquiries concerning the State and Condition of all such *Parsonage Houses* as are repair'd at the charge of the Ministers, and also of the *Glebes,* whether their Houses be preserved in due Reparation, and the Glebes improv'd and occupied in a Husbandlike Manner.

VII. That you enquire from time to time, whether any Person be receiv'd and allow'd to officiate, who has not a Testimonial or License from me, or my Predecessors, for that Government, or coming from some other Government or Governments in the Plantations, did not moreover bring with him proper Testimonials of his good Behaviour from the time that he first arriv'd in the Plantations: And if any be receiv'd and employ'd who has no License; or, having a License, doth not also produce such Testimonials; that you give me notice of it by the first Opportunity.

VIII. That you inform me, what steps are or shall be taken towards the obtaining an Act of Assembly, for Presentments of Crimes and Vices to be to the Temporal Courts twice every year; according to the purport of a late Clause, which has been added to the Instructions of every Governour in the Plantations : To the End that I may be able to inform his Majesty and the Council, in what Manner and to what Degree, the Suppression of Vice and Immorality among the Laity is provided for in that Government by the Temporal Laws ; pursuant to his Majesty's gracious Intention in sending the said Instruction.

IX. That you give me Notice, from time to time, of any Hardships or Oppressions that you find the Clergy to labour under, in relation to the *Rights* which they are entitled to by the Laws and Constitution of the Government.

X. That you take all proper Opportunities to recommend to the Clergy a loyal and dutiful Behaviour towards the present Government, as vested in his Majesty King *George,* and establish'd in the Illustrious House of *Hanover;* and that they pay all due Submission and Respect to the Governour sent by him, as well in regard to his Commission and Character, as to engage his Favour and Protection to the Church and Clergy.

These are the Things which I would suggest to you, as general Rules that may be proper to be observed in the Exercise of your Jurisdiction, leaving it to your own Prudence and Judgment to apply them to particular Cases, as there Shall be Occasion. And so, commending you to the good Providence of God, and to his gracious Direction in this and all your other Affairs, I remain,

Sir,

Fulham Sept.
28 1728.

Your assur'd Friend and Brother,
EDM.' LONDON.'

3.

THE METHOD OF PROCEEDING AGAINST IRREGULAR CLERGYMEN.

The Place of Judicature to be, either some convenient part of the Church where the Commissary is Incumbent, or where the Party prosecuted dwells.

Prosecution to be either *ex Officio mero, i.e.* by the Office assigning a Promoter, or by Accusation ; if the latter, such voluntary Promoter to give a Bond of 20 l. by way of Security to pay Costs, if he fail in the Proof.

The Proceeding to be in a Summary way, as follows : The Citation to be under the Commissary's Seal, to appear at a Time and Place certain. Such Citation to be served by a Person who can at least Read and

Write, and who shall make oath that He duly serv'd it, and left a Copy or Abstract thereof with the Party.

If he could not serve it upon the Party, then a Process *Viis* & *Modis* is to be hung on the Church Door where the said Party officiates, or on the Door of the House wherein he dwelt, returnable the next Court-day appointed for that Cause. And here it is to be remember'd, that when a Cause is once Instituted, the Courts are to be held regularly every ten Days.

If there be no Appearance after Service of the *Viis* & *Modis*, He is to be pronounc'd Contumacious, and in *pœnam Contumaciæ*, the Witness[es] are to be admitted, sworn, and examined, and their Depositions publish'd, and a Day assign'd for Sentence.

On the day of Appearance, *Articles* are to be given, and the *Issue* required, *viz.* Whether he confess or deny the Charge. If He confess, Punishment to be inflicted according to the Nature and Quality of the Offense, either by Admonition, Suspension, or Deprivation, together with the Costs necessarily expended.

If he deny the Charge, then Witnesses are to be produced, who being sworn to speak the Truth, and the whole Truth, and nothing but the Truth, indifferently, between the Parties concern'd, shall be examin'd by a Notary Publick (if conveniently may be) or by a Person skilful in taking Depositions, and in the Presence of the Commissary, and His Assessors *only;* eight and forty Hours being first allow'd to the Defendant, to enquire into the characters of the several Witnesses, and to frame such Interrogations as He shall think proper.

The Depositions are to be kept private, till all the Witnesses are examin'd; and when the Examination of a Witness is finish'd, both as to his Deposition on the *Articles*, and his Answers to the Interrogatories, the whole to be read over to him by the Examiner in the Presence of the Judge and his Assessors, and the Witness ask'd, whether it be agreeable to his Mind, and whether it be all true? and if he answer affirmatively, he is to sign it.

Witnesses duly Summon'd and not appearing, or appearing, and yet refusing to undergo their Examinations, altho' their necessary Expences are allow'd them, may be compelled thereto by Ecclesiastical Censures.

The Defendant to be at Liberty, by himself, or any other Person acting as Proctor or Advocate for him, before the Depositions are publish'd (which must not be till the next Court-day after the Examinations are finish'd) to give in a Defensive Plea.

If the Office, on admitting such Plea as relevant, find it necessary to give a further Allegation in order to Support the *Articles*, to do it within seven days, and make Proof thereof within a fortnight; and then no farther Pleadings, but the Cause to stand concluded and assign'd for Sentence the next Court-day.

If there be not Proof sufficient in Law, the Defendant is to be dismiss'd with his Costs.

Appeal to be within fifteen Days to the Judges appointed by the King's Commission; the Appellant depositing the Sum of ten Pounds, and making Oath that he will *bonâ fide* prosecute the same within 20 days. A Copy thereupon of all the Proceedings in the said Cause shall be deliver'd to him (he being at the Charge of Copying) in order to their being transmitted under the Commissary's Seal, and attested to be true Copy by the Person acting as Register.

The Register is to enter all Proceedings in a Book kept for that Purpose, and to preserve carefully all Original Processes, Articles, Decrees, &c.

4.

INSTRUMENTS AND OTHER THINGS REFERR'D TO IN THE METHOD OF PROCEEDING.

Nº 1. Citation.

N. N. Reverendi in Christo Patris ac Domini Domini Edmundi, Permissione Divinâ London' Episcopi, Commissarius legitime constitutus, Universis & singulis Clericis & Literatis quibuscunque in & per totam Provinciam —— ubilibet constitutis, Salutem. Vobis conjunctim & divisim committimus ac firmiter injungendo mandamus, quatenus Citetis seu citari faciatis peremtoriè P. P. parochiæ —— Rectorem sive Incumbentem, quòd legitimè compareat coram nobis in Ecclesiâ de —— loco*que ;* judiciali ibidem, die sexto aut —— post Citationem hujusmodi eidem P. P. in hac parte factam, certis Articulis, Capitulis, sive Interrogatoriis, meram Animæ suæ Salutem, morumque & excessuum suorum reformationem & correctionem concernentibus, & præsertim propter [the Crime] ei objiciend' & ministrand' ulteriusque factur' & receptur' quod justum fuerit in hac parte sub pœna Juris & Contemptûs ; & quid in præmissis feceritis nos debitè certificetis unâ cum præsentibus. Dat. &c. [Commissary's Name and Seal to be set to this, and to every other Instrument in the Course of the Proceeding.]

Indorsement : This Citation was personally serv'd on the within-named P. P. by shewing to him the Original under Seal, and at the same time delivering to him an *English* Note, containing the effect hereof, this Day of   in the Year of our Lord   by me A. B.

Juratis fuit praefatus A. B. super veritate præmissorum Coram me N. N. Commissario.

The Form of the ENGLISH *Note is to be thus :* you are hereby Cited to appear at the Church of   on the   Day of   before the Reverend   Commissary, to answer to such Articles as shall then be objected to you.

[The Apparitor's Name.]

N? 2.   Citation *Viis* & *Modis.*

N. N. Reverendi in Christo Patris ac Domini Domini Edmundi Permissione Divinâ London' Episcopi Commissarius legitimè constitutus, Universis & Singulis Clericis & Literatis quibuscunque in & per totam Provinciam——ubilibet constitutis, Salutem.   Cum nos N. N. Commissarius antedictus ritè & legitimè proceden' quendam P. P. Ecclesiæ parochialis de——Rectorem, ad diem, horas, locum & effectum subscriptos, subque modo & formâ inferius descriptis, ad petitionem A. B.

If it be a Vol-   Promotoris Officii nostri in hac parte legitimè assignati,
untary Promo-   allegantis eumdem P. P. alias per Mandatarium in hac
ter, then Pro-   parte legitimè deputatum, animo & intentione eum
motoris volun- personaliter citandi ad effectum infra scriptum Sæpius
tarii in hac   diligenter quæsitum fuisse, ita tamen latitasse & in præ-
parte.   senti latitare, quominus personaliter apprehendi vel citari
queat, prout Coram nobis debitè in hac parte allegatum extitit, citand' & ad Judicium evocand' fore decreverimus justitiâ mediante ; vobis igitur Conjunctim & divisim Committimus ac firmiter injungendo mandamus, quatenus Citetis seu citari faciatis peremptorii præfat' P. P. personaliter si sic citari vel apprendi poterit, & ad eum sic citand' tutus vobis pateat accessus ; alioquin publicæ citationis edicto per affixionem præsentium hujusmodi in Valvis sive Foribus exterioribus Domûs solitæ habitationis dicti P. P. vel in Valvis sive Foribus exterioribus Ecclesiæ parochialis de——palàm & publicè in sua forma Originali aliquandiu proposit' verâque presentium hujusmodi Copiâ ibidem dimissâ & relictâ aliisque viis, modis atque mediis legitimis, quibus melius aut efficacius de Jure quovismodo poteritis, ita quod hujusmodi nostra Citatio ad ejus sic citandi notitiam de verisimili pervenire valeat, Quòd legitimè compareat coram nobis in Ecclesia parochiali de—— locoque judiciali ibidem die——die——Mensis——inter horas——

de justitia responsur' certis Articulis, Capitulis, sive Interrogatoriis, meram Animæ suæ Salutem Concernen' ulteriusque factur' & receptur' quod justum fuerit in hac parte, sub pœna Juris & Contemptûs et quid in præmissis feceritis nos debité Certificetis una cum præsentibus. Dat' —— die Mensis —— Anno*que;* Dom.

Indorsement: This Decree was duly executed by affixing the same for some time on the outward Door of the Dwelling-house or Habitation of the within-named P. P. —— or on the publick door of the Parish Church of —— and afterwards by leaving in the room thereof an Authentick Copy of the said Decree, the —— day of —— in the Year of our Lord ——

Juratis fuit præfatus —— super veritate præmissorum, coram me N. N.

N.º 3.   Forms of Articles.

The General Preface to all *Articles* against Irregular Clergymen.

In Dei Nomine Amen. Nos Reverendi in Christo Patris ac Domini Domini Edmundi Permissione Divinâ London' Episcopi Commissarius legitimè constitutus. Tibi A. B. Clerico, [add here, the Place of which he is Incumbent] Articulos, Capitula, sive Interrogatoria omnia & singula, meram Animæ tuæ Salutem, morumque & Excessuum tuorum reformationem & correctionem concernentia, ad promotionem —— objicimus & articulamur, conjunctim & divisim, prout sequitur.

For Officiating without License.

Imprimis. We Article and Object to you the said A. B. that you do know, believe, or have heard say, that by the 48th Canon of the Constitutions Ecclesiastical, it is amongst other things provided, ordained, and decreed, as followeth. "That no Curate or Minister shall be permitted to serve in any place, without Examination and Admission of the Bishop of the Diocese, or Ordinary of the Place having episcopal Jurisdiction, in writing under his Hand and Seal."

2. We Article and Object to you the said A. B. that notwithstanding the Premises in the next precedent Article mention'd, You the said A. B. have on divers Sundays, or Lord's days, happening within the months of   in the Year of our Lord   and more particularly on Sunday the   day of   on all, some, or one of the said Lord's days or Sundays aforesaid, without Examination, or Admission, or Approbation of the Bishop of *London* in writing under his Hand and Seal, of your Honesty, Ability, and good Conformity to the Ecclesiastical Laws of the

Church of *England,* presumed and taken upon you to serve the Cure of Souls of the Parishioners of the Parish of   by reading the Prayers of the Church of *England* by Law Establish'd, and by Preaching of Sermons; and performing other Duties; in Contempt of the Laws, Canons and Constitutions ecclesiastical aforesaid.

3. We Article and Object to you the said A. B. that by reason of the Premisses in the foregoing Articles deduced, you have incurred canonical Punishment and Censure, and were and are by us and our Authority canonically to be punished.

For marrying without BANNS *or* LICENSE.

Imprimis. We Article and Object, that you the said A. B. do know, believe, or have heard, that by the Laws and Constitutions Ecclesiastical, and more especially by the 62^{d} Canon, it is among other things provided, ordain'd, and decree'd, " That no Minister, upon pain of Suspension *per triennium ipse facto,* shall celebrate Matrimony between any Persons, without a Faculty or License, except the Banns of Matrimony have been first publish'd three several Sundays or Holydays in the times of Divine Service in the Parish Churches where the said Parties dwell, according to the Book of Common Prayer."

2. That notwithstanding the Premisses, you the said A. B. in the months of   Anno Dom.   have celebrated or rather Prophaned divers Marriages in the Parish Church aforesaid, and particularly upon   between A. B., and C. D. without a Faculty or License in that behalf lawfully granted or obtain'd, or Banns of Matrimony first duly Publish'd; in manifest contempt of the Laws, Canons, and Constitutions aforesaid, to the evil example of all good Christians.

3. We Article and Object that all and singular the Premisses were and are true.

4. We Article and Object that you the said A. B. by reason of the Premisses have incurr'd the Penalty in the Canons and Constitutions Ecclesiastical aforesaid mention'd and were and are to be suspended *per triennium.*

For Neglect in Catechising.

[This may be applied to the omitting any other Duties in the Church.]

Imprimis, We Article and Object to you the said A. B. that you were and are a Minister in Holy Orders of Deacon and Priest, and for   years at least have been and are Incumbent of the Parish Church of   and   during all the said time have had, and at present have, the Cure of Souls of the Parishioners and Inhabitants of the said Parish of   and for and as such a Person as in this Article is described, you the said A. B. have been and are commonly accounted, reputed, and taken.

2. *Item*, We Article and Object to you the said A. B. that you know, believe, or have heard say, that by the Laws, Canons, and Constitutions Ecclesiastical of the Church of England, and especially by the 59th Canon of the Canons and Constitutions aforesaid, it is, amongst other Things therein order'd and appointed, " That every Parson, Vicar, or Curate, upon every Sunday and Holy-day before Evening Prayers, shall half an Hour or more, examine and instruct the Youth and ignorant Persons of his Parish, in the Ten Commandments, the Articles of the Belief, and in the Lord's Prayer and shall diligently hear, instruct, and teach them the Catechism set forth in the Book of Common Prayer."

3. We Article and Object, that notwithstanding the Premisses in the next precedent Article mention'd, and that you the said A. B. have been by the several Parishioners, divers times within the two years last past, requested to hear, instruct, and teach the Youth and ignorant Persons of the said Parish, the Catechism set forth in the Book of Common Prayer, upon several Sundays and Holy-days within the time aforesaid, you have, in contempt of the said Canon and Constitution, wilfully neglected your Duty herein, to the great Scandal of all good Christians.

4. We Article and Object to you the said A. B. that by reason of the Premisses in the foregoing Articles mention'd and deduced, you have incurr'd Ecclesiastical Punishment and Censure, and were and are by us, and the Authority given to us, canonically to be punished and corrected.

For Refusing to Bury.

[The like, in case of denying or delaying to baptise, mutatis mutandis.]

Imprimis, We Article and Object, that according to the 68th Canon of the Constitutions Ecclesiastical, " Whatever Rector, Vicar, or Curate of any Parish shall refuse or delay to bury any Corpse that is brought to the Church or Church-yard (convenient Warning being given him thereof before) shall be suspended for the Space of three Months."

2. *Item*, We Article and Object, that, notwithstanding the Premisses, you the said A. B. having convenient Warning thereof, did on the Day of   in the year   refuse and deny to bury the Corpse of C. D. a deceas'd Parishioner, and did not bury the same, but did refuse to give the Corpse of the said C. D. Christian Burial, by reading the

Form prescrib'd in the Book of Common Prayer for the Burial of the Dead, to the great Neglect of your Duty and the Scandal of the Christian Profession.

3. We Article and Object to you the said A. B. that by reason of the Premisses, you are and ought to be canonically punish'd and corrected.

For IMMORALITIES *of Several* KINDS.

*　　　*　　　*　　　*　　　*　　　*　　　*[1]

That in the Months of *April, May, June, July, August, Anno Dom.* in all, some, or one of the said Months, you the said A. B. have been very much addicted and given to prophane Cursing and Swearing; and have several times in a most wicked, prophane, and impious Manner spoke, use, and uttered several wicked and execrable Oaths and Curses within the Town and Village of　　and this is true, publick and notorious; and thereof there was and is a publick Voice, Fame, and Report, in the said Town and Village.

That in the Months of *April, May, June, July, August, Anno Dom.* in all, or some, or one of the said Months, you the said A. B. did resort to and frequent divers Taverns and Ale-houses, and did remain in such Taverns and Ale-houses several Hours together, and at very unseasonable Times: And that you the Said A. B. during the said time, was much addicted and given to excessive Drinking, and have been several times very much fudled and drunk within the said Town and Village; and thereof there was and is a publick Voice, Fame, and Report, in the said Village.

N. B. One or other of these Forms of Articles, with very little variation, will serve for any Case not expressly mention'd; adding to these, severally, and to others of the like kind, the 4ᵗʰ Head of the Articles for Neglecting to Catechise.

N° 4. *Compulsory for* WITNESSES.

N. N. Reverendi in Christo Patris ac Domini Domini Edmundi Permissione Divinâ London' Episcopi Commissarius legitimè constitutus, Universis & singulis Clericis & Literatis quibuscunque in & per totam Provinciam de —— ubilibet constitutis, Salutem. Cum nos in quodam negotio Officii sive Correctionis quod coram nobis in Judicio inter A. B. parochiæ —— Promotorem dicti Officii ac partem hujusmodi Negotium

---

[1] Passages relating to other immoralities are omitted.

promoven' ex una, & P. P. partem contra quam idem Negotium promovetur partibus ex altera, vertitur & pendet indecisum, ritè & legitimè proceden' quosdam A. B. C. D. testes (ut asseritur) valde necessarios ad proband' contenta in quibusdam Articulis aliàs ex parte dicti A. B. in eodem negotio datis, ministratis & admissis, qui requisiti, oblatisq*ue ;* eas viaticis expensis, venire recusabunt, nisi Compulsorium ad diem horas locum & effectum subscriptas subq*ue ;* modo & formâ inferius descriptis ad petitionem partis præfati A. B. Citand' & ad Judicium evocand' fore decreverimus (Justitia Mediante ;) Vobis igitur conjunctim & divisim committimus, ac firmiter injungendo mandamus, quatenus Citetis seu Citari faciatis peremptoriè præfator' A. B. C. D. quod compareant & quilibet coram [compareant coram] nobis in Ecclesia Parochiali —— locoque judiciali ibidem die —— Mensis —— inter horas ejusdem diei, juramentum a Testibus præstari Solitum & Consuetum subitur' & præstitur' ac Testimonium Veritati quam in hac parte noverint perhibitur', ulteriusq*ue ;* factur' & receptur' quod justum fuerit in hac parte, sub pœna Juris & Contemptûs, & quid in Præmissis feceritis nos debitè Certificetis unâ Cum Præsentibus Datis —— die —— Mensis —— Anno Domini

Indorsement : This Compulsory was personally serv'd on the withinnamed A. B. C. D. by shewing to them and each of them this Original under Seal, and delivering to them, and each of them, at the same time, an *English* note containing the effects thereof, this Day of in the year of our Lord by me

Jurat' fuit præfatus super veritati præmissorum coram me N. N. Commissario.

The Form of the ENGLISH NOTE *is to be thus :*

You are hereby cited to appear on the Day of in the Church of before the Reverend Commissary, to give your Evidence in a Cause of Correction, instituted against the Reverend Mr. Minister of

[The Apparitor's Name.]

Nº 5. *Sentence.*

In Dei Nomine Amen. Auditis, visis, & intellectis ac pleneriè & mature discussis per nos N. N. Reverendi in Christo Patris ac Domini Domini Edmundi Permissione Divinâ London' Episcopi Commissarium legitimè Constitutum, Meritis & Circumstantiis cujusdam Negotii Officii sive Correctione Morum quod coram nobis in Judicio inter A. B. parochiæ

Promotum officii nostri & partem dictum negotium promoven' ex unâ, & P. P. Clericum Rectorem Rectoriæ & Ecclesiæ parochialis de partem contra quem idem Negotium promovetur partibus ex altera vertitur & pendet indecis. ritè & legitimè procedend' parteque dicti A. B. Sententiam ferri & justitiam fieri ; parte vero P. P. [Here the Judge is to say, pars P. P. *quid petis*, and according to his Prayer to fill up the Blank, either (Usually understood to be an acquiescence in the Sentence the Judge shall give) Justitiam, or (an intention to appeal) Sententiam] instanter respective postulan' & peten' Rimatoque primitus per nos toto & integro processu alias coram nobis in hujusmodi negotio habito ac facto & diligentur recensito, servatisque per nos de jure in hac parte servandis, ad nostræ Sententiæ Definitivæ sive nostri finalis Decreti probationem in hujusmodo negotio ferend' sic duximus procedend' fore, & procedimus in hunc qui sequitur modum : Quia per Acta, inactitata, deducta, allegata, exhibita, proposita & probata in hujusmodi negotio, comperimus luculenter & invenimus, partem præfati A. B. Intentionem suam in quibusdam Articulis, Capitulis sive Interrogatoriis ex parte sua in hoc negotio datis ministrat' & admissus, aliisque propositis & Exhibitis deductam, quæ quidem Articulos, Capitula sive Interrogatoria alioqua proposita & Exhibita pro his lectis & infertis habemus & haberi volumus sufficienter & ad plenum quod infra pronunciand' fundasse & probasse, nihilque saltem effectuale ex parte aut per partem præfati P. P. fuisse & esse in hac parte exceptum, deductum, allegatum, exhibitum, propositum, probatum, aut confessatum, quod intentionem ejusdem A. B. in hac parte elideret seu quomodolibet enervaret : Idcirco Nos. N. N. Judex antedictus, Christi nomine primitus invocato ac ipsum solum Deum Oculis nostris præponentes & habentes, déque & cum consilio Reverendorum Virorum C. D. & E. F. cum quibus in hac parte communicavimus matureque deliberavimus, prædictum P. P. clericum tempore articulato fuisse & in præsente esse Rectorem Rectoriæ & Ecclesiæ parochialis de   ac temporibus & diebus in hac [parte] articulatis [This to be varied as the case stands] officium suum ministeriale & coram animarum parochianorum suorum infra parochiam prædict' inhabitan' sæpius neglexisse, seu saltem secundum Leges Canones & Constitutiones Ecclesiasticas in ea parte editas, provisas & promulgatas, non perfecisse, juxtas probationes legitimas coram nobis in hac parte judicialiter habitas & factas, pronunciamùs, decernimus & declaramus, præfatum igitur P. P. pro ejus excessibus & delictis debitè & canonicè ac juxta Juris in ea parte exigentiam in præmissis corrigend' & puniend' nec non ab Officio & Beneficio suis per spatium —— suspenden' fore debere pronunciamus, decernimus &

declaramus sique per Præsentes suspendimus, & pro sic Suspenso in
facie Ecclesiæ palàm & publicè, denunciand' declarand' & publicand'
fore etiam pronunciamus, decernimus & declarimus necnon præfatum
P. P. in expensis legitimis ex parte & per partem A. B. in hujusmodi
negotio factis & faciendis eidemque seu parte suæ solvend' condemnand'
fore & condemnare debere etiam pronunciamus, decernimus & declaramus, sique per præsentes condemnamus, easdemque expensas ad
Summam taxamus, dictumque P. P. ad solvend' seu solvi faciend' realiter
& cum effectu prænominato A. B. seu parti suæ dictam summam prætaxatam citra vel ante   sub pœna majoris excommunicationis
Sententiæ monend' fore decernimus ; Quam quidem excommunicationis
Sententiam in eundem P. P. non solventem summam prætaxatam sub
modo & formâ prædictis, Nos Judex antedictus [ex nunc prout ex tunc
& ex tunc prout ex nunc] ferimus & promulgamus in hiis Scriptis præ-
fatumque P. P. in casu prædict' pro . . . sive Excommunicato in facie
Ecclesiæ palam & publicè denunciand' & declarand' fere decernimus
per hanc nostram Sententiam Definitivam sive hoc nostrum finale Decre-
tum, quam sive quod ferimus & promulgamus in hiis Scriptis.

N. N.

N° 6. *Appeal.*

In Dei Nomine Amen.   Coram vobis N. N. Reverendi in Christo Patris
ac Domini Domini Edmundi Permissione Divinâ London' Episcopi
Commissario legitimè constituto, Ego P. P. Clericus, Incumbens, Eccle.
Paroch. de   animo appellandi, deque nullitate & iniquitate omnium
& singulorum infra Scriptorum æque principaliter querelandi, dico,
allego, & in hiis Scriptis in Jure propono, Quod licet Ego præfatus
P. P. per hos   annos ult' Elapsos fuerim & sim Clericus Sacris
Diaconatûs & Presbyteratûs Ordinibus insignitus, ac dictæ Ecclesiæ
parochialis ritè & legitimè approbatus, & licentiatus, & admissus, ac
Curæ Animarum parochianorum sive Inhabitantium de   prædict'
per totum & omne tempus prædict' diligenter secundùm talentum
mihi a Deo datum inservierim, vixerimque sobrie & honestè, nihiloque
commiserim aut omiserim, propter quod ad aliquod Forum Ecclesiasti-
cum trahi, aut à Curâ Animarum Parochianorum sive Inhabitantium
dictæ parochiæ de —— sive executione Officii ministerialis dictæ parochiæ de —— amoveri aut privari debuerim aut debeam, præfatus tamen
N. N. Reverendi in Christo Patris ac Domini Domini Edmundi
permissione Divinâ London' Episcopi Commissarius, Juris & Judiciorum ordine in hac parte minime observato, sed penitùs spreto &

postposito, de facto cum de Jure non potuit neque debuit (ejus Reverentia semper salva) utcunque procedens, Articulos quosdam prætensos, Capitula, sive Interrogatoria, vel quandam prætensam materiam omnino, inconcluden' & de jure non admittend' ad petitionem . . . admisit, ac Testes de & super Articulis, Capitulis, sive Interrogatoriis, vel materia prætensa prædict' paribus nullitate & iniquitate recepit ac sententiam quandam prætensam in Scriptis (uti prætenditur) definitivam, omnino tamen nullam, & de Jure prorsus invalidam pro parte & in favorem dicti A. B. ac contra & adversus me præfatum P. P. sine probationibus sufficien' & de jure in ea parte requisitis, ac contra omnem Juris ordinem, de facto cum de Jure non potuit neque debuit, legit, tulit & promulgavit, per quam inter alia me præfatum P. P. ab executione Officii mei Ministerialis, sive Curâ animarum parochianorum sive Inhabitantium Ecclesiæ parochialis de —— praedict' sine aliquâ causâ saltem legitimâ (ejus Reverentiâ semper salvâ) utcunque omnino monuit, jussit, & mandavit, & mihi ad inserviend' curæ Animarum Parochianorum sive Inhabitantium prædict' sine Causæ cognitione, saltem juxta Juris in hac parte exigentiam, expresse interdixit, meque ab Officio & Beneficio meis per spatiam —— suspendend' fore decrevit, & me præfatum P. P. in expensis prætensis litis ex parte dicti A. B. factis, condemnavit, easdemq*ue;* expensas ad summam minis excessivam & immoderatam taxavit, in præjudicium meum non modicum & gravamen. Unde Ego præfatus P. P. sentiens me ex præmissis Gravaminibus, Nullitatibus, Qui iniquitatibus, Injustitiis, & Injuriis, aliisq*ue;* actis, factis & gestis, iniquis, ex prætenso processu præfati Reverendi Commissarii Colligibilibus, indebitè prægravari, ac loesum, gravatum & injuriatum fuisse & esse, ac justè timens me in futurum [invidiis] lœdi & graviari posse ; ab eisdem & eorum quolibet, & præsertim ab admissione quorundam prætensorum Articulorum, Capitulorum, sive Interrogatiorum, contra me per præfat' A. B. dat' exhibit' & ministrator' a dictâ prætensâ Sententiâ ex parte dicti A. B. ut præfertur, lectâ, latâ, & promulgata, & a Condemnatione me P. P. in expensis ex parte A. B. uti prætenditur, factis & faciendis, à minis excessivâ & immoderatâ taxatione earundem prætensarum expensarum, & a Monitione prætensa in me fact' ad desistend' ab executione Officii mei Ministerialis in per spatium   ac ab omnibus & singulis exinde sequen' ad [Insert here the Names of the Judges of Appeal appointed by his Majesty's Commission] in hiis scriptis appello, deque ; nullitate & iniquitate omnium & singulorum præmissorum æquè principaliter dico & querelor, [apostolóque ;] peto primo, secundo & tertio, instanter, instantius, & instantissime me mihi edi, dari, fieri, tradi, & deliberari cum effectu; & protestor quod non sunt quindecem dies adhuc plenè elapsi, ex quo Gravamina praedicta erant mihi illata. Protestor deniq*ue;* de corrigendo & reformando has meas Appellationem & Querelam ipsasq*ue;* in meliorem & competentiorem formam redigendo, deque intimando easdem omnibus & singulis quibus Jus exigit in hac parte intimari, juxta Juris exigentiam & Juris peritorum consilium, prout moris fuerit.

Interposita fuit hujusmodi Appelatio   die mensis   anno Domini   per praefatum P. P. qui Appelavit, Apostolos petiit, cæteroque; fecit & exercuit in omnibus & per omnia, prout in suprascripto Appellationis Protocollo continetur; præsentibus tunc & ibidem, unà cum me Notario Publico Subscripto

Testibus   Ita   Testor

Registarius.

N. B. An Appeal may as properly be interpos'd before a Notary Public, as in the Presence of the Judge, with this Alteration only in the Beginning thereof, viz.

In Dei nomine Amen. Coram vobis Notario Publico, publicâque & authenticâ personâ, ac Testibus fide dignis hic præsentibus, Ego P. P. &c.

VII. A TYPICAL LICENSE FROM THE BISHOP OF LONDON TO A COLONIAL CLERGYMAN.

Hazard's *Pennsylvania Register*, Vol. III. 354. For the form of the Commission to a Commissary see Appendix A, No. vi., pp. 294, 295.

Edmund, by divine permission, Bishop of London, to our beloved, in Christ, Robert Jenney, Dr. of Laws, Clerk. Greeting.

We do hereby give and grant to you, in whose fidelity, morals, learning, sound doctrine, and diligence we do fully confide, our license and authority to continue only during our pleasure, to perform the ministerial office in Christ Church in Philadelphia, in the Colony of Pennsylvania, in reading the Common Prayer, and performing other ecclesiastical duties belonging to the said office, according to the form prescribed by the Book of Common Prayer, made and published by the authority of parliament, and the canons and constitutions in that behalf lawfully established and promul[ga]ted, and not otherwise or in any other manner, (and you having first before us subscribed the articles, and taken the oaths which in this case are required to be subscribed and taken.)

In witness whereof we have caused our Episcopal Seal to be hereto affixed, dated at Whitehall, the 31st day of March in the year of our Lord 1742 and in the nineteenth year of our translation.

EDMUND (L. S.) LONDON.

VIII. LETTER FROM A. SPENCER TO BISHOP SHERLOCK STATING THE RESULT OF HIS MISSION TO THE AMERICAN COLONIES FOR THE PURPOSE OF SOUNDING PUBLIC OPINION ON THE QUESTION OF INTRODUCING BISHOPS.

From the Manuscripts in the Fulham Library.

My Lord,

June 12, 1749.

I made it my business to converse with Several Merchants and Gentlemen of Philadelphia and New York about what your Lordship mentioned to me. Their chief objection against a Suffragan Bishop is, That he will be invested with such a Power as would be inconsistent with the Privileges of the People in those Parts and even interfere with the Rights of the several Proprietaries.

I replied, that I believed that he would have no more Power over the Laity, than what the Commissaries in the Colonies had already; by that the Advantages of having a Suffragan Bishop would be so great, that I could not think any man of Piety and virtue, who considered them, would oppose so laudable a Design. Being desired to give my Reasons I proceeded thus, — That a Suffragan Bishop being on the Spot could be fully satisfied whether the Lives and Conversation of the Persons desiring to be admitted to the Ministry, were in Fact as mentioned in their Recommendatory Letters; and that he would be such a check on their future Behaviour, as to deter them from those gross Irregularities, which the Laity are too apt to charge them with.

In a Word, I found the Gentlemen I conversed with unanimously to agree that if the Affair was on such a Footing, as I had endeavored to represent it, they would be so far from opposing such a Design, that they would rather heartily concur with your Lordship in promoting so good a Scheme.

I shall always think myself [happy] in receiving and obeying your Lordship's Commands. If, therefore, my Lord, you think proper to honour me with any more Orders, your Lordship may direct to Mr. Richard Burgiss in Rochester where I may be [found] till the middle of next month.

IX. EXTRACTS FROM THE REPORT OF A COMMITTEE FOR PREVENTING THE ESTABLISHMENT OF BISHOPS IN THE COLONIES.

From a Pamphlet in the Fulham Library.

It was reported, & generally believed that there was a design on foot to Erect two New Bishoprics, in the West Indies, this the Deputies thought, and have since been well assured, would be very disagreeable to many of our Friends in those parts & highly Prejudicial to the Interest of several of the Colonies. They therefore Appointed two of their Body to wait on Some of his Majesty's principal servants, and to acquaint them with their Sentiments on this Subject, which was accordingly Done [this was in 1749], & the Persons deputed were very civilly received, & whatever the Event May be, the Part the Deputation has Acted has been so kindly taken abroad, that the House of Representatives of the Province of Massachusetts Bay, have returned them their Thanks, in a Message signed by their speaker. . . .

The Committee this year [1750] again Renewed their utmost Endeavors to prevent the introducing a Vicar General, or Bishop into America, & hitherto the Design and Attempt of that kind has not Succeeded.

X. BISHOP SHERLOCK'S CIRCULAR LETTER TO THE COMMISSARIES, OF SEPTEMBER 19, 1750, WITH SOME HITHERTO UNPUBLISHED REPLIES.

Chandler's *Johnson*, Appendix, 166, 167, and the Fulham Manuscripts.

I.

Rev. Sir,

I have no excuse to make for the silence I have observed towards you and the other Commissaries in the plantations, but only this, that I waited in hopes of giving you an account of a settlement of Ecclesiastical affairs for the Colonies, in some shape or other. I have been far from neglecting the affairs of your Churches, and have been soliciting the establishment of one or two bishops to reside in proper parts of the plantations, and to have the conduct and direction of the whole. I am sensible for myself that I am capable of but little service to those distant Churches, and I am persuaded that no Bishop residing in England ought to have, or willingly to undertake this province. As soon as I came to the See of London, I presented a Memorial to the King upon this subject; which was referred to his principal officers of state to be considered. But so many difficulties were started, that no report was made to his Majesty. After this I presented a petition to the King in Council of like purport. His Majesty's journey to Hanover left no room to take a resolution upon an affair that deserves to be maturely weighed. This lies before the King and Council, and will, I hope, be called for when his Majesty returns to England, this is a short state of the case.

You will see by this I am not yet able to say anything as to the effect of these applications : but as in all events a new patent must be granted, either to the Bishop of London, or to a new Bishop, I desire to be informed by you how the jurisdiction has been carried on during the time that the late Bishop of London acted under a patent from the Crown. I know the jurisdiction so granted extends only to the Clergy; but with respect to this there seems to me to be some defects in the patent. But I will not write them out to forestall your judgement, but shall be much obliged to you for any observations upon this head which your experience has furnished you with ; which I shall endeavor to make use of for the service of the Churches abroad.

I am, Sir, Yours, &c.

2.

Reply of Commissary Garden of South Carolina, to Sherlock's Circular Letter, mainly relating to the Trial of George Whitefield.

From the Manuscripts in the Fulham Library.

My Lord

I have received the honour of your Lordship's Letter of 20th Sept[br] last past, in which you are pleased to mention the several steps you had taken in soliciting the Establishment of one or two Bishops to reside in proper Parts of & govern the Episcopal Churches of England in America ; & also the uncertain State in which that Affair still depends. Your Lordship is also pleased to desire me to inform you, how the Jurisdiction was carried on during the time that the late Bishop of London acted under a Patent from the Crown ; & also of any Observations, which my experience may have furnished me with, respecting some Defects which your Lordship apprehends in the said Patent, even as restricted only to the Clergy.

The Episcopal Churches in America, are greatly beholden to your

Lordship, for your Pious & Assiduous endeavors to obtain for them so essential a part of their Being, as that of a Bishop or Bishops personally presiding over, & governing them. In their present Condition they are certainly without a parallel in the Christian Church, in any age or country from the beginning.

When my late Lord of London, sent me his Commission appointing me his Commissary, pursuant to his Patent from the Crown, he therewith also sent me some printed Papers, intitled *Methodus Procedendi contra Clericos Irregulares in Plantationibus Americanis;* (which doubtless your Lordship will find among the records of your See) containing, first, his Lordship's Appointment of a Commissary; 2dly his Directions to the Commissary, 3dly The Method of Proceeding &c 4^{thly} Instruments, & other Things, referrd to in the Method of Proceeding; being Extracts from *Clark's* praxis, Oughton's Ordo Judiciorum &c. Pursuant to the said Directions, I always held an Annual Visitation of the Clergy of this Province, on the 2nd Wednesday after Easter-day at Charlestown; & took that Opportunity punctually to comply with all the other Particulars of his Lordship's 5th & following Directions.

Whether any of his Lordship's Commissaries in the other Colonies, ever Proceded against any irregular Clergymen I know not; but as to myself I proceeded against 4, vizt, *Wintely, Morrit, Fulton,* & *Whitefield.* The two Former chose to resign their Livings rather than stand their Trials; & the two Latter I suspended; the one (Fulton) from his Office & Benefice; & the other (Whitefield) only from his Office, being a Vagabond Clergyman having no Benefice to be suspended from.

In all these proceedings (my Lord) I did not observe any Defect in the Royal Patent, but several Difficulties occurred & perplexed me with respect to the Laws. On Process instituted against Whitefield, for Transgressing the 38th Canon of the Church, or as a Revolter after Subscription, he exhibited in writing *recusatio Judicis* or a refusal of me for his Judge; alledging for Causes, that I was his Enemy, & had printed and preached against him with great Bitterness & Enmity; and referring the Same to Six Arbiters, Three of whom he named on his part, who were two Independents, & one french Calvinist, & all of them his Zealous Admirers. On this Event several Difficulties occurr'd as vizt First, Whether, as the Law only prescribes *probi viri* i.e. as explain'd, *indifferentes* & *docti*, for arbiters, I might not reject those named, as *non* indifferentes, for the reasons above mention'd. (2dly) Admitting that I had taken no exception to the Three persons nam'd, but had nam'd Three others on my part to join them for Arbiters, put the Case (as it certainly would have turn'd out) of their Coming to no agreement or Conclusion, what then was to be done? or what was to become of the principal Cause. The Laws are silent as to such a Case, nor do I find it either put or resolv'd by *Clark, Oughton, Conset,* or any other. I could neither see nor be advised, that it was in my power to proceed in Case of their non Agreement, & so the Cause instituted must have dropt, & Whitefield, escaped without Censure. Again (3dly) supposing the Arbiters had agreed and given Judgment against me, who in that Case should be Judge in the Cause instituted? I find this Query put by the above nam'd Authors, but not otherwise resolv'd than by a *dicunt aliqui; arbitri recusationis :* And this again Queried, *quo Jure ?* & so the point left moot or undecided. Amidst these Difficulties, and for reasons inserted at length in the Proceedings transmitted to my late Lord of London, I repell'd his Recusation ; on which he interposed an Appeal, to the Lords named in the Royal Patent, & had the same granted him ; but which he either wilfully or ignorantly neglected to Prosecute until the Juratory Term assaign'd, viz! the space of Twelve Months was expired, & then the Process against him was carried on here. Witnesses were Examined and Sentence of Suspension from his Office was pronounced, & still stands in Force against him. — But this Sentence having had no effect upon him for his Reformation and Submission, I should have long since proceeded, pursuant to the Canon, to that of Excommunication, but for a Defect in the Law, which would have rendered it as ineffectual as the other, viz!, that the Writ *de Excommunicato capiendo* could not be issued against him here, because the Statutes of Queen Eliza^{bth} on which that Writ is grounded, do not extend to America.

These my Lord, were the Difficulties which occurr'd to me, in the Execution of my late Lord of Londons Jurisdiction in this Province. And I am firmly of Opinion, that if they are not some way or other removed, a Commissary's Office or Authority will be of little avail against any Irregularities of the Clergy. For, First, as it will be easy for any irregular Clergyman to except against the Commissary for his Judge by alledging Enmity, specially on a Prosecution *ex Officio Mero,* so neither will it be a difficult matter for him, to name Two or Three persons for Arbiters, who will stand it aught against the Commissary, as an unfit person for his Judge, and so by a disagreement of the Arbiters, Suspend the Arbitration without decision, & consequently, as far as I can perceive, defeat the whole process. Or (2dly) In case the Arbiters decide against the Commissary, the Law not providing who shall succeed for

Judge to carry on the Process, it must therefore also of course drop & come to nothing.

Concerning *dilapitation* either of Churches or Parsonage Houses, I had no occasion to inquire, for by a particular Law of this Province the Clergy are exempted from that charge which is defray^d partly by the Publick & partly by the Parishioners. But whether, had there been occasion, I could have carried on a Process for *dilapitation* I am doubtful; the Patent not being so explicit on that head, & seeming rather to confine the Authority to the *inquirend' de moribus.* — But it is high time to put an end to this long Epistle containing all I can offer in answer to your Lordship's; & therefore humbly craving your Blessing & Protection, I remain

My Lord
Your Lordship's most
dutiful Son & Obed^t Humble Servt
A GARDEN

So Caro*
Charlestown Feby^y 1st 1750.

3.

COMMISSARY GARDEN TO BISHOP GIBSON, JANUARY 28, 1741.

From the Manuscripts in the Fulham Library.

I have herewith transmitted to your Lordship, an authentick Copy of my farther & final Proceedings against Mr. Whitefield, by wch I have suspended him from his Office pursuant to the 38th Canon. I had kept the Court on regular Adjournments for five months after the expiration of the Juratory Term, waiting for some Order or other in the Affair. But understanding by your Lordship's Letter, that Whitefield had deserted his Appeal (notwithstanding his solemn oath, in open Court, *bona fide* to prosecute it) I saw it my Duty to proceed to a definitive Sentence, wch accordingly I have done; & wch if the Lords Appellees approve not, they may annul; & either way the affair will be at an end as far as I can carry it to any effect on this side of the Water.

I have wrote your Lordship so fully on the Subject of the unruly Man, & the Prosecution I have now finished, in my former Letters, that I have nothing farther to add save only that I could have wished, that the Council your Lordship employed had, on the Expiration of the Juratory Term, transmitted a proper certificate from the Offices, that Whitefield had deserted his appeal; w^ch (if I am rightly informed) is the Method in Cases of appeals in Civil Matters from America, and would not have been denied them.

4.

REPLIES OF THE TWO LEADING EPISCOPAL CLERGYMEN OF BOSTON TO
BISHOP SHERLOCK'S CIRCULAR LETTER.

From the Manuscripts in the Fulham Library.

I.

*Rev. Timothy Cutler, Rector of Christ Church, to the Bishop of
London.*

April 24, 1751.

Your Lordship's Letter of September 19th containing a Copy of a
general Letter from your Lordship to the Commissaries of our late Right
Reverend Diocesan, I received just at the end of February last. . . . I
doubt I can relate nothing in the Jurisdiction exercised here during the
time the late Bishop of London acted under a Patent from the Crown.
Once our Commissary went to New London, upon some business about
the late reverend Mr. Morris : but Mr. Morris voluntarily ended all by
quitting the Place. The Commissary also went to Newbury upon some
Difficulties about a new Church there : but there was no formal Hearing,
nor is there any Issue. The unhappy Case of Mr. Roe belonging to the
Chapel [King's Chapel] might have had a formal Consideration if he
had not immediately departed to England. And this quashed the Consideration of another affair relating to him, which his Lordship referred
to the Cognizance of ye Commissary of South Carolina, to which Mr.
Roe was ordered to repair. As to that of Mr. Whitefield judicially considered by that Commissary, your Lordship may have a perfect account
from him at your pleasure. I can add no more upon this head, than
that upon the Commissaries' call, there have been annual meetings of
the Clergy, mainly taken up in relating the State of our Parishes, and in
consulting and advising one another. And I cannot suppose that what
I have mentioned respecting New England hath raised any uneasy
Speculations or Remarks among our Dissenters.

＊　　　＊　　　＊　　　＊　　　＊　　　＊　　　＊

I have, my Lord, with several of my Brethren, subjoined to the Proposals of sending Bishops, one or more, to reside in America, our humble
Opinion of that affair ; and beg leave to add further what follows :

That in all Probability, this Objection, tho' not openly avow'd, yet
not very latent, outweighs all the rest, That the Church of England growing very much in its imperfect State, would much more grow, compleated

by the Residence of a Bishop; that our increase would be out of the Societies of the Dissenters, perhaps to the breaking up of some of them, or to their greater Burden in supporting of them; that these Colleges would be Nurseries of Episcopal Clergymen; That many Churchmen scattered throughout almost all our Towns, but very much concealed for the sake of a quieter and more agreeable Subsistence among their neighbors, might take heart to shew themselves; and that civil Preferments would not be so confin'd as they are at present.

* * * * * * *

Wherever Bishops are placed in America, we ought all to thank God for it. But I lay myself very low for your Lordship's pardon, [ ] of a few Remarks upon Barring the Settlement of Bishops in places where the Government is in the hands of Dissenters as in New England &c.

That in these Places, the Members of the Church, and the Church itself is peculiarly injured; and there we eminently need a Bishop to appear in our Favor, and upon Occasion to represent our Case home.

That universal experience tells us, That the nearer the Church is to Dissenters, the most it prevails, their Prejudices wear away, misrepresentations are taken off, or prevented, People better know what the Church is, and better esteem it. This is evident from the monstrous Ideas of our Church in our distant Country Towns, which have no place in those bordering on us.

II.

Rev. Henry Caner, Rector of King's Chapel, to the Bishop of London.

From the Manuscripts in the Fulham Library.

May 6, 1751.

I had the Honour of your Lordship's Letter of the 19th September last, with a Copy inclosed of one written to the late Bishop of London's Commissaries: In which your Lordship required the Information of your Clergy in these Parts " how the Jurisdiction has been carried on during the Time that the late Bishop of London acted under a Patent from the Crown." As I have never seen a Copy of the late Bishop's Patent nor even of the Instructions given to his Commissary in this District it is impossible for me to say anything on the Subject. Indeed it has been generally apprehended here, that the late Commissary had no Authority to act at all, as I am told he never qualified himself, by exhibiting his Commission to the Governor, or other proper Officer, and by taking Oath before such Officer for the due Execution of his Trust which I think the Laws here require of every Person in cases of this or a like Nature. . . .

[Caner, like Cutler (see above, p. 317), objects to any concession whereby no bishops would be sent to New England; but is willing to concede that their jurisdiction shall not extend to the laity.]

5.

REPLY OF DR. JENNEY, COMMISSARY OF PENNSYLVANIA, TO SHERLOCK'S CIRCULAR LETTER.

From the Manuscripts in the Fulham Library.

Dated at Philadelphia May 23, 1751.

May it please your Lordship

It was the 15 of this Month before I had the Honor to receive your L^dships Letter by Mr. Craig, dated at London ye 20th of Sep^tbr 1750, wherein your L^dship condescends to acquaint me with your Endeavors to settle ye Ecclesiastical Affairs of ye Colonies, particularly your Application to his Majesty for ye Establishment of two Bishops, which lies still before ye Council undetermined.

Your L^dship commands me to inform you how ye Jurisdiction has been carried on for ye Time past, of which I am afraid my Account will not be very aggreable. The patent of ye late B^p did not seem to justify his Commissary in any Judicial Proceeding :[1] The Laity laughed at it, & ye Clergy seemed to dispise it, nor did there appear at Home a Disposition to shew any Regard to it : The Commissary was no otherwise regarded there than to be made ye Instrument of conveying Letters, Books &c to ye Missionaries, as he lives conveniently for that purpose in ye Chief place of Commerce where ye Ships from & for London are for ye most part only to be found. One Instance of ye Laity's Contempt of my Commission I have found in two gentlemen (one a Lawyer) who insulted me most rudely for not condemning a Clergyman unheard, & refusing to send to ye hon^ble Society their charge against him without giving him an Opportunity (which he earnestly requested) of justifying himself against it. Your L^dship observes that ye B^p of Londons Jurisdiction was by ye Patent extended only to ye Clergy : But even ye Clergy seemed not to take much Notice of it. One has given me under his

---

[1] Cf. Commissary Garden of South Carolina on this head, above, p. 313.

Hand that my Commission from ye B^p was far from being unexceptionable : Another spoke of it with such a sneer as plainly Discovered a Contempt : Both of these were in my District, but one of them is now dead. Besides ye Clergy Settled here we have some Ministers whom we may call Vagabonds having come without License or appointed Settlement. There are also some who come hither for their Health (chiefly from ye hotter Climates) Some of these are exceeding faulty in their Behaviour, & some deistical both in their preaching & Conversation. And although many of these who do so exceedly misbehave do not belong to this province ; Yet if ye Commissary does not take notice of them he is laughed at by ye profane, & blamed by those who are religious : But he is obliged to bear ye Reflections of both through an Apprehension that his Commission will not bear him out if he should proceed against them.

There is also a great Inconvenience arising to our ministers, & Irregularities proceeding ye Licenses for marriages being issued out of ye Office of ye Governors Secretary & directed to any protestant Minister : Some Justices of ye Peace pretend that this Direction includes them, & upon that pretence take upon them to marry. In our neighboring (ye Jersies) they are expressly directed to any protestant Minister or Justice of ye Peace, though some of ye latter are very mean Fellows, Butchers, and low-lifed Traders, & some of ye best of them are but Common Farmers and plow men. And by these means it comes to pass that we have very irregular & unlawful marriages amongst us.

It is said of Mariland that ye Ld Baltimore will not suffer ye B^p of London's Commissary even to read his Commission in that Province : And as to this Province of Pennsylvania ; one of ye greatest men in our Government asserted in Vestry, That our Church is only tolerated by M^r. Penn ye Proprietour ; & he thinks himself justified in saying so by ye Words of that clause in ye Proprietours Charter which was put in for ye Security of our Church and he proceeded so far as to assert that neither ye Cannons nor Rubrick have any Force in this province.

As ye Jersies are divided from this province by nothing but ye River Delaware, & this City stands upon ye Banks of that River, I submit to your L^dship whether it would not be more convenient for ye Missionaries of West Jersey next adjoining to be annexed to Pennsylvania under one Commissary, than to New York which is at so great a Distance.

It wou'd be of considerable Service to ye Church & her Ministers here to find some means to make ye Governors hearty in our Interest.

I cannot recollect at present anything more that has fallen in with my Observation with Regard to that Part of the Colonies that I have been concerned with as the Bishop of Londons Commissary to trouble your L^{d}ship with.

I pray God to give Success to your L^{d}ships pius endeavors for the Service of the Church.

And I am,

May it please your L^{d}ship,

Y^r L^{d}ships

Most dutiful Son & obedient

humble Servant

Rob^T Jenney.

XI. CORRESPONDENCE BETWEEN THE BISHOP OF LONDON AND THE ENGLISH MINISTRY, RELATIVE TO THE INTRODUCTION OF BISHOPS INTO THE AMERICAN COLONIES, 1749–50.

From the Newcastle Papers in the British Museum, Home Series, 32719–21.

I.

THOMAS SHERLOCK, BISHOP OF LONDON, TO THE DUKE OF NEWCASTLE.

September 3, 1749.

I will own to your Grace, what my fatal mistake was, I thought, (and I have not changed my opinion) y^t I had so much of his Mat^{ys} favours; and was in hopes that I had so much interest in y^r Grace that I might prevail to have Bps abroad & some help for myself at home — But if I ask too much in desiring assistance, I am sure I shall undertake *too much* to enter upon the business of America without assistance, and I hope y^r Grace will obtain the King's leave for me to confine myself to the care of my proper diocese of London. I will doe nothing to disoblige the King, I owe too much to him, But I hope his Majesty will (I doubt not but he will) consider the case of an old, and, give me to say, a faithful servant.

2.

DUKE OF NEWCASTLE TO THE BISHOP OF LONDON.

September 5, 1749.

The appointing Bishops, . . . is a great, & national consideration; had been long under the Deliberation of great, & wise men, heretofore; and was, by them laid aside; and ought not to be resumed, for personal considerations; or, at all, be looked upon in that Light. Whatever my Opinion is or may be, upon that Point; I am sure you cannot think, It can proceed from any want of Friendship, or Regard for you.

3.

BISHOP OF LONDON TO THE DUKE OF NEWCASTLE.

September 7, 1749.

I reckoned (perhaps misreckoned) that I was proposing a scheme for the *publick service*, to enable not only myself but every Bp. of London to execute with some tolerable degree of care, the extensive commission he is to have in his Majesties foreign dominions, in the due Execution of w^{ch}, the King's Honour is concerned; and wch the Religion of the Country, the prosperity of the Ch: of England; always esteemed the Bulwark agst Popery; the members whereof are the only set of Xtians in the King's dominions who own the Supremacy of [the Crown]

With respect to the Settlmt of Bps abroad, your Grace's Observation has great justness and Dignity in it: that it ought not to be resumed on a *Personal Consideration*.

I am sensible that I have shewn so much concern for the success of this scheme, and have amongst other considerations so often suggested that the care of the plantations was too much for one Bp to discharge with benefit to others or credit to himself, and brought with it an Expense, not reasonably imposed on one Bp who had no more relation to the plantations than others had; That I may well have fallen under the Suspicion of y^r Grace, & others, that my Concern in this case has been selfish. But whatever handle I may [have] given to such suspicions, yet I must have lived to little purpose, if I am capable of thinking that so great & material an affair was to be determined by regard to me, or any other man living: I did indeed flatter myself that I shou'd not be the worst Solliciter in the case for the favour I had with y^r Grace. — But let not the reasons of real weight be overlooked, & sink under suspiceons, I will not trouble you with setting forth these Reasons: But permit me to say one thing; that there is not, and I think, there never was, a Xtian Ch: in the world, in the condition the Ch: of England is now, in the Plantations; obliged to send from one side of the World to the other, to get ministers ordained to officiate in their Congregations, — As to the reasons relating, (not to myself only, but) to the Bishop of London, I have said no more than my Predecess^r said daily to me & to many others: he was as able to dispatch business, as any who were before him, and as any who may probably come after him, but he felt & complained of the burden. — There is one kind of selfishness wch has perhaps influenced me ; or has more of vanity than Interest in it : I shou'd, indeed think it the glory of my life, if I c'd be the instrument, even in the lowest degree of putting the Ch. abroad upon a true and primitive foot.

As to the Views I have had in this whole affair, I have nothing to accuse myself if in the warmth of prosecuting, I have, either in speaking or writing on this subject, so far forgot myself or y^r Grace, as to have fallen into any Impropriety, I hope you will pardon it ; and permit me to assure you that, tho' you have many abler friends, you have none more heartily & sincerely concerned to your honour & Prosperity, or more sensible of your favours than, etc.

4.

BISHOP OF LONDON TO DUKE OF NEWCASTLE.

March 23, 1749/50.

My Lord Duke,

Your Grace will receive together with this, a Representation of the State of the Church of England in America, which I intend to lay before the King in Council. At present the Church there is without any Government or Inspection, & it is absolutely necessary to put an end to this State which will be a State of Confusion. I laid the Representation before my Lord Chancellor, and tho' he has difficulties as to the main point, yet I had the Satisfaction to know from his Lordship, that the address and the Style of it had nothing to give Offense. — If I shou'd not succeed in the thing I have most at Heart, yet I promise myself that some attention will be given to this Address, and that after Due Consideration of the State of the Church abroad, his Majesty will give such directions as may make his gracious intentions of protecting and Supporting the Church of England, effectual in his foreign Dominions.

As to what relates to myself, I put it all out of the Case, and will resign myself to his Majesty's pleasure. But there are many reasons why I shou'd desire a resolution by Authority, and I hope your Grace, recollecting what has passed will not think me too hasty in presenting this address next Week, that I may know his Majesty's pleasure before he goes abroad.

I am
My Lord, Your Grace's
Most obedient & most humble Servant
THO : LONDON.

5.

DUKE OF NEWCASTLE TO THE BISHOP OF LONDON.

March 25, 1750.

My Lord,

I had the Honour of your Lordship's Letter of the 23ᵈ Insᵗ enclosing a Representation of the State of the Church of England in America, which your Lordship proposes to lay before the King, in Council. I have read the Representation over, with great Attention; and entirely agree with my Lord Chancellor, that It is wrote with great Clearness & Decency; and is far from containing anything, that can give offense. As to the Point of Establishing Bishops in the West Indies, your Lordship knows I have always thought It. of such Importance, that It required the most mature Consideration; and the Opinion is not lessen'd by what appears to have passed, both here, & in the West Indies, relative to this Point. If the Commission, to Bishop Gibson, was defective; that may easily be rectified, if It shall be thought proper to pursue the same Method: But, at present, I understand from My Lord Chancellor, your Lordship proposes to meet some of the King's Servants, to consider this important Question. I shall, with greatest Pleasure, attend any Evening, that is not already appointed for other Business. The only vacant Evening, this week, with me, is Thursday; I doubt whether my Brother can come that Night: If He can, I will fix that Evening with Him. In the Meantime I should hope, your Lordship would not present the Address to the King in Council, till after his Majesty's principal Servants have had a Meeting with you, upon it. I beg your Lordship to be assured, that I shall consider this Question, with the utmost Attention; as an Affair of this high Moment, and so strongly recommended by your Lordship, deserves. You cannot wonder, that one, so little inform'd of these things, as myself, should have his Doubts, upon a Question, which has been often agitated; and which the wisest & best, men have hitherto, not thought proper to determine, in the way, you propose.

I am always, with greatest Respect,
My Lord, your Lordship's, &c
HOLLES NEWCASTLE.

6.

HORATIO WALPOLE TO THE BISHOP OF LONDON.

May 29, 1750

My Lord,

Your Lordship having been pleased to communicate to me sometime since in confidence a paper containing a State of ye Church of England in his Majesty's Dominions in America with your Lordship's inferences & reasonings upon it as motive for having Suffragan Bishops settled in some of these Colonys to perform certain Ecclesiastical functions necessary to promote & support ye Establishment of that Church these I carefully perused and considered the whole with that intention & disposition as became a Member of ye Church of England whose Education & profession have always been agreeable to her form and Doctrine.

But your Lordship may remember that when I returned you that paper, I took ye liberty to tell you that however desirable, and reasonable a Scheme for settling Bishops for some purposes in ye American Colonys might be abstractly considered, yet having weighed this measure, with a due regard at ye same time to what appears to be ye inclination of those colonies, and what might be ye consequence of it as a matter of State to our present happy Establishment, I was apprehensive that ye carrying it only so far as to be laid before ye King & Council might be attended with very Mischievous effects to ye Government.

For with respect to ye Inclinations of ye people in America it does not appear by your Lordships Deduction of what had passed there in Favor of ye Church of England, that ye Governours and those of that persuasion themselves were at all desirous of having Bishops sent thither for any purposes whatsoever; many indeed of ye Colonys and Islands not only prefer, but have encouraged & countenanced by various Acts ye forms and Doctrines of the Church of England, & they will admit none to be capable of a benefice untill they have testimonials of their being qualified according to the Canons of that Church by having taken Deacons & Priests Orders; and your Lordship wou'd draw from thence the following inferences

1° That they wou'd not be unwilling a Bishop shou'd reside amongst them

2° That it can never be thought reasonable that those who profess ye established Religion, & are Episcopal Churches shou'd be denied ye benefit of Episcopal Administration which according to their Religious Principles they think necessary for them

3° That ye Episcopal Churches in America want their first & most necessary Member a Bishop to reside with them & have waited with for ye consent ye Crown.

Now with humble Submission to your Lordships better Judgement I do not think these inferences your Lordship makes from ye Attachment of many of ye Colonies to ye Church of England are Conclusive to prove that they are desirous of having ye Residence of a Bishop, for they confine all their Orders, & Acts to ye Authority of ye Bishop of London acting by his Commissary there.

They have never that I have learnt made any formal application, or even Intimated to ye Crown for ye residence of Bishops wth them; they have vested the care of these matters that want ye Inspection & Authority of a Bishop upon ye Spot in other hands; they have required that their Minister shou'd be ordained here according to the Cannons of ye Church to be certified by the Bishop of London, & all transactions relating to ye Clergy they refer to his Lordship or his Comissary to whom they readily Submitt but they have never yet given ye least hint to him or any of ye Officers of State here, as if they wanted ye Mission, or ye Residence of a Bishop amongst them ; they have declared by Several Acts of Assembly against Ecclesiastical Laws, & Jurisdiction to enforce or establish any mulct or Punishment, they seemed therefore to have conceived some jealousy of that Church power, and I am afraid a stronger Inference may be made from thence of their having no Inclination to have a Bishop, than can be made from other Acts in favor of ye Church of England that they desire to have one

It is true that they have never complained, as your Lordship observes, of ye Bishop's Comissary, nor have they ever intimated their concern at his not having sufficient power, & authority to govern the Clergy there, which rather shows that they are content with a Comissary, than that they wish to have a Bishop in his place ; and indeed my Lord from your own State of ye case all ye Acts of the Colonys and encouragement in support of the Church of England with respect to Ecclesiastical Discipline, Doctrine, & Authority extend no farther than what might be legally delegated by a Bishop of London to a Comissary residing

I took ye Liberty to observe to your Lordship, from Your own paper, that ye Bishops Compton, Robinson, & Gibson to whose departm^t as Bishop of London ye care of ye Church in America belonged, all Prelates zealously and rigorously attached to ye Church of England carryed their desire of having the Doctrine and Governm^t, Settled in ye West Indys under their Authority as far as they possibly could, & nothing more cou'd be obtained but a Superintendency over the Church & his Clergy there by Comissarys to be appointed by them.

And had it been thought prudent to have gone any farther by sending Suffragan Bishops to ye West Indys Queen Ann, & her Ministry, especially at ye latter end of her reign as they were not wanting in zeal for ye Church to undertake, cou'd not have wanted power to carry through so pius a design

I told your Lordship that I cou'd very well remember what was in agitation, on this subject by Bishop Gibson in 1725 ; Lord Townshend was so good a friend to that Orthodox Prelate, as well as to ye Church, that it is natural to believe that such a Scheme for his Benefit wou'd have been pursued, & put in execution had not ye wisdom of those two great men thought unadvisable, & however desirable yet a Dangerous Step with Respect to ye Peace, & Quiet of ye State ; And therefore my Lord independent of what may be ye disposition of ye Governours & of great Numbers in ye West Indys attached to ye Rites, & doctrine of the Church of England ; I cou'd not forbear letting your Lordship know that I apprehended as soon as a Scheme of sending Bishops to ye Colonys altho' with certain restrictions shou'd under your Lordships Authority & Influence be made publick it wou'd immediately become ye Topick of all conversation ; a matter of controversy in ye Pulpitts, as well as by Pamphletts, & Libells, with a Spirit of bitterness & acrimony that prevail more frequently in disputes about Religion as ye Authors and Readers are differently affected than on any other Subject.

The Dissenters of all Sorts whom I mention with no other regard or concern than as they are generally well affected, & indeed necessary Supports to ye present establishment in State, & therefore shou'd not be provoked, or alienated against it, will by the instigation & complaints of their brethren in ye Colonys altho' with no Solid reasons be loud in their discourses & writings upon this intended innovation in America, and those in ye Colonys will be exasperated & animated to make warm representations against it to ye Government here, as a design to establish Ecclesiastical power in its full extent among them by Degrees ; altho' ye first step seems to be moderate & measured, by confining ye Authority of ye Bishops to be planted amongst them to certain Colonies & Functions.

The High Church party here / for immediately ye distinction of High Church & Low Church wch has occasioned great Mischiefs in this divided Country in former Reigns, and has happily laid a Sleep for some Years, will be revived / I say ye High Church party & especially a cer-

tain great Nursery of Learning, and others that are dissaffected to
yᵉ present Establishmᵗ of which your Lordship must allow there are too
many among those of yᵉ Church persuasion, may perhaps cover your
Lordship with great encomiums, for your extended & unexampled Zeal
in behalf of yᵉ Church of England, but will treat with yᵉ Severest reflexions those and especially yᵉ k——g & his ministers who shall not readily
give into yᵉ promoting of so pious a design.

The Low Church party that are all well affected to yᵉ Present Governmᵗ will not be sparing of their Censure & Reflexions upon your
Lordship & others, that are for propagating & promoting a Scheme
which they will say is Calculated to sett up Hierarchy & Church power
in yᵉ Colonys, & to create dissention & confusion among a People that
are now happy & quiet in their Civil & Religious State.

And your Lordship will pardon my friendly freedom for adding that
many persons of Consideration who have a true Value for your Lordship's great Learning & Understanding, are not without jealousy of your
extraordinary Zeal & desire to increase Ecclesiastical Power in this
Country, and that jealousy my Lord will carry with it an apprehension
that this first motion for settling Bishops in America to perform certain
functions only as Ordination & Confirmation is laying a foundation for
giving them gradually yᵉ same Authority & power as yᵉ Bishops here
enjoy & exercise in all other respects; wᶜʰ there is no doubt but your
Lordship thinks are all strictly just & reasonable, and ought not to be
altered or diminish'd, and consequently you must think that they ought
to take place in yᵉ Colonys, and if it was reasonable & practicable to
attempt yᵉ Establishment of them there at present, and this apprehension
will in a great degree have yᵉ same effect & be attended with yᵉ same
consequences of ill humour & discontent as if Ecclesiastical Government was now to be settled there in its full extent.

But if this scheme cannot be carry'd into Execution without being
laid before yᵉ Parliament ; has your Lordship considered yᵉ great dilemma
& difficultys yᵉ K——g & yᵉ administration will be put under in that
respect, & shou'd it be brought thither; however the Court may be
disposed, I am afraid it will not be canvassed without yᵉ greatest heats
& animositys, & perhaps a Division among those that are best affected
to his Majesty's Governmᵗ in both Houses, these Animosities & Divisions
will flow from yᵉ Parliament into yᵉ Country, & all contests in yᵉ Choice
of Magistrates, or for Members of Parliament will be again Governed
by that Odious & pernicious distinction of High Church & Low Church,
and this puts me in Mind of Bishop Atterbury's Policy who when a

certain Sermon of Doct[r] Hoadleys was printed in 1718 said to his
intimate friends that condemned it, *it was no matter what y* Doctrine
was ; y* publication of it was a very lucky event in favour of y* Right
Line as it wou'd create Divisions amongst those attached to y* present
establishment for he added, y* best means to be employed to get rid of
y* present R—— family would be to put y* Controversy upon some
Religious points ;* and altho' we seem to be in a State of perfect tranquility I am sorry to say it, but I am afraid it is too true that y[e] affection
to this family is not so Universal and prevalent, as to make it prudent,
to set on foot the most plausible Scheme for an Innovation in religious
matters even in y[e] Colonys as might / w[ch] I am firmly persuaded this
would / hazard a division among the best friends there as well as in this
kingdom.   I cou'd say a great deal to show that Jaco——sm is rather
encreased than diminished since y[e] Suppression of y[e] last unnatural
Rebellion in 1745, w[ch]. is a thing rather to be secretly lamented than
publicly declared, but this Observation shou'd make all wise men such as
your Lordship, that are well affected to this Government, very Cautious
in Starting & pursuing y[e] most desirable project that may create new
disputes, & tend to disturb y[e] present calm & peaceful Situation of
affairs.

Indeed my Lord I was so vain as to Imagine my Conversation with
your Lordship on this Subject had, had some effect upon you, & you
seemed then inclined to Suspend, your intention of laying your Scheme
before the King, & afterwards when you mentioned it to His Majesty,
& he was pleased to refer y[e] Matter to y[e] Consideration of His Privy
Council, you lodged your paper with y[e] Lord President declaring to
Several that you had done your duty & having discharged your Conscience, you shou'd let it rest there to be Considered by the Council
when they shou'd think proper.

And as the matter stood thus when His Majesty went abroad I
must own my Lord that I was Surprised & Concerned to hear that at a
late meeting of y[e] Society for propagating y[e] Gospel, your Lordship
having stated to them what had passed, & proposed that, while this
matter was pending in Council, y[e] Society shou'd write a letter to y[e]
several Governours in the West Indys, and by Stating to them y[e] several
objections Supposed to have been made against y[e] intended Scheme
of Settling Bishops there, and y[e] answers that might be made to remove
those objections, to conclude with desiring to know their Opinions &
y[e] disposition of y[e] Colonys, with respect to y[e] putting it in Execution.

Now my Lord, as this is a Matter of State, and has been referred by his Majesty to be considered in Council, & your Lordship is one of that Body It seems to be not entirely consistent with ye prudence of one in that Station unless so desired by the Council, to resume an affair of this Importance in ye Society for propagating ye Gospel, and under a Notion of Supposed objections to it, and Supposed answers framed by your Lordship, or if you please by that Society, to write a plausible letter to the Governours for their Sentiments upon a matter of State, under ye Consideration of ye Council, there may possibly be other objections such as I have mentioned before relating to ye Government besides what may be Stated in your Lordship's letter, and even with respect to ye answers to those objections that you suppose to have been Suggested, can your Lordship and that Society undertake to make those answers good ? Can you undertake to promise that no coercive, or other Ecclesiastical power besides Ordination & Confirmation, shall ever be proposed & pressed upon ye Colonys when Bishops have been once settled amongst them, or beyond what is at present exercised by the Bishop of London's Commissary?

Can ye Society undertake that ye maintenance of ye Bishops in ye West Indys shall be no Burthen to ye Colonys? are they to determine what that expence is to be? & how is it to be supply'd? or is it intended that it shall be done by a Voluntary Contribution out of ye Bishopricks in England?

But for what end or purpose is the Opinion of ye Governours, or ye people in America to be asked at this juncture? While the Consideration of this matter is before ye Council, who may and I suppose will advise his Majesty to do what is best for ye good of his Subjects & his Government when the whole case & the consequences of it shall have been examined & taken into Deliberation by them; but Suppose my Lord ye Governors in America being consulted, & influenced perhaps in a great measure by the weight of your Lordship's Character, your Station as Bishop of London, & your Credit with the King & the Ministry, shou'd in their Answer be of Opinion that ye Scheme for Episcopacy in ye West Indys under ye Limitation & explanations proposed by your Lordship, wou'd not be inconvenient, but even beneficial; & shou'd on ye other side the Majority of ye Council be of Opinion for reasons of State that ye Execution of it may, notwithstanding the favorable Sentiments of ye Governours in behalf of it, be prejudicial to his Majesty's Governm^t, has your Lordship well weighed ye Consequences that may result from an affair so Circumstanced & perplexed, & the Embaras-[ment] that his Majesty & his Council may be under in coming to a

Decision upon it, which whatever it may be, in all likelihood will occassion great heats & Controversys as partys are in this Notion unhappily divided & differently affected.

Shou'd not your Lordships wisdom & moderation as a Prelate, so much recomended in ye Gospel to ye followers of our Saviour; and Quality of a Privy Councellor prevail with you to forbear taking this Step untill you shou'd See what is like to be done upon it by ye Council.

If they shou'd be dilatory in taking it under their Consideration, it wou'd be an Indication to your Lordship of their not caring to come hastily to a Determination in a matter of so much Consequence & difficulty, & should be an Inducement to let your Spiritual Zeal yield to your Temporal Prudence, & make you rest contented after having discharged your Conscience as Bishop of London in having laid the matter before his Majesty.

Should ye Council upon his Majesty's return home take it under their Consideration and be desirous, as a Material point in their deliberation, to know ye Sentiments of the Governours, & of ye Colonys upon it, there is no doubt but what they will give directions for that purpose, & therefore my Lord, as you was pleased to impart this matter for settling Episcopacy in America early to me, you will excuse ye Liberty I take in exhorting you for ye sake of publick peace, & ye Interest of this happy Establishment not to proceed any farther in it; for I can't help repeating my fears that, if 2000 copys of your projected letter to ye Governours, with a State of ye Supposed objections & answers relating to your Scheme, shou'd be forthwith printed, as I am told your Lordship has proposed, it wou'd Stir up great feuds & animositys, in Canvassing by Virulent Pamphlets, ye Question on both sides, & I can't but hope that your Lordship when you have cooly weigh'd ye Consequence of such Commotions will give a pause to your present good Intentions; & wait with patience the return of his Majesty, to learn ye Sentiments & proceedings of his Council upon what you have lodged with them without making it immediately ye Subject of discourse or debate either in this Country or in America. The thing itself is new, & therefore deserves Serious Consideration; it is not of so pressing and urgent a Nature, as to hazard any great inconvenience from being Suspended; precipitation may, but Delay cannot be dangerous in this Case, I am &c.

COCKPIT,
May 29, 1750.

7.

HORATIO WALPOLE TO THE DUKE OF NEWCASTLE.

COCKPIT, June 7, 1750.

My Lord/

My unalterable attachment to his Maj^{tys} person and Government [prompted me] to write ye letter (of wch your Grace has a copy enclosed) to the Bishop of London.

The Subject, and occasion of it are so fully sett forth in ye Contents as to want no farther explanations.

I dare say your Grace is persuaded that both his L^{rdp} & I have ye same good intentions for his Majestys interest & Service, And I must own that his Superior talents make me diffident of my own Sentiments, when they do not fall in with his; And if I am mistaken in my judgement, on a matter of so much consequence to ye State, I hope it will be attributed to my abundant zele, & concern for ye Peace, & happiness of his Maj^{tys} Reign.

Your Grace will be so good as to manage this Confidence, of an accidental, & private Correspondence between ye Bishop & me with your usual discretion, because if my apprehensions are at all well-founded, the proposal of so great a man to settle Episcopacy in the Colonys should be as little known as possible to ye Publick; I am with great respect

My Lord
Y^r L^{rdps} most obedi't &
most humble Servent
H. WALPOLE.

8.

DUKE OF NEWCASTLE TO HORATIO WALPOLE.

June 24, 1750.

Sir,

July 5

I am extremely oblig'd to you, for the Honor of your Letter, and your Goodness, in Sending me a Copy of one, that you had wrote to the Bishop of London, upon His Lordship's Scheme, for Settling Bishops in the West Indies. I have read it over, with great Attention; and think, you have stated the Case, with great Clearness, and Judgement, that the Considerations, there suggested, are of the utmost Importance; and ought to be thoroughly weighed, before this Scheme is carried into Execution. I always had very good Doubts, upon This Measure, from the First Proposal, and I have told His Lord^p, from the Beginning; And I was so happy, as to make Some of the same Inferences, from the

Proofs, He alledg'd, of the Sense, & Inclination, of the Colonies, & Islands, That you have done ; which I sent His Lord?, in a Letter I wrote to Him, immediately after I had His Paper. I own, I think, There is great Weight, also, in the Consequences, You so judiciously suggest, that This Affair may have at Home, in reviving old Disputes, & Distinctions, which are, at present, quiet ; and, perhaps, creating new Divisions amongst Those, Who Sincerely mean the Good of His Majesty's Government and the Good of Their Country. For These Reasons, I am persuaded, The Lords of the Council, will fully consider all These Points, before any material Step is taken in this Affair. I was extremely sorry to hear, That the Society, for propagating the Gospel, had been concerned in it : But I find Since, That That is Stopped. Your zeal for his Majesty's Service, and Government is too well known, and acknowledg'd, for it to be proper for me to say any Thing upon it. You will allow me, however to observe, That you have shew'd, very usefully, upon this occasion. . . .

9.

HORATIO WALPOLE TO THE DUKE OF NEWCASTLE.

July 14, 1750.

Your Grace's favorable reception (so fully exprest in ye honour of ye letter of ye 5th of July :) of my Sentiments upon ye Bishop of Londons Scheme for settling Episcopacy in ye West Indys, requires my best acknowledgements, and gave me no small satisfaction, I can assure your Grace, as corroborating with yours my opinion in a matter of so much importance to ye Peace & Quiet of his Majestys Government ; wch all good Subjects should promote, and render as easy to him, as it has been constantly mild, & prosperous to them, as well as greatly admired & respected by foreign Powers. . . .

XII. BISHOP SHERLOCK'S REPORT ON THE STATE OF THE CHURCH OF ENGLAND IN THE COLONIES.

New York Colonial Documents, VII, pp. 360–369, from *Plantations General Entries* (B. T.), XVI, p. 9.

To the KING in Council

Some considerations humbly offered by Thomas Bishop of London relating to Ecclesiastical Government in His Majestys Dominions in America.

The first Grant the Crown made of lands in America was dated the 10th April in the 4th year of James the 1st anno 1606 and made to the two Virginia Companies.

The King grants that each of them should have a Council, wch sho^d govern and order all matters & causes within the same several Colonies, according to such Laws Ordinances and Instructions *as sho^d in that behalf be given and signed by His Majesty's hand or sign manual & pass under the Privy Seal of England.*

1606. On the 20th Novr 1606 the King in pursuance of the right reserved to himself, gave divers orders under his Sign manuall and the Privy Seal, one of which was as follows: "That the President Council and Ministers should provide that the true word and service of God should be preached planted and used, *according to the Rites and Doctrine of the Church of England.*"

1609. The second grant was made separately to the first Virginia Company dated May 23^d in the 7th of the said King 1609 wch orders that there sho^d be a Council resident here and gives them power to establish *all manner* of laws concerning the governm^t of the said Colony, with power to punish, pardon, &^c according to such ordinances constitutions &^c as by such Council should be established; so always as the *said Ordinances* &^c as near as conveniently might be agreeable to the *Laws, Statutes, Government and Policy of the Realm.*

1620. The third Grant was made to the 2^d Virginia Company (then called the Council at Plymouth) and bears date Novr 3^d 18th James I. Anno 1620, and is to the same effect with the former, with this addition that all persons who sho^d pass in any voiage to the said country sho^d take the *Oath of Supremacy,* which was meant to exclude Papists from settling in America.

The affairs of the Company went on but slowly, & after twelve years and a great sum of money spent, the Colony consisted but of 600 persons, men women and children. Under these circumstances nothing was done and nothing could be expected to be done towards settling the Church there.

In 1620. there were but five Clergymen in the Plantations. The Comp^y had ordered an 100 acres in each of their burroughs (wch were in number eleven) to be set apart for a glebe, and for a further maintenance laid upon every planter a certain portion of tobacco to be paid to the Minister.

The next care was to get more Clergymen to go abroad to the Plantations, and this was to be provided for by the Virginia Council that sat at London. The *Bishop of London* was a great promoter of the Plantations and had collected and paid in £1000 towards the College in Virginia, and was himself one of the Council for Virginia. The Company therefore, as it was natural for them to do, applied to the Bishop of London, a member of their own Society, *for his help and assistance in procuring Ministers.* And this is the first instance I meet with of the Bp. of London's concern in the Ecclesiastical affairs of the Plantations.

1624 But so little was done towards settling the Church that it appears by the report of the General Assembly of Virginia in the year 1624. that divers of those who acted as Ministers *had no Orders.* In this Assembly there passed laws consisting of 35 articles. The first seven related to the Church and Ministry, but not the least intimation that the Bp. of London had any authority or jurisdiction there.

By Proclamation 15th July 1624. the Virginia Company &[c] was suppressed; and from that time the King has appointed Governors.

1626. S[r] George Yardly was appointed Governor of Virginia; his instructions bear date 19th April 1626. The 2[d] Article relates to religion and is as follows : —

" That in the first place you be careful, " That Almighty God may be duly and daily served, both by your self and the people under your charge, which may draw down a blessing on all your endeavours."

1650. S[r] William Berkely was Governor. His instructions bear date 1650. The first article relates to Religion : —

" That in the first place you be careful Almighty God be duly and daily served, *according to the form of Religion established in the Church of England.*

" Let every Congregation have an able Minister, build for him a convenient Parsonage House with 200 acres of glebe land. Suffer no innovation in matters of religion, and be careful to appoint sufficient and conformable Ministers to each congregation."

1675. At a Committee of Trade and Plantations 21st Jan. 1675. I find the following entry : —

" Their Lordships desire that enquiry be made touching the Jurisdiction which the *Bp. of London* hath over the Foreign Plantations; in order to w[ch] see the Charter of Virginia and New England, or by any other order since, but most probably about the year 1629. when Bp. Laud was in Chief Authority."

What gave rise to this inquiry I cannot find, but as there was nothing relating to this jurisdiction to be found, there does not appear any return to be made to this Enquiry. And the part allotted to the Bp. of London in the next Governor's instructions shows that the Bp. was not thought to have any *jurisdiction;* for he has nothing but a mere Ministerial Office appointed him, as appears in Lord Culpepers Instructions in 1679.

1679. Thomas Lord Culpeper was Govern' of Virginia. His instructions bear date 6ᵗʰ Septʳ 1679. The 15ᵗʰ articles decrees that God be duly served, *The Book of Common Prayer as is now established, read each Sunday and Holy Day, and the Blessed Sacrament administered according to the rules of the Church of England.*

The 16ᵗʰ article " And our will and pleasure is that no Minister be preferr'd by you, to any Ecclesiastical Benefice in that Our Colony *without a Certificate from the Lord Bp. of London, of his being conformable to the Doctrine of the Church of England.*"

JAMAICA.

1661. Lord Windsor was Governor of Jamaica ; his instructions bear date March 21ˢᵗ 1661. The 11ᵗʰ article concerns religion : — "You are to give the best encouragement you can to such conformable Ministers of the Gospel as now are or shall come and be sent unto you. That Christianity & the Protestant Religion *according to the Doctrine and Discipline of the Church of England,* may have a due reverence and exercise among you."

1681. Sʳ Thomas Lynch was Governor. His instructions bear date

1681. The 38ᵗʰ Article relates to religion : — " Our will and pleasure is that no Minister be preferr'd by you without *a Certificate from the Bp. of London,* of his being *conformable* to the Doctrine of the Church of England."

And you are to enquire whether any Minister preaches or administers the Sacrament without being in *due Orders;* whereof you are to give notice to the Bp. of London.

What the Bp. of London could do upon such notice, does not appear. The Plantations being no part of his Diocese, nor had he any authority to act there.

1685. At the Committee of Trade 15ᵗʰ April 1685. a letter from the Bp. of London proposing, 1ˢᵗ " That he may have all *Ecclesiastical Jurisdiction* in the West Indies, excepting the disposal of parishes, licences for Marriage &ᵉ Probate of Wills.

2ᵈ " That no Schoolmaster coming from England, be received without Licence from His Lordship, or from other His Majesty's Plantations without they take the Governor's licence.

3ʳᵈ " That orders may be given for establishing the Donation of Sᵗ Andrews Parish in Jamaica."

" Whereupon their Lordships agree to take these proposals into further consideration when my Lord Bp. of London shall be present."

At the Committee of Trade the 27 Apr. 1685.

"The Proposals from the Bp. of London contain'd in a letter to M[r] Blathwayt are again read, His Lordship being present; which being approved, their Lordships agree to move His Majesty that the Governors of His Majesty's Plantations have instructions according to the two first particulars, and that a clause be added to S[r] Philip Howard's instructions, to that effect; as also for applying the Donation at S[t] Andrews Parish in Jamaica to the proper Uses."

In consequence of this application from the Bp. and the Resolution of the Board, a clause was added in the same year in S[r] Philip Howards instructions, as follows : —

And our will and pleasure is, that *no Minister be preferr'd* by you, to any Ecclesiastical benefice, *without a certificate from the R[t] Rev[d] the Bp. of London,* of his conforming to the *Doctrine* and *Discipline* of the Church of England.

"*And to the end the Ecclesiastical Jurisdiction of the s[d] Bp. of London may take place in that our Island, as far as conveniently may be, we do think it fit that you give all countenance and encouragem[t] in the exercise of the same excepting only* the Collating to Benefices, granting licences for Marriage, and Probate of Wills, which we have reserved to you our Governor and the Commander in Chief for the time being.

And we do further direct that no Schoolmaster be hence forward permitted *to come from England* and to keep school within that our Island, *without the licence of the said Bishop.*"

The like Instructions were given to other Governors.

Under this authority Bishop Compton,[1] Bp Robinson,[2] and Bp. Gibson[3] for the first two or three years after he was promoted to the See of London, exercised the *Ecclesiastical Jurisdiction* in the Plantations ; with exception to the Collation of Benefices, Marriage Licences & Probate of Wills w[ch] were reserv'd to the Governors at the respective Colonies.

1725. In the year 1725 Bp. Gibson desirious of having a more explicit authority and direction from the Crown, for the exercise of

---

[1] HENRY COMPTON, was consecrated bishop of Oxford, April 18th, 1674, and translated to London, in 1675.

[2] JOHN ROBINSON, was consecrated Bishop of Bristol, 19th of November, 1710, and succeeded Bishop Compton, in the see of London, 1713.

[3] EDMUND GIBSON, was consecrated Bishop of Lincoln, February 12, 1715, and succeeded Bishop Robinson, in the see of London, in 1723. He died in 1748. *Percival's Apostolic Succession.* — ED.

the said Jurisdiction, applied to the King in Council for that purpose. The Petition was referred to the Attorney and Solicitor General & by their report their opinion appears to be that the authority by wch the Bps. of London had acted in ye Plantacôns was insufficient, and that the Eccl͞ial Jurisdiction in America did belong neither *to the Bishop of London*, nor to *any Bp. in England* but was solely in the Crown in virtue of the *Supremacy*, and that the most proper way of granting to any person the exercise of such jurisdiction, was by Patent under the Broad Seal. Accordingly, a Patent was granted to Dr Gibson late Bp. of London, but it was granted to him *Personally* & not to him as Bp. of London and his successors; so that the Patent expired with him and the Jurisdiction is now solely in His Majesty.

By the grant to Dr Gibson his exercise of the Jurisdiction was subjected to certain limitations and restraints, and 'tis not clear what powers he had in virtue of the s^d grant. The Patent gives him authority by himself or Commissaries (1) To *visit* all Churches in which the Rites & Liturgy of the Church of England were used. (2) To *Cite* all Rectors Curates and Incumbents and all Priests and Deacons in *Church of England Orders, et non alias quascumque personas,* cum omni et omnimodo jurisdictione potestate et coercione ecclesiasticâ, in premissis requisit. and to enquire *by Witnesses duly sworn* into their morals &^c with power to *Administer* Oaths in the Ecclesiastical Court, and to Correct & punish the said Rectors &^c by suspension excommunication &^c (3) A power to appoint Commissaries for the exercise of this Jurisdiction and to remove them at pleasure. (4) An appeal is given, to all who shall find themselves aggrieved by any sentence, before the Great Officers of State in England

Observations on this Patent.

1. A power is given to *visit all churches,* but he has no power to *cite* the Churchwardens or any of the Parishioners to appear; and should any of them appear voluntarily he has no right to give them any orders relating to the Church or Church affairs; his whole power and jurisdiction being confined to the Clergy only.

2. He has power to cite all Priests and Deacons & to examine into their conduct *provided they have Church of England Orders;* but if a man should counterfeit Episcopal Orders and administer the Sacraments, he has no power to proceed ag^st him

3. He has power to examine into the Conduct of the Clergy, upon the *Oath of Witnesses,* and power to *administer Oaths* for the purpose;

but he has no power to *cite* any man, at least no *Layman* to give testimony before him : yet the Laymen may be many times necessary witnesses as in such cases ; and they see daily how their Curate behaves, which other Clergymen, who serve distant parishes can give no account of.

4. The Bishop has power to appoint Commissaries to exercise such jurisdiction as is granted him by the Patent, and as the Bp. of London cannot be supposed to reside in America, he can do nothing by himself, as soon as he has appointed Commissaries, the Bishop can neither direct, nor correct, their judgment. No appeal lyes to the Bp. nor indeed can there ; for in judgment of Law, the Commissary's Sentence is the Bp's sentence, and the Appeal must go to a higher Court.

But this shows at the same time how very improper it is to give such power to a Bp. of England, which he cannot execute, but must be obliged to give it over to somebody else, as soon as he has it. So that the Bp. receiving with one hand what he must necessarily give away with the other, remains himself a Cypher without any authority power or influence.

If these observations are well founded the Bishop's jurisdiction, as under the Patent, seems to be defective.

But the Episcopal Churches in America suffer greater hardships still, by being under a Bishop who never can reside among them. There are some things necessary to such Churches wch the Bp. only can do himself. Such for instance are *Confirmation* and *Ordination,* which are not acts of jurisdiction or transferable to Commissaries, but are acts peculiar to the *Episcopal* Order and the Episcopal Churches abroad are *totally* deprived of Confirmation. As to Orders, since the Bp. *only* can give them, there is not in this vast tract of land, one who can ordain Ministers for the Church of England. In which respect the Dissenters of all kinds, upon the mere foot of Toleration are in a better case : for they all appoint Ministers in their own way, and were the Dissenters in New England and elsewhere in America, to send all their Ministers to be ordained by their Brethren in England, they wo^d think it a great hardship and inconsistent with the rights they claim by Toleration.

From these considerations it appears that several Colonies abroad where the Church of England is established, are, with respect to their religious principles, put under great difficulties. They are absolutely deprived of confirmation for all their youth and children, and they are oftentimes ill supply'd with Ministers to perform other duties of religion among them ; for as the families settled in the country and which are able to provide otherwise for their children, will not send their Children at a great expence and hazard to be ordain'd in England, where they often (as by experience has been found) catch the Small Pox, a distemper more fatal to them than to others, and several who have come over hither for Orders have dyed here of this disease. In consequence of this the Plantations are furnished with such Ministers from hence, as can be prevail'd upon to go among them, or such as are forced through necessity to seek a maintenance in a foreign country. And they are chiefly *Scotch* & *Irish* who offer themselves for this service; and there is reason to apprehend that the Scotch Episcopal Clergy who cannot be employed at home, may think of settling in the Plantations; which may be attended with bad consequences in regard to the government.

The Churches abroad of the Episcopal Communion have been under a necessity of submitting to these difficulties; for as Protestants they cannot apply to Popish Bishops for Confirmation or Orders; and as Episcopal Churches they could resort for Orders only to English or Irish Bishops. But since the Moravians have been recognized by Parliam^t to be a Protestant Episcopal Church and have liberty to settle in His Majesty's American Dominions, should the Churches abroad admit of Ordination by Moravian Bps. it may be attended by consequences not easily foreseen, but easily prevented by suffering the Episcopal Churches of England in America to have one or more Suffregan Bishops residing among them.

As the Dissenters at home and abroad may possibly think themselves concern'd in this question; it is necessary to observe that Bps. abroad are not desired in behalf of an *inconsiderable* party there, and that the Independents and other Dissenters do by no means (as the case is sometimes mistaken to be) make the body of the Inhabitants in His Majesty's American Dominions. But previously to stating how the fact is at present, it is proper to recollect how the law stands with respect to the establishment of the Church of England in America, according to the royal Charters and Instructions given to the King's Governors abroad herein before mentioned.

For the Church of England being establish'd in America, the Independents and other Dissenters who went to settle in New England, co^d only have a Toleration and in fact they had no more, as appears by their several Charters, and more particularly in Rhode Island Charter, granted in the 14th year of Chas IInd.

Thus stands the right of the Church of England in America. And in fact, at least one half of the Plantations are of the established Church, and have built Churches and Minister's houses and have by *laws of their respective Assemblies* (confirm'd by the Crown) provided maintenance for Church of England Clergy, & no others are capable of having benefices among them.

This is the case of S° Carolina, N° Carolina, Virginia, Maryland, Jamaica, Barbadoes, Antegoa, Nevis, and the rest of the Caribbee Islands.

On the other side — Pennsylvania is in the hands and under the governm[t] of the Quakers, and New England and the adjoining Colonies are in the hands of the Independents. But in some of them are great numbers of Churchmen.

It is sometimes said that it wo[d] be hard to send Bps: among the Dissenters in America; many of whom left their own Country to get from under their power.

If Bps. were proposed to be established in Pensilvania and New England, with *Coercive Powers*, there wo[d] be some colour in the complaint. But as it never has been propos'd to settle Bps. in those Colonies, nor in any other Colonies, with *Coercive* powers, there is no ground for it. And whatever prejudices the Independents of New England may have to Bps. themselves, surely it can never be thought reasonable that because the Northern end of America is possessed chiefly by the Independents, therefore the Southern and Midland parts and the Islands, who profess the Established Religion of England and are Episcopal Churches, sho[d] be denied the benefit of Episcopal administration, which according to their religious principles they think necessary to them.

If the Supremacy of the Crown be (as it has been often styled) a rich jewel in the Crown of England, it should be considered that the Supremacy is maintained and obeyed by the *Establish'd Church only*. Dissenters of all kinds are discharged from all regard to it, and are at full liberty to act for themselves in religious affairs, without taking the consent or even advice of the Crown: and therefore they make what Ministers they please. But the Episcopal Churches of England in America want their first and most necessary Member, a Bp. to reside with them; and have waited with patience for the consent of the Crown; and their bretheren at home, the Bps. of England and the Society for Propagating the Gospel, have often been intercessors to the Crown on their behalf.

The objections to settling Bishops in the Plantations are chiefly these two.

1. It is doubted whether it will be agreeable to the People there.

2. It is doubted whether any maintenance can be had for such Bishops.

As to the first point: As no Bishops are propos'd to be settled in Pensilvania, or New England, or the Colonies thereto belonging, it is to no purpose to enquire of their inclination; they are not concern'd *themselves* and have no right to judge for *others*. This question therefore can relate only to those parts where the Church of England is established and profess'd, and with respect to them and to know clearly what their sentiments are, it is necessary to consider Episcopacy with respect to the *Duties* belonging to it as an *Order* in the *Christian Church*, and with respect to the *Powers* of *Jurisdiction* derived to it from the *Civil Magistrate*.

In the first view, their own laws will shew that they have no objection. To begin with —

South Carolina. By Acts of Assembly there, all Churches and Parishes are to be served by Ministers *Episcopally ordained.* (vide the Act called the Church Act) & with respect to the Schoolmaster of their own Free School, it is enacted that he shall be of the religion of the *Church of England* and conform to the same. (Vide Free School Act) and by an Additional Act to the Free School Act, special encouragement is given to the Ministers recommended by the *Bp. of London.*

North Carolina. It is enacted that all Statute Laws made in England for the *Establishment of the Church, shall be in force here.*

Virginia. Enacted, that no Minister be admitted to officiate in this country, but such as have received *Ordination* from some *Bishop in England.*

Maryland. All places for Public Worship according to the *Usage of the Church of England,* shall be deemed settled and established Churches.

Barbadoes. *The Church of England established* by Act of Genl Assembly; and the maintenance, provided for the better encouragem^t of the Clergy, is appropriated to the *Orthodox Ministers of the Church of England.*

Antegoa. By act of Assembly, none capable of being presented to Benfices, unless they produce testimonials that they are *qualified according to the Canons of the Church of England; by having taken Deacons and Priests Orders.*

Nevis. By Act of Assembly Maintenance provided for Ministers of the *Church of England,*

Leeward Islands. By Act of Assembly, the Governor may suspend an

Incumbent giving notice thereof to the *Bp. of London,* that *his Lordship* may give such directions therein, as to him shall seem meet.

Jamaica. None to be capable of a Benefice unless they produce testimonials that they are qualified according to the *Canons of the Church of England by having taken Deacons and Priests Orders.*

By these Acts of Assembly it is plain that they have no objection agst Bishops, in the religious view, so far from it, that they admit no Minister to serve in the Churches supported by Publick Maintenance, but such as are Episcopally ordained. And it cannot be supposed that they wo^d be unwilling a Bp. should *reside* among them, where his authority & influence might be of great use in the due governm^t & direction of the Clergy; provided. that a Bp. *residing* with them had power to do no more than they are now desirous sho^d be done by a Bishop at a distance.

But the difficulty arises from the 2nd view; and the question is, how far they will be contented to admit the jurisdiction wch the Bps. in England have in many cases, by and under the Crown.

As the first planters in America were members of the Church of England, and carried over with them a regard to the government and discipline of their Mother Church; there is no doubt to be made but that they would very willingly have continued under the same Ecclesiastical Government & Discipline in America, under which they had been bred in England, had they had any Bps. among them at their first settlement abroad. But being destitute of Bps. and for some years deprived of *Publick Church Communion* for want of Ministers regularly ordain'd; it is more to be wondered at that they have adhered so steadily to the Communion of the Church of England with respect to Episcopal Ordination and the established Liturgy, than that they have some prejudice against Ecclesiastical Courts and Jurisdictions of Bps. of which they have seen and known so little for many years. Many things which are under the care and authority of Bps. in England, are things necessary to be done by somebody, and where there are no Bps. they must be done by some other authority. Such are the repairs of Churches and the providing books and other necessaries for the service, the Instituting and inducting Incumbents, the repairs of Glebe Houses, the Probate of Wills, Licence for Marriage, examining and approving Clergymen, and Schoolmasters, and the correction of vice and immorality by coercive power. As the Colonies had no Bps. to discharge these duties they were necessitated to provide for them otherwise. And therefore these powers are placed by several Acts of Assembly, partly in the Churchwardens, partly in Justices of the Peace, and partly in the Governors of the respective Provinces.

That these provisions were made for *want* of a Bp. among them, and not out of dislike to *Episcopal Authority* appears from the Act of Assembly of the Leeward Islands before mentioned, by which the Governor is empowered to suspend Clergymen, but it passed under an obligation of giving notice to the Bp. of London, and of taking his directions. Had there been a Bp. among them, can it be supposed the[y] would not have referr'd the matter *directly* to him?

The present generation of men in the Colonies being born and bred under this Constitution, it is natural to suppose that they are attached to the custom of their country, and would be alarm'd at the apprehension of having their powers remov'd out of their hands, in wch the law of their country had plac'd them, and put into the hands of a Bp. with whose power in these cases they are unacquainted : and therefore these powers exercis'd in the Consistory Courts in England are not desired for Bps. residing in America.

But these Colonies however unaccustomed to *Episcopal Jurisdiction* have always been brought up in an opinion that their Clergy must be *Episcopally* Ordained. And it is not to be supposed that they had rather have their Children come to England for Orders than to have a Bp. among them to Ordain them at home, and as they are members of the Church of England and have received it's liturgy, they cannot look into it without seeing that for want of a Bp. among them they and their Children are debarr'd from Confirmation

That there have been jealousies in some of the Plantations of an Ecclesiastical Jurisdiction, is certain from some Acts of their Assembly. In the Church Act of Antegoa (wch passed July 1st 1692.) it is enacted, *that no Ecclesiastical Law or Jurisdiction shall have power to enforce confirm or establish any penal mulct or punishment in any case whatsoever.*

There is the like clause in the Church Act of *Jamaica.*

If by Penal Mulct or Punishment is to be understood the imposing fines upon offenders, it is hard to say what gave occasion to this Proviso ; it could not be to guard against the Ecclesiastical Law of England, for the Ecclesiastical Court in England neither does nor can impose Fines.

There is the same Law in *Barbadoes* against Penal Mulcts by Ecclesiastical Law. But whatever gave occasion to it, it is certain it never was meant ags^t the Authority exercis'd by the Bp. in the case of religion or in the government of the Clergy ; for it is declared in a subsequent statute that the s^d clause sho^d not extend to the exercise of Ecclesiastical Jurisdiction over the Clergy, according to the tenour of *His Majesty's Commission to the Bp. of London.* The construction upon these two Acts must be this ; that they are not willing to receive Ecclesiastical Courts with *Coercive* Powers, but are desirous of receiving Bishops as an *Order* of the Christian Church, to inspect the conduct and behaviour of the Clergy, and to perform the duties of their Office in examining and ordaining Ministers for the service of the Church.

Let them at least have such Bps. among them as they are willing to receive.

There have been Commissaries acting under the Bp. of London, ever since Bp. Compton's time, and no complaint has been made of their power being too great or any ways burdensome to the Country ; and if Suffragan Bishops with the same Ecclesiastical Powers that the Commissaries have had, were settled in the Plantations, it could make no alteration with respect to the Civil Governm^t or to the people, but it will enable the Church of England there to do what all Churches of all denominations have thought necessary to their very being, to provide a succession for the Ministry among themselves : a right which the Established Church of England in the Plantations has been long deprived of, and wch as far as I can judge, no other Christian Church in the world ever wanted. Every sect of Christians, under the Toleration, claims it as their right, and exercises it ; and it seems but reasonable to hope that an Established Church should enjoy the rights of a Church in equal degree at least with tolerated societies of Dissenters.

The other objection is, — How shall Bishops in America be maintained? Not by *Tax* or imposition on the *People* certainly. If Bps. were to be sent them, and the country laid under contribution, Bishops would be received as *Excise Men* and *Taxgath[er]ers ;* and this apprehension in the people abroad, of being burden'd with the maintenance of Bishops, would be the readiest way to raise an opposition in the Colonies to the settlement of the Bps. among them.

Nor ought the Crown to be burdened with the maintenance of such Bps, or put to more expence than what already lyes upon the Crown in providing Clergy for the Plantations. And yet there will not want means to provide a decent support for them by annexing some preferments abroad to these Bishopricks and by giving the Bp. a capacity of receiving Benefactions from such as will be ready to promote so good a design.

But as the care to maintain them will be premature till His Majesty's pleasure is known as to the appointing them it may wait His Majesty's determination.

As the Bp. of London is generally supposed to be the Bp. principally if not only concern'd in the Plantations: He desires to say one word for himself, and to assure Your Majesty that however necessary to the state of Religion & the Churches abroad, he apprehends the settlem^t of Bps, in America to be, and however sensible he is that with the Authority granted to the late Bishop of London, he co^d by no means answer the good purposes intended by Your Majesty; yet he submits himself to your Royal Pleasure, and whatever part you in your royal wisdom shall think fit to allot to him, he will discharge it to the best of his ability.

[Indorsed]

Rec^d with the Bishop's lrê of 19 Feby. 1759.
Read Feb^ry 21. 1759.

XIII. REV. THOMAS BRADBURY CHANDLER TO THE BISHOP OF LONDON, STATING HIS REASONS FOR WRITING THE APPEAL TO THE PUBLIC.

From the Manuscripts in the Fulham Library.

ELIZABETHTOWN, NEW JERSEY,
October 21, 1767.

Having been prevailed upon to draw up, and publish, a Pamphlet on the Subject of an American Episcopate, I have taken the Liberty to send your Lordship a Copy of it, which is the Occasion of my being troublesome at this Time. The most that I can say in Favor of the Performance is, that it expresses the Opinion of the Clergy in most of the Colonies, of the Case of the American Church of England, and represents some of those Reasons and Facts, upon which their Opinion is founded. There are some other Facts and Reasons, which could not be prudently mentioned in a Work of this Nature, as the least Intimation of them would be of ill Consequence in this irritable Age and Country: but were they known, they would have a far greater Tendency to engage such of our Superiors, if there be any such, as are governed altogether by political Motives, to espouse the Cause of the Church of England in America, than any contained in the Pamphlet. But I must content myself with having proposed those only which could be mentioned safely, and leave the Event to Divine Providence.

I could heartily wish, My Lord, that my feeble Attempt might be a

Means of engaging some Person at Home, who can command the Attention of the Public, to take the Cause in Hand, and set it forth to Advantage. Even my Appeal it is hoped may have some good effect here ; but I fear it will hardly bear reading on the other side of the Atlantic.

XIV. LEGISLATION OF THE PARLIAMENT OF GREAT BRITAIN TO PROVIDE BISHOPS, PRIESTS, AND DEACONS FOR THE CHURCH OF ENGLAND IN THE UNITED STATES OF AMERICA.

I.

An Act to impower the Bishop of *London* for the Time being, or any other Bishop to be by him appointed, to admit to the Order of Deacon or Priest, Persons being Subjects or Citizens of Countries out of his Majesty's Dominions, without requiring them to take the Oath of Allegiance as appointed by Law.

Statutes at Large, 24 George III. Cap. XXXV.

Whereas, by the Laws of this Realm, every Person who shall be admitted to Holy Orders is to take the Oath of Allegiance in Manner thereby provided : And whereas there are divers Persons, Subjects or Citizens of Countries out of his Majesty's Dominions, inhabiting and residing within the said Countries, who profess the Publick Worship of Almighty God according to the Liturgy of the Church of *England*, and are desirous that the Word of God, and the Sacraments, should continue to be administered unto them according to the said Liturgy, by Subjects or Citizens of the said Countries, ordained according to the Form of Ordination in the Church of *England;* be it enacted by the King's most Excellent Majesty, by and with the Advise and Consent of the Lords Spiritual and Temporal, and Commons, in this present Parliament assembled, and by the Authority of the same, That, from and after the passing of this Act, it shall and may be lawful to and for the Bishop of *London* for the Time being, or any other Bishop by him to be appointed, to admit to the Order of Deacon or Priest, for the Purposes aforesaid, Persons being Subjects or Citizens of Countries out of his Majesty's Dominions, without requiring them to take the Oath of Allegiance.

II. Provided always, and be it hereby declared, That no Person, ordained in the Manner herein before provided only, shall be thereby enabled to exercise the Office of Deacon or Priest within his Majesty's Dominions.

III. Provided always, and be it further enacted, That in the Letters Testimonial of Such Orders, there shall be inserted the Name of the Person so ordained, with the Addition of the Country whereof he is a Subject or Citizen, and the further Description of his not having taken the said Oath of Allegiance, being exempted from the Obligation of so doing by virtue of this Act.

2.

An Act to impower the Archbishop of *Canterbury*, or the Archbishop of *York*, for the Time being, to consecrate to the Office of a Bishop, Persons being Subjects or Citizens of Countries out of his Majesty's Dominions.

Statutes at Large, 26 George III. Cap. LXXXIV.

Whereas, by the Laws of this Realm, no Person can be Consecrated to the Office of a Bishop without the King's License for his Election to that Office, and the Royal Mandate under the Great Seal for his Confirmation and Consecration : And whereas every Person who shall be so consecrated to the said Office is required to take the Oaths of Allegiance and Supremacy, and also the Oath of due Obedience to the Archbishop : And whereas there are divers Persons, Subjects, or Citizens of Countries out of his Majesty's Dominions, and inhabiting and residing within the said Countries, who profess the Publick Worship of Almighty God, according to the Principles of the Church of *England*, and who, in order to provide a regular Succession of Ministers for the Service of their Church, are desirous of having certain of the Subjects or Citizens of those Countries consecrated Bishops, according to the Form of Consecration in the Church of *England*: Be it enacted by the King's most Excellent Majesty, by and with the Advice and Consent of the Lords Spiritual and Temporal, and Commons, in this present Parliament assembled, and by the Authority of the same, That from and after the passing of this Act, it shall and may be lawful to and for the Archbishop of *Canterbury*, or the Archbishop of *York*, for the Time being, together with such other Bishops as they shall call to their Assistance, to consecrate Persons, being Subjects or Citizens of Countries out of his Majesty's Dominions, Bishops, for the Purposes aforesaid, without the King's License for their Election, or the Royal Mandate, under the Great Seal, for their Confirmation and Consecration, and without requiring them to take the Oaths of Allegiance and Supremacy, and the Oath of Obedience to the Archbishop for the Time being.

II. Provided always, That no Persons shall be consecrated Bishops in the Manner herein provided, until the Archbishop of *Canterbury*, or the Archbishop of *York*, for the Time being, shall have first applied for and obtained his Majesty's License, by Warrant under his Royal Signet and Sign Manual, authorizing and empowering him to perform such Consecration, and expressing the Name or Names of the Persons so to be consecrated, nor until the said Archbishop has been fully ascertained of their Sufficiency in good Learning, of the Soundness of their Faith, and of the Purity of their Manners.

III. Provided also, and be it hereby declared, That no Person or Persons consecrated to the Office of a Bishop in the Manner aforesaid, nor any Person or Persons deriving their Consecration from or under any Bishop so consecrated, nor any Person or Persons admitted to the Order of Deacon or Priest by any Bishop or Bishops so consecrated, or by the Successor or Successors of any Bishop or Bishops so consecrated, shall be thereby enabled to exercise his or their respective Office or Offices within his Majesty's Dominions.

IV. Provided always, and be it further enacted, That a Certificate of such Consecration shall be given under the Hand and Seal of the Archbishop who consecrates, containing the Name of the Person so consecrated, with the Addition, as well of the Country whereof he is a Subject or Citizen, as of the Church in which he is appointed Bishop, and the further Description of his not having taken the said Oaths, being exempted from the Obligation of so doing by virtue of this Act.

APPENDIX B.

LIST OF THE ARCHBISHOPS OF CANTERBURY AND BISHOPS OF LONDON DURING THE SEVENTEENTH AND EIGHTEENTH CENTURIES.[1]

ARCHBISHOPS OF CANTERBURY.

Richard Bancroft	1604
George Abbot	1611
William Laud	1633
William Juxon	1660
Gilbert Sheldon	1663
William Sancroft	1677
John Tillotson	1691
Thomas Tenison	1695
William Wake	1716
John Potter	1737
Thomas Herring	1747
Matthew Hutton	1757
Thomas Secker	1758
Frederick Cornwallis	1768
John Moore	1783–1805

BISHOPS OF LONDON.

Thomas Ravis	1607
George Abbot	1609
John King	1611
George Monteigne	1621
William Laud	1628
William Juxon	1633
Gilbert Sheldon	1660
Humphrey Henchman	1663
Henry Compton	1675
John Robinson	1713
Edmund Gibson	1723
Thomas Sherlock	1748
Thomas Hayter	1761
Richard Osbaldeston	1762
Richard Terrick	1764
Robert Lowth	1777–1787

[1] Stubbs, *Registrum*, 2d ed., 111-146; Le Neve, *Fasti*, I., 26-31, II., 303-306; Perceval, *Succession*, Appendix, 106-121; Abbey, *English Church and Bishops*, II., Appendix, pp. 357, 359 (for eighteenth century).

APPENDIX C.

A LIST OF SPECIAL WORKS.

THIS bibliography aims to include all books, manuscripts, pamphlets, newspapers, periodicals, broadsides, official records, or other collections of material which contain important information regarding the relations between the Anglican Episcopate and the American Colonies. It has not been thought necessary to repeat here the titles of works which are necessarily consulted by students of any phase of American colonial history.

Among the great American and English libraries the author has found the following most useful: the Harvard University Library, the Boston Public Library, the library of the Massachusetts Historical Society, the Boston Athenæum, the John Carter Brown Library of Providence, the Bishop of London's library at Fulham, the Archbishop of Canterbury's library at Lambeth, the British Museum, and the Public Record Office at London. The Fulham and Lambeth libraries and the British Museum were especially rich in hitherto unpublished manuscripts and rare pamphlets, some of which are to be found printed in appendices to this work.

For all matters relating to the history of the Episcopal Church in America the student is primarily and chiefly indebted to Francis Lister Hawks and William Stevens Perry, pioneers in this field both as historians and historiographers. The value of their histories, for the purposes of the present writer at least, consisted mainly in the documents or extracts there printed. But these collections, largely made up of transcripts from the Fulham and Lambeth manuscripts and the letter books of the Society for Propagating the Gospel, are not altogether adequate. In the first place, they contain practically no material on New Hampshire, Rhode Island, New York, New Jersey, the Carolinas, or Georgia — the printing of the Carolina series was begun, but, owing to a lack of funds, was never finished. In the second place, many documents of an inter-colonial character, such as did not primarily concern any of the particular colonies included in the collection, find no place. And finally, even in the case of particular colonies, there are a few important omissions.

Oftentimes, too, the extracts given are provokingly short for the purposes of the present study.

Besides the manuscripts and pamphlets in the English libraries enumerated above, and the printed collections of Perry and Hawks, the records of the various colonies furnish much valuable and interesting material. Specially worthy of note are the documents relating to the Colonial History of New York, the New Jersey Archives, the Pennsylvania Archives, and the Colonial Records of North Carolina. It is unfortunate that the North Carolina Records have no index; but the serious student will be well repaid for turning the ten thousand odd pages of this extremely valuable work.

The publications of some of the historical societies contain much that is of use. This is particularly true in the case of the Massachusetts, Virginia, New York, South Carolina, and Protestant Episcopal Historical Societies.

Another fertile source, especially on the subject of the attempt to introduce bishops, are the publications of the Society for Propagating the Gospel, notably the series of annual sermons and abstracts of proceedings. Of these latter the John Carter Brown Library has a complete set.

ABBEY, C. J. The English Church and Bishops in the Eighteenth Century. 2 vols. London, 1887.

An Address from the Clergy of New York and New Jersey to the Episcopalians in Virginia. New York, 1771.

The Humble Address of the Right Honorable the Lords Spiritual and Temporal, in Parliament assembled, presented to her Majesty the Queen, on Wednesday, the Thirteenth Day of March, 1705, relating to the Province of South Carolina, and the Petition therein mentioned, with her Majesty's Most Gracious Answer thereunto. pp. 4. London, 1705.

An Advertisement. [Being an Attack on Mayhew's Observations.] Providence, 1763.

The American Whig, A Collection of Tracts from the Late Newspapers, etc. 2 vols. John Holt, New York, 1768, 1769.

ANDERSON, J. S. M. History of the Colonial Churches. 3 vols. London, 1848.

An Appendix to the Life of Archbishop Secker. American edition. New York, 1774.

APTHORP, EAST. Considerations on the Character and Conduct of the Society for the Propagation of the Gospel. Boston, 1763.

APTHORP, EAST.   A Review of Dr. Mayhew's Remarks on the Answer to his Observations, etc.   London, 1765.

BALDWIN, SIMEON E.   The American Jurisdiction of the Bishop of London in Colonial Times, American Antiquarian Society, *Proceedings,* New Series, xiii. 179–221.   Worcester, 1900.

BEACH, JOHN.   A Calm and Dispassionate Vindication of the Professors of the Church of England.   1749.

BEACH, JOHN.   A Continuation of the Calm and Dispassionate Vindication of the Church of England against Mr. Noah Hobart.   Boston, 1751.

BEARDSLEY, E. E.   History of the Episcopal Church in Connecticut [1635–1865].   2 vols.   New York, 1883.

BEARDSLEY, E. E.   Life and Correspondence of Samuel Johnson, D.D., Missionary of the Church of England in Connecticut and First President of King's College.   Boston, 1881.

BEARDSLEY, E. E.   Life and Times of William Samuel Johnson, LL.D.   New York, 1876.

BLACKBURNE, FRANCIS.   A Critical Commentary on Archbishop Secker's Letter to Horatio Walpole.   London, 1770.

BRADFORD, ALDEN.   Memoir of the Life and Writings of the Reverend Jonathan Mayhew.   Boston, 1838.

BRAY, THOMAS.   The Acts of Dr. Bray's Visitation held at Annapolis in Maryland, May 23, 24, 25, Anno 1700.   [Dedicated to the Bishop of London.]   London, 1700.

BRAY, THOMAS.   A Memorial representing the Present State of Religion on the Continent of North America.   London, 1701.

BROWNE, ARTHUR.   Remarks on Dr. Mayhew's Incidental Reflections relative to the Church of England as contained in his Observations, etc.   By a Son of the Church of England.   Portsmouth, 1763.

CANER, HENRY.   A Candid Examination of Dr. Mayhew's Observations concerning the Character and Conduct of the Society for the Propagation of the Gospel.   [With an Appendix containing a Vindication of the Society by one of its Members — Samuel Johnson.]   Boston, 1763.

CASWALL, HENRY.   America and the American Church.   2d ed.   London, 1851.

CASWALL, HENRY.   The American Church and the American Union.   London, 1861.

CHANDLER, THOMAS B.   An Appeal to the Public in behalf of the Church of England in America.   New York, 1767.

CHANDLER, THOMAS B. An Appeal defended: or, The Proposed Episcopate Vindicated. New York, 1769.

CHANDLER, THOMAS B. An Appeal farther defended, in Answer to the Farther Misrepresentations of Dr. Chauncy. New York, 1771.

CHANDLER, THOMAS B. A Free Examination of the Critical Commentary on Archbishop Secker's Letter to Mr. Walpole [by F. Blackburne]. With a copy of Bishop Sherlock's Memorial. New York, 1774.

CHANDLER, THOMAS B. The Life of Samuel Johnson, the First President of King's College in New York. New York, 1805.

CHAUNCY, CHARLES. An Appeal to the Public Answered, in behalf of the Non-episcopal Churches in America. Boston, 1768.

CHAUNCY, CHARLES. A Reply to Dr. Chandler's Appeal defended. Boston, 1770.

CHAUNCY, CHARLES. A Letter to a Friend containing Remarks on Certain Passages in a Sermon preached by the Rt. Rev. John, Lord Bishop of Llandaff, before the Society for the Propagation of the Gospel at their Anniversary Meeting, 20 Feb., 1767, in which the Highest Reproach is undeservedly cast on the American Colonies. Boston, 1767.

CLARK, SAMUEL A. History of St. John's Church, Elizabethtown, N. J., from 1703 to the Present Time. New York and Philadelphia, 1857.

COLLIER, JEREMY. Ecclesiastical History of England. 2 vols. London, 1708-1714.

CORNELISON, I. A. The Relation of Religion to Civil Government in the United States. New York and London, 1895.

CUTTS, E. L. A Dictionary of the Church of England. London, 1887.

DALCHO, FREDERICK. An Historical Account of the Protestant Episcopal Church in South-Carolina from the First Settlement of the Province to the War of the Revolution. Charleston, S.C., 1820.

ELIOT, ANDREW. Remarks on the Bishop of Oxford's [Secker's] Sermon before the Society for the Propagation of the Gospel in Foreign Parts. Boston, 1740. [Also in Massachusetts Historical Society Collections, Vol. II, 2d Series, pp. 190-216. Extracts were published in England by Rev. Francis Blackburne.]

EVANS, H. D., ED. Bishop Christopher Wordsworth's Theophilus Americanus. Philadelphia, 1859.

FLEMING, CALEB. A Supplement to a Letter to a Friend, by a Presbyter in Old England. London, 1768.

FOOTE, H. W. Annals of King's Chapel. [2d vol. completed by H. H. Edes.] 2 vols. Boston, 1882-1896.

FOWLER, WILLIAM C. Article on Charles Chauncy (1705–1787) in Charles Chauncy, his Ancestors and Descendants. (New England Historical and Genealogical Register.) October, 1856. Vol. X., pp. 323–329.

FULLER, THOS. Church History of Britain to 1648. Ed. J. L. Brewer. 4th ed. 6 vols. Oxford, 1845.

GWATKIN, THOMAS. A Letter to the Clergy of New York and New Jersey, occasioned by an Address to the Episcopalians in Virginia. Williamsburgh, 1772.

HARTWELL, BLAIR, AND CHILTON. The Present State of Virginia. London, 1727.

HAWKINS, ERNEST. Historical Notices of the Missions of the Church of England in America to 1783. London, 1845.

HAWKS, F. L. Contributions to American Church History. 2 vols. I. Virginia. II. Maryland. New York, 1836–1839.

HAWKS, F. L. Efforts to obtain a Colonial Episcopate before the Revolution. In Protestant Episcopal Historical Society Collection, I. 136–157. 2 vols. New York, 1851–1853.

HAWKS, F. L., AND PERRY, W. S. Documentary History of the Church in the United States. Connecticut. 2 vols. New York, 1863–1864.

HAWKS, F. L., AND PERRY, W. S. No. 1 of South Carolina [incomplete]. New York, 1862.

HEYLYN, PETER. Cyprianus Anglicus, or the History of the Life and Death of William Laud. 2d ed. London, 1671.

HOBART, NOAH. A Serious Address to the Members of the Episcopal Separation in New England. Boston, 1748.

HOBART, NOAH. A Second Address to the Members of the Episcopal Separation in New England. [Appendix by Moses Dickinson.] Boston, 1751.

HOOKER, RICHARD. An Account of the Jurisdiction of the Bishop of London in the Foreign Plantations. *Weekly Miscellany*, Vol. I., No. 11, pp. 79–86. [Only 2 vols. of this Magazine appeared.] London, 1736–1738.

HOYT, A. H. Sketch of the Life of T. B. Chandler [1726–1790]. Boston, 1873. [Reprinted from the *New England Historical and Genealogical Register* for July, 1873, Vol. XXVII., pp. 227–236.]

HUMPHREYS, DAVID. An Historical Account of the Society for the Propagation of the Gospel. London, 1730. Reprinted New York, 1853. [The chapter on South Carolina is printed in Carroll's Historical Collections.]

INGLIS, CHARLES. A Vindication of the Bishop of Llandaff's Sermon. New York, 1768.

JOHNSON, SAMUEL. Elements of Philosophy. [The English edition contains at the end a letter entitled, Impartial Thoughts on an American Episcopate.] London, 1754.

JONES, HUGH. The Present State of Virginia. London, 1724.

LAUD, WILLIAM. Autobiography. Oxford, 1839.

LEAMING, J. A Defence of the Episcopal Government of the Church. New York, 1766.

LE NEVE, JOHN. Fasti Ecclesiæ Anglicanæ, or a Calendar of the Principal Ecclesiastical Dignitaries in England and Wales, etc. 3 vols. Oxford, 1854.

A Letter to the Reverend Father in God The Lord B——p of L——n, occasioned by a letter of his Lordship's to the L——ds of T——e, on the Subject of an Act of Assembly passed in the Year 1748, entitled an Act to Enable the Inhabitants of this Colony to discharge their Publick Dues in Money for the Ensuing Year. From Virginia. Pub. 1767.

LIVINGSTONE, WILLIAM. A Letter to John, Bishop of Llandaff, occasioned by his Sermon, February 20, 1767, in which the American Colonies are loaded with Reproach. London, 1768.

McCONNELL, S. D. History of the American Episcopal Church, from the Planting of the Colonies to the End of the Civil War. New York, 1891.

MAYHEW, JONATHAN. Observations on the Charter and Conduct of the Society for the Propagation of the Gospel. London and Boston, 1763.

MAYHEW, JONATHAN. Defence of the Character and Conduct, etc., against a Candid Examination of Dr. Mayhew's Observations, etc., and against a Letter to a Friend. Boston, 1763.

MAYHEW, JONATHAN. Remarks on an Anonymous Tract, entitled an Answer to Dr. Mayhew's Observations, etc. Boston, 1764. London, 1765.

MILLER, SAMUEL. Memoirs of Rev. John Rogers. New York, 1813.

Minutes of a Convention of Delegates from the Synods of New York and Philadelphia and from the Associations of Connecticut, held annually, 1766–1775. Hartford, 1843.

MOTLEY, DANIEL ESTEN. Life of Commissary James Blair, Founder of William and Mary College, Johns Hopkins University Studies in Historical and Political Science, Series XIX., No. 10. Baltimore, 1901.

PERCEVAL, A. P. An Apology for the Doctrine of Apostolic Succession. New York, 1839.

PERRY, G. G. A History of the Church of England. Appendix on the Church of England in America by J. A. Spencer. New York, 1879.

PERRY, WILLIAM STEVENS. Bishop Seabury and Bishop Provost. 1862.

PERRY, W. S. The Connection of the Church of England with Early American Discovery. Portland, Me., 1863.

PERRY, W. S. The Episcopate in America. New York, 1895.

PERRY, W. S. Historical Collections relating to the American Colonial Church. 5 vols. I. Virginia. II. Pennsylvania. III. Massachusetts. IV., V. Maryland, Delaware. Hartford, 1870–1878.

PERRY, W. S. The History of the American Episcopal Church [1587–1883]. 2 vols. Boston, 1885.

PORTEUS, BEILBY. A Review of the Life and Character of Archbishop Secker. London, 1797.

ROYCE, M. S. Historical Sketch of the Church of England and of the Protestant Episcopal Church in the United States. New York, 1859.

A PROTESTANT DISSENTER OF OLD ENGLAND. The Claims of the Church of England Seriously Examined, in a Letter to the Author [Thomas Secker] of an Answer, etc. London, 1764.

SECKER, THOMAS. An Answer to Dr. Mayhew's Observations on the Charter and Conduct of the Society. London, 1764.

SHERLOCK, THOMAS. A Letter to the Rt. Hon. Horatio Walpole. London, 1769.

SHARPE, GRANVILLE. Memoirs, Ed. Prince Hoare. 2d ed. 2 vols. London, 1820. *Ibid.,* 1828.

SHERLOCK, THOMAS. A Circular Letter to the Commissaries, 19 September, 1750. [In Appendix to Chandler's *Johnson;* also in his *Free Examination.*]

SOCIETY FOR PROPAGATING THE GOSPEL. Abstracts of the Proceedings of the Society appended to the Sermon preached at the Annual Meetings held in the parish church of St. Mary-le-Bow. [1701 to 1783, *passim.*]

SOCIETY FOR PROPAGATING THE GOSPEL. An Account of the Society. London, 1706.

SOCIETY FOR PROPAGATING THE GOSPEL. A Collection of Papers. London, 1715.

SOCIETY FOR PROPAGATING THE GOSPEL. Classified Digest of the Records, 1701–1892. Compiled by C. F. Pascoe. 3d ed. London, 1893.

SOCIETY FOR PROPAGATING THE GOSPEL, The Results of 180 Years' Work of. London, 1882.

STEVENS, ABEL. A History of the Religious Movement of the Eighteenth Century called Methodism. 3 vols. New York, 1858–1861.

STILLÉ, CHARLES J. Address at the Bicentennial of Christ Church, Philadelphia, in a Memorial of the Proceedings. Published by the Christ Church Historical Association. Philadelphia, 1896.

STUBBS, WILLIAM. Registrum Sacrum Anglicanum. 2d ed. Oxford, 1897.

TIFFANY, C. C. A History of the Protestant Episcopal Church in the United States of America. New York, 1895. [There is a good bibliography of works relating to the history of the American Episcopal Church on pp. xvi.–xxiv.]

TURELL, EBENEZER. Life and Character of the late Reverend Dr. Benjamin Coleman. Boston, 1749. [Contains the Letter of the Hampshire clergymen to the Bishop of London.]

TYERMAN, L. The Life of the Rev. George Whitefield. 2 vols. London, 1876–1877.

Virginia's Cure, Dedicated to Sheldon, Bishop of London, and Morley, Bishop of Winchester. 1662.

WELLES, NOAH. The Real Advantages which Ministers and People may enjoy, especially in the Colonies, by Conforming to the Church of England, Faithfully considered and represented in a Letter to a Young Gentleman. 1762.

WELLES, NOAH. A Vindication of the Validity and Divine Right of Presbyterian Ordination. New Haven, 1767.

WETMORE, JAMES. Vindication of the Professors of the Church of England in Connecticut. 1747.

WHITE, WILLIAM. Memoirs of the Protestant Episcopal Church in the United States. [Ed. B. F. De Costa.] New York, 1880.

WILBERFORCE, SAMUEL. History of the Protestant Episcopal Church in America. New York, 1849.

INDEX.